The ENCYCLOPEDIA of RECREATIONAL DIVING

PADI®

This book is printed on environmentally friendly, chlorine-free, recyclable paper to support Project AWARE and the environment.

Library of Congress Card Number 90-060546
ISBN 1-878663-02-X

Published by PADI
1251 East Dyer Road #100, Santa Ana, CA 92705-5605 USA

Printed in the United States of America

10 9 8 7 6 5 4 3 2 1

PRODUCT NO. 70034 (Rev. 1/93, 8/96) Version 2.0

Acknowledgements

Revised edition developed by
Drew Richardson, Julie Taylor Shreeves, Gary Van Roekel, Al Hornsby

Based on first edition developed by
Alex Brylske, Al Hornsby, Drew Richardson, CK Stewart

Editor-in-Chief
Drew Richardson

Editor
Karl Shreeves

Assistant Editors
John Kinsella, Riad Yakzan

Continuity Editing
Lori Bachelor

Copy Editing
Jeanne Bryant, John Kinsella, Riad Yakzan

Section Authors
One: Alex Brylske, revised by Karl Shreeves
Two: Karl Shreeves
Three: Riad Yakzan, Harry Averill, revised by John Kinsella
Four: Charles Seaborn, Wayne Brown, revised by John Kinsella
Five: John Kinsella, Al Hornsby, Karl Shreeves, Riad Yakzan

Contributors, First and Revised Editions
Paul S. Auerbach, M.D.
    Director, Emergency Department, Vanderbilt University Medical Center
Susan Bangasser, Ph.D.
    Co-author, *Women Underwater*
Hugh D. Greer III, M.D.
    Neurologist, Santa Barbara Medical Foundation Clinic
Wolf Krebs, V.M.D.
    Department of Ophthamology, College of Physicians & Surgeons of Columbia
    University
Tom S. Neuman, M.D.
    Director, Hyperbaric Medicine Center, San Diego Medical Center
Stephen Pauley, M.D.
    Otolaryngologist
Michael R. Powell, Ph.D.
    Head, Environmental Physiology/Biophysics Group, Space Biomedical Research
    Institute, NASA, Johnson Space Center

Raymond E. Rogers, D.D.S.
    Senior Technical Consultant, Diving Science & Technology
Barry Shuster, M.B.A.
    Director, Marketing, Divers Alert Network
Chris Wachholz, R.N.
    Director, Special Projects, Divers Alert Network

Section Review, First and Revised Editions
Bruce Bassett, Ph.D.
    President, Human Underwater Biology Inc.
William A. Johnston, Ph.D.
    Research Engineer, The Aerospace Corp., Los Angeles
Eric Maiken, Ph.D.
    University of California Irvine, Department of Physics
Michael R. Powell, Ph.D.
    Head, Environmental Physiology/Biophysics Group, Space Biomedical Research
    Institute, NASA, Johnson Space Center
PADI Training, Education and Memberships Department

Technical Assistance, Illustrations and Stock Photography

Absymal Software	Oceanic
Catalina Cylinders	RJE International
CisLunar	Scubapro
Dacor	Sea & Sea
Dive Rite	Sea Quest
DiveComm	Seatec
Forte	Sherwood
Hardsuits International	Sport Divers Mfg.
Henderson	Tekna
Ikelite	U.S. Divers Corporation
Mares	

Illustrations
Greg Beatty, Harry Averill, Joe De La Torre, Johnny Kwan

Photography
Wayne Brown, Al Hornsby, Frank Palazzi, Charles Seaborn, Karl Shreeves,
Bob Wohlers, Riad Yakzan

Graphic Design and Production
Jeanne Bryant, Dail Schroeder, Joy Zuehls

Contents

Three: Dive Equipment

Four: The Aquatic Realm

Five: The Future of Diving

The Chemistry and Physics of Diving

One

Metric and imperial references appear throughout the Encyclopedia for Recreational Diving. When measurements must be precise (such as the boiling point of water), the metric and imperial are equivalent in the respective systems. However, when measurements are approximate, the figures may be rounded to read more conversationally. In these instances, the measurements may not be equal. Therefore, to simplify the mathematics, measurements may not be identical when comparing metric and imperial examples.

Introduction

Few experiences can compare with the thrill of exploring inner space. The oceans, which comprise more than 70 percent of the planet, make the earth unique in the solar system — perhaps even the universe. Yet, while people have walked on the moon, they have only begun to explore this water planet.

As air-breathing animals, humanity is adapted to life on land. People are used to the phenomena that surround them. They expect to hear and see in a predictable manner. They are familiar with how the body functions in air.

Underwater, divers find a new world where the rules appear different. The diver experiences new sensations, and the underwater world affects the body in ways that may influence its most basic functions.

Yet while diving is unique and sometimes puzzling, it needn't be frightening. The same physical laws that govern the universe topside apply underwater. Pressure and the unique properties of the amazing substance called "water," require some understanding, but they *are* understandable and predictable.

To provide a basis for understanding the physical properties of inner space, this section discusses the chemistry and physics of diving. Unfortunately, the terms "chemistry" and "physics" can cause undue apprehension among those not acquainted and comfortable with mathematics and the sciences. They tend to conjure images of scientists who speak incomprehensibly and use impossibly difficult equations. As a result, fundamentally simple concepts are often viewed as quite difficult, and understandable only by those with "Ph.D." following their names.

Nothing could be further from the truth. As the following section demonstrates, chemistry is simply the study of the composition, structure and properties of substances, while physics is nothing more than the study of how matter and energy behave. With logic, common sense and a few basic arithmetic skills, anyone can understand the physical laws and chemical processes that govern the world in general, and the underwater world in particular.

Overview

To lay a foundation for understanding the physics of diving, this section begins with a look at the nature, composition and states of matter. It explores the most basic unit of matter — the atom: How do these tiny particles interact? The subject looks at other questions as well: What is an atom made of? What does it look like (if you could see it)? How do substances combine? What determines whether a substance is a solid, liquid or gas? What is energy?

The section then turns to the special interests of the diver, beginning by examining the unique structure and properties of water. It explains why life on earth could not exist if water were not unique in its molecular structure, and different from other liquids. This and other answered questions include: What is the special relationship between water and heat? Why does ice float (other substances *sink* when they freeze)? Why does water appear blue at times and green at others? Why do objects appear closer or sometimes farther away than they really are when seen underwater? Why is it possible to hear sounds up to 24 kilometres/15 miles away underwater? How does the specific gravity of an object affect its buoyancy?

With regard to pressure, this section looks at how two Renaissance Italians inspired an investigation into the nature of the "sea" of air that surrounds the earth, and at the answers to questions that affect the diver, such as: How much pressure is exerted on a diver at 30 metres/100 feet, and why doesn't that pressure crush the diver?

From pressure, the next area to consider is gases — those that comprise the atmosphere, and others than affect divers: Why does every air-breathing animal on earth depend on tiny oceanic plankton? Why does breathing helium make a diver's voice unintelligible? What is enriched air? What is heliox? What is the most abundant element in the universe, and what is its role on earth?

This section also looks at gas behavior, including the development of the kinetic gas theory and the General Gas Law, which predicts gas pressure, volume and temperature. Down-to-earth explanations of these classic gas laws, along with examples, demonstrate how they apply to diving: How many molecules strike every square centimetre/inch of a container each second? What is a mole? If the temperature of a scuba tank changes a few degrees, how much will the internal pressure change? How can a perfectly safe gas mixture become poisonous if it is breathed under water? Do gases still exert pressure even when they are dissolved in a liquid?

This chapter of the *Encyclopedia of Recreational Diving* attempts to make chemistry and physics informative, understandable and relevant to diving. Hopefully, it makes these subjects enjoyable. In fact, by the end of this subsection, they will probably seem amazingly simple.

Matter

"Matter" is the substance that makes up the universe. To date, physicists and chemists have identified and agreed upon slightly more than 100 distinct varieties of matter. These distinct forms of matter are called "elements." Of the approximately 100 elements, 90 occur naturally. The remaining have been produced in the laboratory. At the most basic level, all substances, whether living or nonliving, are composed of elements in various proportions and combinations.

By definition, an element is a substance that cannot be decomposed into any simpler substances by chemical process. Water clearly demonstrates the fundamental nature of elements. It is composed of two elements: 1) oxygen and 2) hydrogen. Through various chemical processes, water can be reduced to these two component elements, but no chemical process can further reduce the elements.

Elements can be changed or decomposed via nuclear fission and particle acceleration, but then they no longer retain the properties of elements. In fact, these processes may produce such dramatic changes that the element may turn from matter into energy, which is the principle of atomic energy. Therefore, an element is the most basic form of distinct matter.

Elements are comprised of atoms. An atom is the smallest portion of an

The periodic table of elements
An element is comprised of atoms and cannot be decomposed into a simpler substance. Each element is shown by its chemical symbol; with its atomic number above and its atomic weight below.

1 H 1.008																	2 HE 4.00
3 Li 6.94	4 Be 9.01											5 B 10.8	6 C 12.0	7 N 14.0	8 O 16.0	9 F 19.0	10 Ne 20.2
11 Na 23.0	12 Mg 24.3											13 Al 27.0	14 Si 28.1	15 P 31.0	16 S 32.1	17 Cl 35.5	18 Ar 39.9
19 K 39.1	20 Ca 4.01	21 Sc 45.0	22 Ti 47.9	23 V 50.9	24 Cr 52.0	25 Mn 54.9	26 Fe 55.6	27 Co 58.9	28 Ni 58.7	29 Cu 63.5	30 Zn 65.4	31 Ga 69.7	32 Ge 72.6	33 As 74.9	34 Se 79.0	35 Br 79.9	36 Kr 83.8
37 Rb 85.5	38 Sr 87.6	39 Y 88.9	40 Zr 91.2	41 Nb 92.9	42 Mo 95.9	43 Tc (99)	44 Ru 101.1	45 Rh 102.9	46 Pd 106.4	47 Ag 107.9	48 Cd 112.4	49 In 114.8	50 Sn 118.7	51 Sb 121.8	52 Te 127.6	53 I 126.9	54 Xe 131.3
55 Cs 132.9	56 Ba 137.3	see below 57-71	72 Hf 178.5	73 Ta 180.9	74 W 183.9	75 Re 186.2	76 Os 190.2	77 Ir 192.2	78 Pt 195.1	79 Au 197.0	80 Hg 200.6	81 Tl 204.4	82 Pb 207.2	83 Bi 209.0	84 Po 210	85 At (210)	86 Rn (222)
87 Fr (223)	88 Ra (226)	see below 89-103	104 Rf (261)	105 Ha (260)													

57 La 138.9	58 Ce 140.1	59 Pr 140.9	60 Nd 144.2	61 Pm (147)	62 Sm 150.4	63 Eu 152.0	64 Gd 157.3	65 Tb 158.9	66 Dy 162.5	67 Ho 164.9	68 Er 167.3	69 Tm 168.9	70 Yb 173.0	71 Lu 175.0
89 Ac (227)	90 Th 232.0	91 Pa (231)	92 U 238.0	93 Np (237)	94 Pu (242)	95 Am (243)	96 Cm (247)	97 Bk (245)	98 Cf (251)	99 Es (254)	100 Fm (253)	101 Md (256)	102 No (254)	103 Lw (257)

element capable of exhibiting the specific properties of that element. (The word "atom" comes from the Greek root meaning "uncuttable.") Atoms are so small that if laid side by side, it would take several million atoms to equal the thickness of this page.

Atoms are, in turn, composed of still smaller components that include negatively charged *electrons*, positively charged *protons*, and particles that have no electrical charge at all, called *neutrons*. Positive and negative charges attract, and it's this attraction that maintains the unity of the atom. Additionally, since the total number of protons and electrons is equal (at least in nonionized atoms — more about this later), the atom as a whole has a neutral (no) charge.

The neutrons and protons are located in the center of the atom, in what is referred to as the "nucleus." The protons provide the nucleus with a positive charge, around which the negatively charged electrons move in what is called an "orbital cloud." The high-speed action of the orbiting electrons is why atoms are sometimes described as "fuzzy little balls." In terms of size, the diameter of the electron cloud is 100,000 times larger than that of the nucleus. To illustrate, if a hydrogen atom were about six kilometres/four miles in diameter, the nucleus would be about the size of an orange. However, since the protons and neutrons are about 2000 times heavier than the electrons, the nucleus accounts for 99.9 percent of the atom's mass.

The total mass of the particles within an atom is referred to as the atom's *atomic mass*. Generally, it is the number of protons within the nucleus that dis-

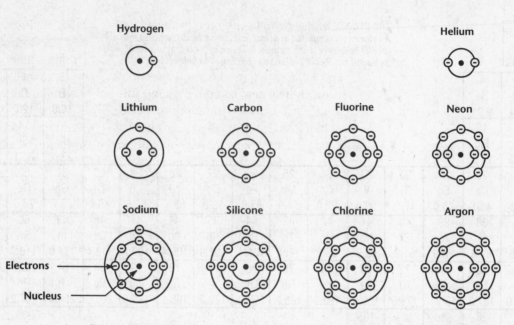

Atom diagrams. The number of protons in the nucleus equals the number of electrons orbiting the nucleus.

Electrons orbit the nucleus in predictable layers or shells. Each shell, this atom has three, can accommodate a specific number of electrons.

tinguishes individual elements. This number is referred to as the element's *atomic number.* Some atoms of the same element may have differing numbers of neutrons, although they contain the same number of protons. These variations on the same element are referred to as *isotopes.*

Through various means, atoms combine with each other to form *molecules.* Molecules comprised of different elements are referred to as "compounds." A molecule is the smallest particle of a com-

pound capable of retaining the properties of that compound. In addition, atoms of the same element sometimes combine to form molecules of the same element. An example of this is the element nitrogen, which combines to form the two atom nitrogen gas molecule found in air. Such a molecule is called a *di-atomic* molecule.

Often, compounds exhibit properties entirely different from those of the component elements. Again, water is an excellent illustration of this concept. Both

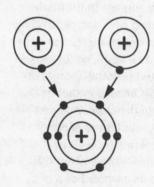

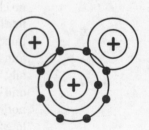

Two hydrogen atoms bond chemically with one oxygen atom to form a water molecule.

of the component parts of water — oxygen and hydrogen — are highly reactive gases in their natural state. Yet, when combined to form the compound water, an entirely new, completely stable substance is formed — a substance (liquid) that is radically different from either of its elemental parts (gases). Similarly, molecular elements (like nitrogen gas) may behave differently from the same element in the form of separate atoms.

Atoms that comprise a given molecule are linked through *chemical bonds.* The formation of a chemical bond is re-

Sodium   Chlorine   Sodium Chloride (Salt)

Ionic bonding occurs when two atoms with opposite charges bond through mutual attraction. Here, the sodium atom transfers an electron to the chlorine atom. The sodium atom now has more protons than electrons and, consequently, a positive charge. The chlorine atom now has a negative charge due to the extra electron and the two atoms bond.

ferred to as a *chemical reaction.* Only those atoms with compatible atomic structures can form chemical bonds. This compatibility depends upon the atoms' electron configurations.

Electrons circle the nucleus in predictable, organized orbits or "shells," with each shell capable of accommodating only a certain number of electrons. How reactive an atom is depends upon the number of electrons in its outermost shell. If this shell is full, the atom will not readily combine with others and is referred to as "stable." Examples of highly stable atoms are the inert gases sometimes used in diving, such as helium and neon.

Other atoms combine more readily, but only with certain other elements. In essence, these atoms combine with each other to "complete" their outer electron shell, which can hold more electrons than the atom has. This may be accomplished by either *ionic* or *covalent* bonding.

An example of ionic bonding is common table salt — sodium chloride (written

"NaCl"). The sodium atom has only one of its 11 electrons in its outer shell. The chlorine atom, on the other hand, has its outer shell almost full with seven electrons, but it can hold up to eight. Therefore, chlorine can take sodium's lone outer electron and complete its own outer shell. Doing this gives the chlorine atom one more negatively charged electron than it has positively charged protons, so that the atom has a net negative charge. Conversely, the sodium atom, having given up its electron, now has one more proton than electrons and therefore a net positive charge results. Since each atom now has a charge, (negative and positive, respectively), they are called *ions.* The two oppositely-charged ions attract each other, forming the ionic bond that creates the compound sodium chloride.

Some atoms will neither entirely give up nor take electrons to complete their outer shells. Instead, they share the electrons required to complete their shells. This is referred to as covalent bonding, and the most common example is the water molecule.

In the case of water, oxygen and hydrogen — two highly reactive elements — combine into a stable compound. To become stable, oxygen requires two electrons to complete its outer shell. Each hydrogen atom has only one electron, and each merely needs one more to complete its shell. (The innermost electron shell can accommodate only two electrons.) By combining with two atoms of hydrogen, oxygen receives — in a sharing arrangement — the two electrons it needs, while each hydrogen atom receives the single electron it needs. As a result of this proportional combining (two hydrogen atoms to every one oxygen atom), water is expressed by what is probably the most commonly recognized chemical symbol — H_2O. This molecular arrangement also gives water other unique properties, which will be detailed later.

States of Matter

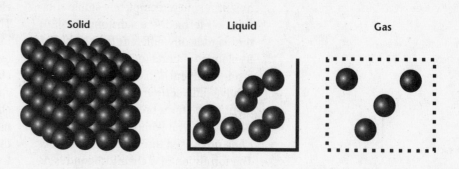

| Solid | Liquid | Gas |

Molecules in a fixed, rigid pattern are solid. Molecules move readily about each other in a liquid state. Molecules are spread even further apart in a gas.

Elements and compounds may exist in one of three states: 1) solids, 2) liquids or 3) gases. Water, for example, can exist in its natural state (liquid), as ice (solid) or as steam (gas).

The state in which a substance exists depends upon how close and how rigid the molecules are that comprise the substance. Typically, the most important factor affecting this is temperature (pressure is also a factor, but less important in most cases), because *heat* is simply the motion of molecules. Temperature is actually a measure of the amount of activity exhibited by the molecules that comprise a substance. The more active the molecules, the "warmer" the substance. As molecular activity decreases, the substance is said to "cool."

Substances with molecules arranged in fixed, aligned patterns are solid. As the temperature rises, the molecules begin to slip from their fixed po-

sitions and move readily about one another, creating a liquid state. Finally, if temperature increases further, molecules will grow further apart and actually leave the surface of the substance, forming a gas. As one may expect from the examples of ice, water and steam, the solid state (ice) represents the coldest condition and the gas state (steam) the warmest.

With respect to pressure, solids and liquids are considered (within the practical realm of diving) incompressible. Gases, however, are highly compressible. The molecules that constitute a gas occupy approximately one thousandth of the total volume of a container at any one time, at room temperature and normal atmospheric pressure. This explains the tremendous degree of compressibility of matter in a gaseous state, and it is the property of gases that has a strong bearing on diving.

Energy

Energy is "the capacity to do work." So, the concepts "energy" and "work" are interrelated. Work is defined as the application of a force through a distance. In the metric system, force is measured in terms of ergs and joules. An erg is the amount of work needed to move one gram one centimetre against the force of gravity (gravitational acceleration); a joule is 10^7 ergs. In the imperial system, energy is measured in terms of foot-pounds. A foot-pound is the amount of work done by a one-pound force, when the point on which it acts moves through a distance of one foot. One joule equals approximately .7375 foot pounds. (Note: These definitions apply loose terminology that consider "weight" and "mass" as interchangeable. Within the context of diving, this is acceptable, though in a pure physics sense, they are not. Mass is constant and weight is a property of mass that varies with gravity.)

Aside from nuclear reactions, energy can neither be created nor destroyed, but rather transformed into five forms: 1) heat, 2) light, 3) electrical, 4) chemical and 5) mechanical.

1. Heat energy, as mentioned previously, is the motion of molecules that make up a substance. The more motion, the greater the heat energy, and vice versa. It should be noted that all energy is eventually turned into heat, and that in the process of converting energy from one form to another always causes some of the energy to dissipate as heat.

2. Light is energy in the form of electromagnetic radiation. The best example is the light energy from the sun. An example of energy transformation is photosynthesis in plants, which transforms light energy into chemical energy.

3. Electrical energy results from the interaction of negatively charged electrons and positively charged protons. A battery is a good example; it stores potential electrical energy until used in an appliance, such as a flashlight.

4. Chemical energy is stored within a substance's molecular composition. A common example of this is gasoline. When it reaches a critical temperature, gasoline reacts with oxygen in a chemical reaction that releases heat energy.

5. Mechanical energy is energy that results from motion or the possibility of motion — it is the result of an object's position or condition. If an object is retained in a position so that, if released, it could do some sort of work, the object is said to have *potential* energy. Once in motion, the object is said to have *kinetic* energy. An example of both types can be found in a spring. When in its static, tense position, the spring has potential energy. Once in motion (either expanding or contracting) the energy is kinetic, that is, released and in motion.

The Metric System and Absolute Zero

Part of understanding the language of chemistry and physics involves understanding the measuring system used by those fields. This system is the metric system, which is the standard means of measurement throughout much of the world, but not necessarily as familiar for people living in areas using the imperial system (feet, pounds, gallons, etc.). For those, a brief overview of the metric system may be useful.

In scientific applications, the metric system is easier to use than the imperial system because it is based upon units of ten. This simplifies matters when converting from one scale unit to another.

By understanding the meanings of prefixes used in the metric system, it's simple to follow:

kilo = one thousand (Greek — used in larger units)

milli = one thousandth (Latin — used in smaller units)

centi = one hundredth

deci = one tenth

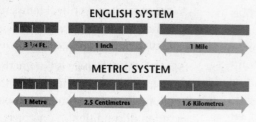

ENGLISH SYSTEM

3 1/4 Ft.   1 Inch   1 Mile

METRIC SYSTEM

1 Metre   2.5 Centimetres   1.6 Kilometres

Metric compared to imperial measurements.

The basic unit for the measurement of length is the metre. One metre equals 39.37 inches. Smaller scales are measured in decimetres (dm) or tenths of a metre; in centimetres (cm) or hundredths of a metre; and in millimetres (mm) or thousandths of a metre. For longer lengths, the kilometre is used. A kilometre is 1000 metres or approximately six-tenths of a mile.

Units of area are expressed as a square of the unit of length. Thus, a rectangle 10cm x 50cm has an area of 500cm^2 or expressed another way, .05m^2. Volume is expressed in terms of the unit of length cubed, such as m^3. Additionally, 1000 cubic centimetres (cc) is referred to in the metric system as a *litre*. In the case of a box 10cm x 20cm x 30cm, it is said to have a volume of either 6000cc or 6 litres. This could also be expressed as 6,000,000mm^3.

The standard metric unit for the measure of mass (used generally as weight) is the gram (g). One gram is equal to the mass of one cc of pure water. One kilogram equals 1000 grams. Therefore, a kilogram equals the mass (weight) of one liter of water, which weighs about 2.2 pounds in the imperial system. As in the case of measuring length, smaller units are expressed as: decigrams (dg), centigrams (cg) and milligrams (mg).

Expressed still another way:

1kg = 1000g = 1,000,000mg   or   1g = 0.001kg = 1000mg

Divers using the metric system to measure gas pressure typically express pressure in *kilograms per square centimetre* (kg/cm^2). However, they sometimes also use the expression *millimetres of mercury* (mmHg). The metric system uses the term *bar* to express the pressure of one atmosphere or 760mm Hg.

Those using the metric system usually employ the Celsius system for the measurement of temperature. As a result, this is also the most common system in scientific measurement. Celsius is based upon water. Water freezes at 0°C (as opposed to 32°F) and boils at 100°C (as opposed to 212°F). To convert a given value from one system to another, use the following formulas:

To convert from Celsius to Fahrenheit: (degrees C x 1.8)+32

To convert from Fahrenheit to Celsius: (degrees F -32) x .555

In place of 1.8 and .555, some people find it easier to remember 9/5 and 5/9, respectively.

Occasionally, temperatures may be expressed in terms of absolute zero, especially when making calculations that apply gas laws. Absolute zero is the temperature at which there is no heat at all; that is, there is no molecular movement at all, or more accurately the molecules reach *zero-point-motion*. To express absolute zero, the Kelvin scale is used when working from degrees Celsius, and the Rankine scale when working from degrees Fahrenheit. 0 Kelvin equals -273°C; 0° Rankine equals -460°F. (Note that Kelvin measurements omit the degree mark.)

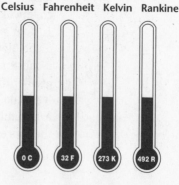

Celsius   Fahrenheit   Kelvin   Rankine

0 C   32 F   273 K   492 R

The freezing point of water on the Celsius, Fahrenheit, Kelvin and Rankine scales.

Converting a Celsius reading to Kelvin simply requires adding 273°C. Hence, 0° Celsius equals 273 Kelvin. To convert a Fahrenheit reading to Rankine simply requires adding 460°. Hence, 0° Fahrenheit equals 460° Rankine.

Water

Divers are primarily concerned with physical phenomena underwater, and comprehending physics and chemistry in water requires an understanding of the properties of water itself.

Water is actually a very simple chemical compound, yet it exhibits unusual properties that make it very special. It consists, as stated earlier, of two

on the other. This creates a slight negative charge at the oxygen end and a slight positive charge at the hydrogen end.

As a result of this configuration, water is referred to as a polar molecule because each molecule can, in turn, now attract other water molecules in much the same way magnets can attract the opposite poles of each other. Therefore, water has a dual bonding characteristic. While its atoms are chemically bound via covalent bonding, water molecules are further bound together via a weaker electrical (polar) attraction, referred to as a *hydrogen bond*, to form liquid water.

It is this weaker hydrogen bond that gives water many of its unique and significant properties. For example, without the polar phenomenon, water molecules would tend to separate very readily — as do other substances of similar molecular weight. If this were true, at room temperature water would be a gas rather than a liquid. One can only imagine how different the world would be if this were true — life as we know it couldn't exist.

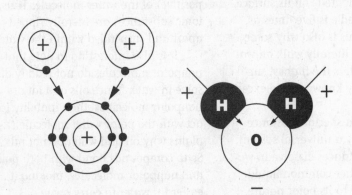

Water molecules are referred to as polar because they exhibit a dual bonding characteristic. While its atoms are bound covalently, water molecules are further bound via a weaker electrical (polar) attraction, referred to as a hydrogen bond.

hydrogen atoms combined with one oxygen atom. The oxygen atom draws the shared hydrogen electrons closer to its nucleus than do the hydrogen atoms, causing a molecule with two hydrogen atoms on one side and an oxygen atom

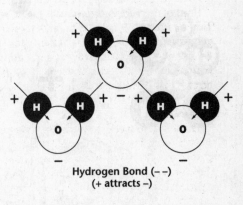

Hydrogen Bond (– –)
(+ attracts –)

Physical and Chemical Properties

Due to hydrogen bonding, a "skin" forms over the surface of water, resulting in surface tension. This means a needle can actually float on its surface.

The first important property of water is that it is *cohesive*. This means that, due to hydrogen bonding, a "skin" forms over the surface of water, resulting in *surface tension*. This phenomenon is observed almost every day — it causes water droplets to hold together and bead. Surface tension is so great that a needle can actually be "floated" on its surface, even though a needle is five times as dense as water! This is also why some insects are able to literally walk on water. In fact, water has the highest surface tension of any known liquid except liquid metals.

Water is also a special substance because it is nearly a universal solvent. In fact, more substances dissolve in water than in any other common liquid. This, again, is due to its polar nature.

When a substance is placed in water, molecules begin to react according to their polarity. Positively charged portions of the molecule are attracted to the oxygen side (which is negative) of the water molecule, and the negatively charged portion of the molecule is attracted to the hydrogen side (which is positive) of the water molecule. Thus, ionic substances are literally ripped apart and suspended within the water.

It is also interesting to note that nonpolar molecules do not readily dissolve in water. Since oils and fat are nonpolar molecules, their inability to react with the polar water molecule explains why oil and water do not mix. Soap compounds bond with both polar and nonpolar molecules, making it easier for water to carry away oils.

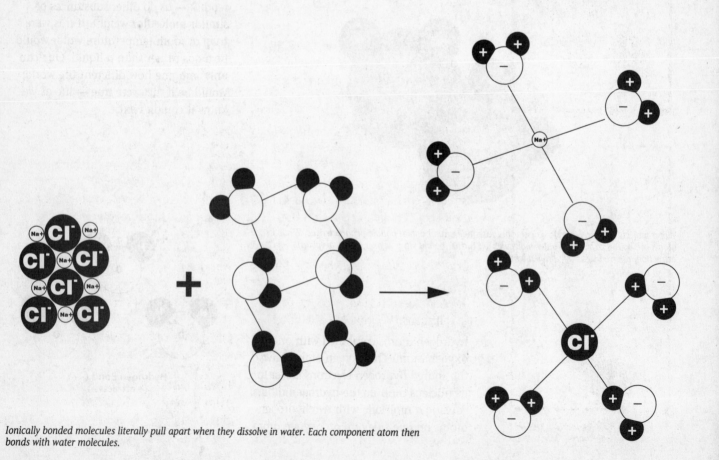

Ionically bonded molecules literally pull apart when they dissolve in water. Each component atom then bonds with water molecules.

Water and Heat

Solid

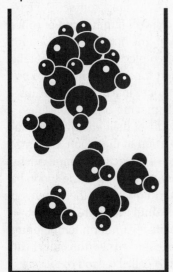

Liquid

Gas

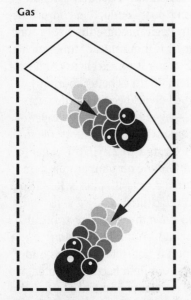

Water as a solid, liquid and gas. Due to water's polar nature, it is less dense as a solid than as a liquid. This is the reason ice floats.

Other important properties of water relate to the effects of heat. Water has one of the highest heat capacities of all naturally occurring substances (ammonia is one of few exceptions), which is why it chills divers at temperatures that would be comfortable in air. Heat capacity is a measure of the amount of heat that must be removed from a substance to cool it a measurable amount. Here, again, water's polar nature is responsible. When heating water, a significant amount of heat must first be used to break the hydrogen bonds before heat can increase the kinetic energy of the water molecules. Because of this high heat capacity, water serves an important balancing function in maintaining the relative stability of the world's climate. It also explains why the temperature variation within a body of water is always less than within a similar volume of air.

Compared to other liquids, water tends to evaporate very slowly when exposed to heat — slower, in fact, than any other common liquid. This phenomenon is referred to as having a *high heat of vaporization*. This phenomenon is due to the fact that before water will evaporate, sufficient heat must be introduced to it to break hydrogen bonds between its molecules. Similarly, water has a *high latent heat of fusion*. This means that when water freezes, it releases large quantities of heat. Conversely, when ice melts, the water absorbs large quantities of heat.

Another important property of water is its density-temperature relationship. As most other liquids cool, they become more dense and turn into solids. The liquid solidifies as the molecules slow and get closer together. The solid is more dense than the liquid, and sinks and accumulates on the bottom of the liquid as the freezing process continues.

Water, however, behaves differently. As it cools, water becomes more dense, *but* only until it reaches 4° Celsius/39° Fahrenheit. At this point, water's polar molecules begin to align themselves as a crystal — ice — in a pattern that takes up *more* space than it does as a liquid. As a result, ice has a *lower* density than water, so that although it's a solid, it floats rather than sinks. Floating ice tends to insulate the water beneath it, slowing the freezing process compared to other liquids. If it were not for this property of water, and if ice sank rather than floated, massive portions of the planet's oceans would be frozen solid. In fact, most of the earth's water might be frozen. It's also this property that causes water to remain 4° Celsius/39° Fahrenheit year-round in some deep lakes.

To examine the relationship between heat and water requires making an important distinction between *heat* and *temperature*. Although they're commonly thought of as being the same, they are not. *Heat* is the total kinetic energy of the molecules within some mass, whereas *temperature* is a measure of the average degree of molecular motion within the mass. Two substances may have the same temperature but have quite different amounts of heat — total kinetic energy. Comparing air and water, suppose someone placed a kettle of air at room temperature on a 95°C/ 200°F stove. The kettle and the air in it would heat to 95°C/200°F very rapidly. Conversely, if the kettle were full of water, it would take significantly longer to reach 95°C/200°F. This is an example of how much more heat water requires to reach the same temperature as air.

Therefore, temperature and heat have different systems of measurement. Temperature is measured in degrees Celsius, Fahrenheit, Kelvin or Rankine. Heat is measured in British Thermal

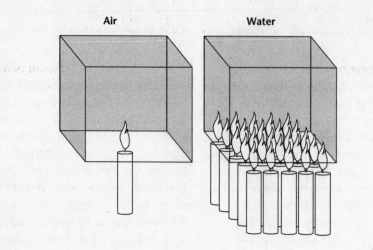

Air   Water

To raise a given volume of water to a specific temperature requires 3200 times as much heat as raising the same volume of air to an equal temperature.

Units (BTUs) or calories. A calorie is the amount of heat required to raise one cubic centimetre of water one degree Celsius; a BTU is the amount of heat required to raise a pint (one pound) of water one degree Fahrenheit.

From the previous example, it should be obvious that one calorie would raise a cubic centimetre of air more than one degree Celsius, and that one BTU would raise a pound of air more than one degree Fahrenheit. In fact, if there are two equal *masses* of water and air, to raise the temperature in each by an equal amount, one needs four times as much heat for the water as for the air. On the other hand, more than 3200 times more heat would be needed to raise the temperature of the water than would be needed to raise the temperature of air when dealing with equal *volumes*!

The reason for water's superior ability to absorb heat is that it is denser than air. Density is a measure of mass or quantity of matter, per unit of volume. For example, a litre of water weighs one kilogram, and the same volume of air weighs 1.3 grams. Therefore, to equal the density of water, air would have to be *approximately* 770 times denser (.0013kg x 770 = 1.0 kg). To use

the imperial system, a cubic foot of water weighs approximately 62.4 pounds, but a cubic foot of air weighs only about .081 pounds. Therefore, to equal the density of water, air would have to be *approximately* 770 times more dense (.081 x 770 = 62.37).

Furthermore, to understand the effects of heat on a diver, the means by which it is transmitted from place to place must be considered. Such transmission occurs in three different ways: 1) conduction; 2) convection and 3) radiation.

Conduction refers to the transmission of heat via direct contact. An example is a spoon in a hot cup of coffee. Even though the handle of a spoon may be cool when placed in the cup, it takes only a short time for the handle to become too hot to touch. This is because the rapidly moving coffee molecules transfer some of their energy to the submerged portion of the spoon. In turn, the heated — or excited — molecules in the submerged portion of the spoon begin transferring some of their energy up the handle until the entire spoon obtains a relatively uniform temperature. A substance that easily transmits heat this way is a called a good *conductor*.

Air is actually a good *insulator* because of its poor conduction characteristics. Conversely, because the heat capacity of water is thousands of times greater than air, water is an excellent conductor (more than 20 times better than air). Submerged divers become chilled very quickly — even in water at a temperature that may be quite comfortable in air. For example, in 21°C/70°F water (a very comfortable air temperature), an unprotected diver will quickly lose heat and become chilled.

Convection involves heat transmission via fluids. A fluid is the state of matter that is not solid — liquids and gases. When a fluid becomes heated, it becomes less dense and tends to rise. As heated fluid rises, cooler fluid replaces it. This sets in motion a continuous flow that draws heat away from whatever the fluid surrounds. Take, for example, an unprotected diver in water. As the diver's body heats the water in contact with the skin, the water becomes less dense and rises, so cooler water replaces it, and the cycle continues. For this reason, there is *always* cold water cooling a diver, even when motionless.

Radiation refers to heat transmission via electromagnetic waves. This is the kind of heat felt from the sun or a fireplace. This form of transmission affects divers the least underwater.

Water and Light

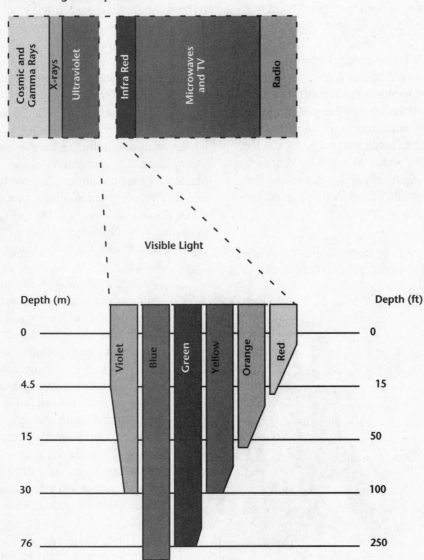

Electromagnetic Spectrum

Visible light penetration in clear water.

The human eye sees by collecting light reflected from an object, converting this energy into electrical impulses and transmitting them to the brain via the optic nerve. Since the behavior of light alters as it passes through water, what a diver sees underwater differs compared to above water. Water affects light through turbidity, diffusion, absorption and refraction, each of which affects visibility differently.

Although only an average of 20 percent of sunlight reaches an approximate depth of 10 metres/30 feet in clear water, there's enough penetration to sustain photosynthesis to depths approaching 100 metres/300 feet in open sea. On the other hand, high concentrations of suspended particles in the water can keep light from reaching even 3 metres/10 feet.

The relative concentration of suspended particles is referred to as *turbidity*. Suspended particles may be organic, as with plankton, or inorganic, as with stirred up sediment (silt). Turbidity may result from healthy and natural phenomena, such as rainwater runoff, or result from artificial, unhealthy phenomena, such as pollution.

Even extremely clear water scatters and deflects light, a phenomenon called *diffusion*. Diffusion reduces the amount of light reaching a certain depth, and it tends to disperse the available light, making it more even. This reduces or even eliminates shadows underwater.

The concept of *absorption* first requires an understanding of the nature of light energy, and how the eye perceives it. Electromagnetic energy (of which visible light is one form) travels in *waves*; the length of these waves is determined by their energy. Wavelength determines the type of electromagnetic energy. Some wavelengths of electromagnetic energy are not visible, such as ultraviolet light, infrared light, X-ray, microwaves and cosmic ray.

The human eye sees only a narrow segment of the electromagnetic spectrum — a range of about 400 nanometres (nm) to about 760nm. Differences in wavelengths within this range the eye perceives as colors. When light strikes an object, the object absorbs some wavelengths and reflects others; the eye perceives the object's color based on the reflected wavelengths. When *all* possible wavelengths of visible light reflect off something at once, the eye sees the color white. When *no* (or very few) wavelengths of visible light reflect, the eye sees the "color" (actually a *lack* of color) black.

Owing to the fact that light energy travels in wavelengths, it's easy to predict water's tendency to absorb light. As light penetrates water the absorption process begins by filtering out wavelengths with the least energy — the red end of the visible spectrum. In fact, as most divers realize, reds tend to disappear very quickly during descent. After red, water absorbs oranges and yellows. Hence, at depth, objects that are red, orange or yellow appear black or gray because the wavelengths responsible for these colors are absorbed by the water column. At depth, there is little or no light of the appropriate wavelength to reflect off a red, orange or yellow object.

Clear water provides maximum transparency to wavelengths of approximately 480nm — what the eye perceives as blue. However, in turbid water, maximum transparency shifts to wavelengths of approximately 530nm — or yellow-green. This phenomenon explains why blue dominates clear water, and why yellow-green dominates turbid water. (See Section Two, The Physiology of Diving, "The Physiology of Color Perception: How Divers See Colors Under Water.")

Absorption affects the visibility of something underwater by contrast as well as by color because it's easier to see something that stands out against its background. Experiments have shown that turbidity, depth, salinity, particle size and pollution all affect light absorption by water, and therefore contrast as well. This is because anything that affects color filtration properties will affect what colors will contrast with each other.

This is one reason dive equipment manufacturers often use fluorescent colors. Fluorescent colors are conspicuous un-

Color contrast affects underwater visibility. The blue wet suit blends with the background, the black wet suit stands out.

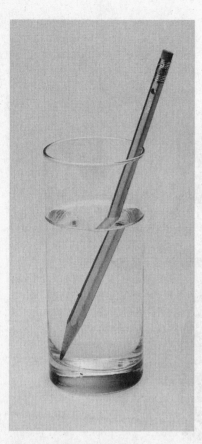

Because light travels at different speeds in different substances, its angle shifts as it passes from one medium to another. This is called refraction and it makes a pencil in a glass of water appear broken.

derwater because their wavelengths aren't common underwater, and because fluorescents don't simply reflect color, but *emit* color when stimulated by light of any shorter wavelength (the phenomenon of *fluorescence*). This is why fluorescents retain their colors at depth, and they're not restricted to dive gear — the *Corynactus* anemone, for example, appears red at depth because they contain natural fluorescents. When not displayed against another fluorescent color, fluorescent colors increase contrast, making objects more visible.

Another factor related to vision underwater is how the eye adapts to low light levels. The eye adapts by opening the pupil to admit more light, but after the pupil is open all the way, it continues to adapt by switching from day vision to night vision cells (photoreceptors) in the eye (called "cones" and "rods" respectively, due to their shape). This process increases the eye's sensitivity to light, but decreases the ability to distinguish fine detail and color. These adaptations begin to occur in as little as ten minutes in low light, although they

may require more than 30 minutes when going from bright conditions to near total darkness. To assist in this adaptation process, particularly when night diving, some divers (especially in the military) wear red goggles or prepare under red light for 10 to 20 minutes before entering the water.

The last property of light that concerns divers is *refraction*. This is the tendency of light to bend as it passes from one medium to another — such as from air to water. Refraction results when light travels at different speeds through various substances due to different densities. For example, light travels through air much faster than through water, so its angle changes when it goes from air into water (unless entering at a 90 degree angle), or vice versa.

To see clearly underwater, divers wear masks. Light must travel through water, glass and air to reach the diver's eyes. During each interface, the light wave refracts since each medium has a different density. As a result, objects appear closer by a ratio of about 4:3 according to their actual and apparent distance. For instance, an object that is actually four metres/yards away will appear to be only three metres/yards away. New divers sometimes miss when reaching for something due to refraction; with experience, most divers learn to correct unconsciously.

The tendency to underestimate distance due to refraction is very interesting because the apparent distance may be reversed at greater distances, so that under certain conditions, objects appear *farther* away than they actually are. This phenomenon — called *visual reversal* — depends upon depth and seems to result from decreased brightness and reduced contrast, as well as an absence of familiar visual/distance cues found on land. In highly turbid water, even relatively close objects can appear farther away than they are. As a general rule

Refraction makes objects underwater appear closer by a ratio of approximately 4:3.

in estimating distance, the closer the object, the more likely it will appear closer than it actually is due to refraction. The more turbid the water, the more likely it will appear farther away than it actually is due to visual reversal.

The magnification effects of refraction may not affect apparent distance, but size. The magnification factor of 25 percent may make things look bigger, rather than closer, but again, divers learn to compensate for this just as they

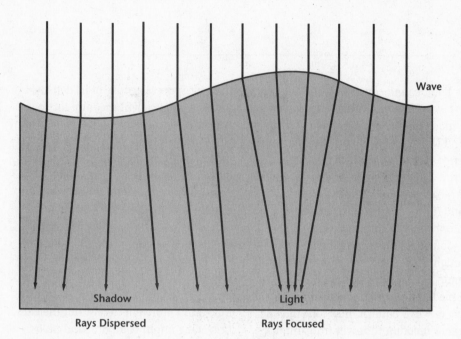

Light ripples are caused by waves concentrating and dispersing light on the bottom. Wave crests focus light rays; troughs disperse light rays, causing shadow.

learn to compensate for apparent distance. It should be noted that apparent closeness and apparent size both result from refraction; the difference is simply how the diver's mind interprets the image — either as a normal sized object that's apparently closer, or as an apparently larger object.

Refraction also causes the constantly changing light ripples appearing on the bottom. These ripples are most noticeable on flat, sandy bottoms and are caused by a lens effect of surface waves. As a wave passes overhead, the cresting portion refracts light and concentrates them on a bright spot on the seafloor.

Reflection also affects underwater visibility. When light encounters something it cannot penetrate, as mentioned, the substance absorbs and/or reflects the light, depending upon wavelengths. Light may also reflect from a substance it can penetrate, including water, if it strikes at a shallow angle. This is why it's brightest underwater from approximately 10 a.m. to 2 p.m. — with the sun directly overhead, light strikes the water at a steep (near perpendicular) angle and most penetrates. With the sun lower in the sky, much of the light reflects off the surface, with proportionately less light entering. This is why underwater photographers and videographers consider 10 a.m. to 2 p.m. the ideal time for shooting.

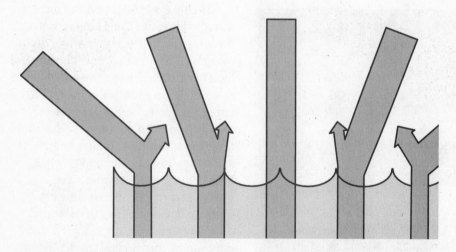

Maximum penetration occurs when light enters the water perpendicularly. The shallower the angle of penetration, the more light is reflected off the surface.

Water and Sound

Like light, sound consists of and travels in, waves. However, while light waves are made up of electromagnetic energy, sound waves are made up of acoustical energy, which is a form of mechanical energy. Electromagnetic energy (such as light) can exist apart from matter; sound (and other mechanical energy) can only exist within matter.

Sound results when an object, through action (such as vibration), sets in motion a wave or pattern of waves in the medium in which it is present. This wave or wave pattern may continue into another medium that will transmit it. For instance, a sound in water, if it has sufficient energy, may continue into the air. Once the wave comes in contact with the eardrum, the energy is "heard" and perceived as sound.

Unlike light, sound travels best in dense media, such as solids or liquids. This is because the molecules that comprise media such as these are densely packed and can easily transmit the wave motion from one molecule to the next. Conversely, sound cannot travel in a vacuum (absence of matter), such as

in outer space. Because of its density, water is an excellent medium for sound transmission. In fact, at 15°C/58°F, fresh water transmits sound at approximately 1410 metres/4625 feet per second, while seawater at the same temperature transmits sound at approximately 1550 metres/5084 feet per second. This is approximately four times the speed of sound in air.

It should be noted that from a pure physics point of view, it's not really the *density* of water that allows it to transmit sound more effectively, but the *elasticity*. One might compare sending a wave down a taut rope by snapping it with snapping a taut rubber band; a wave travels along the rubber band faster and farther because of it's elastic quality. Since in nature dense materials usually have superior elasticity, it's common to attribute good sound transmission to the fact the material is denser. This is "loosely" accurate and simpler to explain, so it's a suitable guideline for diving purposes, even if not technically or universally accurate. (Lead and carbon, for example, are quite dense but don't transmit sound well because they have little elasticity.)

In any event, as a result of sound's increased transmission speed in water, divers hear quite well underwater and over much greater distances than on land (particularly lower frequency sounds). As an example, ships with listening equipment are able to detect sounds emanated underwater from distances as far away as approximately 24 kilometres/15 miles, and divers often hear boats that are beyond sight.

The speed of sound underwater makes it difficult to discern the sound direction. The brain determines sound direction by interpreting the difference between when a sound reaches each ear and relative intensity, but this is based

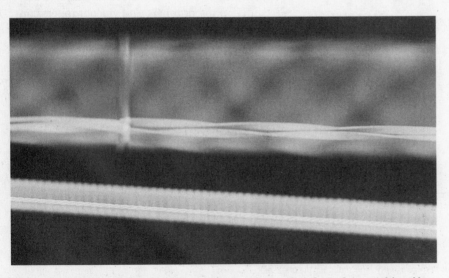

A wave travels along a rubber band faster and farther than along a piece of string because of the rubber band's elastic quality. The elastic property of water, rather than its density, makes it a good sound conductor.

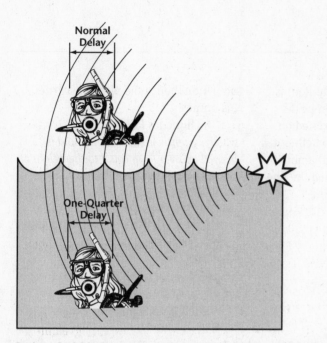

Because sound delay between ears is one quarter of what it is at the surface, a diver perceives sound as coming from all directions at once.

on sound in air. Underwater, the high speed of sound means that perceptually, sound reaches both ears simultaneously and with equal intensity. Hence, sound appears to be coming from all directions, which results in the illusion that sound comes from directly overhead. Nonetheless it is interesting to note that

evidence suggests that under the proper conditions (proper frequency selection, duration and rise/decay time), divers are able to use sound to aid underwater navigation, and the brain does manage to determine its direction.

Because sound travels well in water, one may wonder why humans can't talk underwater. Vocal cords produce sound by vibrating as exhaled air passes over them, but sound waves in air do not transfer efficiently to water. This is why a submerged diver — even one near the surface — can't hear above water noises unless they're very loud. Over the years, different devices have attempted to increase the efficiency of sound transfer from air to water to allow divers to speak, but so far none of these have been widely accepted. Electronic underwater communication equipment has been quite successful because it turns human voice sound into a signal that's received electronically, but in essence this is underwater two way radio, not the human voice carried through water. (See Underwater Communication Equipment in the Equipment Section.)

Another sound transmission variable relates to differing water temperatures, such as in a thermocline. As mentioned earlier, as a substance changes temperature, its density changes also. Also when sound waves pass through media of differing densities such as from air to water, they lose a considerable amount of energy crossing the interface. So, sound transmission can be greatly affected by a thermocline, or any other place where waters of different temperatures meet. For example, it may be possible to hear a sound quite well in one layer of water, yet difficult or impossible to hear the same sound in another water layer only a metre/few feet away. How significantly water temperature affects sound transmission depends on the degree of temperature change and the sound.

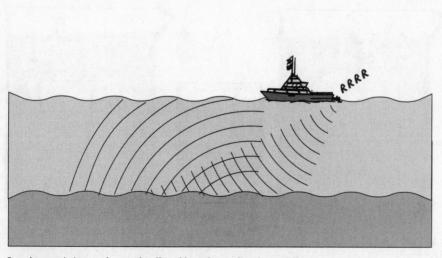

Sound transmission can be greatly affected by a thermocline due to different water densities.

Buoyancy

The force that causes objects to float is called *buoyancy*. Buoyancy can be described as an upward force exerted on any object placed in a fluid, whether it sinks or floats. The Greek mathematician Archimedes first explained the phe-

nomenon, hence the principle carries his name:

Archimedes Principle: *Any object wholly or partly immersed in a fluid is buoyed up by a force equal to the weight of the fluid displaced by the object.*

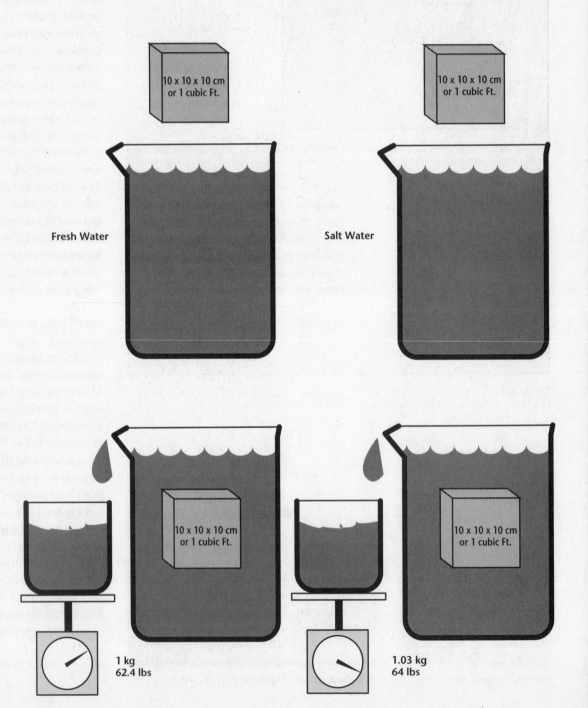

Fresh Water

Salt Water

10 x 10 x 10 cm
or 1 cubic Ft.

10 x 10 x 10 cm
or 1 cubic Ft.

10 x 10 x 10 cm
or 1 cubic Ft.

10 x 10 x 10 cm
or 1 cubic Ft.

1 kg
62.4 lbs

1.03 kg
64 lbs

Because the density of the fluid displaced by identical objects is greater in salt water, the object is buoyed up by a greater force in salt water than in fresh.

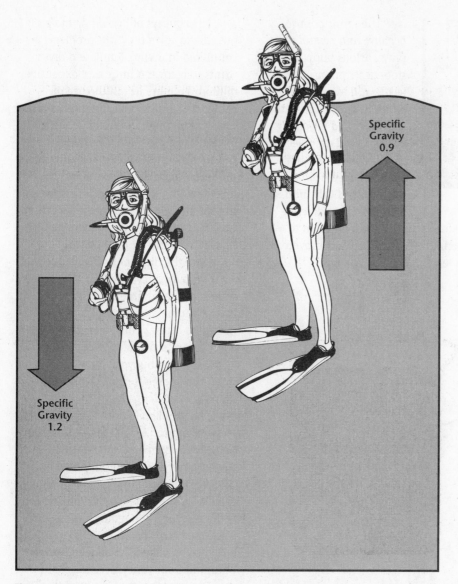

Specific
Gravity
0.9

Specific
Gravity
1.2

The use of a weight belt to offset the buoyancy dive equipment creates allows a diver to submerge. The BCD allows the diver to vary displacement and consequently buoyancy.

explains why a diver needs more weight when diving in salt water. One litre of pure fresh water weighs one kilogram; or in the imperial system, pure water weighs 62.4 pounds per cubic foot. On the other hand, due to the dissolved salts, seawater weighs approximately 1.03 kg per litre/64 pounds per cubic foot. The additional weight and density of seawater make it generate more buoyancy for a given displacement compared to fresh water.

The tendency for solid and liquid substances to float or sink in water is measured as *specific gravity*. Specific gravity compares the density of a given substance to pure water by forming a ratio of the densities. Since pure water is the standard of measure, the ratio of pure water to pure water is 1:1. Therefore, pure water has a specific gravity of 1.0. Substances with a value less than 1.0 are, by definition, less dense than pure water and will float in pure water. Substances with values greater than 1.0 are more dense and will sink in pure water. (Gases are measured on the basis of the density of air at standard temperature and pressure — termed STP — which is 273K/518°R at 1.0 atmosphere absolute.)

In the human body, buoyancy characteristics depend upon the proportion of various body tissues, because each tissue has a different specific gravity. For example, fat tissue has a specific gravity of between 0.7 to 0.9; bone approximately 1.9; and muscle 1.08. Depending upon factors such as the ratio of fat to muscle, a human body has a specific gravity near 1.0, but some individuals may be slightly higher than 1.0, and tend to sink, or lower than 1.0, and tend to float in pure water. However, dive equipment — particularly a wet suit or dry suit displaces considerably more water without a corresponding weight increase. The net result is usually a substantial buoyancy increase, requiring a weight system to allow the diver to submerge.

Archimedes' principle holds true for all objects in all fluids (in diving, the fluid in question is usually water, of course). However, for a given object with a specific volume and weight, variations in buoyancy will result from variations in the density of the fluid in which the object is immersed. The more dense the fluid, the more buoyancy results for a given displacement.

This variation includes the seemingly insignificant difference in the density of salt water and fresh water, and

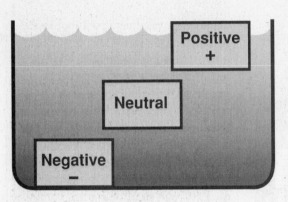

The three states of buoyancy.

The terms *positive*, *negative* and *neutral* simplify various buoyancy state descriptions. An object that floats is called *positively buoyant*; one that sinks is called *negatively buoyant*, and an object that neither floats nor sinks is called *neutrally buoyant*. It is this third condition that divers strive for because it enables them to minimize the energy expended overcoming a tendency to float or sink.

The concept of buoyancy makes it possible to solve practical problems encountered in diving. Suppose a diver wants to recover a large and expensive outboard engine lost in the ocean. (Note: for simplicity in the mathematics, metric and imperial figures in the following example are *not* equivalent.) If the engine weighs 100 kg/300 lbs out of the water, how much additional buoyant force (that is, buoyancy in addition to that already caused by the fact the engine is in water) must be applied to float the engine off the bottom?

First, the diver must determine the existing buoyancy, which is equal to the weight of the volume of water displaced by the engine. Supposing the engine displaces 20 litres/2 cubic feet. 20 litres/2 cubic feet of seawater weighs 20.6 kg/128 lbs, so the buoyant force acting upon the engine is also 20.6 kg/128 pounds.

The problem can be viewed as one of opposing forces; 100 kilograms/300 pounds of downward force (gravity — the engine's dry weight) opposed by 20.6 kg/128 lbs of upward force (buoyancy). For the engine to become neutrally buoyant, the remaining negative buoyancy must be offset: 100 kg/300 lbs - 20.6 kg/128 lbs = 79.4 kg/172 lbs of additional buoyancy needed.

Disregarding the weight of the lifting device (lift bag or drum), determining how much water to displace and offset the remaining negative buoyancy becomes a matter of dividing the negative buoyancy by the weight of seawater: 79.4 kg ÷ 1.03 kg per litre = 77.1 litres of water to displace, or 172 lbs ÷ 64 lbs per cubic foot = 2.7 cubic feet of water to displace. In practice a diver would displace the water by adding this air volume to the lifting device.

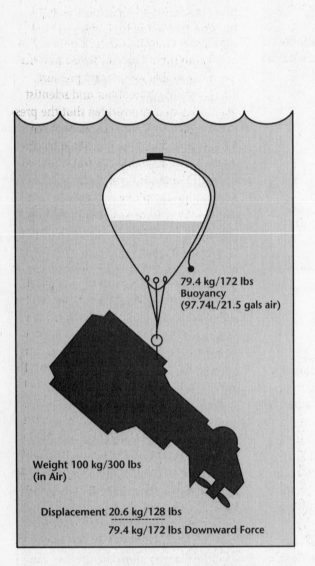

79.4 kg/172 lbs
Buoyancy
(97.74L/21.5 gals air)

Weight 100 kg/300 lbs
(in Air)

Displacement 20.6 kg/128 lbs

79.4 kg/172 lbs Downward Force

If the outboard's weight and displacement are known, it is possible to determine the amount of buoyant force needed to lift it.

Pressure

Pressure is the term used to describe the force or weight acting upon some unit of area. Mathematically it can be expressed as:

$$\text{Pressure} = \frac{\text{Force}}{\text{Area}}$$

Most divers are familiar with pressure expressed as kilograms per square centimetre (kg/cm^2) or pounds per square inch (psi), both of which describe pressure based on weight per given area. Underwater, two different sources exert pressure: the weight of the atmosphere upon the water, and the weight of the water column itself.

Scientists have understood for a long time that air has substance (as can be deduced when one feels the wind against one's face). The Renaissance scientist Galileo first demonstrated that air has weight, even though the body doesn't normally perceive that weight. Building upon this, Evangelista Torricelli, an Italian mathematician, reasoned that if the atmosphere surrounds everything and humanity lives at the bottom of this "sea of air," then the body must be under a constant pressure.

In the classic experiment with a sealed, inverted tube of mercury, Torricelli demonstrated that the atmosphere had sufficient pressure to hold 760 millimetres/30 inches of mercury in a vacuum tube. This confirmed that air has measurable weight and pressure. Later, French philosopher and scientist Blaise Pascal demonstrated that the pressure exerted by the atmosphere at sea level equals the pressure exerted by approximately 10 metres/33 feet of seawater. Since water pressure is the weight of water per unit volume, it's easy to demonstrate that 10 metres/33 feet of seawater exerts the same pressure as the atmosphere.

In the metric system, one litre of seawater weighs 1.03 kg, which in volume equals 1000 cm^3 and forms a cube 10 cm by 10 cm by 10 cm (10 cm x 10 cm x 10 cm= 1000 cm^3). The bottom of the cube, against which all the water pressure exerts, would be 100 cm^2 (10 x10 =100). To find out the pressure per/cm^2, divide 1.03 kg by 100 cm^2, which equals 0.0103 kg/cm^2. This means each 10 cm of seawater exerts a pressure of .0103 kg/cm^2. To convert this to pressure per metre, multiply by 10 (1 metre = 100 cm; 100 cm ÷ 10 cm = 10), for .103 kg/cm^2 pressure for each metre of seawater.

Dividing this pressure into atmospheric pressure per square centimetre

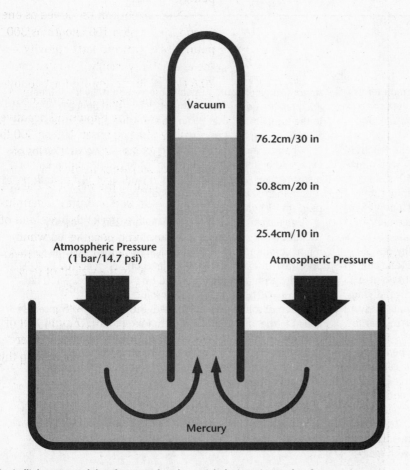

Vacuum

76.2cm/30 in

50.8cm/20 in

25.4cm/10 in

**Atmospheric Pressure
(1 bar/14.7 psi)**

Atmospheric Pressure

Mercury

Torricelli demonstrated that the atmosphere has weight by inverting a tube of mercury into a pan. Atmospheric pressure held 760 mm/30 inches of mercury in the tube.

shows how many metres of seawater equals one atmosphere of pressure. One atmosphere exerts 1.03 kg/cm^2 ÷ .103 kg/cm^2 per metre = 10 metres. Therefore, 10 metres of seawater exerts the same pressure as the atmosphere.

In imperial units, one cubic foot of seawater weighs 64 pounds. The bottom of a cubic foot, against which all the water pressure exerts, would be 144 in^2 (12 in x 12 in = 144 in^2), To find how much

pressure is exerted per square inch for each foot of seawater, divide 64 lbs by 144 This shows that each foot of seawater exerts a pressure of .445 lbs/in^2.

Dividing this pressure into atmospheric pressure per square inch shows how many feet of seawater equals one atmosphere of pressure. 14.7 psi ÷ .445 psi per foot= 33 feet. Therefore, 33 feet of seawater exerts the same pressure as the atmosphere.

Pressure Terminology

To avoid error and confusion, there are some common terms used to express pressure. These terms include: *atmospheric pressure, barometric pressure, gauge pressure, absolute pressure* and *ambient pressure.*

Atmospheric pressure is the pressure exerted by the weight of the atmosphere at sea level and although it varies with atmospheric conditions, it is accepted universally as 760 millimetres of mercury (mmHg) or 14.7 psi. This may simply be referred to as one atmosphere ("atm" or "ATM") of pressure. In metric system countries, the pressure of one atmosphere is also expressed in *bar*, and is commonly used to express cylinder pressure. Although there's technically a slight difference between a bar and 760 mmHg/14.7 psi (one bar =14.5 psi), one bar is usually considered equal with no attempt to account for the difference. For most practical diving applications, most people find it simplest to calculate pressure problems using atmospheres/bar, then convert the answer to another pressure measurement if necessary.

Barometric pressure is synonymous with atmospheric pressure except that it varies according to atmospheric conditions such as weather. High- and low-pressure centers associated with settled or unsettled air are examples of this concept. This is seldom used in diving applications.

Gauge pressure is the pressure designation that uses atmospheric pressure as its zero point. It is defined as the difference between atmospheric pressure and the pressure being mea-

sured. Gauge pressure may be observed on a diver's submersible pressure gauge, for example. Before that gauge is attached to the tank, it indicates 0. Yet, the pressure on the surface is not zero, it is 1 bar/14.7 psi.

When gauge pressure readings are used, they are commonly expressed by indicating the letter "g" at the end of the unit of measurement (except bar). Thus, a reading of 14.7 pounds per square inch of gauge pressure would be expressed as "14.7 psig," or "1 bar gauge."

Absolute pressure is a pressure designation that uses a vacuum as its zero point. It is the *total* pressure exerted, which might commonly be derived by adding gauge and atmospheric pressure. For example, if at sea level an SPG read 100 bar/1470 psig, the absolute pressure would be 1 bar/14.7 psi + 100 bar/1470 psi = 101 bar/1484.7 psi absolute pressure.

When absolute pressure is used, the letter "a" is commonly added to the unit of measurement (except bar). Thus, 14.7 pounds per square inch of absolute pressure would be expressed as "14.7 psia," or "1 bar absolute." When measuring pressure in atmospheres, the abbreviation is "ata" or "ATA," for "atmospheres absolute."

Ambient pressure is roughly synonymous with absolute pressure; it means "surrounding" pressure, as in "What is the ambient pressure when a diver reaches 24 metres/80 feet in the ocean?"

Pressure and Liquids

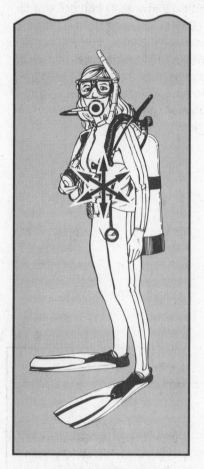

The human body is made primarily of water, which is incompressible. Pressure transfers through it directly and equally in all directions so the diver only feels the pressure in the body's air spaces.

Although all matter is compressible under enough pressure, within the pressure ranges encountered by recreational divers, water is considered incompressible for practical purposes. Any outside pressure applied to the surface of water (or other liquid) transfers equally in all directions through the liquid. This is the principle by which a hydraulic lift operates, and is called *Pascal's principle*.

Because body tissues consist primarily of water, pressure transfers through them directly and equally in all directions, with no direct effect. Hence, the human body can endure the tremendous pressures exerted on it underwater, and the diver only feels the pressure in the body's air spaces.

During descent, water pressure increases at a rate of one bar per 10 metres/one atmosphere per 33 feet in salt water, or one bar per 10.3 metres/one atmosphere per 34 feet in fresh water. Because water is incompressible, this value remains constant regardless of depth. In addition to the water pressure (also called *hydrostatic pressure*), atmospheric pressure exerting force on the surface of the water also reaches the diver. Therefore, to determine the ambient or absolute pressure at any given depth, one must add the hydrostatic pressure to the atmospheric pressure.

For example, to determine the ambient pressure at 30 msw (metres of seawater)/99 fsw (feet of seawater):

Metric

30 msw ÷ 10 msw = 3 bar

3 bar water pressure + 1 bar atmospheric = 4 bar absolute pressure

or

Imperial

99 fsw ÷ 33 fsw = 3 atm

3 atm water pressure + 1 atm atmospheric = 4 atmospheres absolute pressure (4 ata)

In seawater, each 10 metres/33 feet produces 1.03 kg per cm^2/14.7 psi of hydrostatic pressure. To determine absolute pressure in kg/cm^2 or psi at any depth of seawater, divide the depth by 10 (for metric) or 33 (for imperial), then add 1 to the result (for the atmosphere of air) to get the absolute pressure in bar/ata. Multiply this by 1.03 for kg/cm^2 absolute or 14.7 for psia.

For example, at the depth of 240 msw/792 fsw, the absolute pressure is 25 atmospheres: (240 divided by 10 plus 1 = 25; 792 divided by 33 plus 1 = 25). This equals 25.75 kg/cm^2 absolute (25 x 1.03 = 25.75) or 367.5 psia (25 x 14.7 = 367.5).

Gases

Many elements exist as gases in their natural state, and because gases mix easily, in nature, gases normally occur mixed rather than in isolation. On earth, the most common gas mixture is air, which consists of nitrogen, oxygen, argon, carbon dioxide, neon, helium, krypton, hydrogen, xenon, radon, and carbon monoxide among others. However, many of these gases exist in such

small portions that they are normally inconsequential. So, from a practical point of view, it's only necessary to address those gases that affect diving, either in respiration or through special applications to diving. These gases include: oxygen, nitrogen, carbon dioxide, carbon monoxide, helium, hydrogen, argon and neon.

Under normal conditions, the com-

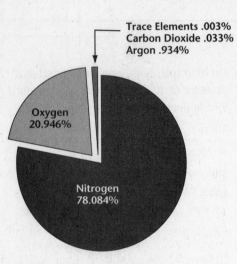

The Atmosphere's gas composition.

Trace Elements .003%
Carbon Dioxide .033%
Argon .934%

Oxygen
20.946%

Nitrogen
78.084%

position of dry air remains quite uniform and is made up (by volume) of the following:

Nitrogen	78.084%
Oxygen	20.946%
Argon	0.934%
Carbon Dioxide	0.033%

The remaining components of air — neon, helium, krypton, hydrogen, xenon, radon and carbon monoxide — are referred to as rare gases and account for only 0.003% of the atmosphere. With respect to diving, these have little or no effect when breathing compressed air. In fact, it's normally adequate to treat air as 79% nitrogen and 21% oxygen and ignore other gases.

Nitrogen

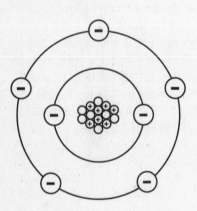

The nitrogen atom.

Nitrogen, as an element, reacts readily with other substances and occurs in many natural compounds. As a gas, two nitrogen atoms join to form a single nitrogen molecule (N_2), which is an "inert" gas so far as its applications to diving are concerned (it should be noted that especially among plants, nitrogen gas is not inert and takes part in important biochemical processes). Nitrogen is the most abundant component of the atmosphere, but it isn't used during respiration.

In diving, breathing nitrogen can cause several problems. While it is not used chemically in the respiratory process, nitrogen (and to a varying extent all other inert and reactive gases) interfere with signal transmission through the central nervous system when breathed under pressure, causing nitrogen narcosis. (See Section Two, The Physiology of Diving.) In addition to its narcotic effect, nitrogen dissolves into body tissues when breathed under pressure during a dive, and must be kept within limits to prevent it from coming out of solution and forming bubbles within the body (decompression sickness) when the pressure is released at the end of the dive. Any inert gas breathed by a diver causes the same concern.

$$\frac{1\text{bar} \times 500 \text{ liter}}{302 \text{ K}} = \frac{6.5 \text{ bar} \times V_2}{278 \text{ K}}$$

Oxygen

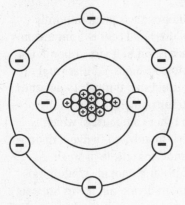

The oxygen atom.

Oxygen is a very reactive element that readily combines with other elements to form many different compounds. Oxygen is also one of the most plentiful elements on earth, accounting for 20.946% of the atmosphere. The vast abundance of this gas is due primarily to the tiny yet prolific phytoplankton that thrive in the shallow lighted zone of all the world's oceans. These phytoplankton — primarily dinoflagelettes and diatoms — produce more than 85 percent of the world's oxygen. Without these tiny creatures, life as we know it could not exist.

Like nitrogen, in its gaseous form oxygen combines with itself so that two atoms create the oxygen gas molecule O_2. However, unlike nitrogen gas, oxygen gas remains very reactive and the body uses it during metabolism (the process by which food is converted to energy to support life).

Although the body needs oxygen to live, under pressure oxygen can become toxic. When breathing air within recreational depth limits, this isn't an issue, but when using *enriched* air (air that has more than 21% oxygen — commonly 32% or 36% oxygen) a diver can reach depths at which oxygen toxicity can occur. (See Section Two, The Physiology of Diving, for more information about oxygen toxicity.)

Carbon Dioxide

Carbon dioxide is another active compound that dissolves well in seawater. As a result, seawater contains a concentration of carbon dioxide far exceeding that found in air. In its normal concentration in the atmosphere, carbon dioxide is odorless, colorless and tasteless, though in high concentrations, it has an acid odor and taste. This is what gives a carbonated beverage its distinct smell and taste, and why the same beverage tastes different after it "goes flat."

One of the main sources of carbon dioxide is the waste product from animal respiration (plant respiration in light is called *photosynthesis*, which consumes carbon dioxide and gives off oxygen). Another important source is air pollution. Divers are primarily concerned with controlling carbon dioxide levels, since, as discussed in Section Two, The Physiology of Diving, too much or too little can cause physiological problems.

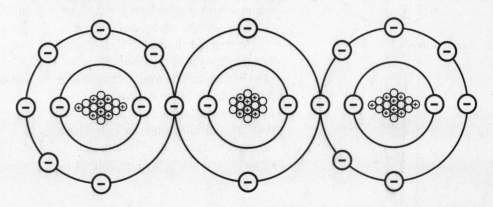

The carbon dioxide molecule.

Carbon Monoxide

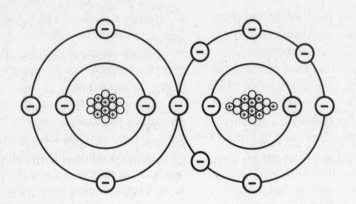

The carbon monoxide molecule.

Carbon monoxide is predominantly man-produced and results from incomplete combustion of hydrocarbon fuels. It is highly poisonous, odorless and tasteless, making it difficult to detect in isolation. Fortunately, it commonly occurs with other compounds, which is why divers are advised to avoid diving with air that has a taste or smell. Although carbon monoxide contamination is rare in diving air, it can happen, usually due to compressors that are either improperly placed (resulting in pumping exhaust gases into the dive cylinder) or lubricated with inappropriate substances that partially combust and form carbon monoxide during the heat of compression.

Helium

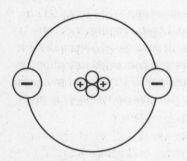

The helium atom.

Helium is so rare that it was not known to exist in significant quantity until 1895. Some estimates suggest that commercial helium sources will be exhausted shortly into twenty first century. An extremely light gas (second only to hydrogen), helium is inert and doesn't even combine with itself to form a two-atom gas molecule like nitrogen or oxygen.

In diving, helium is used as a substitute for nitrogen in the breathing mixtures of deep commercial, technical and military divers because it does not produce the narcotic effects under pressure that are associated with nitrogen. These mixtures include heliox (helium and oxygen), and trimix (helium, nitrogen and oxygen).

Because of its light molecular weight, helium mixtures are easier to breathe than nitrogen-oxygen mixtures at a given depth, but there are problems associated with helium use in diving. First, divers breathing heliox and trimix have to contend with extensive and complex decompression procedures. These procedures not only require special dive tables for the heliox or trimix in use, but may require the diver to switch to different gas blends during decompression. Obviously, this is beyond the needs and limits of mainstream recreational diving.

The second problem is a result of helium's light molecular weight, which makes sound travel faster in a heliox mixture. This increased speed makes a diver's voice sound garbled and unintelligible when using voice communication. Fortunately, electronic communication devices can restore this unintelligible speech to an understandable form.

Third, helium conducts heat well, so a helium mix is not used for dry suit inflation. This means that the diver must use a different gas for insulation (see Argon) in a dry suit. However, using a different dry suit gas raises a decompression concern in which gases dissolved in the body try to dissolve out of the body through the skin when the diver is surrounded by a gas different from the breathing gas. This theoretical problem (called *isobaric counterdiffusion*)

occurs when a diver breathes a slowly diffusing gas while immersed in a rapidly diffusing gas. This is avoided by choosing an appropriate dry suit gas, (such as air or argon) or by using a wet suit.

Finally, at extreme pressures helium is associated with a physiological phenomenon called high-pressure nervous syndrome (HPNS), which causes muscular tremors, dizziness and nausea at extreme depths. This can be partially offset by putting nitrogen in the breathing mix, so that nitrogen narcosis "calms" the nervous system. Again, it should be noted that the use of helium and the effects of HPNS are well beyond the realm of mainstream recreational diving.

Hydrogen

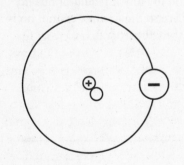

The hydrogen atom.

Hydrogen, the lightest of all gases, is believed to be the most abundant substance in the universe. Because it is so plentiful (it can be obtained easily by using electricity to separate the hydrogen from oxygen in water), it may be a substitute for helium in deep technical, commercial and military diving as helium becomes scarce and expensive. It's also thought that hydrogen does not have the HPNS problems associated with helium.

The problem with hydrogen is that it is very reactive, to the point that in air, it is explosive. This danger can be eliminated by restricting the oxygen percentage in the diver's breathing mix-

ture to 4% or less. As discussed later in this section under Dalton's Law, this is sufficient oxygen for dives deeper than 30 metres/100 feet. Shallower than 30 metres/100 feet, the diver would need to use another mixture, such as an oxygen-nitrogen mixture.

Hydrogen diving is still considered experimental, and again, is well outside the needs and limits of recreational diving. Due to its reactive nature, handling hydrogen and even switching to a hydrogen mix during a dive requires special caution and procedures to prevent an explosion. No one should handle hydrogen without special training.

Neon

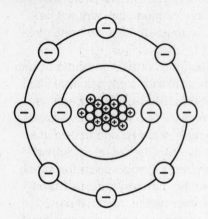

The neon atom.

Neon is another inert gas that is known for its ability to conduct electricity while emitting a bright red glow. For this reason, even today, electric signs of all varieties are often referred to as "neon signs."

Although the use of neon in diving has been limited primarily to experimental applications, it does hold great promise as a possible substitute for helium in mixed-gas diving. Neon does not cause changes in speech, nor does it appear to be very narcotic like nitrogen. However, because neon has a heavier molecular weight than helium, it causes greater breathing resistance and cannot be used as deep as helium.

Currently, neon is very expensive, but it is obtainable by distilling air — a common process for industrial gas suppliers. As helium becomes scarce and the demand for neon rises, gas production may eventually make neon more cost effective than helium.

Argon

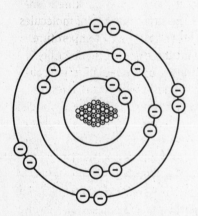

The argon atom.

Although physiologically inert, argon is a heavy gas, with strong narcotic properties. Argon has almost no application as a breathing gas because a diver using it will experience narcosis in as little as 6 metres/20 feet of water, and because it is very dense and hard to breathe.

However, argon is an excellent insulator because it has large mass and large molecules, giving it low specific heat. Technical, commercial and military divers sometimes use it in their dry suits because it insulates better than air or enriched air. This practice does have some concerns: First, there's been little scientific testing of decompression in which a heavy gas surrounds a diver while breathing a different, light gas. Second, the diver must take steps to prevent trying to accidentally breathe from an argon gas system underwater. To accomplish this, argon inflation systems have a different valve from that used for air, enriched air or other breathing gases, and the argon regulator has no mouthpiece so that a diver cannot accidentally breathe from it.

The Behavior of Gases

The *kinetic gas theory* explains the behavior of gases under conditions of varying pressures and temperatures. As discussed in the Energy segment, "kinetic" (derived from the Greek word "chaos") means "motion." This aptly describes the behavior of gases, which relates primarily to the motion of their molecules.

Gas molecules are relatively distant from one another, but constantly moving. This somewhat understates the phenomenon considering that in a container confining gas at room temperature at 1 ata pressure, more than 2,000,000,000,000,000,000,000,000 molecules per second strike each six square centimetres/square inch of that

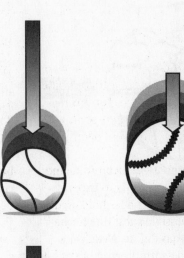

Just as a light tennis ball must travel faster than a heavy baseball to produce equal impact, a light molecule must move faster than a heavy one to exert equal pressure.

container. Gas pressure refers to the collective impact of these molecules.

Further, gas kinetic energy relates to the speed at which the molecules move and the mass of the individual molecules. The speed is, in turn, affected by temperature, which excites molecular motion. The mass of the molecule depends upon the gas in question. In essence, the more heat applied, the faster the molecules move and the more often they strike the sides of the container — and therefore exert more pressure. However, a heavier molecule can strike the container at a slower speed and exert the same force (pressure) as the lighter, high-speed molecule because of its mass.

It helps to think in terms of a tennis ball and a baseball hurled against a wall. If both are propelled by an equal force, the lighter tennis ball will travel

faster. Yet, when both hit the wall, they will have an equal force of impact because the heavier weight of the baseball carries the same energy. So, the same energy applied to either ball yields the same impact (pressure), even though the balls travel at different speeds.

This interrelationship of speed and weight makes all gases behave in similar ways if held under similar temperature and pressure. For example, a light gas such as helium, when heated, will have its molecules accelerate to greater speeds than a heavier gas, such as oxygen. Nonetheless, the heavier gas, though unable to travel as quickly as the light gas, through its weight will exert the same pressure increase relative to the heat applied as the light gas. Hence, the kinetic gas theory states that the kinetic energy of any gas at a given temperature is the same as the kinetic energy for the same number of molecules of any other gas at that temperature. (Note that these principles describe "ideal" gases, and are generally accurate for all gases within the pressures and temperatures experienced by divers. However, all gases vary to some extent in their behavior; helium, for example, compresses easily and when compressed into a scuba cylinder, will yield pressures that vary from those predicted for an ideal gas.)

In addition to temperature and pressure, the behavior of gases is also related to volume. Imagine a volume of gas contained in a balloon. Squeeze the balloon, and its volume reduces. As the volume reduces, the molecules that comprise the gas come closer together. The closer the molecules, the more frequently they will collide with each other and the side of the balloon. The increased frequency of collision results in greater pressure being exerted. Conversely, stretch the balloon, and the volume increases (without adding any additional gas molecules) the additional space means fewer collisions and a pressure decrease.

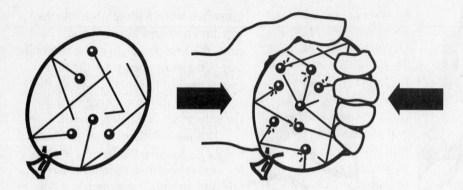

If the volume of a gas is reduced, gas molecules collide more often and pressure increases.

22.4 litres of gas consists of 602.257 billion trillion molecules! This number is more typically expressed as 6.02257 x 10^{23} and is referred to as *Avogadro's number*. Avogadro's number of particles of any given substance is referred to as one *mole*.

As a result of the common behavior among gases identified by the kinetic gas theory, a single unifying rule, termed the Ideal *General Gas Law*, can be derived to predict the behavior of any gas. Expressed mathematically, the General Gas Law is:

$$P V = n R T$$

wherein P is the absolute pressure; V the volume; n the number of moles of gas; R the universal gas constant of 8.314 joules per degree Kelvin (a joule is equal to 0.24 calories or 0.74 foot-pounds of energy); and T the absolute temperature. This single law encompasses both Boyle's and Charles' laws, which can be looked at independently.

The last aspect of the kinetic gas theory has to do with the number of gas molecules that will occupy a particular space. In 1811, Italian scientist/philosopher Amedeo Avogadro discovered an interesting phenomenon. He calculated that a certain volume at the same temperature and pressure always has the same number of gas molecules, no matter what gas the volume holds. Later it was determined that at 0°C and 1 ata,

Boyle's Law

Sir Robert Boyle was a seventeenth century Irish scientist who was greatly influenced by the work of Torricelli. While Torricelli first determined the pressure exerted by the atmosphere, Boyle wanted to find out what happens to a quantity of air if the pressure changes.

Boyle's now-famous experiment involved a U-shaped glass tube sealed at one end. Into this tube he poured mercury until there was an equal quantity in each end. Since the level of mercury on either side of the tube was level and equal, the pressure inside the closed end must have been equal to the pressure being exerted by the atmosphere at the open end.

Boyle then began adding mercury to reduce the volume in the closed end. He found that to reduce the volume by half, he had to add 76 centimetres/30 inches more of mercury. Since Torricelli had established that atmospheric pressure equals 76 centimetres/30 inches of mercury, an additional 76 centimetres/30 inches meant that the pressure

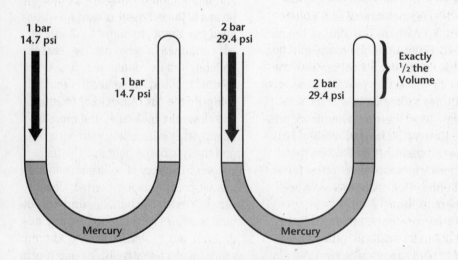

Robert Boyle demonstrated that gas volume is inversely proportional to pressure. When pressure doubled on mercury in a u-shaped tube, the gas volume opposite halved.

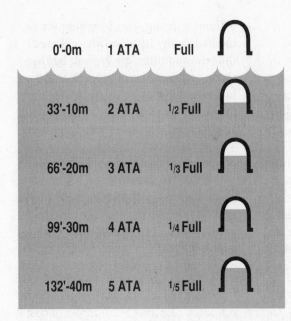

0'-0m	1 ATA	Full
33'-10m	2 ATA	1/2 Full
66'-20m	3 ATA	1/3 Full
99'-30m	4 ATA	1/4 Full
132'-40m	5 ATA	1/5 Full

The effects of Boyle's law on air volume during descent.

needed to halve the closed volume was double that of atmospheric pressure. Therefore, the pressure in the closed end must likewise be twice that of the atmosphere. What Boyle had demonstrated was that *if the temperature remains constant, the volume of a gas is inversely proportional to the absolute pressure*; that if the pressure was increased, the volume must decrease proportionately and vice versa.

As can be demonstrated mathematically, some very simple relationships predict how a given gas volume will behave under pressure. Boyle demonstrated that it takes approximately 9 metres/30 feet of water to exert the same pressure exerted by the atmosphere. (In actuality, it takes 10 msw/33 fsw, or 10.3 mfw/34 ffw). Therefore, every 10 metres/33 feet of descent in seawater adds the pressure of one additional atmosphere. Furthermore, a gas volume in a flexible or inverted open container will expand or contract in a precise relationship to the depth (pressure). In fact, a given volume will be reduced to 1/2 the volume at two atmospheres absolute pressure (10 msw/33 fsw); 1/3 at three atmospheres 20 msw/66 fsw); 1/4 at four atmospheres (30 msw/99 fsw) and so on.

This constant relationship can be used to determine the new volume when any given volume is taken to a different depth. For example, suppose a volume of 280 litres/10 cubic feet is taken from the surface to 30 metres/99 feet. The absolute pressure is four atmospheres (three of water, one of air), so expressing this as a fraction, the numerator (top number) is the original volume, and the denominator (bottom number) is the number of atmospheres. The result is 280/4 = 70 litres, or 10/4 = 2.5 cubic feet.

A concise statement of these results

is made possible by applying Boyle's Law mathematically:

$$P V = K$$

wherein P is the absolute pressure of a gas; V is its volume; and K a constant. As an illustration, assume a volume of 1 (a litre or a cubic foot — it doesn't matter) at the surface. This is expressed mathematically as:

(P)		(V)		(K)
1 ata	x	1 litre/ft^3	=	1

If this balloon is taken to 20 metres/66 feet (3 ata) in seawater, then:

$$3 \text{ ata} \times V = 1 \text{ litre/ft}^3$$

Using algebra to isolate V yields:

$$V = 1/3 \text{ litre/ft}^3$$

The formula shows the volume would be reduced to 1/3 of its surface size. Suppose this same balloon is now taken to 40 metres/132 feet (5 ata) in seawater. How would this affect the volume compared to the surface volume?

At 5 ata, the formula would read:

$$5 \text{ ata} \times V = 1$$

therefore:

$$V = 1/5$$

Because a constant is solved for in all cases, the formula can be rearranged to make it more useful for finding how pressure or volume changes from one depth to another. The first pressure can be called P_1 and the first volume can be called V_1, giving:

$$P_1 \times V_1 = K$$

Likewise, in the second depth, the pressure can be called P_2 and the volume is called V_2, giving

$$P_2 \times V_2 = K$$

Both instances are equal to the same constant (K), so:

$$P_1 \times V_1 = K = P_2 \times V_2$$

or

$$P_1 \times V_1 = P_2 \times V_2$$

Another example illustrates the usefulness of the formula when the depth doesn't coincide with an even atmosphere of pressure. (Note: Metric and imperial figures in the example are approximately, but not exactly equal to simplify the mathematics):

A diver is attempting to salvage an object from a depth of 26 metres/85 feet in seawater. Since the diver doesn't have a lift bag available, inner tubes will be used to accomplish the task, but the diver must be sure the tubes will hold the volume of air required to lift the object — and yet not burst as the air expands during ascent. The diver has already determined that 29 kilograms/64 pounds of buoyant force will be required to free the object from the bottom. To find out how much the air will expand upon surfacing:

P_1 The absolute pressure at 26 msw/85 fsw is approximately 3.6 ata (26/10, or 86/33 = 2.6 atm of water, + 1atm of air = 3.6 ata).

V_1 The volume required to lift the object is about 28.1 litres/1 cubic foot (1 litre of water weighs approximately 1.03 kg, so 29 kg ÷ 1.03 = 28.1 litres; 1 cubic foot of seawater weighs approximately 64 pounds.)

P_2 is 1 ata (the pressure at the surface).

V_2 is the unknown value.

Applying the known values to the formula, we now have:

metric

3.6 ata x 28.1 litres = 1 ata x V2

or

101.2 litres = V_2

imperial

3.6 ata x 1 ft³ = 1 ata x V_2

or

3.6 ft³ = V_2

The diver now knows that if the inner tubes can hold 101.2 liters/3.6 ft³ of air, they will bring the object to the surface

without bursting. This formula may be applied to any instance where three of the four quantities are known. Furthermore, any measure of volume or absolute pressure may be used, provided they're used consistently throughout. The previous example could have been worked out using kg/cm² or psia instead of ata.

While the pressure and volume of a gas are *inversely* proportional, the pressure and density of a gas are *directly* proportional. If the gas volume is reduced, the space between the gas molecules must likewise be reduced and the gas becomes more compact or denser because the same number of molecules share less space.

This density relationship is similar to that demonstrated earlier concerning volume. At two atmospheres, a given air volume is twice as dense as at the surface. At three atmospheres, it is three times as dense, and so on. This explains why a diver uses cylinder air supply more rapidly with depth: A diver takes a breath of air, but a full breath of air at two atmospheres takes in twice the number of air molecules, so each breath takes twice as much from the tank as at the surface. Therefore, the diver's air supply lasts only half as long as at the surface. As the diver descends, this relationship continues as predicted by Boyle's law.

At three atmospheres, the air supply will last only one-third as long as at the surface; at four atmospheres only one-fourth, and so on. This gives divers a useful way to make rough air duration estimates; however exact predictions are impossible because: 1) an individual's air consumption rate can change drastically due to factors such as cold and stress; and 2) a diver rarely remains at one depth the entire dive.

Clearly, Boyle's law has many applications related to diving. During every dive, divers take with them gas-filled

Depth	Pressure	Gas Volume	Density	
0'-0m	1 ATA	1	x1	
33'-10m	2 ATA	1/2	x2	
66'-20m	3 ATA	1/3	x3	
99'-30m	4 ATA	1/4	x4	
132'-40m	5 ATA	1/5	x5	

Depth	Pressure	Gas Volume	Density	
0'-0m	1 ATA	1	x1	
33'-10m	2 ATA	1/2	x2	
66'-20m	3 ATA	1/3	x3	
99'-30m	4 ATA	1/4	x4	
132'-40m	5 ATA	1/5	x5	

The effects of pressure on gas density.

containers — BCDs, tanks, dry suits, masks — and have gas-filled spaces in their bodies — sinuses, ears and lungs. Even the tiny bubbles that comprise wet suits continually expand and contract as pressure changes as described by Boyle's law.

Charles' Law

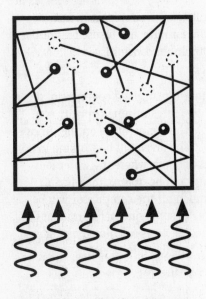

Charles' Law states that if gas temperature rises and volume stays constant, pressure increases. If temperature rises and pressure stays constant, volume increases.

Boyle's experiments dealt solely with the effects of pressure and volume. He did not consider the effect of a third factor — temperature. The influence of temperature on gas behavior was first explored by the French scientist Jacques Charles (although much of his work was published later by a colleague, Joseph Gay-Lussac).

Through experimentation, Charles found that if the pressure of a gas is kept constant within a container, the volume of the gas increases as the temperature increases. If the volume remains constant, the pressure increases when the temperature increases.

Stated another way: The amount of change in either volume or pressure of a given gas volume is directly proportional to the change in the absolute temperature. As a general rule, one can assume that for every 1 degree C change, a full scuba tank changes .6 bar. For every 1 degree F change, a 5 psi change occurs. For more precise calculations, and to fully understand its implications, Charles' law can be combined with Boyle's law and expressed as:

$$P \times V = K \times T$$

or

$$\frac{P \times V}{T} = K$$

wherein P is absolute pressure; V is volume; T is absolute temperature; and K is constant. This equation is very similar to that described by Boyle's law. As with Boyle's law, this formula can be rearranged to make it more useful in determining pressure/volume/temperature changes

$$\frac{P_1 \times V_1}{T_1} = K$$

and

$$\frac{P_2 \times V_2}{T_2} = K$$

then:

$$\frac{P_1 \times V_1}{T_1} = K = \frac{P_2 \times V_2}{T_2}$$

or

$$\frac{P_1 \times V_1}{T_1} = \frac{P_2 \times V_2}{T_2}$$

Notice how this reconstruction takes care of all possible factors: pressure, volume and temperature in both the first and second instance. This is the mathematical expression of the General Gas Law. Here are some examples of how the General Gas Law formula may be used:

Metric

A 12 litre cylinder reaches 52°C while being filled to 200 bar. The tank will be used in 7°C water. The tank pressure when the diver enters the water is calculated as follows:

P_1 = 200 bar + 1 bar = 201 bar

V_1 Because the volume does not change ($V_1 = V_2$), the volumes cancel out and can be dropped from both sides of the formula for simplicity.

T_1 52°C + 273°C = 325 Kelvin (K)

T_1 7°C + 273°C = 280 Kelvin (K)

Because the factor of volume has been eliminated, the formula reads:

$$\frac{P_1}{T_1} = \frac{P_2}{T_2}$$

By applying the values, the formula becomes:

$$\frac{201 \text{ bar}}{325 \text{ K}} = \frac{P_2}{280 \text{ K}}$$

or:

$$\frac{280 \text{ K} \times 201 \text{ bar}}{325 \text{ K}} = P_2$$

P_2 = 173 bar absolute - 1 bar = 172 bar gauge

Imperial

An 80 cubic ft tank is filled to 3000 psi. During filling, the temperature of the tank is raised to 125°F. The tank will be used in water at 45°F. The tank pressure when the diver enters the water is calculated as follows:

P_1 3000 psig + 14.7 psi = 3014.7 psia

V_1 Because the volume does not change ($V_1 = V_2$), the volumes cancel out and can be dropped from both sides of the formula for simplicity.

T_1 125°F + 460°F = 585° Rankine (R)

T_2 45°F + 460°F = 505° Rankine (R)

Because the factor of volume has been eliminated, the formula would read:

$$\frac{P_1}{T_1} = \frac{P_2}{T_2}$$

By applying the values, the formula becomes:

$$\frac{3014.7 \text{ psia}}{585°R} = \frac{P_2}{505°R}$$

or:

$$\frac{505°R \times 3014.7 \text{ psia}}{585°R} = P_2$$

P_2 = 2602.4 psia - 14.7 psi = 2587.7 psig

The following examples demonstrate how the formula can be used if volumes do not remain constant.

Metric

A surface-air-supplied commercial diver has a 500 litres/minute capacity compressor. The temperature on the surface is 29°C. The diver will be working in 55 metres of depth where the water temperature will be approximately 5°C. How much air the compressor will be capable of supplying per minute at the specified depth is calculated as follows:

P_1 1 bar absolute

V_1 500 litre

T_1 302 K

P_2 6.5 bar absolute

T_2 278 K

V_2 unknown

or:

$$\frac{278 \text{ K} \times 1 \text{ bar} \times 500 \text{ l}}{302 \text{ K} \times 6.5 \text{ bar}} = V_2$$

or:

$V_2 = 70.81$ litres/min

Imperial

A surface-air-supplied commercial diver has a 75 ft³/minute capacity compressor. The temperature on the surface is 85°F. The diver will be working in 187 feet of depth where the water temperature will be approximately 40°F. How much air the compressor will be capable of supplying per minute at the specified depth is calculated as follows:

P_1 14.7 psia

V_1 75 ft³

T_1 545°R

P_2 98 psia

T_2 500°R

V_2 unknown

$$\frac{14.7 \text{ psia} \times 75 \text{ ft}^3}{545°R} = \frac{97.9 \text{ psia} \times V_2}{500°R}$$

or:

$$\frac{500°R \times 14.7 \text{ psia} \times 75 \text{ ft}^3}{545°R \times 97.9 \text{ psia}} = V_2$$

or:

$V_2 = 10.3$ ft³/minute (cfm)

The General Gas Law describes the behavior of a gas (such as pure oxygen) or

Altitude Diving

Altitude diving requires special consideration because there's less air pressure at altitude. This affects dive table use (which requires using special tables to adjust for the change), and even the General Gas Law.

You can calculate the absolute pressure in metres or feet of sea water using the following formula:

Metric

Pressure in msw = $10 \times 2.718^{(-0.038 \times \frac{\text{altitude in metres}}{305})}$

Imperial

Pressure in fsw = $33 \times 2.718^{(-0.038 \times \frac{\text{altitude in feet}}{1000})}$

Or, as a loose rule of thumb, subtract .035 atm for each 300 metres/1000 feet of altitude up to 3000 metres/10,000 feet.

Using this rule of thumb, suppose a diver is diving in a mountain lake at 1800 metres/6000 feet of altitude. The depth gauge has been adjusted for the altitude and reads 10 metres/33 feet (it's calibrated for sea water, so the diver's actually slightly deeper in fresh water, but the concern is *pressure*, not linear metres/feet). If the diver sends up a lift bag with 1 litre of air, what will the air volume expand to on reaching the surface?

P_1 = 1.79 ata (1800 metres ÷ 300 = 6, or 6000 feet ÷ 1000 = 6; 6 x .035 = .21atm; 1 atm - .21 atm = .79 atm atmospheric

pressure. 10 metres/33 feet = 1 atm hydrostatic pressure; 1 atm + .79 atm = 1.79 ata)

V_1 = 1 litre

T_1 = T_2 (No temperature change, so temperature can be removed for simplicity)

P_2 = .79 ata (see above)

So:

1.79 ata x 1 liter = .79 ata x V_2

Or

$$\frac{1.79 \text{ ata} \times 1 \text{ litre}}{.79 \text{ ata}} = V_2$$

2.26 litres = V_2

So, due to lower atmospheric pressure, the gas expansion is greater than at sea level, as dictated by Boyle's and the General Gas Laws.

Dalton's Law

The General Gas Law describes the behavior of a gas (such as pure oxygen) or a mixture of gases (such as air). The General Gas Law applies in either case. However, other gas characteristics become important when breathing gas under pressure; how the body reacts depends upon the gases in the mix, the proportions of each, and the absolute pressure.

When gases mix, they become diffused. This means that even though they may vary in molecular weight and size, due to their constant state of motion they will nonetheless mix evenly within the mixture. Yet within this even mix, each gas continues to demonstrate its own individual behavior in terms of its pressure.

The first person to investigate this phenomenon was the English scientist John Dalton. (Dalton is also noted for describing the structure of matter as being comprised of atoms.) In summarizing his experience with gas behavior within mixtures, Dalton's law states:

The total pressure exerted by a mixture of gases is equal to the sum of the pressures of each of the different gases making up the mixture — each gas acting as if it alone were present and occupied the total volume.

In essence, this means that each gas within a gas mixture acts independently of the others. The individual pressure exerted by a particular component of the gas mixture is proportional to the number of molecules of that particular gas within the mixture. This individual pressure exerted by a component gas is referred to as a *partial pressure* (abbreviated "pp"); as the name indicates, the partial pressure is the part of the total pressure exerted by that gas. Understanding partial pressure is important because, as shown later, both the solubility and diffusion of a gas into body issues are proportional to the gas' partial pressure.

For example, consider air, which, for simplicity, is comprised of 21% oxygen and 79% nitrogen. The pressure is 1 ata, and there are no other gases present. Dalton's law simply says that 21% of the total pressure of the gas mixture will be exerted by the oxygen molecules and 79% of the total pressure will be exerted by the nitrogen molecules. So, if the total pressure exerted is 1 ata, then the oxygen would be responsible for .21 ata (.21 x 1 ata = .21 ata) of the total, and the nitrogen responsible for .79 ata (.79 x 1 ata = .79 ata) of the total. (Again, note that any measure of absolute pressure, such as psia or kg/cm^2 may be used and the principle applies).

Suppose the pressure is doubled to 2 ata with no further gas added. In accordance with Boyle's law, the gas volume is halved. Yet, each of the component gases still exerts a proportional partial pressure to the 79/21 mixture. Therefore, of the total 2 ata, nitrogen continues to exert 79% of the total or 1.58 ata (.79 x 2 ata = 1.58 ata), and oxygen exerts 21% of the total or .42 ata (.21 x 2 ata = .42 ata).

Mathematically, Dalton's law can be expressed as:

P total = pp A + pp B + pp C . . .

and:

pp A = P total x % volume A

An example illustrates Dalton's law: In an air mixture of 1% CO_2, 79% N_2, and 20% O_2, what would the partial pressure of N_2 be at a depth of 40 msw/132 fsw?

% volume (N_2) = 79%

P total = 5 ata (40/10 = 4 +1 = 5 ata; 132/33 = 4 + 1 = 5 ata)

therefore:

pp N_2 = 5 x .79

    or:

pp N_2 = 3.95 ata

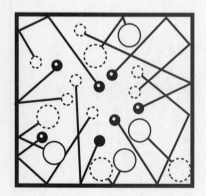

According to Dalton's law, each gas in a mix exerts pressure independently of the others.

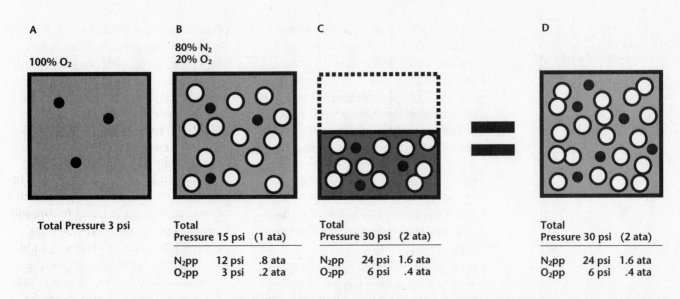

Each gas in a mix exerts a part of the total pressure equal to its proportion in the mix. (A) 100 percent oxygen exerts 100 percent of the total pressure. (B) Oxygen makes up 20 percent of the mix and exerts 20 percent of the total pressure. (C) If the volume is halved, pressure doubles and oxygen still exerts 20 percent of the new total pressure. (D) If the volume stays the same and the pressure doubled, the effect on the oxygen partial pressure is the same as in the previous instance.

If necessary, partial pressure can be calculated in ata and then converted to other pressure expressions. For example, what is pp N_2 in kg/cm² and psi absolute pressure?

3.95 ata x 1.03 kg/cm² = 4.06 kg/cm² absolute pressure

3.95 ata x 14.7 psi = 58.06 psia

Most often in medicine, partial pressures are expressed in terms of millimetres of mercury (mmHg). To convert to millimetres of mercury, multiply atmospheres by 760 (the mmHg of 1 atm). From the above example:

3.95 atms x 760 = 3002 mmHg

The previous discussion of Boyle's law showed that as the ambient pressure increases, the pressure inside a flexible container (such as the lungs) increases. If the container is to maintain its original volume as well, more gas must be introduced to the container. This is what

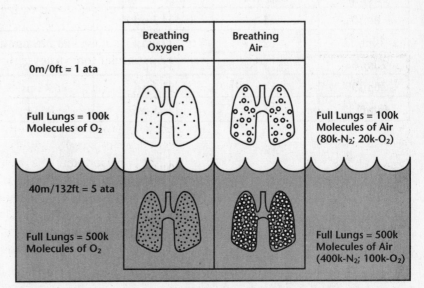

Air breathed at five atmospheres is physiologically the same as pure oxygen breathed at the surface.

happens when a diver breathes from a scuba regulator during descent; the amount of air delivered to the diver increases to maintain lung volume.

While the gas percentages within a mixture remains constant, the number of gas molecules in a given volume increases with the pressure. For example, if a theoretical lung volume at the surface contains 100×10^{21} air molecules, one would assume that 79×10^{21} molecules were nitrogen, and 21×10^{21} were oxygen (using the simplified 79%/21% ratio of nitrogen to oxygen that ignores trace gases). If, on the other hand, one were to breathe pure oxygen at the surface, oxygen would account for all 100×10^{21} molecules.

If the pressure increases fivefold, such as during a dive to 40 msw/132 fsw, 500×10^{21} molecules are needed to maintain the same lung volume. Of this new volume, 395×10^{21} molecules are nitrogen (79% of 500×10^{21}), and 105×10^{21} are oxygen (21% of 500×10^{21}). Looking at just the 105×10^{21} oxygen molecules the diver is breathing, the physiological effect is similar to breathing pure (100×10^{21} molecules of) oxygen at the surface. From a physiological

point of view, the effect of a gas depends upon its partial pressure alone; other gases present or absent are immaterial.

This means that in comparing two gas mixtures, it is possible to compare the effects of a single gas in the mix breathed at a particular depth with the effects of a greater percentage of that gas at the surface. This is called *surface equivalency*, which can have considerable effect when dealing with toxic gases.

For example: a scuba tank is filled and unintentionally, 0.5% of the gas volume is carbon monoxide (CO). While this is undesirable, breathed at the surface this volume of CO isn't likely to be toxic. The partial pressure is .005 ata (1 ata x .005 = .005 ata).

However, if the diver descends to 40 msw/132 fsw (5 ata), Dalton's law shows that the effects of the CO will be more dramatic. The partial pressure is .025 ata (5 ata x .005 = .025 ata), and now has the same physiologic effects as breathing a gas mixture with 2.5% CO at the surface (5 ata x 0.5% = 2.5%) which is a poisonous level. Nothing in the air within the tank changed; the effect results purely from partial pressure as dictated by Dalton's law.

Depth	Bar/ATA	Total Pressure	Partial Pressure	
			N₂ 79%	O₂ 21%
0m/0'	1	14.7 psi	11.613 psi/.79 bar/ata	3.087 psi/.21 bar/ata
10m/33'	2	29.4 psi	23.225 psi/1.58 bar/ata	6.174 psi/.42 bar/ata
20m/66'	3	44.1 psi	34.837 psi/2.37 bar/ata	9.261 psi/.63 bar/ata
30m/99'	4	58.8 psi	46.45 psi/3.16 bar/ata	12.348 psi/.84 bar/ata
40m/132'	5	73.5 psi	58.063 psi/3.95 bar/ata	15.435 psi/1.05 bar/ata

Enriched Air Diving & Dalton's Law

Enriched air "nitrox" (EANx) diving uses air that has had oxygen added to reduce the proportional amount of nitrogen. Popular blends of EANx include 32 percent oxygen/68 percent nitrogen; 36 percent oxygen/64 percent nitrogen, as compared to 21 percent oxygen/79 percent nitrogen found in normal air.

Although diving with enriched air has several considerations that demand special training and certification, the lower fraction of nitrogen means the diver absorbs less nitrogen for a given depth and duration compared to air. This means a longer no decompression limit.

There are special tables available for enriched air diving, but divers also use regular air tables by using a formula to find an Equivalent Air Depth (EAD) for a given depth with a given EANx blend. This is simply a special application of Dalton's Law:

Metric

$$EAD = \frac{(1\text{-oxygen \%}) \times (\text{depth in metres} +10)}{.79} - 10$$

Imperial

$$EAD = \frac{(1\text{-oxygen \%}) \times (\text{depth in feet} +33)}{.79} - 33$$

All this formula does is find the depth at which the nitrogen partial pressure would be the same using air as with the EANx blend in question. Consider that "(1-oxygen%)" defines the percent of nitrogen in the blend. The next part "(depth + 10) metric/(depth + 33) imperial" determines the absolute pressure in metres or feet of seawater. The nitrogen percentage multiplied by the absolute pressure yields the nitrogen partial pressure in metres or feet of sea water, per Dalton's Law.

In the denominator (bottom of the fraction) ".79" is the percentage of nitrogen in air. When this is divided into the nitrogen partial pressure in absolute metres/feet of seawater, the result is the depth at which air would have the same nitrogen partial pressure, with an extra 10 metres/33 feet to account for atmospheric pressure. The final step is to subtract the 10

metres/33 feet, which yields a gauge depth the enriched air diver can use on conventional air tables.

The application of Dalton's Law in enriched air diving involves oxygen partial pressure. The oxygen partial pressure limit is 1.4 ata; at higher partial pressures, the risk of oxygen toxicity becomes unacceptable. The depth at which a diver reaches this limit with air or enriched air is easy to determine using Dalton's Law:

O_2 pp = absolute pressure x O_2%

So for air:

1.4 ata = absolute pressure x .21

or

$$\frac{1.4 \text{ ata}}{.21} = \text{absolute pressure}$$

6.67 ata = absolute pressure

6.67 ata - 1 atm = 5.67 atm hydrostatic pressure

5.67 atm x 10 = 56.7 metres, or 5.67 x 33 = 187 feet.

This shows why oxygen toxicity isn't really a concern when using air within recreational depth limits (max. 40 metres/130 feet). However, if the diver uses EANx36:

1.4 ata = absolute pressure x .36

or

$$\frac{1.4 \text{ ata}}{.36} = \text{absolute pressure}$$

3.89 ata = absolute pressure

3.89 ata - 1 atm = 2.89 atm hydrostatic pressure

2.89 atm x 10 = 28.9 metres, or 2.89 x 33 = 95 feet.

With this enriched air blend, a diver can reach the oxygen partial pressure limit well within recreational depth limits of 40 metres/130 feet.

Henry's Law

Anyone who puts sugar in coffee is familiar with the chemical phenomenon of substances in solution. Sugar sweetens coffee, as well as other drinks, by reducing into particles so small that they can be held and evenly distributed by the liquid. Hence, a solid substance (sugar) can

be held within the molecules of a liquid.

The same is true for gases. Most people have experienced the consequences of this by opening a shaken bottle or can of soda too quickly. Gas bubbles form as they come out of solution within the liquid, causing the soda

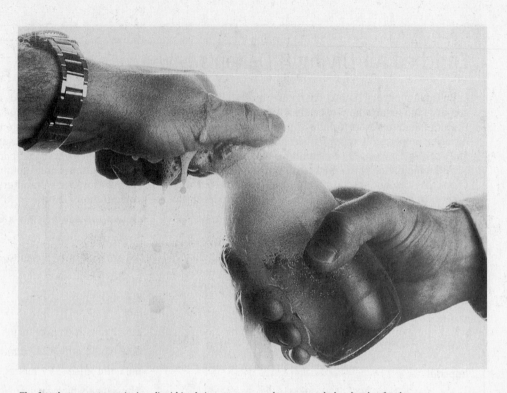

The fact that gases can exist in a liquid is obvious to anyone who opens a shaken bottle of soda.

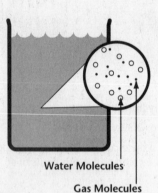

Water Molecules

Gas Molecules

Gas dissolves in liquid by becoming trapped between the liquid's molecules.

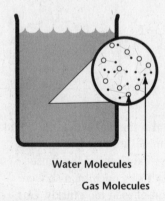

Water Molecules

Gas Molecules

When gas is in solution, it still exerts pressure within the liquid. This is called gas tension.

to spray violently, demonstrating vividly that gas can be contained within liquids and remain there, at least until certain conditions change.

The previous discussion of matter explained that the liquid state lies between a solid and a gas. This means that the relative distance between molecules comprising a liquid is less than that of a gas, but greater than that of a solid. Because of the distance between liquid molecules, there is ample room for gas molecules to become trapped between them. When this happens, the gas is said to be dissolved within the liquid, or in solution.

An interesting aspect of gases in solution is that gas molecules retain their gas properties. Although completely surrounded by the liquid molecules, gas molecules still exert pressure inside the liquid. This pressure exerted within the liquid by a particular gas in solution is called *gas tension*.

How much gas dissolves in a liquid depends upon several factors, which were first explored by William Henry,

an English chemist and physician who was a close associate of John Dalton. Through experimentation, Henry concluded *that the amount of gas that will dissolve into a liquid at a given temperature is directly proportional to the partial pressure of that gas.* Hence, there are at least two factors that affect gas solubility in liquids — pressure and temperature.

For example, suppose a theoretical bucket of water has no gas dissolved in it. Therefore, the gas tension is zero. Once the water comes into contact with a gas, gas molecules rush to penetrate the solution, flowing from high pressure to low pressure just as when someone opens the valve on a scuba tank.

The gas entering the water exerts a pressure (gas tension) that continues to rise until the pressure is equal to the pressure of the gas in contact with the water. In accordance with Dalton's law, each gas dissolved within the water exerts a partial pressure of the total gas tension independent of other gases present. For instance, if the bucket of

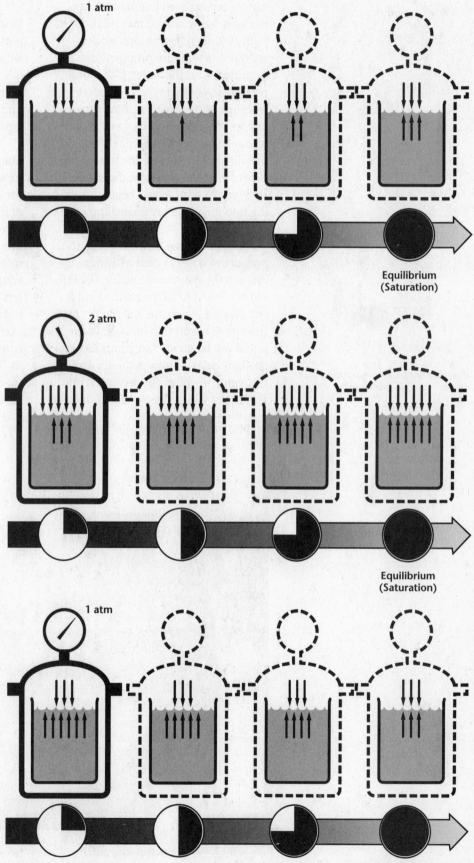

Gas dissolves into a liquid until the gas tension balances with ambient pressure. This is called saturation.

If ambient pressure rises, more gas dissolves into the liquid until reaching saturation at the higher pressure.

If pressure drops and gas tension becomes greater than ambient pressure, the liquid is said to be super saturated and gas will come out of solution until equilibrium is reached again.

If pressure drops quickly, gas coming out of solution may form bubbles within the liquid.

water were exposed to pure nitrogen, nitrogen gas would go into solution until the nitrogen gas tension reaches equilibrium with the nitrogen pressure in contact with the water. If the total pressure in contact with the bucket were now increased by adding pure oxygen, no more nitrogen would go into solution because while the total pressure has increased, the partial pressure of nitrogen would be the same. However, oxygen would begin dissolving into the water until reaching equilibrium.

The difference between the partial pressure of gases in contact with a liquid and the gas tension within the liquid is referred to as the *pressure gradient*. When the pressure gradient is high, the rate of absorption of gas into the liquid will be great. As the number of gas molecules continues to dissolve into the water, the gradient decreases, and the rate at which the molecules dissolve into the water slows.

Eventually the gas tension within a liquid will reach equilibrium with the partial pressure of each gas in contact with the liquid, and no net exchange of gas will occur (although equal numbers of molecules will continue to pass in and out of the liquid). At this point the liquid is said to be *saturated*.

Returning to the bucket of water, imagine that it is placed in a recompression chamber. As the pressure in the chamber is increased, the pressure of the gases in contact with the water is increased. Henry's law explains that more gas will now become dissolved into the liquid until such time that an equilibrium again exists between the gas tension of each gas within the liquid and the partial pressure of that gas exerted on the liquid. So, the more pressure exerted by the gas in contact with the water, the more gas will dissolve in the water. Gas will dissolve into the water until reaching equilibrium (saturation) with the new pressure.

The small bubbles released from water just before it boils are air displaced by accelerated motion of the water molecules.

Now suppose the pressure is released in the chamber. The phenomenon reverses. Less pressure in contact with the water means that the gas dissolved within the water will now have a greater gas tension than the gas in contact with it. Thus, the pressure gradient favors the gas flowing out of the water. The water is said to be supersaturated, or containing more gas than it can keep in solution at that pressure.

Because the gas again seeks equilibrium with the surrounding pressure, gas comes out of solution until the gas (or each gas in the mix) has pressure equal to the gas in contact with the water. As long as the pressure reduction occurs gradually and the pressure gradient isn't too high, the dissolved gas will come out of solution without forming gas bubbles. If the pressure decrease occurs rapidly, causing a large pressure gradient, or if other factors are present (such as agitating the water vigorously) the gas may come out of solution faster than it can diffuse into the surrounding gas. The gas will form bubbles.

This is what happens when someone shakes a soda bottle and then opens it, and, as discussed in Section Two, The Physiology of Diving, this roughly describes how a diver's body absorbs and releases nitrogen.

Besides pressure, temperature affects gas solution into liquids. In diving physiology, temperature normally has little consequence because the body temperature stays within a relatively narrow range. However, based on the behavior of molecules under differing pressure conditions, it's easy to understand how temperature affects gas solubility.

Specifically, as heat enters a liquid, molecular motion increases. As the molecules move faster, they require more space to move, leaving less space for gas molecules to occupy. Therefore, the higher the temperature, the less gas a liquid can hold in solution. This explains the small bubbles released just before water boils when heated. The accelerated water molecules displace the dissolved air, so that the air diffuses into small gas pockets in the surfaces of the container to form small bubbles that eventually rise out of the water .

Returning to gas absorption and the human body, although the bucket of water provides a simple model of the phenomenon, there are some important differences.

First, not all tissues absorb gas at the same rate. This is because tissues vary in their degree of permeability (ability to let gas pass across the tissues). The absorption rate also depends on the blood circulation to various tissues, which may in turn be affected by variables such as temperature or exercise.

Another important distinction between the bucket of water and human tissues is that different gases have differing solubility in different tissues, and different tissues dissolve gases more readily than others. For example, given an equal quantity of blood tissue and fat tissue, when equilibrated to surface pressure the fat tissue holds more nitrogen molecules in solution, though both have the same tissue pressure (.79 ata partial pressure of nitrogen, for simplicity). However, to be technically accurate, living tissue is never saturated at exactly the ambient pressure because oxygen consumption creates a pressure difference). During a dive, different body tissues absorb nitrogen at different rates. Given enough time, all tissues reach equilibrium (saturation), but during the short duration of a typical dive, some areas of the body will saturate while others will not.

Predicting how inert gases enter and leave the body is more complex, but divers need reasonably accurate predictions to avoid decompression sickness. Among other topics, Section Two, The Physiology of Diving, discusses how the phenomenon of Henry's law is applied to the construction of decompression models.

The Physiology of Diving

Two

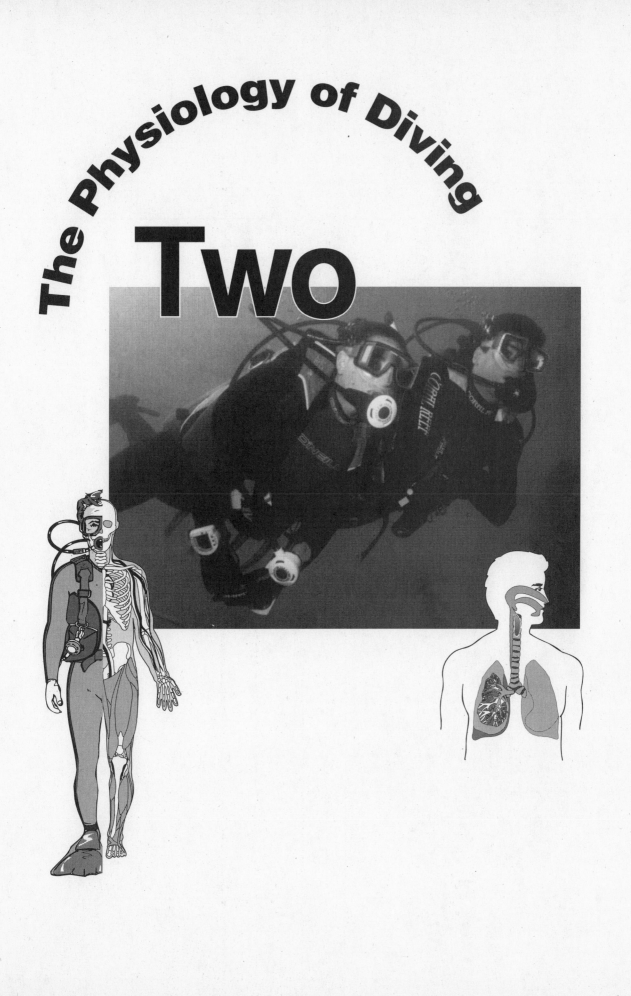

Introduction

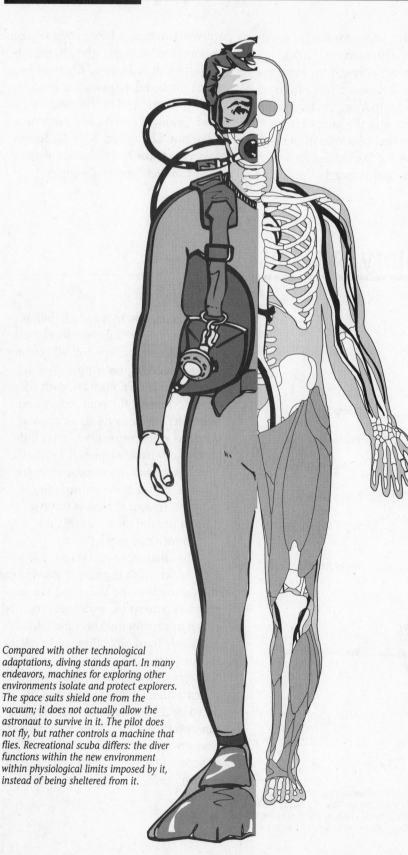

Compared with other technological adaptations, diving stands apart. In many endeavors, machines for exploring other environments isolate and protect explorers. The space suits shield one from the vacuum; it does not actually allow the astronaut to survive in it. The pilot does not fly, but rather controls a machine that flies. Recreational scuba differs: the diver functions within the new environment within physiological limits imposed by it, instead of being sheltered from it.

Of all the life-forms on Earth, only humans have the means to leave the environment to which they're adapted for more than a few brief moments. Technology rockets people into space and plunges them into the depths of the oceans, allowing them to venture into realms nature never equipped them for.

Compared with other technological adaptations, though, diving stands apart. In many endeavors, machines for exploring other environments isolate and protect explorers. The space suits shield one from the vacuum; it does not actually allow the astronaut to survive in it. The pilot does not fly, but rather controls a machine that flies. Recreational scuba differs: the diver functions within the new environment within physiological limits imposed by it, instead of being sheltered from it.

Scuba equipment does not breathe for the diver, but allows the respiratory system to function underwater. Fins don't move the diver, but adapt the feet so the diver can move efficiently. Technology *meshes* with human physiology, and the doors to the underwater world open.

It's all the more remarkable considering the diver's body: billions of cells, each a single unit of life working interdependently as tissues, organs and systems to create a complex, single unit greater than the sum of its parts. Yet as complex as this structure seems, the human body functions according to the same clear, simple principles that govern the rest of nature. What makes the body remarkable is how these thousands of basic and simple actions occur simultaneously to maintain life.

Diving physiology studies the functions of the body underwater. It examines how the body responds to this environment, as well as the problems the body can have in the underwater world, and the consequences of those problems.

Overview

To form a basic understanding of diving physiology, the first section, Circulatory and Respiratory Systems, focuses on the two body systems most directly influenced by the underwater environment. Being familiar with the normal structure, function and responses of these systems provides the foundation for understanding how they respond to the under-water environment. Next, Physiological Responses to Nitrogen, and Physiological Responses to Thermal Changes, examine the body's responses to nitrogen under pressure, and to temperature in water. Finally, Physiological Responses to Pressure Change on Body Air Spaces looks at how the body handles pressure directly influencing its air spaces.

Circulatory and Respiratory Systems

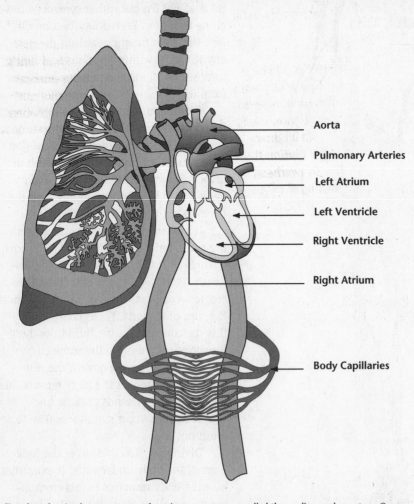

Aorta

Pulmonary Arteries

Left Atrium

Left Ventricle

Right Ventricle

Right Atrium

Body Capillaries

Together, the circulatory system and respiratory system are called the cardiovascular system. Oxygen rich blood from the lungs enters the left heart, which pumps the blood to the body via the aorta. The blood flows through the arterial system, branching into smaller arteries until reaching the capillaries, where it exchanges oxygen for carbon dioxide. The oxygen poor blood returns to the lungs through the veins, ready to begin the cycle again.

The human body moves itself, builds itself, repairs itself and reproduces itself, all through various specialized systems of tissues and organs. Although every system has its own purpose, each relies on the others for the body to function normally. The body needs all systems, but some can "break down" with little immediate effect, whereas the failure of other systems causes rapid and severe damage, or death. A strained muscle, for example, seldom threatens survival, but without prompt medical attention, a heart attack can mean death.

The circulatory and respiratory systems, which work together to provide gas and nutrients to the body, and to eliminate waste, react to conditions produced by the underwater environment more noticeably than any other body systems. Because the entire body relies on these two systems for virtually uninterrupted gas exchange, responses in them induced by the underwater environment can affect every cell in the body. The systems are so interlinked that few of their responses to diving occur independently of each other.

Circulatory System

The circulatory system transports fuel, materials and oxygen from the respiratory and digestive systems to the body tissues, and carries material wastes and carbon dioxide from the tissues for elimination. Although all these functions are essential, the movement of gases to and from the respiratory system is the most urgent and most relevant to diving.

The Need for Oxygen

All living cells in the human body engage in *oxidative metabolism*, the process in which each cell uses oxygen to convert chemical energy into usable energy required for life. Deprived of oxygen, some tissues can temporarily "suspend" operations for up to several hours and still survive; others rapidly die without it.

The brain and nervous system demand a continuous oxygen supply, higher than that demanded by other body tissues, and begin to die within minutes without it. The oxygen requirements of nerve tissue consume about one-fifth of the oxygen the circulatory system transports.

Blood

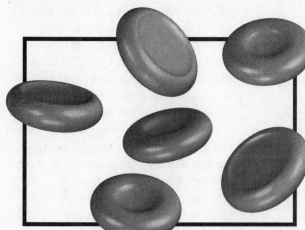

Red blood cells (erythrocytes) carry the majority of the oxygen required by body tissue via hemoglobin, a protein that easily bonds and unbonds with oxygen.

To meet the complex demands on the circulatory system to supply oxygen and materials, to remove wastes and waste gases, and to mobilize the body's defensive system, human blood functions as a multifaceted liquid tissue. Blood consists of several distinct components to accomplish its different functions.

Plasma is the actual liquid that carries nutrients, chemicals and other blood components. It also carries dissolved gases, including some of the waste carbon dioxide produced by the cells, and nitrogen as it fluctuates with the partial pressure of breathed nitrogen. (See Physiological Responses to Nitrogen, which discusses the body's interactions with dissolved nitrogen in detail.)

Although plasma accounts for about half the weight of blood and carries some dissolved gases, it carries little dissolved oxygen at surface pressures. Red blood cells (*erythrocytes*) carry the majority of the oxygen required by body tissue via *hemoglobin*, a protein that easily bonds and unbonds with oxygen. Without hemoglobin, the blood would have to circulate the plasma about 15-20 times faster to supply even a resting body with sufficient oxygen. Red blood cells make up about 45 percent of the blood.

Hemoglobin carries and releases oxygen efficiently because variations in oxygen partial pressure influence its capacity to remain bonded with oxygen. The blood circulates through the lungs where it encounters higher oxygen partial pressure. High partial pressure increases oxygen's ability to bond with hemoglobin, consequently, oxygen diffuses into the red cells to bond with hemoglobin.

When the blood reaches the tissues where metabolism has reduced the oxygen partial pressure, oxygen unbonds from the hemoglobin for use by the tissues because its ability to maintain the bond declines at lower partial pressures. With much of the oxygen released, hemoglobin can now bind reversibly with carbon dioxide to be carried to the lungs for elimination. An enzyme in the red blood cell also participates in a reversible chemical reaction that transports

carbon dioxide in the plasma in the form of bicarbonate.

Once the blood returns to the higher oxygen partial pressure of the lungs, again the hemoglobin bonds easily with oxygen, and releases carbon dioxide. The carbon dioxide reaction in the plasma reverses, breaking down the bicarbonate and releasing the carbon dioxide, which then diffuses into the respiratory system to be eliminated. By transporting carbon dioxide in the form of bicarbonate, the circulatory system can carry larger amounts than by direct solution of carbon dioxide into the plasma. About five percent of the carbon dioxide the blood carries is in solution in the plasma, about 20 percent combines with hemoglobin and about 75 percent transports in the form of bicarbonate.

Cardiovascular Structure

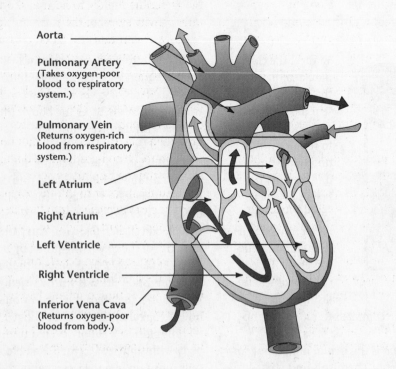

Aorta

Pulmonary Artery
(Takes oxygen-poor
blood to respiratory
system.)

Pulmonary Vein
(Returns oxygen-rich
blood from respiratory
system.)

Left Atrium

Right Atrium

Left Ventricle

Right Ventricle

Inferior Vena Cava
(Returns oxygen-poor
blood from body.)

The human heart is essentially a four-chambered organic pump composed of muscle tissue and divided longitudinally. The atria receive blood coming into the heart and pump it into ventricles. The ventricles pump blood away from the heart. Blood from the respiratory system enters the left heart, which pumps the blood to rest of the body. Because the left side of the heart supplies the entire body with blood, it is larger and stronger than the right heart.

The heart, arteries, veins, and capillaries make up the *cardiovascular system*. Basically, the *heart* moves the blood, which travels through the *arteries* to tissues throughout the body. Arteries branch into the tiny *capillaries*, in which the blood and tissues exchange gases and material. The capillaries lead to the *veins*, which return the blood to the respiratory system and heart to begin again. A closer look at this system forms the foundation for understanding the cardiovascular system's role in diving physiology.

The human heart is essentially a four-chambered organic pump composed of muscle tissue and divided longitudinally. The upper chambers on each side, called *atria* (atrium — singular) receive blood coming into the heart and pump it into *ventricles*, the chambers below. The ventricles pump blood away from the heart.

Oxygen-rich blood coming from the respiratory system enters the left side of

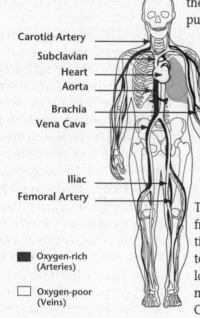

Carotid Artery
Subclavian
Heart
Aorta
Brachia
Vena Cava
Iliac
Femoral Artery

■ Oxygen-rich (Arteries)
□ Oxygen-poor (Veins)

Major arteries and veins of the cardiovascular system.

the heart (left heart), which pumps the blood into the *aorta*, the largest artery in the body. Because the left side of the heart supplies the entire body with blood, it is larger and stronger than the right side (right heart).

The *carotid arteries* branch off the aorta almost immediately and supply blood to the brain. Tracing the arterial system away from the heart, the arteries continue to branch into smaller arteries until they reach the capillaries, the actual site of gas and material transfer with the tissues. Capillaries are microscopic, with diameters so small that blood cells pass through single file, and walls so thin that gases and materials diffuse readily through them to and from other body tissues.

Capillaries lead through the tissues they supply, then branch together into the veins, which branch together returning oxygen-poor blood to the right side of the heart. The right side of the heart pumps blood into the *pulmonary arteries*, which lead to the pulmonary capillaries inside the lungs. The oxygen bonding with hemoglobin and carbon dioxide release from the blood actually occurs in the pulmonary capillaries. Oxygen-rich blood leaving the pulmonary capillaries flows into the *pulmonary veins* and back to the left atrium to begin another cycle.

Blood Pressure

Blood pressure is the force of the heart and the pressure it makes, recorded by physiologists as diastolic and systolic pressures.

On each heart beat, blood surges into the arteries, creating the *pulse* and *blood pressure*. Pulse rate measures the frequency of heart rate, which in the average adult at rest is 60-80 beats per minute. Although the heart never stops beating, except in emergency medical conditions such as a heart attack, it rests between beats.

Blood pressure is the force of the heart and the pressure it makes, recorded by physiologists as *diastolic* and *systolic* pressures. Blood flows into the arterial system in pressure surges that coincide with heart contractions. The systolic pressure is the surge, or high point as the heart contracts, and diastolic pressure is the lull after the surge, or low point when the heart relaxes.

Blood pressure and pulse increase during exercise, stress or fright, but normally decline rapidly to normal shortly after activity stops, or the stress or fright ends. The heart rate and blood pressure increase in response to exercise as muscle tissues use more energy and increase their metabolism, increasing the demand for oxygen. This is why exercise also corresponds with an increased breathing rate. How the body monitors and controls blood-gas levels is discussed shortly with the respiratory system.

During stress or fright, the *adrenal gland* releases *adrenaline* into the circulatory system as part of the body's survival response. Adrenaline stimulates the heart, constricts blood vessels and increases the breathing rate to prepare the body to flee or fight a threat. This response occurs instinctively due to perception; that is, a threat doesn't have to be real to trigger survival responses.

Recommendation: Both stress and moderate exercise are common in recreational diving. For this reason, individuals with high blood pressure or a history of cardiac difficulties should consult an appropriately qualified physician before participating in recreational diving.

The Respiratory System

Basic respiratory system structure, with lung cutaway showing bronchi and alveoli.

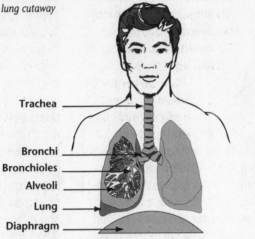

Trachea

Bronchi

Bronchioles

Alveoli

Lung

Diaphragm

The respiratory system functions with the circulatory system by providing the blood with an appropriate environment for gas exchange. Broadly, the respiratory system brings oxygen into the body and carries waste carbon dioxide out of the body. It also carries nitrogen to and from the body, which is particularly relevant to the diver.

Respiratory System Structure and Function

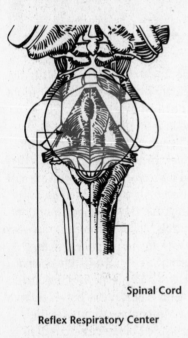

Spinal Cord

Reflex Respiratory Center

Breathing starts when the body detects a carbon dioxide increase and/or an oxygen decrease in the blood. The reflex respiratory centers at the base of the brain have primary command of breathing.

Following the sequence of events in the respiratory system simplifies understanding the physiology of breathing. Breathing starts when the body detects a carbon dioxide increase and/or an oxygen decrease in the blood. The *reflex respiratory centers* in the brain have primary command of breathing. When carbon dioxide increases above a specific level, the respiratory centers stimulate breathing.

The *peripheral chemoreceptors* monitor oxygen levels and signal the respiratory centers when the partial pressure of oxygen declines below a specific level. This "low oxygen" signal from the peripheral chemoreceptors, combined with the presence of high carbon dioxide, triggers the reflex respiratory centers to stimulate breathing.

Carbon dioxide, however, primarily controls breathing — not oxygen. If the peripheral chemoreceptors detect low oxygen, but the reflex respiratory centers find carbon dioxide acceptable, the respiratory center may not stimulate breathing. On the other hand, even if oxygen levels are normal, an overabundance of carbon dioxide will cause the reflex respiratory centers to stimulate breathing.

Upon detecting high carbon dioxide, the respiratory center stimulates the *diaphragm*, a large muscle that separates the chest cavity from the abdominal cavity, to flex downward, increasing the chest's internal volume. The volume change and pressure decrease causes air to flow inward to maintain pressure equilibrium inside and outside the lungs.

Air enters and passes through the mouth, nose and sinuses, which moisten and filter the air. From the oral and nasal passages, the air travels past the *epiglottis* in the throat into the *trachea* (windpipe). The epiglottis acts as a valve between the trachea and the *esophagus* (which leads to the stomach) to prevent inspiration of food or liquids. The trachea branches into the right and left *bronchi*, which lead into the lungs.

Commonly likened to balloons, the lungs are actually more like two large sponges inside the protective rib cage. Within the lungs the bronchi continuously branch down to smaller air passages, called *bronchioles*. The bronchioles terminate at the *alveoli*, which are air sacs surrounded by pulmonary capillaries. This is where gas exchanges with the blood.

Gas moves between the alveoli and the capillaries through the microscopically thin gas-permeable membranes that make up the alveolar and capillary walls. Thus, oxygen and carbon dioxide exchange freely between the blood and alveoli without the blood coming directly in contact with the air. The actual mechanism of gas movement is simple diffusion — the natural tendency of a gas to move from an area of high concentration to an area of low concentration. Without diffusion, this fundamental life process could not take place.

To provide maximum contact area for rapid gas diffusion, the alveoli and capillaries, because of their large num-

bers, if opened and spread out, would be the size of a typical living room floor. In spite of this large area, the respiratory and circulatory systems normally use only 10 percent of the available oxygen in each breath. Mouth-to-mouth resuscitation works because exhaled air still contains 90 percent of its original oxygen and is sufficient to sustain life.

Breathing rate fluctuates with the body's carbon dioxide production. At rest, the average person breathes 10-20 times per minute, but during exercise, the rate increases as the muscular system more rapidly consumes oxygen and produces carbon dioxide. The reflex respiratory center maintains the higher breathing rate until carbon dioxide levels return to normal.

The inspired air volume fluctuates, increasing with the breathing rate at times of high oxygen demand/high car-

Nasal Passages

Epiglottis

Esophagus

Trachea

Bronchi

Air passages into the respiratory system. Air flows through the mouth, nose and sinuses, which moisten and filter the air, past the epiglottis in the throat into the trachea (windpipe). The trachea branches into the right and left bronchi, which lead into the lungs.

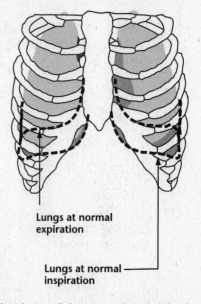

Lungs at normal expiration

Lungs at normal inspiration

Physiologists call the amount of air inhaled and exhaled during normal breathing the tidal volume.

bon-dioxide production. Physiologists call the amount of air inhaled and exhaled during normal breathing the *tidal volume. Vital capacity* is the maximum volume that can be inspired after total expiration, and *residual volume* is the air left in the lungs after complete exhalation.

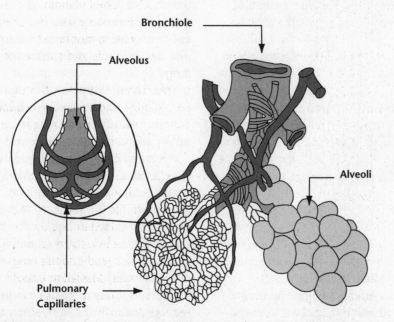

Bronchiole

Alveolus

Alveoli

Pulmonary Capillaries

Enlarged detail of alveoli, which are air sacs surrounded by pulmonary capillaries. This is where gas exchanges with the blood.

Circulatory and Respiratory Responses to Diving

The previous discussion reviews normal circulatory and respiratory system functions, but while these continue during a dive, when a diver descends, either breathing compressed air or holding his breath, both systems respond to the new environment. It is the body's ability to respond that makes diving possible.

Responses to Breathing with Equipment

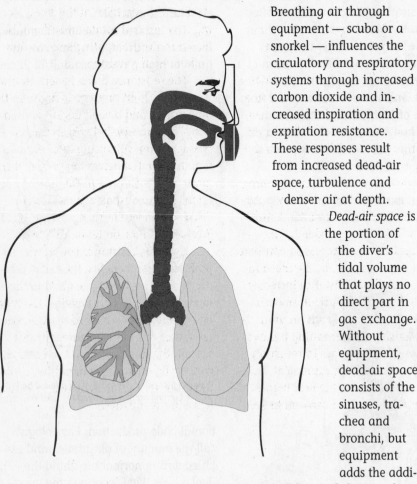

Dead-air space is the portion of tidal volume that plays no part in gas exchange. Dead-air space consists of the sinuses, trachea and bronchi; equipment adds the volume of the snorkel or regulator.

Breathing air through equipment — scuba or a snorkel — influences the circulatory and respiratory systems through increased carbon dioxide and increased inspiration and expiration resistance. These responses result from increased dead-air space, turbulence and denser air at depth.

Dead-air space is the portion of the diver's tidal volume that plays no direct part in gas exchange. Without equipment, dead-air space consists of the sinuses, trachea and bronchi, but equipment adds the additional volume of the snorkel or regulator to the dead-air space.

At inspiration, the first air drawn into the alveoli is the air left in the passages from the previous expiration. This air is high in carbon dioxide and mixes with fresh air drawn in, so alveolar air is always higher in carbon dioxide than fresh air. With the addition of the snorkel, regulator or other breathing device, the dead air on each breath increases, influenced further by an approximate 15 to 20 percent reduction in tidal volume caused by water pressure compressing the thorax.

With the tidal volume decreased and the dead-air space increased, dead air becomes a larger percentage of each breath, and carbon dioxide in alveolar air increases correspondingly. The increase depends upon the tidal volume and the dead air space volume, and therefore can range from insignificant to substantial. Within limits, the diver's physiology compensates for the higher carbon dioxide through both an involuntary and a voluntary response.

Increased alveolar carbon dioxide raises carbon dioxide in the bloodstream, although there is no substantial decrease in the oxygen level. Nonetheless, the reflex respiratory center stimulates the diver to breathe more frequently and/or more deeply to eliminate the excess carbon dioxide. In some individuals it seems that with experience, the reflex respiratory center becomes tolerant of a slightly higher-than-

When air flows through smooth passages, it can travel with an uninterrupted, laminar flow. In rough air passages, such as dive equipment, the trachea and bronchi, friction with the side passages makes the flow turbulent. The air moves faster in the center of the flow column, leading to swirls that rotate away from the flow direction, increasing resistance.

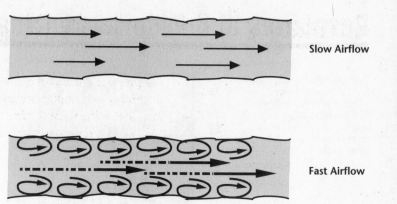

Slow Airflow

Fast Airflow

normal carbon dioxide level. This seems most common among divers who make long breath-hold dives, such as when hunting underwater.

The voluntary response — one made consciously by the diver — is deep breathing to maximize the tidal volume. Taking advantage of as much volume as possible per breath reduces the proportion of dead air, allowing as much fresh air as possible to reach the alveoli.

While using scuba, deep breathing requires an additional voluntary adaptation as a consequence of the denser air the scuba delivers at depth. The denser air becomes, the less smoothly it flows at a given speed, as the speed increases, breathing resistance increases.

When air flows through smooth passages, it can travel with an uninterrupted, *laminar* flow, meaning it moves as a continuous column. In rough air passages, such as dive equipment, the trachea and bronchi, the flow becomes turbulent from friction between the air

and the passage sides. This drag causes the air to move faster in the center of the flow column than at the sides, leading to swirls that rotate away from the flow direction, disrupting smooth flow and increasing resistance.

The resistance has a benefit in that it causes a slight pressure increase in the bronchioles and alveoli during exhalation. This increase helps keep the air passages from collapsing after exhalation, although a percentage will still collapse after each breath. Diving considerations due to air-passage collapse are discussed under Physiological Effects of Pressure Change on Body Air Spaces.

However, resistance causes more problems than benefits; the faster the air moves, the denser the air, and the more irregular the air passage, the more energy must be consumed to overcome resistance due to turbulence. For this reason, the diver responds by relaxing, conserving energy and breathing slowly to minimize resistance caused by turbulence in the airways.

Recommendation: To minimize the effects of dense air and dead-air space, the diver should breathe deeply and slowly while using scuba.

Responses to Breath-Hold Diving

Bradycardia, or slowing of the heart is triggered by cold moisture in contact with the face, but what causes the resulting decline in heart rate in water is not fully understood.

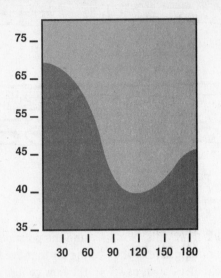

The respiratory and circulatory systems respond to diving without scuba as well as with scuba. While breath-hold diving, such as when snorkeling, the body responds to ensure survival during cessation of breathing (called *apnea*) and to ensure that breathing eventually resumes.

During apnea, the circulatory system taps oxygen stored in the lungs, muscles and blood to supply tissue oxygen needs. With no place to vent, carbon dioxide builds in the circulatory system, causing the reflex respiratory center to stimulate the diaphragm. The diver feels this stimulation as an urge to breathe. The initial urge is weak, but successive urges grow stronger as the body consumes oxygen and produces carbon dioxide, until the diver must surface for air.

How long a diver can go without breathing depends on several physiological responses. The extent of these responses varies significantly from individual to individual, meaning the length of time different divers can hold their breaths will vary also.

An involuntary response found in breath-hold diving is *bradycardia*, or slowing of the heart. This is a similar response to conditions produced in diving

mammals, but though bradycardia reduces circulation, it does not seem to significantly reduce oxygen consumption as it does in diving mammals. Physiologists know that apneaic bradycardia is triggered by cold moisture in contact with the face, but what causes the resulting decline in heart rate in water is not fully understood.

The bradycardia response to apnea has sometimes been called the *mammalian diving reflex* because it is found in diving mammals such as whales, seals and porpoises. The diving reflex in humans is believed to have helped prevent deaths in near-drowning accidents of youths in water below 10°C/50°F. In these incidents, the near-drowning victims have recovered with resuscitation, even after periods of 20 minutes or more without breathing. There were no apparent after effects.

Physiologists believe the diving reflex pools the blood in the brain and heart, distributing the limited oxygen supply only to critical areas. That cold water on the face seems to trigger the response explains why the diving reflex has been noted less in warm-water near-drowning accidents than in cold water. Some experts believe that cooling of the brain accounts for some of the phenomonon.

Voluntary actions can increase breath-hold time. One is diver relaxation. By moving efficiently and unhurriedly, the diver exercises less, and thereby reduces oxygen consumption and carbon-dioxide production.

Intentional hyperventilation produces significant increases in breath-hold time. By taking three or four deep, rapid breaths prior to breath-holding, the diver drops respiratory carbon dioxide below normal levels, which subsequently produces a circulatory carbon-dioxide decline. The tissues must therefore produce more carbon dioxide before reaching the level that stimulates breathing.

Physiological Rationale of the First Aid and Medical Treatment for Near-drowning

According to most studies, drowning is the most frequent cause listed for death in scuba diving accidents. Although the final physiology (drowning) is similar in almost all accidents, the actual incident that leads to it may differ many ways. For example, a diver becoming exhausted on the surface (before or after the dive), or a diver running out of air and panicking can lead to drowning (which may also have lung overexpansion injury complications). Other conditions that can cause loss of consciousness, such as diabetes, epilepsy, hypothermia or cardiac arrhythmia, can also lead to a drowning incident. This is why people with conditions that predispose them to loss of consciousness are advised not to dive.

Before discussing the physiology of this phenomenon, it is probably worth defining *drowning* and *near-drowning*. Simply stated, in a drowning incident, the victim dies. In a near-drowning incident, the victim survives at least temporarily.

In either type of incident, a victim may or may not inhale water. Approximately 15 percent of drowning and near-drowning victims don't inhale water, possibly because during immersion they reflexively close their larynx. In essence, these individuals suffocate. If ventilation can be reestablished prior to irreversible circulatory or neurologic injury, such a person usually has a speedy and relatively uneventful recovery.

For the remaining 85 percent of victims, the course of a near-drowning incident differs. These victims inhale varying quantities of water, which in turn causes lung injuries that persist long after the rescuers take the individual from the water. With rare exception, it makes little difference whether the victim inhales fresh water or salt, because the final physiological consequences are the same, though the mechanisms differ somewhat.

The most important effect of fresh or salt water inhalation is *hypoxemia*. Hypoxemia is abnormally low blood oxygen, which results in inadequate oxygen reaching body tissues (hypoxia).

The brain is the most sensitive to a lack of oxygen, which is why unconsciousness is almost universal in near-drowning episodes. Also important to hypoxemia that occurs due to the victim not breathing while underwater is water aspiration, which causes lung injury that may not manifest itself for several hours. Someone rescued from near-drowning may be revived and appear fully recovered, only to suffer hypoxemia hours (or sometimes days) after the actual incident. This is called *secondary drowning*. Without appropriate therapy, secondary drowning can cause hypoxemia to continue, and is frequently fatal.

Given that hypoxemia during and after the accident causes the tissue injury, the most important first aid for the near-drowning victim is prompt rescue breathing and/or CPR if necessary , then emergency oxygen. Many victims of near-drowning have suffered cardiac arrest and recovered fully without noticeable permanent residual effects.

It's generally not worth trying to drain water from the lungs, but a rescuer will want to protect the upper airway (mouth, nose and throat) to keep it free of obstructions, as well as to prevent inhaling any more water. Near-drowning patients may vomit after rescue since they often swallow water; a rescuer will want to keep a patient from inhaling it.

Since pulmonary (lung) damage and hypoxemia resulting from near-drowning can persist for hours or days following an incident, it is extremely important that all near-drowning victims receive emergency medical treatment for a more detailed evaluation, and receive oxygen if available en route to emergency medical care.

Physiologists once thought that the near-drowning injury mechanism depended upon whether the victim aspirated salt versus fresh water. Today this has little bearing upon patient treatment, except under extremely unusual circumstances, even though salt and fresh water injure the lung differently. With sea water, it seems that sand, diatoms, algae, and other microscopic material combine to irritate the lung lining and interfere with oxygen transfer. With fresh water, the lung loses chemical components, also affecting oxygen transfer. In either case, less oxygen reaches the blood to supply the tissues, which is why the most important treatment for a breathing near-drowning patient is emergency oxygen.

In scuba diving accidents, the actual primary injury may not be clear. A diver can suffer, for example, an air embolism, lose consciousness and then near-drown. In the first few moments of a rescue, it may be impossible to decide what happened, but this doesn't really play an important role in handling the emergency.

Fortunately, near-drowning, lung expansion injuries, or decompression sickness call for the same response: Provide rescue breathing and/or CPR as needed, and emergency oxygen. Get the patient to emergency medical care as soon as possible.

The most important effect of fresh or salt water inhalation is hypoxemia. Hypoxemia is abnormally low blood oxygen, which results in inadequate oxygen reaching body tissues (hypoxia). This is why emergency oxygen is the specific first aid for near-drowning.

MFA *PADI Rescue Diver Manual*

Diving Problems with Circulatory and Respiratory Systems

Although the circulatory and respiratory systems function remarkably well during diving, a land-based physiology can't be expected to make the transition to the underwater environment perfectly. Human circulatory and respiratory systems may develop difficulties due to equipment complications, failure to make voluntary responses to changing pressure, or a diver's ignorance concerning the behavior of the body.

Carotid-Sinus Reflex

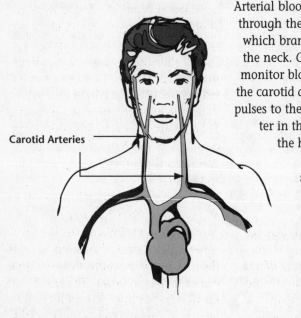

Carotid Arteries

An excessively tight dry suit, wet suit, hood or other equipment that constricts the carotid arteries may cause the carotid-sinus receptors to stimulate the cardioinhibitory center to slow the heart. This can cause unconsciousness.

Arterial blood reaches the brain through the carotid arteries, which branch up each side of the neck. *Carotid-sinus receptors* monitor blood pressure within the carotid arteries and send impulses to the cardioinhibitory center in the brain to regulate the heart.

When the carotid-sinus receptor detects high blood pressure, it stimulates the cardioinhibitory center, which slows the heart rate. When the carotid sinus receptors detect low blood pressure, it stops stimulating the cardioinhibitory center, which in turn stops sending signals to the heart. The heart rate then increases.

If a diver wears an excessively tight dry suit, wet suit, hood or other equipment that constricts the neck, the carotid-sinus receptors may incorrectly interpret the excess local pressure as high blood pressure and stimulate the cardioinhibitory center to slow the heart. The reduced heart rate slows blood flow to the brain, but continued pressure on the neck continues to stimulate the carotid-sinus receptor as though blood flow were still high. Eventually, a diver may lose consciousness due to the reduced blood supply reaching the brain. In most cases, a diver feels discomfort and lightheadedness before the constriction leads to serious problems.

Hypercapnia

Heavy work underwater can produce carbon dioxide faster than the respiratory system can eliminate it. The elevated carbon dioxide stimulates a high breathing rate, which at depth, requires considerable effort to overcome resistance from turbulence. This additional respiratory effort further increases carbon dioxide production, creating more demand for increased breathing. This vicious cycle stops when the diver ceases activity and the respiratory system catches up with gas-exchange.

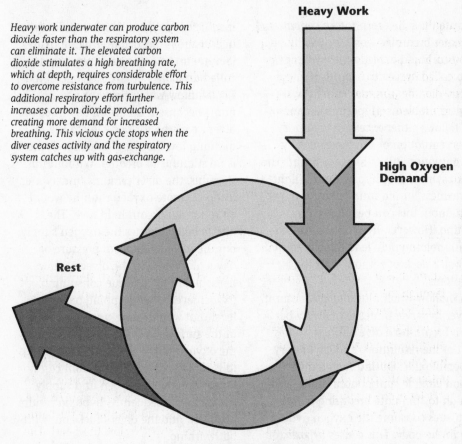

Heavy Work

High Oxygen Demand

Rest

Labored Breathing

Hypercapnia (also called *hypercarbia*), or excess carbon dioxide, can result from several causes. It most commonly occurs when a diver fails to breathe slowly and deeply enough, resulting in a small tidal volume and a high proportion of dead air to fresh air in the alveoli. Carbon-dioxide levels in the alveolar air and in the bloodstream increase, causing headache, confusion and accelerated breathing until the diver resumes deep breathing. Unchecked, elevated carbon dioxide can eventually lead to loss of consciousness. Some forms of scuba, such as some types of closed and semiclosed scuba (rebreathers) and full face masks, have been associated with hypercapnia due partly to comparatively large dead air spaces. In conventional open circuit scuba used in recreational diving, hypercapnia due to dead air spaces is rare, though not unheard of.

If a diver attempts heavy work underwater, muscle tissue can produce carbon dioxide faster than the respiratory system can eliminate it. The elevated carbon dioxide causes the reflex respiratory center to stimulate a high breathing rate, which, due to the denser air breathed at depth, requires considerable effort by the diaphragm and other respiratory muscles to overcome resistance from turbulence. This additional respiratory effort further increases carbon dioxide production, resulting in a yet higher demand for increased breathing. This vicious cycle stops when the diver ceases all activity and the respiratory system catches up with body gas-exchange needs.

An inappropriate technique called *skip-breathing* can cause hypercapnia. Skip-breathing is holding the breath while scuba diving in an effort to extend the air supply. In reality, this technique causes a diver's circulatory carbon dioxide to increase, until it actually stimulates faster breathing and depletes the supply faster. High carbon dioxide levels due to air supply contamination have been known to cause hypercapnia also, but fortunately, contaminated air is rare in recreational diving. Hypercapnia from contaminated air leads to the same symptoms as hypercapnia from improper breathing.

Hypocapnia

Because the reflex respiratory center regulates breathing based primarily on blood carbon-dioxide levels, *hypocapnia* (also called *hypocarbia*), or insufficient carbon dioxide, can also cause physiological problems. Hypocapnia generally follows either excessive voluntary hyperventilation or unintentional hyperventilation due to stress or fright. The initial symptom of hypocapnia is lightheadedness during unintentional hyperventilation; this can be followed by fainting. However, hypocapnia during breath-holding may lead directly to *shallow-water blackout* without warning symptoms.

Shallow-water blackout can occur if a diver hyperventilates excessively before a breath-hold dive and eliminates most of the respiratory and circulatory carbon dioxide. During such a dive, the carbon dioxide cannot accumulate fast enough to stimulate breathing before the tissues consume the oxygen available in the body. This causes *hypoxia*, or insufficient oxygen, which rapidly damages tissue — particularly nerve tissue. (Severe, tissue damaging hypoxia is called *anoxia*.)

Shallow-water blackout gets its name because it occurs on ascent as the diver nears the surface. Due to the remaining low carbon-dioxide level, there is no stimulus to breathe. Without this stimulus, the diver remains underwater, using far more oxygen than he would on a normal breath-hold dive. The diver's body depletes the oxygen supply, but the increased partial pressure of oxygen at depth in the alveoli allows hemoglobin to continue consuming oxygen even after dropping below a level that would cause unconsciousness at the surface. When the diver ascends, the oxygen partial-pressure in the lungs falls rapidly, so the hemoglobin can no longer bond with oxygen and supply the body. Consequently, hypoxia results instantly, and the diver blacks out without warning.

Carbon Monoxide Poisoning

Although carbon monoxide poisoning happens most often outside the realm of diving, carbon monoxide in the underwater environment tends to be more serious and more complex because of increased pressure. In diving, carbon monoxide poisoning generally originates from a contaminated air supply, where it may be unnoticed by a diver because carbon monoxide lacks both odor and taste. (Fortunately, it *usually* occurs along with various oil-derived hydrocarbons that have a strong smell or taste.)

Hemoglobin bonds with carbon monoxide more than 200 times more readily than with oxygen, but does not unbond as easily. Once carbon monoxide enters the bloodstream, it can take eight to 12 hours for the circulatory system to eliminate it. In addition, carbon monoxide bonds with enzymes in the blood.

As a diver breathes air contaminated by carbon monoxide, blood hemoglobin reaching the alveoli bonds with the carbon monoxide, forming carboxyhemoglobin; this "locks" the hemoglobin molecule, making it incapable of carrying oxygen. The strong bond between carbon monoxide and hemoglobin keeps the carbon monoxide bonded as the blood circulates through the tissues, unlike oxygen. As the diver continues to inhale carbon monoxide, more and more hemoglobin bonds with it, so as circulation continues, fewer and fewer uncontaminated red bloods cells are available to carry the oxygen. Unchecked, this causes hypoxia despite continuing circulation and respiration because the blood can no longer supply oxygen to the tissues.

At depth, this condition can be further complicated because increased pressure dissolves oxygen into the blood plasma. Although at the surface blood plasma does not carry sufficient dissolved oxygen to support the body's tissues, higher oxygen partial pressure while breathing at depth greatly increases oxygen dissolved in the plasma. This action helps meet the tissue oxygen requirements and delays the onset of symptoms warning the diver. When carbon-monoxide poisoning symptoms do occur — headache, confusion, narrowed vision — the diver ascends, blacking out from hypoxia at shallow depths because there is no longer sufficient pressure to dissolve adequate oxygen into the plasma. If all divers obtained air at the same source, the situation can be complicated further by the fact that all will suffer from carbon monoxide poisoning simultaneously.

Carbon monoxide poisoning may cause a victim's lips and nail beds to turn bright red. Hemoglobin bonded with oxygen appears red, and hemoglobin bonded with carbon monoxide appears even redder than usual. Contaminated blood is highly visible as it flows through capillaries of the lips and nails, which are close to the surface of the skin. However, this isn't always apparent, especially underwater where color absorption and dive equipment may hide this sign.

Although carbon monoxide rarely contaminates a diver's air supply, it should be noted that smoking is another source. Physiologists have found that smoking raises normal carbon-monoxide levels in the blood three to 12 times, which impairs oxygen transport and carbon-dioxide elimination. Circulation increases so uncontaminated red blood cells can meet tissue gas-exchange requirements, raising blood pressure and heart rate. This is why smoking stimulates the heart. It takes 10 to 12 hours for gas exchange to return to normal after smoking.

Oxygen Toxicity

Within recreational diving limits using air, it's nearly impossible to have oxygen toxicity problems. However, commercial diving, technical diving, and recreational diving with *enriched* air (a.k.a. nitrox — air with oxygen added to reduce the nitrogen content) have the potential to cause oxygen toxicity. Recompression treatment, when needed, usually involves breathing pure oxygen under pressure, too, and can give rise to the toxic effects of high oxygen concentrations.

There are actually two types of oxygen toxicity; one involves the symptoms in the respiratory system, and the other involves the nervous system. *Pulmonary oxygen toxicity*, or the *Lorrain Smith effect* (after one of early researchers who investigated it) results from a lengthy exposure to oxygen partial pressures of 0.5 ata to 1.4 ata (see the Physics section for more on gas partial pressures). *Central nervous system* (CNS) oxygen toxicity is not directly related to respiratory- or circulatory-system problems, but is discussed here for clarity. CNS toxicity tends to be almost unpredictable beyond the fact that it occurs at high oxygen partial pressures. Oxygen partial pressures from 1.4 ata to 1.6 ata fall in the "gray" contingency range, and above 1.6 ata, CNS risk is considered hazardous.

Pulmonary oxygen toxicity occurs as excess oxygen reacts throughout the body, causing a wide number of possible symptoms. Lung irritation seems the most immediate and noticeable, although physiologists are unsure exactly how elevated oxygen partial pressure affects the lungs. Theories suggest that extended exposure causes the alveoli to collapse, or that the oxygen pressure causes changes in enzymes in the lungs. Whatever the cause, pulmonary oxygen toxicity reduces the vital capacity and, if unchecked, lessens the lungs' ability to transfer oxygen to the blood.

How fast pulmonary toxicity develops depends on the oxygen partial pressure, the length of exposure and the susceptibility of the individual. It is considered a predictable phenomenon; divers

use several methods based on oxygen partial pressure and breathing time to keep oxygen exposure within acceptable levels (see the Tracking Oxygen Exposure sidebar).

Recreational divers using air (approximately 21 percent oxygen) within recreational depth and no stop limits virtually cannot reach an exposure level where pulmonary toxicity would be expected. At 15 metres/50 feet the oxygen partial pressure of air is approximately 0.53 ata; oxygen problems would be expected only after more than 94 hours on an isolated exposure. At 40 metres/130 feet, the partial pressure is approximately 1.04 ata; it would require more than 12 hours before pulmonary oxygen toxicity were likely.

Using enriched air, on the other hand, makes pulmonary toxicity possible, though still unlikely, when making dives within no decompression limits. A recreational diver using enriched air would most likely approach oxygen exposure limits when using a blend with

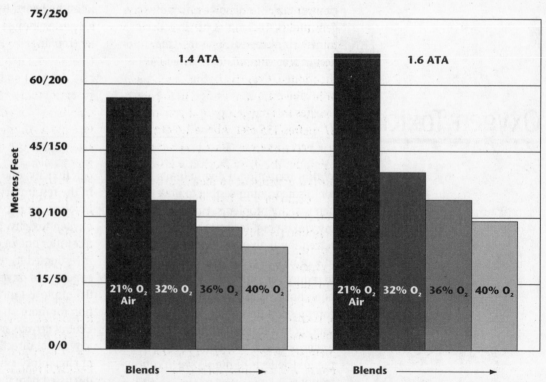

Depths at which different blends of air and enriched air reach oxygen partial pressures of 1.4 ata and 1.6 ata. Divers breathing air within recreational depth limits of 40 metres/130 feet won't reach the 1.4 ata limit or 1.6 ata contingency limit. Divers using enriched air, however, can reach these partial pressures within recreational depth limits.

36 percent to 40 percent oxygen and making more than three repetitive dives. Technical, commercial and military divers making dives that require enriched air and/or pure oxygen for decompression are more likely to reach oxygen exposure limits. However, by tracking exposure, divers (recreational or otherwise) can stay within accepted limits.

Even if a diver experiences pulmonary toxicity, the situation isn't serious unless oxygen exposure continues. Burning in the chest and an irritated cough usually signal the onset of toxicity and progressively worsen with continued exposure until symptoms become serious. On the other hand, a diver who notices symptoms and discontinues diving can expect the condition to resolve itself in a few days with no aftereffects or long-term consequences.

Central nervous system oxygen toxicity involves the whole body and requires much less time than pulmonary toxicity for symptoms to occur, but the oxygen partial pressure must be higher. This makes CNS toxicity highly unlikely for the recreational diver using air within recreational depth limits. As mentioned, CNS risk becomes unacceptable above 1.4 ata; using air, the diver reaches this oxygen partial pressure at 57 metres/185 feet. Above 1.6 ata, CNS risk becomes immediate and hazardous; using air, the diver reaches this oxygen partial pressure at 66 metres/218 feet.

Using enriched air, however, a diver can easily exceed 1.4 or 1.6 ata partial pressure. For this reason, the special training required for enriched air diving includes learning how to determine the maximum depths for differing enriched air blends. For example, using EANx32 (enriched air with 32 percent oxygen), a diver would reach the 1.4 ata limit at 33 metres/110 feet — well within the 40 metre/130 foot limit for recreational diving. Using EANx36, a diver would reach the same limit at 29 metres/95

feet. It's worth noting that using pure oxygen, a diver would reach 1.4 ata at 4 metres/13 feet, and 1.6 ata at 6 metres/20 feet. This is one reason why recreational divers never use pure oxygen in their cylinder (technical divers use pure oxygen for decompression at very shallow stages; this requires special training and poses substantially more potential risk than recreational diving).

Physiologists are unsure of what causes central nervous system toxicity. Theories suggest the high concentration of oxygen can temporarily overwhelm the body's defenses and interfere chemically with enzymes used by the tissues for metabolism, leading to central nervous system symptoms including lip-twitching, muscular trembling, nausea, epileptic-like convulsions and unconsciousness.

CNS toxicity is considered life-threatening in many diving situations because of possible sudden convulsions and unconsciousness. Although these conditions pose no direct threat themselves, a convulsing diver using a conventional regulator may lose the mouthpiece, leading to a high probability of drowning. This is why recreational enriched air divers learn to stay well within oxygen limits. Commercial divers, for example, may breathe gas blends with oxygen partial pressures higher than 1.4 ata, but usually do so in a chamber or wearing a full face mask. In these cases, a convulsion poses much less risk because drowning isn't likely.

Breathing 100 percent oxygen at surface pressures poses virtually no risk of CNS toxicity because the partial pressure is only 1.0 ata. Pulmonary toxicity would require more than 12 hours continuous exposure before serious symptoms would be expected. This is why rescuers in medical emergencies can administer oxygen to patients without concern for potential oxygen poisoning. Hospitals normally reduce the oxygen concentration if a patient will require extended exposure to high oxygen levels.

Tracking Oxygen Exposure

Divers using enriched air (nitrox) or other high oxygen level gas blends need to track their oxygen exposure to stay within accepted limits. Depending upon the diving circumstances (recreational or technical diving, for example), divers may use one or more methods.

Most physiologists consider attempts to predict Central Nervous System (CNS) on a partial pressure/time basis unreliable. For this reason, divers — whether recreational, commercial, research, or technical — avoid CNS toxicity by staying well within a maximum partial pressure of approximately 1.4 ata. (Depending upon the circumstances, nonrecreational divers decompress at an oxygen partial pressure as high as 1.6 ata.)

Pulmonary/whole body toxicity, on the other hand, has shown to be reliably predictable based on time and partial pressure exposure. For recreational purposes, most divers find it simplest to stay with the single exposure limits established by the U.S. National Oceanic and Atmospheric Administration (NOAA):

NOAA Oxygen Limits for single exposures

PO_2 in ata.	Time
0.6	720 min
0.7	570 min
0.8	450 min
0.9	360 min
1.0	300 min
1.1	240 min
1.2	210 min
1.3	180 min
1.4	150 min
1.5	120 min
1.6	45 min

For increased utility when making multiple dives or multi-level dives, the NOAA limits can be applied as a percent of allowed exposure. This is the basis of the DSAT Oxygen Exposure Table distributed by PADI, and some other tables/procedures used in the dive community.

The NOAA limits were developed for use by research divers who may be diving for several days continuously. However, this methodology causes problems for commercial divers who may be involved with long decompressions at high oxygen partial pressures. In these instances, commercial divers use the Repex method, developed by R.W. Hamilton, Ph.D., to stay within pulmonary limits.

The Repex method calculates in doses called Oxygen Toxicity Units (OTUs), whereby

$$OTUs = \text{time in minutes} \times [(PO_2 - 0.5) \div 0.5]^{0.83}$$

The allowable number of OTUs daily depends upon the cumulative oxygen exposure over multiple days. For example, for a single day, the diver may have 850 OTUs, but if a diver will be diving each day for 10 days, the limit is approximately 300 OTUs. The NOAA limits, which accommodate multiple day exposure, allow a maximum of 300 OTUs and is consistent with the Repex method.

Recommendations to help minimize circulatory and respiratory problems:

1. *Divers should be careful not to wear wet suits or other equipment in such a way as to apply pressure to the carotid-sinus nerve.*

2. *Divers should breathe slowly, deeply and continuously, and should avoid overexertion to help their respiratory and circulatory systems avoid problems from dead-air space, dense air and increased carbon dioxide.*

3. *Hyperventilation before a breath-hold dive should be limited to two or three breaths to avoid shallow-water blackout.*

4. *Divers should only have their tanks filled at reputable dive stores and resorts to minimize the possibility of contaminated air. Pure oxygen should never be used by recreational divers, and enriched air nitrox should only be used by divers trained and certified in enriched air diving (except under instructor supervision).*

5. *Divers using enriched air should stay well within oxygen exposure limits.*

6. *The effects of smoking are undeniably detrimental, and divers should avoid it. If the habit cannot be eliminated altogether, divers should abstain from smoking 10-12 hours before and after diving to prevent interference with normal gas exchange. Smokers should consult an appropriately qualified physician before engaging in diving, especially if they smoke a pack of cigarettes or more daily.*

Physiological Responses to Nitrogen

The previous section has shown how the circulatory and respiratory systems respond to diving, but the discussion involves only those two systems. Beyond these responses, the circulatory and respiratory systems deliver increased amounts of dissolved nitrogen (or other inert gases in nonrecreational diving) to the body during a dive, which becomes distributed throughout the body with potential effects on every tissue. This section examines how the body responds to increased nitrogen, and the consequences if a diver exceeds the body's ability to handle it.

Nitrogen Absorption and Decompression

More than 140 years have passed since physiologists first started studying decompression sickness (DCS), a painful condition that first appeared in laborers who worked in pressurized mines. Subsequently, laborers employed in pressurized caissons placed on river beds for bridge construction developed the condition.

Early physiologists determined that excess nitrogen forms bubbles in the body that cause decompression sickness, but they were still puzzled. Why did some exposures to excess nitrogen (dives or pressurized work environments) create DCS, while others do not? Why can the same exposure produce the condition in one person and not in another?

With research, hyperbaric physiologists have learned a great deal about how the body responds to nitrogen, but new questions replace those asked by early physiologists: Can bubbles develop without DCS? What is the state of nitrogen when the body eliminates it — in solution or in bubbles? Decompression models provide a reliable way to avoid decompression sickness, but how closely do they actually approximate human physiology? The answers have only come to light in the last 25 years, and even today the explanations aren't complete.

Pioneer Dive Table Physiologists

In 1670, Robert Boyle looked into the eye of a snake he had depressurized in a chamber. A bubble grew in its eye, which Boyle neither understood nor explained, but dutifully, he recorded. This record stands as history's first mention of decompression sickness (not by name), though it took until the 1870s before anyone understood the bubble's significance.

Decompression sickness appeared in humans for the first time in 1841, after French coal miners began digging in the world's first pressurized mine. Physicians B. Pol and T.J.J. Wattelle clinically described DCS in 1854 after studying the miners, noting that *leaving* pressure caused the condition, and *returning* to pressure relieved it. Since they didn't understand cause, this struck Pol and Wattelle rather like getting burned by taking your hand *out* of a fire, and having the burn go away when you stick your hand back in. Pol and Wattelle recorded the signs and symptoms of DCS, but couldn't adequately explain it.

Before long, the condition cropped up in workers laboring in pressurized caissons on bridge foundations. The caissons used compressed air to hold back water while work progressed on the river bottom. Workers leaving the caissons often developed decompression sickness, which became known as "caisson workers disease." Workers building piers for the Brooklyn Bridge compared the contortions sufferers twisted into trying to ease pain with the "Grecian Bend," an awkward fashionable posture of women of the period. From this the workers dubbed decompression sickness "the bends."

The unexplained disease struck divers and workers seemingly without pattern or reason, until a French physiologist, Paul Bert, turned his attention to it in the 1870s. Collecting medical reports on decompression sickness cases from caissons and from helmet divers, Bert started digging for the cause of caisson disease.

Experimenting with respiration, Bert concluded that the gas components of air act chemically with the body in proportion to the pressure. Bert determined that nitrogen absorbed by the body under pressure sometimes forms bubbles when the pressure is released.

In 1878, Bert published his theory in *La Pression Barometrique*, an 1100-page book that was published in English in 1943. Bert recommended that divers and caisson workers surface slowly, and if "bent," to go back down and come up again more slowly. Bert's theory seemed verified in 1893 during construction of a tunnel under the Hudson River. Workers who were struck by DCS were treated in an on-sight recompression chamber, reducing both symptoms and fatalities. Although Bert's recommendations represented a major advance in decompression medicine, the systemization of bubble formation into time and depth tables wouldn't happen for 30 years.

In 1906, Prof. John Scott Haldane, M.D., F.R.S., a physiologist interested in gas effects on the body, turned his attention to decompression sickness in Royal Navy helmet divers. Already Haldane had made more significant contributions to respiratory science than might be expected of one man. Haldane had improved mine conditions relating to gases and emergency treatment and, working with J.G. Priestley, "accidentally" discovered that carbon dioxide regulates the normal breathing cycle — a cornerstone in respiratory physiology.

Armed with Paul Bert's *La Pression Barometrique* and other pressure studies, Haldane along with A.E. Boycott and G.C.C. Damant began experimenting with goats. Theorizing that the body could hold a fixed quantity of excess nitrogen in solution, Haldane used the goats to demonstrate how much excess nitrogen the body could hold before "bends" bubbles resulted. The goat experiments were successful.

Next Haldane experimented with Royal Navy volunteer divers. Before experimenting, however, Haldane demanded changes in the divers' helmet equipment, including better pumps that supplied cleaner air to deeper depths. When Haldane concluded his project, he and his team's recommendations regarding hoists and suit design became Royal Navy standards.

Instrumental in the safety changes was his son, J.B.S. Haldane, who later pioneered oxygen poisoning research with Royal Navy closed-circuit scuba used in submarine escape during World War II. (About the same time, Kenneth Donald began similar studies for the purposes of training combat swimmers to use closed-circuit scuba to plant mines on enemy ships. These studies would ultimately position Donald as the world's most recognized authority in oxygen toxicity; he and J.B.S. Haldane consulted as they both explored the effects of oxygen under pressure.)

In 1670, Robert Boyle looked into the eye of a snake he had depressurized in a chamber. A bubble grew in its eye, which is history's first mention of decompression sickness.

Haldane's experiments took divers to record depths and surfaced them without decompression sickness. As dives validated Haldane's theories, volunteers reached record depths on nearly a daily basis, down to 64 metres/210 feet. After bringing the divers up from "undivable" depths without decompression sickness, Haldane published the first dive tables in 1907. The *Journal of Hygiene* published "The Prevention of Compressed Air Illness," written by Boycott, Damant and Haldane in 1908; to this day, the paper is considered the groundwork of decompression theory.

Today the work Bert and Haldane pioneered continues. Diving-medicine specialists continuously research and improve dive tables and decompression-sickness treatment, seeking to make diving safer and minimize the risk of decompression sickness. Nonetheless, the vast majority of dive computers and dive tables have their roots in Haldane's original model, with comparatively minor modification considering his work took place about a century ago.

J.S. Haldane's work with Royal Navy helmet divers led to the first dive tables, which were published in 1907.

Nitrogen Absorption

Nitrogen absorption by the body is a direct consequence of Henry's Law (discussed in section One, The Chemistry and Physics of Diving), which states that the quantity of gas dissolved in a liquid is proportional to the partial pressure of the gas. The human body is primarily liquid, so gases dissolve into it just as they dissolve into water. Because human physiology arranges its mass as tissues, however, the gas solution into the body is more complex than solution into water.

The effects of Henry's Law on physiology in recreational diving relate primarily to nitrogen, because nitrogen gas is physiologically inert and not used by the body. Oxygen diffusion under pressure, below oxygen toxicity limits, doesn't raise decompression concerns be-cause the tissues metabolize or otherwise use the oxygen. Other gases found in air exist in trace amounts, and their absorption is inconsequential.

Commercial, technical and military divers often use gas mixtures containing helium to prevent or reduce nitrogen's narcotic effects (discussed under Nitrogen Narcosis, this section). The mechanisms involving nitrogen absorption in recreational diving generally apply to any inert gas used by divers, although absorption and release times vary with different gases due to varying solubilities.

Henry's Law states that the human body will dissolve nitrogen in proportion to the surrounding pressure. At the surface, the body is *saturated*, meaning it contains as much nitrogen as it can hold in solution at surface pressure. As pres-

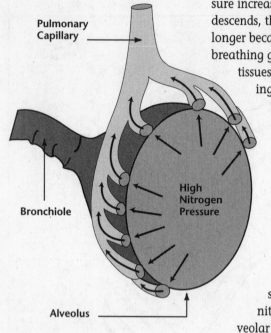

Pulmonary
Capillary

Bronchiole

High
Nitrogen
Pressure

Alveolus

Nitrogen diffuses from the alveolar air through the alveolar and capillary membranes into solution in the plasma in much the same way oxygen diffuses from alveolar air to reach the blood.

sure increases, such as when the diver descends, the body isn't saturated any longer because more nitrogen from the breathing gas can go into solution in the tissues, and begins to do so according to Henry's Law. If a diver were to remain at a given depth long enough, eventually the gas going into solution in the diver's body would reach equilibrium with the surrounding pressure. The body would be saturated again.

Solution into body tissues transpires through the circulatory and respiratory system. As the diver descends, nitrogen partial pressure in alveolar air increases, making it higher than the tissue pressure (pressure of nitrogen already dissolved) in blood plasma. The nitrogen diffuses from the alveolar air through the alveolar and capillary membranes into solution in the plasma in much the same way oxygen diffuses from alveolar air to reach the blood. The higher the pressure difference (*pressure gradient*) between the nitrogen in the alveolar air and the nitrogen in solution in the plasma, the faster nitrogen dissolves into the plasma.

As the plasma circulates to the body tissues, the nitrogen pressure in the plasma is higher than the nitrogen pressure in the rest of the tissues. Nitrogen therefore diffuses from the plasma into the tissues. As stated, if a diver maintained a depth and could stay long enough, the tissue pressures would eventually become saturated and unable to absorb any more nitrogen at that depth. Recreational divers, and even divers in most technical, commercial, research and military diving situations, do not

reach body saturation, which requires twelve or more hours at depth.

As tissue pressures climb, becoming closer to ambient pressure, the pressure gradient drops, slowing the rate of nitrogen absorption. Theoretically, saturation occurs exponentially, that is, it takes much less time for tissues to reach 50 percent saturation than to go from 50 percent saturation to saturated. Physiologists call the time required to reach 50 percent saturation in a theoretical tissue the *tissue halftime*, in that it takes one halftime for a theoretical tissue to absorb half the nitrogen remaining to reach saturation. This is an important cornerstone discussed in the development of dive tables.

The rate tissues absorb nitrogen is not the same in all tissues, thus different tissues have different halftimes. Some tissues, such as blood, absorb rapidly and contain relatively little nitrogen before they saturate. These are (theoretically) *fast* tissues. Other tissues, like fat, absorb a lot of nitrogen and therefore have long halftimes. These are (theoretically) *slow* tissues. The amount of circulation a tissue receives also affects how quickly or slowly it absorbs nitrogen.

Theoretically, saturation occurs exponentially. The time required to reach 50 % saturation in a theoretical tissue is the tissue halftime. In one halftime, a theoretical tissue absorbs half the nitrogen remaining to reach saturation. A five minute halftime, as shown, would be 98.4% saturated after 30 minutes, or six halftimes. For practical purposes, a theoretical tissue is considered saturated (100%) after six halftimes.

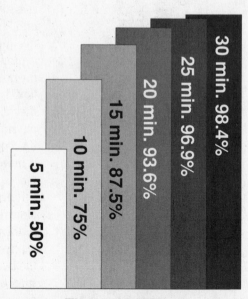

5 min. 50%
10 min. 75%
15 min. 87.5%
20 min. 93.6%
25 min. 96.9%
30 min. 98.4%

Tissue Half Times

The amount of nitrogen absorbed by a diver relates directly to the dive's depth and duration. The deeper a diver descends, the greater the ambient pressure and the relative pressure gradient between the nitrogen pressure in the lungs and the nitrogen pressure in the tissues become. With the higher gradient, the tissues absorb nitrogen more rapidly than at shallower depths. Also, the longer a diver remains under pressure, the more time the body has to absorb nitrogen.

The additional nitrogen dissolved into a diver's tissues has no significant physiological effects at recreational diving depths, as long as the diver remains underwater or more precisely, under pressure. As a diver ascends however, pressure decreases on the body. Because the diver's body has been absorbing nitrogen throughout the dive, the diver eventually ascends to a depth where tissue pressure exceeds the surrounding pressure. The tissues are then *supersaturated*, that is, they contain more dissolved nitrogen than they can hold at the ambient pressure. The tissue pressure exceeds the surrounding pressure so nitrogen begins to dissolve out (exsolve) of the tissues and the body begins to eliminate it, which is where potential decompression sickness problems arise.

Nitrogen Elimination

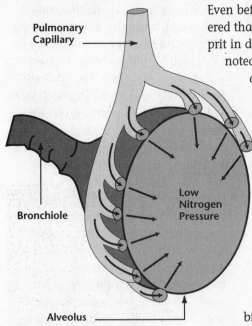

Pulmonary Capillary

Low Nitrogen Pressure

Bronchiole

Alveolus

Upon ascending, the tissue pressure of the blood exceeds the ambient pressure in alveolar air. Nitrogen diffuses from the blood into the alveolar air.

Even before early physiologists discovered that dissolved nitrogen was the culprit in decompression sickness, they noted that the condition developed *after* the victim left pressure, rather than while under pressure. Eventually, physiologists developed theories as to how the body responds to supersaturation.

Early physiologists quickly noted, through experimentation, that the body can tolerate some degree of supersaturation without complications, but if the pressure gradient between tissue pressure and ambient pressure exceeds a reasonable level, decompression sickness develops.

Original Theory — Originally, physiologists believed nitrogen elimination by the body was identical to nitrogen absorption so long as levels were kept within reasonable limits. As a diver reaches a shallower depth, they reasoned, the tissue pressure of the blood exceeds the ambient pressure in alveolar air. Nitrogen diffuses from the blood into the alveolar air, which in turn causes the blood tissue pressure to drop. Nitrogen from the other body tissues diffuses into the blood, which carries the nitrogen to the lungs to dissolve into alveolar air.

This original concept, which was based on experimentation by J.S. Haldane, stated that tissues would hold nitrogen in solution as long as the tissue nitrogen pressure was no more than 1.58 times the ambient pressure. This was expressed as a critical tissue pressure-to-ambient pressure ratio of 1.58:1, (originally expressed as a 2:1 ratio of ambient pressure-to-ambient pressure, but it's the same ratio). The theory stated that, within this critical ratio, bubbles would not form in the tissues, and the circulatory and respiratory systems would carry away nitrogen in a dissolved state until the body returned to equilibrium. If the critical ratio were exceeded, however, bubbles would form and cause decompression sickness.

Haldane published the first dive tables in 1907 based on this theory. This concept of how the body responds to excess nitrogen continued as the basis for decompression theory until the early 1970s, when technology revealed it to be partially inaccurate.

Current Theory — Although the original conceptions of how the body eliminates excess nitrogen have proven partially correct in that the body does eliminate much excess nitrogen as described, as time passed physiologists realized there were problems with the theory.

The first problem physiologists noted was that the critical ratio, as proved by decompression experiments, was far lower than physics dictates. For some reason, they observed that bubbles form in supersaturated tissue much easier than in supersaturated pure liquids, such as pure water. In fact, in the pure liquid a gas requires at least 200 times as much pressure gradient to form.

The introduction of the Doppler ultrasound bubble detector in the early 1970s by Dr. Merrill Spencer at the Institute of Applied Physiology and Medicine revolutionized decompression research. Using Doppler detectors, which use ultrasound to "see" bubbles moving through the heart and veins, physiologists could look for bubbles in test subjects after a dive, even though they didn't display decompression-sickness symptoms.

Almost immediately, hyperbaric research discovered small bubbles in the bloodstream, even though the divers exhibited no DCS signs. The discovery of "silent" (so named because they don't produce DCS) bubbles led to the current theories on how the body eliminates nitrogen and nitrogen in the *gas phase*, i.e.,

as bubbles of various shapes and sizes in the tissues. Physiologists have found some bubbles within the capillaries tend to be cylindrical and sausage-like, rather than spherical.

According to one current theory, bubbles form after virtually all dives. Microscopic gas pockets called *gas micronuclei* are common throughout the body in tissue walls and surfaces and explain why bubbles form more easily in tissues than in pure liquids. In supersaturated tissues, nitrogen diffuses into these micronuclei, enlarging them until they break free from the tissue surface as tiny bubbles. These bubbles are so small they cause no complications and are not detectable even by Doppler detectors. They travel through the venous system to the lungs, where they are trapped by the pulmonary capillaries. The gas in the micro-bubbles then diffuses into the alveoli.

If there are many microbubbles, they tend to combine, forming larger bubbles, eventually reaching the size of the harmless, but detectable, silent bubbles. Silent bubbles also leave the body by diffusing into the alveoli. Some bubbles grow within tissues. If the number of these silent bubbles is great, they begin to grow and form larger bubbles that cause decompression sickness.

This current theory shows, then, that the body eliminates nitrogen through diffusion as originally thought, but not exclusively and not without some subclinical (symptomless) bubble formation. The fact that microbubbles can form has affected developmental research on the decompression models used in dive tables and dive computers.

Microscopic gas pockets called gas micronuclei are common throughout the body. In supersaturated tissues, nitrogen diffuses into these micronuclei, enlarging them until they break free from the tissue surface as tiny bubbles. These bubbles travel through the venous system to the lungs, where they diffuse into the alveoli.

Liquid

Solid

A   B   C   D

Decompression Models

As mentioned earlier, J.S. Haldane used the original theory of nitrogen elimination to develop a decompression model, which became the basis for the first dive tables, published in 1907. In theory, the model (and hence the tables) prevented decompression sickness by calculating nitrogen levels in the diver's body and controlling the critical ratio.

Modern decompression models used in dive tables and dive computers also calculate nitrogen levels and use critical ratios, although research suggests the models prevent decompression sickness by controlling the tissue microbubble size and quantity, rather than by completely preventing them.

Origin and Growth of Gas Phase within the Body

It wasn't until the research of Paul Bert in the 1870s that physiologists realized that decompression sickness is caused by nitrogen bubbles in the body. Since his discovery, the origin and growth of *gas phase* within the body has been the focus of considerable research.

When speaking of bubble (gas phase) growth, one conceives of the expansion from something small into something larger. One may ask, "From what does this growth originate?" "How small are the smallest gas bubbles?" Even today, these physiologists still don't have all the answers, though evidence seems to indicate that they grow from very small "gas seeds" called *gas micronuclei.*

To experimentally form a gas bubble in a pure liquid requires more than 200 atmospheres of pressure change. This far exceeds the one atmosphere change that J.S. Haldane proposed in 1907 as required to instigate decompression sickness in human divers, and the 0.6 atmospheres widely accepted today. On theoretical grounds, the pressure change that should be necessary to spontaneously form a gas bubble in a pure liquid against the liquid's tensile strength would be *about 1000 atmospheres.* In other words, if a human diver were composed of pure liquid, this diver could descend more than *13 kilometres/6 miles* and ascend directly to the surface without decompression concerns, regardless of bottom time.

Because the maximum depth for direct ascent falls somewhere between 6 metres/20 feet and 10 metres/33 feet (considerably less than 13 kilometres/6 miles), something must assist bubble formation. Physiologists think that small gas pockets in the tissues act as nuclei from which the larger gas bubbles grow. These gas micronuclei explain the 1000-fold pressure discrepancy between observed gas phase in human divers, and what would be predicted in a pure liquid.

Small gas micronuclei are hypothesized to be stabilized in *hydrophobic* (nonwettable) crevices, or stabilized by proteins or other molecules bound to the gas-liquid boundary. Gas micronuclei may originate from the movement of surfaces over another, creating low-pressure areas. This is called *tribonucleation. Reynold's cavitation,* which is the result of moving fluids creating vortices, produces low-pressure areas that may cause gas micronuclei, and it's possible that they're also caused by negative pressures resulting from muscle activity.

The primary factor instigating decompression sickness appears to be the growth of a larger gas phase in the tissues from these gas micronuclei. From experimental evidence, it appears possible to reduce or eliminate these nuclei. Compression experiments performed on agar gels, shrimp and rats indicate that less gas-phase forms during decompression when the subject was first subjected to a rapid increase of pressure. It is hypothesized that this initial pressure increase crushes the gas micronuclei and returns them into solution. This leaves fewer to act as "seeds" for bubbles to grow from during a subsequent decompression.

How many gas micronuclei are present in the body at any one time and whether the number can increase with time is currently unknown, though it appears that vigorous exercise causes them to form. During the decompression phase of the dive, however, dissolved gas will diffuse into the nuclei and result in their growth into bubbles. Thus, during decompression there exists no specific "supersaturation limit" below which gas phase will never form and above which it always forms. Instead, gas phase in the body grows at a rate related to the degree of supersaturation — the diver's time, depth (pressure), number of micronuclei and to some extent, ascent rate. These of course, are controlled by a decompression model — either a table or computer.

Some gas phase growth, no matter how small, will always

take place during the decompression phase of a dive, unless there are no micronuclei. Its limitation by dive table or computer, to a point where the gas phase growth remains minimal, results in the diver being free of decompression sickness. That is, the diver has no overt signs and symptoms of decompression sickness, but has some degree of subclinical gas phase.

Ultrasound devices make it possible to detect this subclinical gas phase, the most common being the *Doppler ultrasonic bubble detector*. It was first developed for diving in the late 1960s and received extensive testing on animal and human subjects during the 1970s. It was in this period that the concept of "silent bubbles" became a working reality.

In numerous experiments, scientists demonstrated that decompressions free of signs and symptoms of decompression sickness, in both humans and animals, could actually produce a gas phase. This precluded the use of Doppler ultrasound detectors to detect decompression sickness, since silent bubbles indicate that there was little physical reality to a critical supersaturation limit. The early concept of a supersaturation limit proved more of a metaphysical entity; the degree of supersaturation governs the degree and rate at which a gas phase will grow, rather than whether it exists.

The bubbles detected by Doppler ultrasound equipment are in the venous system, although they initially form in the muscle capillaries and fat. As gas phase grows in the capillaries following decompression, it enlarges to a point where the tiny gas bubbles break off, enter the venous return and flow with the blood, where they become detectable by Doppler device placed (usually) over the heart.

The site of gas phase growth most responsible for "the bends" (limb pain decompression sickness) is probably the tendons and ligaments around the joints; this gas phase is most likely not located in the capillaries. The bubbles detectable by Doppler devices are related to the actual gas bubbles that are responsible for joint pain, but are not identical. With bubble detection, physiologists monitor "downstream" in the blood flow, and try to postulate what's occurring "upstream."

For Doppler devices to predict decompression sickness, gas bubbles in the venous system must originate in tissues that mirror, as closely as possible, the gas phase formation in the tendons and ligaments. Because the venous gas phase evolves from tissues not directly connected to limb decompression sickness (muscle and fat), the number of bubbles detected in the venous return do not correspond exactly with the magnitude of the pain producing gas phase in the tendons and ligaments. This lack of a one-to-one correspondence prevents using Doppler as "bends detectors" on an *individual* basis, although they are *quite* useful for evaluating decompression profiles when making many test dives with many individuals.

Physiologists can reasonably conclude that decompression profiles that produce a small gas phase (from muscle or fat tissue) would generally produce a small gas phase in tendons and ligaments. On a statistical basis, with many divers and many dives, this has been found to be true. Consequently, Doppler evaluation of decompression schedules has become commonplace. The efficiency of certain decompression schedules can be determined, in a large measure, by determining the gas bubbles quantity, although all dive subjects remain free of decompression sickness.

Curiously, the gas phase, once released into the venous system, is essentially benign. The gas bubbles move with the flow of the blood from tissues toward the heart and are filtered out by the lungs. In the lungs, the gas bubbles dissolve, and the gas diffuses into the alveoli and exhaled. Only in rare cases where a large number of gas bubbles occur in the venous return, such as missed decompressions, for example, can problems arise. Here the number of gas bubbles increases in the blood vessels of the lungs and some, rather than dissolving, pass through the pulmonary capillaries into the arterial side of the circulation where they move on to block blood flow in other organs. If those organs happen to be the spinal cord, brain or the heart, the consequences can be severe.

So, although theories have changed, the basic methodology used in the vast majority of dive tables and dive computers remains essentially the same as that used by Haldane. Some of the variables have changed, and different labels applied, but the Haldanean method remains the foundation for most modern decompression models, including virtually all those used in recreational dive computers. The primary reason is that the Haldeanean method requires comparatively simple mathematics, making it well suited for small, portable dive computers, and that the model is quite reliable within the realm of recreational diving, and even normal commercial and technical diving.

This isn't to say, however, that decompression experts have ignored the dynamics of bubble formation. Several "bubble dynamic" models, based on current knowledge of decompression physiology, attempt to model changes that may occur in a diver's body due to the formation of silent bubbles. Interestingly, these models differ little in their allowable dive time predictions for conservative recreational diving from what a Haldanean model predicts. However, for unrecommended practices (excessive ascent rate, following a shallow dive with a deep dive, etc.), bubble dynamic models become more conservative and predict slower nitrogen elimination due to bubble formation. Recently, some computer manufacturers and decompression software writers have begun including conservatism factors based on bubble dynamic models, but the models are still primarily Haldanean in form. NASA in the U.S. is developing decompression procedures for astronauts based on reduced micronuclei in zero gravity conditions.

While it's accepted that different tissues have different characteristics with respect to nitrogen absorption and elimination, it's important to distinguish between the concept of "tissues" in decompression physiology and in decompression modeling. As mentioned earlier, some tissues absorb more nitrogen than others, and therefore take longer to release nitrogen. To mathematically predict how various tissues throughout the body would absorb and release nitrogen, Haldane developed a model of theoretical "tissues," or theoretical "compartments" based on theoretical tissue halftimes. While Haldane believed there was some relationship between the halftimes he assigned and the body, he didn't intend for any particular theoretical tissue to correspond to any particular body tissue. Rather, Haldane was simply trying to build a mathematical model that replicated the fact that the body doesn't absorb and release nitrogen on a single time scale.

Today, the terms "tissue compartment," "theoretical tissue" and "theoretical tissue compartment" prevail, though some use (somewhat imprecisely) "tissue." Further, comparing models to decompression sickness incidents finds no consistent relationship between symptoms and theoretical tissues, raising doubts whether theoretical

tissues correspond to actual tissues at all. Therefore, a growing number of decompression experts use the term "compartment" with no reference to "tissue" at all. Thus, one could exceed the limits of a five minute "tissue" and in another instance a 480 minute "tissue," and experience, for example, wrist pain in both cases.

Haldane's original model had five compartments with halftimes ranging from 5-75 minutes. Contemporary models have calculated as many as 20 or 30 compartments with halftimes longer than 600 minutes, though the value of going to this length appears to have diminishing value, depending on the type of diving.

In formulating his tables, Haldane assigned the critical ratio of 1.58 nitrogen pressure: 1 ambient pressure to all his tissue compartments, but in the late 1930s, the U.S. Navy discovered this relationship to be inaccurate, ushering in the first of several major changes to the Haldanean method.

U.S. Navy research showed that different model compartments have different critical ratios; fast compartments tolerate much more supersaturation than supposed by Haldane, and slow compartments a bit less. Later, research in the 1950s demonstrated that critical ratio not only varies with each tissue compartment, but may vary within the compartment itself depending on depth. During this same period, the U.S. Navy developed the first repetitive dive procedures that credit the diver for nitrogen released during time at the surface (surface interval) between dives. Prior to this, all dives made in a single day were added together, with repetitive dive limits and decompression stops based on the total time.

In 1965, the Navy developed the concept of the *M value* as an easier way of calculating maximum allowable supersaturation pressures for each compartment. The M value expresses the tissue compartment's maximum allowable

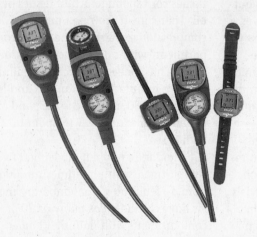

Dive computers can monitor theoretical tissues simultaneously and make recommendations for repetitive dive times based on the individual characteristics of each compartment. In general, this results in more generous repetitive dive times.

pressure in feet of sea water absolute (fswa). This streamlines the mathematical formulation of dive tables by defining the maximum amount of excess pressure in the compartment over ambient pressure and by eliminating the need to calculate variable ratios.

With the Navy's changes, one specific tissue, called the *controlling tissue* or more properly *controlling compartment*, sets the limits for a specific dive and dominates the schedules the dive computer or table recommends. During a single no decompression dive, the controlling compartment depends upon the depth; at deeper depths, the fast compartments rapidly absorb nitrogen, but at shallower depths the M value of a fast compartment may be higher than the depth. In this case, the fast compartment can never control the dive, and the task passes to slower ones.

During a surface interval, if the decompression model will be expressed as a table, for pragmatic use in the field a single compartment controls repetitive dive credit. The usual approach is to use the slowest compartment that could affect a repetitive dive because this is the most conservative approach. Repetitive

dive calculations assume that all compartments faster than the controlling compartment eliminate nitrogen at the same rate as the controlling compartment.

Dive computers can monitor theoretical tissues simultaneously and make recommendations for repetitive dive times based on the individual characteristics of each compartment. In general, this results in more generous repetitive dive times, though the drawback is that some models may permit dives outside what has been demonstrated to work reliably.

Once a decompression model has been calculated mathematically, it is verified experimentally through test dives in hyperbaric chambers and in open water. In some cases, tests precede model development, with model design following the test results. Prior to the Doppler bubble detector, tests were based on the absence of decompression sickness in the test subjects. Newer models have been tested using Doppler ultrasound, or based on Doppler tests, allowing physiologists to control free gas phase (bubble) formation below the levels that produce decompression sickness.

Following successful testing, or affirming that it conforms to successful test dives, the model may be expected to be reliable within the parameters for which it was designed and tested.

 The Recreational Divers Guide to Decompression Theory, Dive Tables and Dive Computers.

Nitrogen Problems

Although dive tables and computers help the diver deal with nitrogen absorption within a limited depth and time, there can be problems. If a diver fails to use a table or computer properly, or fails to use one at all, upon surfacing

nitrogen levels may be beyond the body's ability to safely eliminate it, resulting in decompression sickness. An unrelated concern is that nitrogen can temporarily affect the nervous system at high partial pressures.

Decompression Sickness

As mentioned earlier, most physiologists believe bubbles exist to some degree in the body after all dives (although a few others believe this is unprovable). If the bubbles are few and small, they have no effect, but if they exist in quantity, their volume can be large enough to cause decompression sickness.

Because bubbles can develop in practically any part of the body, decompression sickness can be characterized by dozens of seemingly unrelated symptoms with varying severity. Physiologists understand a few of the factors theoretically predisposing divers to decompression sickness and recognize decompression sickness symptoms, but the exact injury mechanism can often be a mystery. Although bubble formation is responsible, in some forms of decompression sickness, such as limb and joint DCS, physiologists aren't even sure why the diver feels pain. In other manifestations, physiologists don't understand precisely how bubbles affect the body.

What is Decompression Illness?

Although the term "decompression illness" is sometimes used interchangeably with "decompression sickness," there is a difference in the terms.

"Decompression sickness" refers to the conditions caused by inert nitrogen gas coming out of solution within the body. Another set of serious pressure related injuries are lung overexpansion injuries, covered later in this section. These injuries also involve bubbles within the body, but the mechanism by which bubbles get into the body differs.

"Decompression illness" refers to both decompression sickness and lung overexpansion injuries. The reason for a combined term is that in a dive emergency, the first aid for either DCS or lung overexpansion injury is the same. It's not necessary to distinguish between them when helping an injured diver, so emergency care follows protocols for a "single" condition called "decompression illness."

Factors Predisposing Divers to Decompression Sickness

When researchers test dive tables or computers based on a decompression model, the tests obviously can't include everyone who will ultimately use the table or computer. This means that individual variations in physiology can, in rare instances, affect whether a diver suffers decompression sickness. Physiologists still don't understand all factors that may predispose an individual to decompression sickness, and therefore these cannot be taken into account. If a diver's physiology or actions create predisposing factors, a dive table or computer may less accurately model nitrogen absorption and elimination. This can mean the diver has a higher decompression sickness risk, especially if the diver doesn't use the device conservatively. The following factors are generally accepted as predisposing divers to decompression sickness. Little scientific evidence supports or refutes most of these; the concerns are theoretical at present, in that they've not been proved. However, the prudent diver accounts for them when planning dives in any case.

Fat tissue: Fat is a slow tissue, holding a high amount of dissolved nitrogen. A lot of body fat increases the nitrogen retained in the body after a dive. Divers who have a high body fat to lean ratio are, in theory, likely to have more nitrogen after a dive and therefore have slightly greater risk of DCS. However, in recreational diving, the role of body fat has not been closely studied or clarified.

Age: The circulatory and respiratory systems work somewhat less efficiently in an older person, which interferes with gas exchange. With higher body fat and less efficient circulation, older divers may retain more nitrogen following dives than they did when they were younger. Remaining physically fit by regulating fat intake and exercising regularly helps offset this concern to some degree, but age inevitably produces changes in circulation and respiration.

Dehydration: Decompression models are calculated assuming that normal circulation transports nitrogen from the tissues for elimination. Dehydration reduces the quantity of blood available for gas exchange, slowing nitrogen removal from the body. Consumption of diuretics (like caffeine), profuse perspiration, and even the dry scuba air all tend to dehydrate the diver. During metabolism of alcohol, a diver's body uses a great deal of water, thus a diver with a hangover is likely to be partially dehydrated. Dehydration seems frequently associated with DCS cases.

Injuries and illness: Any condition that affects normal circulation can potentially affect nitrogen elimination by the body. Healed injuries may produce local circulation difficulties, and illness can produce a general reduction in circulatory efficiency.

Alcohol: Alcohol consumed before or after a dive alters physiology in favor of decompression sickness. Immediately before a dive, even in relatively small quantities, alcohol tends to accelerate circulation and can cause tissues to carry higher amounts of nitrogen to the tissues during the dive. Following a dive,

Factors that can predispose a diver to decompression sickness include excessive fat tissue, injuries, alcohol and exposure to altitude.

alcohol dilates capillaries, possibly increasing the rate of nitrogen release and contributing to bubble formation. It is also a diuretic.

Carbon dioxide: Elevated carbon dioxide from skip-breathing or improper breathing may interfere with gas transport by the circulatory system by dilating capillaries and increasing nitrogen uptake under pressure.

Cold water: Diving in cold water, or diving with inadequate exposure protection in moderate to warm water, changes normal circulation as the body takes heat-conserving measures. At the start of a dive, circulation carries nitrogen to all parts of the body, but as heat conservation reduces circulation to the extremities, there is less blood to carry away dissolved nitrogen during ascent. Some areas of a diver's body may be carrying more nitrogen than usual upon surfacing due to poor elimination.

Heavy exercise: Exercise while diving accelerates circulation, carrying nitrogen to body tissues more rapidly than normal. After resting, a diver's circulation returns to normal, and so there is no corresponding circulation to accelerate nitrogen elimination.

Altitude and flying after diving: Most decompression models calculate theoretical tissue pressures based on ascending from the dive to atmospheric pressure at sea level. Complications may develop if a diver flies or ascends above sea level in some manner before the body desaturates. Reduced atmospheric pressure at altitude increases the pressure gradient between tissue and ambient pressures, and can possibly cause large-bubble formation in the body. The same complications occur if diving above sea level without accounting for reduced atmospheric pressure on special dive tables or with a computer designed for altitude diving. Once decompression sickness occurs due to altitude exposure, returning to sea level does not usually alleviate it.

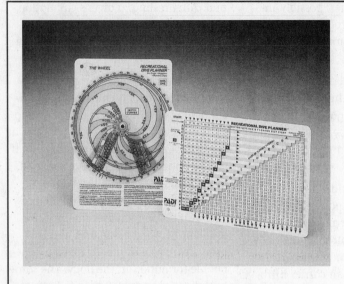

The Recreational Dive Planner

The introduction of the Recreational Dive Planner (RDP) marked a significant departure in no decompression dive planning. Its debut followed three-years development, beginning with research into dive schedules specifically for recreational divers. This was the first such effort specifically for recreational no stop diving.

The ideal in developing dive tables, such as the Recreational Dive Planner, is to create standard tables that give generous dive times and avoid DCS for all divers under all conditions. Unfortunately, this isn't possible because there are too many unknown factors and physiological variations from one individual to the next. Other variables include degree of activity (both during a dive and after surfacing), water temperature, thermal protection, physical condition, anxiety states and equipment. All of these cause problems in table design. People vary considerably in their resistance to pressure stress, not only individually, but within an individual from moment to moment. These factors preclude any practical possibility of custom dive tables formulated for any specific individual, and any practical possibility of general dive tables with zero risk of decompression sickness. Although absolute safety is the goal, it cannot be guaranteed even by unreasonably restrictive bottom times. Because of this, and with maximum safe dive time the objective, the ideal re*alistic* goal is to generate tables that are safe for virtually any diver under almost any conditions. Nevertheless, both divers and table designers must recognize that some possibility of decompression sickness exists on any dive, and that there can never be a perfect dive table.

The RDP applies three principle changes that overcome the majority of difficulties recreational divers had with the (U.S.) Navy tables, which for many years were essentially the only tables recreational divers had access to.

First, it changed the surface interval credit compartment halftime to one specifically suited to recreational no decompression diving. Previously, the halftime used by the Navy suited military or commercial decompression diving. Second,

the number of repetitive groups increased to create better precision and reduce unnecessary time penalties, and third, more conservatism was incorporated in the maximum nitrogen levels permitted.

More Suitable Halftime — Recreational diving defines itself as staying within no decompression limits and staying above a maximum depth of 40 metres/130 feet when using air, or within an oxygen partial pressure of 1.4 ata when using enriched air. Within these limitations, theoretical tissues with relatively long halftimes (slow theoretical tissues) do not approach their saturation limits. It is therefore practical to use a halftime for surface interval credit other than the one the Navy (necessarily) based surface interval credit on.

The Navy's choice of a 120-minute halftime was entirely appropriate for military (decompression) diving, because they had to account for the higher residual nitrogen a diver can have in the tissues following a dive requiring decompression stops. However, for use exclusively with no decompression dives (i.e., recreational use), this long halftime proved unnecessarily restrictive.

Extensive computer analysis examined what halftime would be appropriate for surface interval credit in no stop diving. A 40-minute halftime proved appropriate for almost all reasonable no decompression repetitive profiles. A small percentage of profiles, mainly those that involve repeated, long, shallow dives (less than 15 metres/50 feet), require a halftime longer than 40 minutes, however. With diver safety a primary concern, the RDP model employed a more conservative 60-minute halftime, which covers the vast majority of all common recreational no decompression profiles, and has only slightly shorter bottom times compared to those imposed by a 40-minute compartment halftime. This left a few, very long no stop dives that could bring theoretical tissue compartments with halftimes longer than 60 minutes into play. The RDP handles these dives with two rules (the WX & YZ rules), since an even slower surface interval halftime would have unnecessarily restricted all dives simply to accommodate dive profiles that seldom occur in actual diving circumstances.

More Pressure Groups — Within the scope of no decompression diving, the Navy tables employed 14 pressure groups to represent residual nitrogen after a dive. The RDP increased this number to 26 to eliminate unnecessary rounding when calculating credit for nitrogen outgassing during a surface interval.

More Conservatism — Although the use of the 60 minute halftime for surface interval credit increases repetitive dive time compared to the Navy tables in most instances, the RDP also reduced the maximum allow nitrogen levels permitted in each theoretical compartment. This reduces the no decompression limit on the first dive, compared to the Navy tables limit, which followed physiologist recommendations that recreational divers use more conservative limits than those intended for commercial or military divers. Today, these reduced limits have become virtually standard in the dive community.

Depending on the dive profile, then, the RDP shortens the first dive, but restricts repetitive dives less because the 60 minute elimination halftime gives surface interval credit about twice as rapidly as the Navy table 120 minute halftime. The end result is that the diver more than makes up for a somewhat shorter first dive on subsequent dives, yet maintains an overall more conservative level of body nitrogen if diving at table limits compared to diving at table limits on the Navy tables. Since the RDP's introduction, equipment manufacturers have introduced dozens of dive computers. Almost all dive computers employ a similar approach to conservative maximum nitrogen levels combined with more appropriate repetitive dive credit.

Comparing the Navy tables to the RDP shows the benefit to recreational divers of using a 60-minute elimination halftime and more repetitive groups. Using the Navy tables, typical recreational dives end in a repetitive group from E through H. For these dives, it takes approximately 45 minutes surface interval to change pressure groups and receive credit for nitrogen outgassing on the next dive, approximately one and one half hours to change two pressure groups, and more than two hours to change three pressure groups. It is typical on many recreational dive trips for less than two hours to elapse between dives and, on single-day charters, the surface interval is often less than 45 minutes.

In contrast, the Recreational Dive Planner permits credit for surface interval much more quickly. On the RDP, the diver

	Navy Bottom Time Limit	Recreational Dive Planner Bottom End Time Limit	Pressure Group
Dive 1			
24 meters/80 feet	40 min	30 min	Navy: G
Actual Bottom Time: 30			Dive Planner: R
Surface Interval: 30 minutes: New Pressure Groups:			Navy: G
			Dive Planner: K
Dive 2			
18 meters/60 feet	16 min	26 min	Navy: J
Actual Bottom Time: 15			Dive Planner: R
Surface Interval: 30 minutes: New Pressure Groups:			Navy: J
			Dive Planner: K
Dive 3			
18 meters/60 feet	Not allowed	26 min	

Chart 1

typically changes pressure groups in four or five minutes. After a typical dive and a 30-minute surface interval, the diver changes five to eight pressure groups. This becomes especially significant when making more than two dives. Dives prohibited by the Navy tables become not only possible using the Recreational Dive Planner, but they have reasonable bottom times.

Note that on the second dive, the Recreational Dive Planner allows a significantly longer bottom time than the Navy tables, and on the third dive, the Navy tables do not permit a

dive at all. It's worth noting that modern dive computers offer similar repetitive dive characteristics to the RDP for no decompression dives.

Although today's divers employ multilevel diving routinely, during the RDP's development multilevel diving was in its infancy, and while theoretically valid, had little test or field data to support it. Multilevel diving (allowing a longer dive time by giving credit for slower nitrogen uptake when a diver moves to a shallower depth) more closely resembles the majority of actual recreational dive profiles, so it only made sense to incorporate multilevel diving in the RDP. To make multilevel dive planning practical, The Wheel version of the Recreational Dive Planner was designed for multilevel dive planning (not the table version).

Following its mathematical design, the Recreational Dive Planner underwent manned test dives evaluated using Doppler bubble detection. These dives included test dives in a hyperbaric chamber and open water, with emphasis on repetitive no decompression dives not permitted by the Navy tables but permitted by the RDP. The manned dives also included multilevel dives, making the RDP the first significant body of manned test dive data for recreational repetitive no decompression single depth and multilevel dives. Subsequent testing extended these data to validate the RDP's use for four dives daily for six consecutive days with the same test subjects.

Since its introduction in 1988, the Recreational Dive Planner has become by far the world's most popular dive table. Millions of dives have been planned and made with the RDP, with a demonstrably low decompression illness rate. In addition, many dive computers available draw upon the test data and basic concepts behind the RDP. In 1996, special Recreational Dive Planners for enriched air (EANx32 and EANx36) were introduced.

In all, the Recreational Dive Planner, both The Wheel and Table versions, made these improvements over the Navy tables for recreational divers:

1. The RDP was designed for recreational diving, and uses conservative limits to minimize bubble formation within the body, even at levels that do not cause decompression sickness.

2. The RDP was tested using Doppler technology not available when the Navy tables were developed.

3. The RDP contains more surface interval periods for higher precision when calculating surface intervals.

4. The RDP bases surface interval elimination on a halftime that creates a realistic credit for surface intervals made between no decompression dives.

In addition, The Wheel offers these additional advantages:

5. The Wheel makes it possible to calculate multilevel dives that increase dive time by giving credit for slower nitrogen uptake in shallower depths.

6. The Wheel allows the diver to more closely calculate time and depth profile for greater accuracy, and it incorporates residual nitrogen time into its design, eliminating much confusion in calculating repetitive dives. This feature makes The Wheel much easier and faster to use than conventional tables.

Types of Decompression Sickness

The diversity of DCS symptoms makes diagnosis complex for physicians unacquainted with it. Yet despite the different symptoms, manifestations of decompression sickness tend to share some characteristics.

Decompression sickness tends to be delayed after the dive, and may take as long as 36 hours to manifest. About half of all decompression-sickness cases appear within an hour after the dive and about half take longer. Also, decompression sickness tends to get worse with time until treated.

Physiologists often group decompression sickness into Type I — skin and pain-only symptoms — or Type II — with more significant, sometimes life-threatening symptoms. Generally, cutaneous (skin) and joint pain decompression sickness are regarded as Type I, with all others regarded as Type II. Both may be possible simultaneously, depending on where bubbles form or accumulate in the body.

Cutaneous decompression sickness: Bubbles coming out of solution in skin capillaries can cause cutaneous decompression sickness, which may be characterized by a red rash in patches, usually on the shoulders and upper chest. Although cutaneous decompression sickness is not considered serious by itself, its presence indicates decompression problems and the possibility of more serious symptoms.

Joint and limb pain decompression sickness: Joint or limb pain occurs in approximately 75 percent of DCS cases. As mentioned, the cause of joint pain is unclear, though physiologists believe bubbles growing around or within the tendons, ligaments and related muscles are the immediate cause, even though they don't completely understand the mechanism. Symptoms may be found in more than one place on the same limb, such as the shoulder and elbow; bisymmetrical symptoms are unusual. Like cutaneous decompression sickness, limb pain decompression sickness is considered serious primarily because it may indicate significant decompression problems.

Neurological decompression sickness: Effects on the nervous system produce some of the most serious cases of decompression sickness. Because the nervous system reaches throughout the body, neurological decompression sickness can affect movement or touch, and life-support functions like breathing and heartbeat.

Besides bubbles growing within nervous tissue, physiologists believe that in some neurological cases, bubbles in the venous system may block blood outflow, "backing up" the system and reducing the arterial flow to the affected area.

Pain, frequently in the limbs and joints, is the most common DCI symptom. In approximately 40 percent of cases it is the first symptom reported and the second symptom in approximately 20 percent. Numbness, dizziness, weakness and fatigue are among the next most common symptoms.

Spinal-cord related DCS may be related to this type of blood flow restriction. Neurological DCS involves the spinal cord most frequently, commonly causing numbness and paralysis in the lower extremities that creep upward. In a relatively short time, victims may become paralyzed from the neck down.

Bubbles can also travel to the brain (*cerebral decompression sickness*), causing stroke as they block blood flow. These symptoms may be very similar to those caused by arterial gas embolism (discussed under Physiological Responses of Pressure Change on Body Air Spaces) and include blurred vision, headache, confusion, unconsciousness and death. Symptoms depend upon where bubbles end up in the brain; the similarity between cerebral DCS and arterial gas embolism makes it probable that bubbles pass through the lungs and enter the carotid arteries supplying the brain.

Pulmonary decompression sickness: Decompression sickness manifesting itself in lung capillaries signals the possible onset of life-threatening symptoms of decompression sickness. Fortunately, it is rare. Silent bubbles and microbubbles reaching the pulmonary capillaries normally diffuse into the alveoli, or in rare cases, if present in large quantities, may travel into the arterial system and cause neurological decompression sickness. If bubbles accumulate faster than they diffuse or travel through the pulmonary capillaries, they block and back up blood flow to the lungs. With less blood moving through the lungs, the left side of the heart receives less blood, causing the heart rate to rise and blood pressure to drop. Without treatment, the circulatory system may fail completely.

Assuming the circulatory system continues to function, two possibilities exist. Either blood begins traveling around the blockage through unobstructed pulmonary capillaries and thus maintains circulation until the bubbles diffuse into the alveoli, or the bubbles continue to accumulate faster than they diffuse, interfering with gas exchange in the lungs. This simultaneously reduces oxygen to the tissues and nitrogen elimination.

Pulmonary decompression sickness creates breathing pain, commonly associated with a short, irritated cough. The victim often feels air-starved, which has given pulmonary decompression sickness the nickname "the chokes." Symptoms tend to progress rapidly and may lead to shock.

Other DCS forms: Other forms of decompression sickness occur less commonly than those listed, though they're possible. If bubbles reach the arterial system, blood flow obstruction can produce symptoms that range from dizziness to heart attack, depending on where the bubbles lodge. Decompression sickness has also manifested itself in the equilibrium organs of the inner ear and the gastrointestinal system. The most common DCS symptom is excessive *fatigue*, though physiologists aren't sure what mechanism causes this.

What About the "Hole in the Heart?"

In general terms, minimal bubble formation on the venous side of the circulatory system following decompression appears normal and harmless; bubbles flow with the blood to the lungs, where the pulmonary capillaries trap them, allowing them to diffuse into the alveoli. Problems occur, on the other hand, when bubbles enter the arterial side of the circulatory system because they will flow with the blood until they reach a tissue and block the capillaries, depriving the tissue of oxygenated blood.

One normally expects bubbles in the arterial system only in the case of severe decompression sickness (the bubble quantity in the venous system exceeds what the pulmonary capillaries can trap, and push through to the arterial side), or in the case of AGE (because ruptured alveoli let air escape directly into the arterial system.)

However, some physiologists have become concerned for a minority of divers who may have an *atrial septum defect* (ASD), also called a *patent foramen ovale*, or commonly, a "right-to-left shunt," "heart shunt" or "hole in the heart." An ASD is a remainder from fetal development; a fetus doesn't breathe, so this opening allows blood to bypass the lungs until the baby is born. After birth, the ASD normally closes and grows shut within a year, but in some people, it doesn't close completely. About one quarter of people have an ASD; for the vast majority of these, the ASD normally poses no consequence because a tissue flap grows over the ASD and normal heart pressures keep it in place, effectively separating both sides of the heart. Under some unusual circumstances, the flap will allow blood to transfer from the venous side to the arterial side, and in a very small percentage of people, the ASD is open and a small amount of venous-to-arterial transfer happens frequently. This is called a "resting ASD," because it can happen at rest.

The concern is that presence of an ASD can, in theory, allow normally harmless bubbles passing through the venous side of the heart on the way to the lungs, to bypass the lungs and enter the arterial side through this opening. This would cause the more severe types of DCS.

However, because ASDs normally remain closed, it's also questionable how significant a concern this really is. Divers with ASDs do not appear to be over represented in the decompression accident data (though the data are limited and checking for ASD isn't a standard procedure when treating a diver with DCI).

Studies at the National Aeronautical and Space Administration (NASA) Johnson Space Center (astronauts decompress before making space walks and have similar concerns as divers) in Houston, Texas, have found that in individuals with ASDs, it's very difficult to get bubbles to transfer through an ASD, even when experimenters tried to make it happen

Given the field data, limited experimental data and diving's excellent track record, it would appear the risk of DCS for someone with an ASD is not *significantly* greater than for a diver without one, when adhering to normal, conservative dive practices. It's not even conclusive that a resting ASD is a significant concern, though an individual with a known resting ASD would be best advised to consult a physician knowledgeable in diving before diving, and to dive very conservatively.

Physiological Rationale for First Aid and Treatment of Decompression Sickness

 PADI Rescue Diver Manual; PADI Rescue Diver Video **MFA**

Decompression sickness typically requires recompression treatment, though cutaneous decompression sickness may not, if no other symptoms are present. Rapid recompression treatment has proved highly effective in reducing or preventing permanent injury, while treatment delays have proved highly likely to leave permanent residual injury.

Recompression forces bubbles in the patient's body to a smaller size or back into solution, alleviating symptoms by effectively removing the immediate cause. This restores blood flow to the affected tissues and simultaneously raises available oxygen; treatment then begins a slow decompression, usually accompanied by oxygen therapy, drug therapy and intravenous fluids, while giving accumulated nitrogen plenty of time to safely leave the tissues.

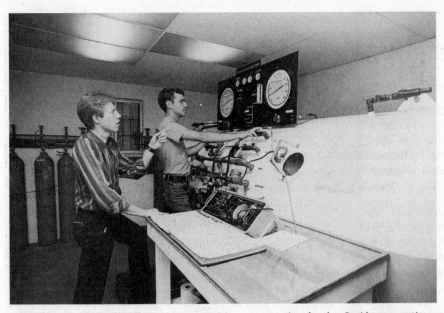

Decompression sickness typically requires treatment in a recompression chamber. Rapid recompression treatment has proved highly effective in reducing or preventing permanent injury, while treatment delays have proved highly likely to leave permanent residual injury.

the blood nitrogen pressure and alveolar gas. This accelerates diffusion of nitrogen from the body to slow and reverse bubble growth, and help in bubble elimination. Second, since DCS injury usually results from localized hypoxia due to obstructed blood flow, breathing oxygen raises blood oxygen levels and maximizes the effectiveness of the blood that does reach the affected tissues.

A breathing patient should lie level on the left side, head supported. Lying on the side helps keep the airway clear should the patient vomit; some patients have abruptly worsened from sitting up, so the patient should be advised not to sit up during first aid or transport until advised otherwise by a physician. A nonbreathing patient should be placed level on the back for rescue breathing and/or CPR.

The priorities of care are to monitor and restore airway, breathing and circulation, administer oxygen and rapidly transfer the diver to a medical facility. The once standard modified Trendelenburg position, which inclined the patient with the feet above the head, is no longer recommended in decompression illness first aid.

The recommended primary first aid for decompression sickness (actually, for decompression illness — in an emergency, there's no benefit in trying to determine whether DCS or lung overexpansion caused the incident) is to *administer oxygen.* Oxygen helps in two ways. First, breathing oxygen lowers alveolar nitrogen partial pressure, increasing the pressure gradient between

The recommended primary first aid for decompression illness is to administer oxygen. A breathing patient should lie level on the left side, head supported. A nonbreathing patient should be placed level on the back for rescue breathing and/or CPR. The priorities of care are to monitor and restore airway, breathing and circulation, administer oxygen and rapidly transfer the diver to a medical facility.

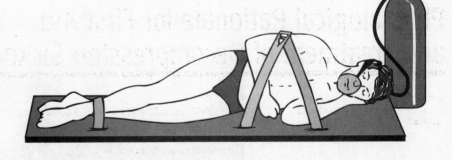

Recommendations for avoiding decompression sickness:

1. *Divers should be familiar with the proper use of dive tables through education by a professional diving instructor. Divers using a computer should follow all manufacturer recommendations. Conservatism is always wise.*

2. *Factors thought to predispose divers to decompression sickness should be avoided. If they are conditions that cannot be avoided, such as age, a diver should use dive tables and computers extra conservatively.*

3. *Divers should be familiar with first aid for decompression illness and the proper procedures for obtaining medical treatment. The best way to be prepared is to complete PADI Rescue Diver and MFA courses taught by a professional instructor.*

Nitrogen Narcosis

When breathing air, nitrogen narcosis develops with an increase in nitrogen partial pressure, typically at approximately 30 metres/100 feet. The exact mechanism surrounding narcosis is not fully understood, but almost any gas can cause anesthesia under high partial pressures.

Deep diving can bring a diver in contact with another difficulty that relates to nitrogen — nitrogen narcosis, a euphoric, anesthetic effect nicknamed "Rapture of the Deep." Although divers experience this most commonly with nitrogen, other gases can create the effect under the broader headings of "inert gas narcosis" or just "narcosis" (since it appears oxygen, which isn't inert, has narcotic properties).

When breathing air, nitrogen narcosis develops with an increase in nitrogen partial pressure, typically at approximately 30 metres/100 feet. The exact mechanism surrounding narcosis is not fully understood, but almost any gas can cause anesthesia under high partial pressures. Theory suggests that nitrogen becomes dissolved in the lipids in neurons (nerve cells), which interferes with signal transmission from neuron to neuron. Older theories suggested that carbon dioxide might have precipitated narcosis, but these ideas have essentially been disproved.

Narcosis may cause a diver to feel drowsy, sleepy and may affect memory of the dive. The diver may feel falsely secure, exercise poor judgment and become uncoordinated. Some divers have reported hallucinations and giddiness.

The effects of narcosis recede quickly upon reaching shallower depths, with no after effects. It's not a dangerous or harmful condition in itself, but is dangerous because it impairs judgment and coordination.

Although enriched air has less nitrogen than air, it should be noted that it appears to have the same narcotic qualities as air. This is because oxygen has about the same theoretical narcotic potential. This hasn't been tested extensively; some divers report reduced narcosis when using enriched air, but animal experiments support the notion that oxygen is narcotic at high pressures.

For more detail on nitrogen narcosis, see the accompanying sidebar: Nitrogen Narcosis.

Although enriched air has less nitrogen than air, it should be noted that it appears to have the same narcotic qualities. This is because oxygen has about the same theoretical narcotic potential. These divers use a computer designed specifically for enriched air diving to monitor depth and time.

Nitrogen Narcosis

It is *nitrogen narcosis*, not decompression sickness, that limits the depth of air diving (in recreational diving, the extremely short no decompression limits below 40 metres/130 feet are a factor, too). The commercial diving industry and the Navy observe a 52 to 54-metre/170- to 180-foot limit for routine surface-supported air diving. Commercial mixed-gas divers descend to depth using air for economy, then shift to heliox; technical divers may use trimix (helium, nitrogen and oxygen). These divers use helium not to prevent decompression sickness, but to prevent the mental dulling and drunkenness — narcosis — that occurs with nitrogen under pressure. (In reality, helium has significant problems of its own — it's expensive; it shortens decompression a little on some dives, but lengthens it on others; and it causes the diver to lose heat so the diver must be heated or surrounded by a different gas if diving in a dry suit. Helium would not be used if nitrogen narcosis were not a problem.)

Physicists describe nitrogen as a physiologically inert gas. This simply means that it takes no part in oxidative metabolism. The body doesn't burn nitrogen as fuel, nor exchange it for or combine it with oxygen. None of the nitrogen breathed is used to build protein. In short, all nitrogen that gets breathed in is eventually breathed out.

Inert, however, does not mean harmless. When nitrogen saturates tissue and comes out of solution too quickly, it forms bubbles and causes decompression sickness. Dissolved in brain tissue, nitrogen acts as an anesthetic gas. Nitrogen narcosis may best be understood by comparison with nitrous oxide. Nitrous oxide (sometimes called "laughing gas") is a commonly used surgical anesthetic, particularly in dentistry. In high concentrations at sea level it causes euphoria, drunkenness and, in a very short time, unconsciousness. These effects are pressure-related. If the pressure is doubled, the time to anesthesia is significantly shorter.

The same concept is true of nitrogen gas. The 0.79 (ata) nitrogen partial pressure in surface air causes no discernible narcosis. Doubling the pressure has little effect, but at three atmospheres (20 metres/66 feet), mental processing slows measurably. Experimental animals, including humans, have been shown to learn more slowly and make more errors in simple tasks when breathing air at three atmospheres. Most human subjects don't notice the impairment at three atmospheres, but most recognize some mental dulling at four atmospheres (30 metres/99 feet), and virtually everyone is affected at 45 metres/150 feet. Deeper than that, divers become unreliable in judgment and performance. It is this effect of nitrogen that determines the depth in which professional divers shift to heliox and limits the operational use of air.

The narcotic potency of a gas is directly proportional to its solubility in lipids, which are primary structural materials in cells. Inert-gas narcosis follows the Meyer-Overton hypothesis, which in contemporary form states, *All gaseous or volatile substances induce narcosis if they penetrate the cell lipid in a definite molar concentration, which is characteristic for each type of ani-*

mal, and is approximately the same for all volatile narcotics.

The lipid solubility of nitrogen is much more than that of helium, so its narcotic potency is accordingly greater. The current hypothesis further states that narcosis occurs at the junction of nerve cells, called *synapses*, where the nitrogen interferes with electrical transfer from neuron (nerve cell) to neuron. This most commonly affects structures in the brain responsible for alertness and coordination.

Anesthesia, it is postulated, occurs when the absorption of the nitrogen molecules into the synaptic membrane lipids causes the membrane to expand. When the membrane expands beyond a critical volume, signal transmission through it fails, resulting in narcosis. This means that the information transferred from one nerve cell to the next processes more slowly.

Nitrogen narcosis effects are frequently compared to alcohol effects. "Martini's Law" is a tongue-in-cheek reference that says that 30 metres/100 feet has the potency of one martini, with each 15 metres/50 feet thereafter equal to an added martini. Most deep air divers will attest to this.

Trainees in commercial diving programs commonly experience bounce dives to 50 metres/165 feet in a hyperbaric chamber as an introduction to pressure. The dive often sounds like the first round at a cocktail party. At 50 metres/165 feet, the trainees begin to talk, giggle and their conversation is light-hearted and frivolous. They begin to tell jokes, and, just as at a cocktail party, the simplest jokes are funnier than they should be. The initiate will recall tingling lips, like the first time the diver drank a martini. As the chamber is depressurized, the effect dissipates rapidly, and by the time it has reached 18 metres/60 feet, intoxication has largely disappeared.

In the water, narcosis behaves somewhat differently. In the absence of socialization, the diver at 50 metres/165 feet is more likely to notice slowness of thinking, slowness of action, shortened attention span and impaired vigilance. The diver may forget well-learned procedures and be indifferent to personal safety. Colorful stories (some of them documented), tell of divers offering regulators to fish, or trying to cut through their own air hoses, or other irrational, intoxicated behavior.

The time course of nitrogen narcosis differs distinctly from alcohol's. Narcosis occurs immediately upon reaching the narcotic depth and subsides promptly as partial pressure decreases. The effect is entirely reversible. Alcohol, on the other, has a slight delay between drinking and intoxication, and intoxication takes hours to end because the body must metabolize and burn it like any other fuel.

Individuals vary in their susceptibility to narcosis, just as they vary in their susceptibility to any form of drug intoxication. At a given depth, some divers will be more impaired than others. However, the variation is not great, and at narcotic depths all subjects will show test decrements in arithmetic, coordination, short-term memory and physiologic tests. Tests don't show consistency in individual response to narcosis. In other words, it's not clear that a group of divers can be selected for a given job on the basis of nitrogen narcosis tolerance.

Adaptation to narcosis occurs both with repeated exposures and with prolonged exposures. A diver who makes repeated deep air dives on succeeding days will become progressively less impaired by narcosis. A great deal of this is simply learning to cope with narcosis, but there appears to be some degree of true acclimation. A diver who has made successive deep air dives and who demonstrates progressively higher test scores (lower narcosis) on succeeding days loses that advantage if diving ceases for a matter of weeks. This means that some physiological acclimation has taken place, and the acclimation decays over time. The "learning to cope" mechanism may be expected to persist longer.

Divers working in prolonged saturation at moderate depths have been shown to adapt to narcosis in a matter of days. Test scores increase from the first day, and by the third or fourth day, approach or equal surface scores.

By and large, divers learn to live with narcosis. Those in commercial diving who make deep air dives adapt by careful planning, practice and by simplifying their tasks. Dive supervisors and tenders provide support, aware that the diver has dulled faculties. There are few reports of accidents directly attributed to nitrogen narcosis. Recreational divers who observe safe-diving practices will not exceed 40 metres/130 feet, thereby only skirting the edges of narcosis. Technical and commercial divers handle higher narcotic levels through more extensive training, support and experience, and switch from air to helium mixes when the depth exceeds approximately 55 metres/180 feet.

Drug interactions with nitrogen, however, apply to recreational divers even much shallower than 40 metres/130 feet. It is generally recognized that the combination of one sedative drug with another greatly increases effects. The danger of combining alcohol and Valium is widely known. Exactly the same considerations apply to combining nitrogen under pressure with other sedatives, particularly with alcohol and tranquilizers. Barbiturates and other sleeping pills are equally dangerous. Drugs that are used to counter motion sickness, hay fever and traveler's diarrhea also increase nitrogen narcosis. Common examples include Marezine, Contac and Lomotil. All of these drugs have an anticholingeric effect, meaning they block transmission of nerve signals.

At sea level, these drugs may have some sedative effect. At depth a synergy may exist, and they can greatly increase the narcotic effect of nitrogen. Alcohol is the worst of all in this regard. Any drug that makes the mouth dry, no matter how innocent its purpose, may increase narcosis at depth. Drugs used for seasickness should be tried before diving, and then with shallow dives to prevent surprise narcosis. Some of these have been documented to cause extreme narcosis at depths as shallow as 18 metres/60 feet.

Recommendations concerning nitrogen narcosis:

1. Divers should gain experience with depths involving narcosis under supervision, preferably in a deep-diving specialty class.

2. The 40 metre/130 foot depth limit for recreational diving has been determined with narcosis in mind. Recreational divers should observe this limit.

3. Some drugs amplify the effects of narcosis; divers taking such drugs while diving (with their physician's approval) should be cautious to avoid narcosis and limit depth.

4. Alcohol amplifies the effects of narcosis, and should be avoided before diving.

Physiological Responses to Thermal Changes

The above-water environment exposes human physiology to a wide temperature range, and accordingly, nature equips the human body with temperature-maintenance mechanisms. The approximately 37°C/98.6°F normal core body temperature is critical to normal chemical processes in human physiology, so that deviation from the normal core temperature more than a few degrees for more than a short period may be life-threatening.

Unlike most other aspects of dive physiology, a diver may be exposed to thermal considerations even before making the first dive. Once in the water, the diver's physiology responds to thermal conditions within a specific range and period; exposure suits aid the diver's body when exposed to cold, but make core temperature maintenance more difficult when exposed to heat.

Responses to Heat

Divers need to be most concerned with excessive heat and physiology more before or after a dive than during the dive.

Divers need to be more concerned with heat and physiology before or after a dive than during the dive. Even relatively warm water cools the body, so the primary concerns with heat result from hot above-water environments, and ironically, especially when the water is *cool* because divers will need exposure suits.

When body temperature rises, either through exposure to a warm environment, heat-produced exercise or a combination of these, the body starts several cooling mechanisms to protect the core temperature.

Initially, skin capillaries dilate, allowing heat from the blood to radiate through the skin. Perspiration follows, cooling the skin — and thus the blood — through evaporation. If the core temperature remains high, the pulse accelerates to circulate blood more rapidly for faster cooling, accompanied by a breathing increase. These responses remain until the core temperature returns to normal, which usually means when the diver stops exercising or reaches a cooler environment. If this doesn't happen rapidly, the body continues its cooling efforts until exhausting its physiological ability to do so (discussed in Thermal Problems).

Responses to Cold

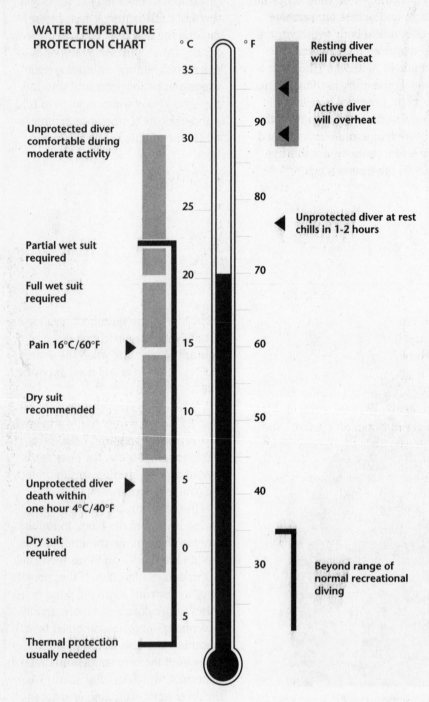

**WATER TEMPERATURE
PROTECTION CHART**

°C   °F

35

Resting diver
will overheat

Active diver
will overheat

90

Unprotected diver
comfortable during
moderate activity

30

25   80

Unprotected diver at rest
chills in 1-2 hours

Partial wet suit
required

Full wet suit
required

20   70

Pain 16°C/60°F   15   60

Dry suit
recommended

10   50

Unprotected diver
death within
one hour 4°C/40°F   5   40

Dry suit
required

0

30   Beyond range of
normal recreational
diving

5

Thermal protection
usually needed

The effects of temperature on the diver.

A diver's physiology also reacts to a temperature drop to protect the core temperature. Water conducts heat more than 20 times faster than air and requires much more heat to raise its temperature, meaning temperatures that are comfortable and warm in the air require heat conservation in water.

Without an insulating exposure suit, for example, the average diver will be dangerously cold in half an hour in 4°C/40°F water, and can expect to survive only two hours in 16°C/60°F water. For the majority of divers, water must be warmer than 27°C/80°F for an enjoyable dive without insulation.

Except in very warm water, an insulating exposure suit does not change the body's methods of responding to cold. By insulating the diver, the insulating exposure suit extends dive time by slowing the cooling process, and making the body's efforts more effective. It cannot, however, eliminate cooling. With or without an exposure suit, a diver's physiology will react to cold identically. What differs is how long these reactions will maintain the core temperature.

Individual physiology also plays a part in the response to cold. Divers with thicker layers of fat tissue are better insulated and tend to lose heat more slowly. Thin people have a greater surface-area-to-body-weight ratio and cool more quickly. Frequent exposure to continuous cold acclimates the individual, increasing the body's ability to retain heat, to some extent.

As the body cools, temperature centers in the hands, feet and head trigger heat-conserving responses that begin with a change in circulation. Blood flow to the extremities (except the head) slows through *vasoconstriction* (constriction of blood vessels) to reduce heat loss from the blood through the skin. This

Divers with thicker layers of fat tissue are better insulated and tend to lose heat more slowly. Thin people have a greater surface-area-to-body-weight ratio and cool more quickly.

results in numbness in the fingers and toes after a long exposure to cold.

If vasoconstriction does not sufficiently maintain the core temperature, the body reacts by triggering shivering, which generates heat through muscle activity and accelerated metabolism. Shivering signals a losing battle with the cold. If a diver fails to leave the water when shivering starts, the body will reach the limits of its ability to maintain the core temperature, causing conditions discussed in Thermal Problems.

A diver extends the body's ability to maintain the core temperature through proper use of exposure suits and diving techniques. The head loses considerable heat because the body can't reduce blood supply to the brain. Therefore, a wet suit hood makes a substantial difference in reducing heat loss. In very warm water, an exposure suit can allow the body to generate heat as fast as it's lost, allowing the diver to remain in the water indefinitely so far as body heat is concerned.

Heat loss through respiration is usually minimal (except in very deep commercial diving), because the trachea and sinuses act as heat-retaining mechanisms. During inspiration, incoming cold air cools the trachea and sinuses as it passes into the lungs. During expiration, the air rewarms these areas, helping the body retain heat. During diving, however, denser cold air can absorb more heat than the body can reclaim in this manner. When diving in colder waters, divers often plan shallower dives to minimize respiratory heat loss, as well as to avoid exposure suit compression that reduces insulation.

The head loses considerable heat because the body can't reduce blood supply to the brain. Therefore, a wet suit hood makes a substantial difference in reducing heat loss.

Thermal Problems

Although the body responds protectively within a specific range to different heat and cold conditions, diving can expose the body beyond its capability to successfully overcome the effects.

Heat Exhaustion and Heatstroke

 Rescue Diver Manual,   *Rescue Diver Video*

Although the body can cool itself in relatively hot conditions, an exposure suit can cause difficulties. Perspiration provides a principle means to dissipate heat, but a wet suit or dry suit prevents this evaporative cooling.

Although the body can cool itself in relatively hot conditions, an exposure suit can cause difficulties. Perspiration provides a principle means to dissipate heat, but a wet suit or dry suit prevents this evaporative cooling. Strenuous activity or a hot environment coupled with an exposure suit can lead to *heat exhaustion*, the condition in which the body works at maximum capacity to keep the core temperature cool.

A diver suffering from heat exhaustion has weak and rapid breathing, a weak and rapid pulse, cool and clammy skin. The diver sweats profusely and dehydrates, with nausea and weakness common. The breathing pattern, high pulse and heavy sweating are all maximum cooling efforts by the body.

If a diver remains hot, or continues to heat, the physiological control mechanisms will eventually fail, and result in *heatstroke*. With heatstroke, the pulse is strong and rapid; perspiration ceases; and the skin is flushed and hot. At this point, the core temperature rises because the body's cooling mechanisms have failed. Brain and systemic damage are likely with heatstroke, and without medical attention, even death is possible. Heatstroke is considered a medical emergency.

Hypothermia

If a diver ignores shivering and continues to lose heat, the core temperature will drop, leading to *hypothermia*, or reduced body temperature. Hypothermia indicates that the body's heat regulation has failed, just as in heatstroke, but in the opposite direction.

As hypothermia advances, uncontrollable shivering and vasoconstriction cease. The diver suddenly feels comfortable as warm blood rushes to the skin. This is a dangerous condition, because although the diver no longer feels cold, the body now loses heat at uncontrolled rate, and the core temperature drops rapidly.

The decline in core temperature causes a decline in mental processes, and the diver becomes drowsy, uncoordinated and forgetful. If hypothermia continues unchecked, the diver loses consciousness, followed by coma and death.

Recommendations on Thermal Problems

1. *To prevent possible heat exhaustion or heatstroke, divers should be careful when donning exposure suits in warm environments. The suit should be put on at the last possible moment and removed if signs of overheating become apparent.*

2. *In warm environments, perspiration can lead to possible dehydration. Divers should consume cool, nondiuretic liquids or commercially available balanced salt solutions to prevent dehydration.*

3. *Exposure suits appropriate to the environment should be worn while diving to prevent excessive heat loss. Divers should leave the water if they begin shivering.*

4. *Heat exhaustion, heatstroke and hypothermia are medical conditions requiring special emergency considerations. Divers should be trained to handle these considerations, preferably through a rescue diver course taught by a professional instructor.*

Physiological Responses to Pressure Change on Body Air Spaces

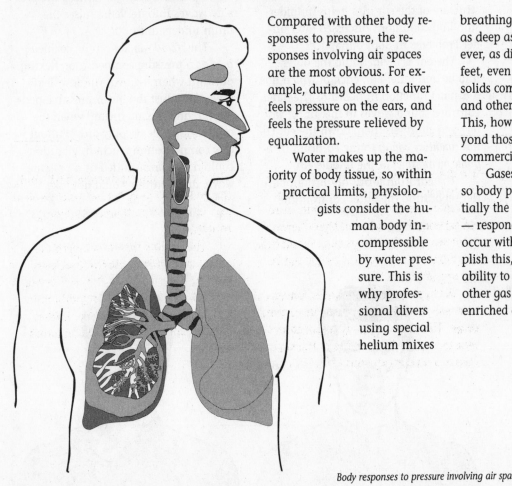

Compared with other body responses to pressure, the responses involving air spaces are the most obvious. For example, during descent a diver feels pressure on the ears, and feels the pressure relieved by equalization.

Water makes up the majority of body tissue, so within practical limits, physiologists consider the human body incompressible by water pressure. This is why professional divers using special helium mixes breathing gases have been able to dive as deep as 450 metres/1500 feet. (However, as divers exceed 600 metres/2000 feet, even "incompressible" liquids and solids compress, which alters protein and other macromolecular structures. This, however, involves depths well beyond those visited routinely by even commercial divers.)

Gases, including air, do compress, so body parts containing air — essentially the ears, sinuses, lungs and mask — respond to air volume changes that occur with pressure changes. To accomplish this, all body air spaces have the ability to admit or release air (or any other gas the diver is breathing, such as enriched air).

Body responses to pressure involving air spaces are the most obvious.

The Ears

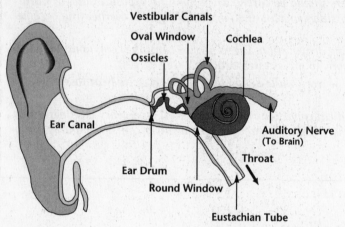

Vestibular Canals
Oval Window
Ossicles
Cochlea
Ear Canal
Auditory Nerve (To Brain)
Ear Drum
Throat
Round Window
Eustachian Tube

Basic structure of the ear.

In as little as one metre/three feet of water, a diver feels pressure in the ears. During descent, the diver voluntarily equalizes to the increasing hydrostatic pressure to avoid discomfort.

The diagram of the ear and a review of its anatomy explains how and why the diver must equalize the ears. Familiarization with the function and structure of the ear also helps in understanding conditions discussed later under Problems in Body Air Spaces.

The ear is divided into the outer, middle and inner ear, each of which has a distinct function in hearing. The outer ear traps sound waves in the air (or water) and channels them down the ear canal (*auditory canal*) to the eardrum (*tympanic membrane*) of the middle ear.

The eardrum forms an airtight barrier separating the outer ear from the middle ear. Sound waves vibrate the eardrum, which is attached to three bones that conduct and magnify vibration, the *ossicles*. Sound vibrations from the eardrum pass into the ossicles, which use mechanical advantage to amplify the vibrations as they pass to the inner ear.

Vibrations transmit from the ossicles into the *cochlea*, an inner-ear organ filled with a liquid called *perilymph*. The ossicles attach to the *oval window* of the cochlea, which flexes in and out in response to ossicle vibration. As the oval window flexes, it pushes against the perilymph, causing pressure waves to oscillate through the cochlea. The pressure waves stimulate auditory nerve endings in the cochlea, turning the pressure waves into nerve impulses the brain understands.

The *round window* on the cochlea acts as a pressure compensator, flexing outward when the oval window flexes inward against the incompressible perilymph, and flexing inward when the oval window flexes outward. Without this compensating reaction, vibration could not be transmitted as a pressure wave, and hearing would not take place.

The eustachian tubes connect the middle ear to the throat. During equalization, air travels from the throat to the middle ear to offset increasing hydrostatic pressure.

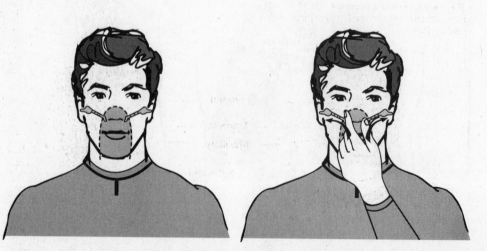

Also located in the inner ear are the vestibular canals (*vestibular endorgans*), which control balance and sense of orientation. Although the canals do not contribute to the hearing process, they connect to the cochlea through the perilymphatic system. For this reason, responses by the ear to pressure changes affect not only hearing, but balance, too.

Responses to pressure by the ear concern the middle ear. The outer ear is open to the environment, therefore always in equilibrium, and the inner ear is entirely fluid filled and incompressible. The middle ear is dry and air filled, but connects to the throat via the *eustachian tube* to permit air flow to and from the air space.

During descent, hydrostatic pressure bears in on the eardrum as it compresses air in the middle ear. The diver compensates for the increased pressure by blowing additional air through the eustachian tube into the middle ear and restoring the volume/pressure balance on both sides of the eardrum.

Recreational divers normally accomplish equalization through the *Val-salva maneuver* or the *Frenzel maneuver*. With both techniques, the diver blows air against a pinched nose, which simultaneously relaxes the tissues surrounding the eustachian tube and forces air through it. With the Valsalva, the diver uses the diaphragm and attempts to exhale against the blocked nose, and with the Frenzel, the diver uses throat muscles to compress air against the pinched nose. The Frenzel minimizes probability of round-window rupture, discussed under Problems in Body Air Spaces, but requires more time to master. Beginning divers learn to equalize by "blowing against a pinched nose," and many new divers initially equalize using the Valsalva maneuver. However, as divers become acclimated to equalizing, most unconsciously begin using the Frenzel maneuver.

During ascent, the middle ear space generally equalizes without conscious action by the diver. Expanding air vents through the eustachian tube to the throat very easily, so the ascending diver usually has to take no action regarding the ears.

The Sinuses

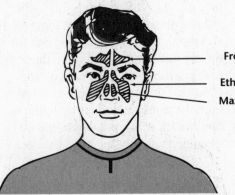

The sinuses. The sinuses equalize automatically with ear equalization in the healthy diver.

Frontal

Ethmoid

Maxillary

Sphenoid

The sinuses of a healthy diver are open and air flows through them naturally. Sinus equalization occurs naturally with middle-ear equalization. No additional effort by the diver is required on either ascent or descent in the response of the sinuses to diving.

The sinuses are more of a concern to the diver with a congestion problem, such as a head cold or allergy. This is covered in more detail under Problems in Body Air Spaces.

The Lungs

When a diver descends free diving increasing hydrostatic pressure reduces lung volume. As the diver ascends, the air reexpands to a little less than the volume at the start of the dive. The slight reduction is due to oxygen taken from alveolar air by the circulatory system during apnea, and air exhaled into the mask and ears for equalization.

The responses to air-volume changes by the lungs vary, depending on whether the diver is breath-hold diving or scuba diving.

Breath-hold Diving

When a diver descends free diving (breath-hold diving), increasing hydrostatic pressure reduces lung volume by compressing the air in the lungs. This causes no problem because the lung is designed to reduce in volume. The volume decrease doesn't differ from exhaling, provided pressure does not reduce lung volume below residual volume. For the average diver beginning descent with full lungs, a breath-hold dive past 40 metres/130 feet would be required to compress the lungs smaller than residual volume. Needless to say, most divers can't free dive that deeply.

As the diver ascends, the air reexpands to a little less than the volume at the start of the dive. The slight reduction from the original volume is due to oxygen taken from alveolar air by the circulatory system during apnea, and air exhaled into the mask and ears for equalization.

Scuba Diving

Scuba equipment delivers air to the diver at ambient pressure, so the lungs equalize to changing depth with every breath. Regardless of depth, lung volume remains approximately the same as when the diver breathes at the surface. As a diver descends, lung volume equalizes with each inspiration, and during ascent, expanding air in the lungs escapes during expiration.

In this instance, equalization is totally automatic, as long as the diver continues to breathe normally. Severe complications may arise if the diver holds the breath using scuba, as discussed under Problems in Body Air Spaces.

Equipment

Any air space applied to the body differs little physiologically from a natural air space, because both require equalization to offset increasing hydrostatic pressure.

During descent, pressure compresses air in the mask. To compensate, the diver blows air through the nose into the mask, keeping internal air pressure and volume in balance with external ambient pressure.

Upon ascent, air expanding in the mask bubbles out past the mask skirt easily, requiring no action by the diver to equalize the mask to the decreasing pressure.

A dry suit creates another air space that usually surrounds the entire body (except the hands and head, in most models, which the diver insulates with wet suit gloves and hood, but some models keep these dry, too). During descent, the dry suit compresses around the body; to compensate, the diver adds air (or other gas) through a low pressure hose from the regulator and tank. During ascent, the diver releases expanding air through a valve on the suit's shoulder.

Problems in Body Air Spaces

All body air spaces respond easily to the underwater environment, provided a diver ensures equalization to the ambient pressure. If the diver fails to equalize air spaces, either descending or ascending, complications and injuries may arise.

Any air space can suffer *barotrauma* (pressure injury) during ascent or descent, but the nature of the injury varies with the physiology of the affected air space. Descending barotraumas are called "squeezes," and involve hydrostatic pressure forcing body tissues into uncompensated air spaces. Ascending barotraumas are called "reverse squeezes," "reverse blocks" or "expansion injuries" (depending on the particular condition) and involve trapped expanding air forcing air spaces apart as hydrostatic pressure declines.

Although particular barotraumas have the potential to seriously injure the diver, divers can avoid all barotraumas easily through proper procedures. Pressure-related injuries follow failure to apply the proper procedures.

The Ears

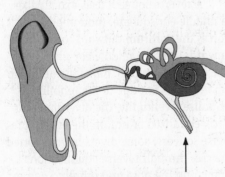

**Eustachian tube blocked
by increased pressure**

If the diver delays equalization, increased pressure in the throat can squeeze the eustachian tube shut, making equalization difficult or impossible.

Assuming a diver knows how to equalize the ears, there may still be reasons for difficulty in doing so. After several rapid depth changes, the throat muscles can tire, or after several months without diving, the diver may be rusty in equalization techniques. Sometimes equipment compresses the throat, such as a tight neck seal on an exposure suit or the straps from a full face mask, partially obstructing the eustachian tubes.

If a diver descends too far without equalizing, increased air-pressure differential between the middle ear and the air in the throat may pinch the eustachian tubes shut, making equalization impossible. The most common cause of equalization problems, however, is congestion due to a cold or allergy.

Mucus and swelling of the mucous membranes that congests the eustachian tubes (due to cold or allergy) blocks air flow to the middle ear, making equalization difficult or impossible. Equalization attempts while congested can force mucus into the middle ear, possibly leading to infections.

Middle-Ear Squeeze — If a diver descends while unable to equalize, the ear experiences sharp pain caused by the hydro-

If a diver descends while unable to equalize, the ear experiences sharp pain caused by the hydrostatic pressure forcing the eardrum in toward the unequalized air space. If this continues without additional air to offset the diminished volume, the hydrostatic pressure forces fluids and blood from the tissues surrounding the middle ear into the ear's air space.

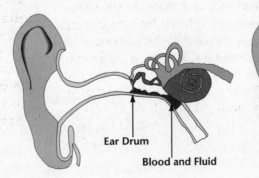

Ear Drum

Blood and Fluid

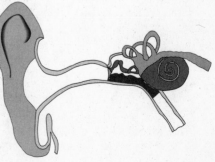

static pressure forcing the eardrum in toward the unequalized air space. If this continues without additional air to offset the diminished volume, the hydrostatic pressure forces fluids and blood from the tissues surrounding the middle ear into the ear's air space. The longer the diver remains unequalized, the more fluid and blood flows into the middle ear.

As this happens, the sharp pain diminishes and the diver's ear feels "full." Liquids in the middle ear dampen vibration that passing through it, diminishing hearing. Middle-ear squeeze usually heals with proper treatment by an otolaryngologist (ears, nose and throat specialist), but failure to receive medical treatment can mean permanent hearing impairment from infection.

Eardrum Rupture — If a diver with unequalized ears descends rapidly, at a rate faster than hydrostatic pressure can force liquids from the tissues into the middle ear, the eardrum may burst inward. When the eardrum ruptures, the diver experiences a sharp pain, followed by immediate relief as the break admits water, instantly equalizing the space. Since the water is colder than normal body temperature, it can create vertigo when it comes in contact with the vestibular canals, but the vertigo passes when body heat rewarms the water.

Generally, a broken eardrum will heal. However, when water enters the middle ear, it may contaminate it with bacteria and foreign organic material, which may very likely cause infection. Treatment by an otolaryngologist minimizes the possibility of permanent hearing damage following an eardrum rupture.

Reverse Squeeze — Reverse squeeze results when the middle ear equalizes on descent, but air fails to exit via the eustachian tube on ascent. This condition occurs most frequently when a diver uses a

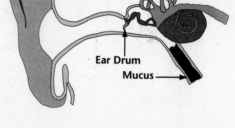

Reverse squeeze results when the middle ear equalizes on descent, but air fails to exit via the eustachian tube on ascent.

nasal decongestant to dive with a cold or allergy, and the decongestant wears off during the dive. It may also occur if a diver with a cold forces the ears to equalize, only to have the eustachian tube block again at depth.

A reverse squeeze feels exactly like a middle-ear squeeze, though pressure forces the eardrum outward rather than inward. Unlike a middle-ear squeeze, the diver's air supply limits the ability to abort the ascent due to the inability to equalize; eventually, the diver must surface, equalized or not. In the event of reverse squeeze, some divers have reported success through reverse equalization (pinching the nose and inhaling against it), but a stubborn reverse squeeze can on rare occasions cause an outward rupture of the eardrum.

Ear Plugs — Ear plugs create air spaces in the ear canals between the plug and the eardrum that cannot be equalized, so diver's can't use them. On occasion, a tight-fitting wet suit hood can create a similar condition, though a diver easily alleviates this problem by pulling the hood away from the ear momentarily, admitting water.

If a diver were to use ear plugs, during descent the eardrum would hurt as pressure forces it outward (as in a reverse squeeze) into the unequalized space. The diver might try to equalize,

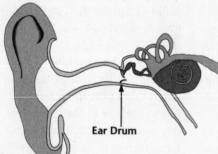

If a diver with unequalized ears descends rapidly, at a rate faster than hydrostatic pressure can force liquids from the tissues into the middle ear, the eardrum may burst inward.

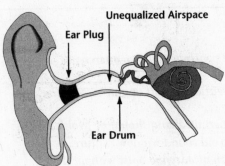

Ear plugs create air spaces in the ear canals between the plug and the eardrum that cannot be equalized.

only to make the pain worse (or rupture the eardrum) because adding air to the middle ear *increases* the pressure difference. At the same time, hydrostatic pressure may force the plug deep into the ear canal.

Round-Window Rupture — Rupture of the round window on the cochlea takes place if a diver delays equalization during descent and then attempts a forceful or lengthy Valsalva maneuver. The physiology causing the round window to rupture is extensive, though easy to understand.

In an unequalized ear, the eardrum flexes inward in response to hydrostatic pressure. The inward movement transmits and amplifies as it travels through the ossicles into the cochlea via the oval window—exactly like a sound wave does. The oval window presses inward, exerting pressure on the perilymph, and the compensating round window flexes outward.

Throughout the body, the nervous system constantly produces *cerebrospinal fluid* that bathes the nerves of the head and spinal cord. The venous system continuously produces and absorbs these

fluids, which include perilymph. During Valsalva, pressure in the chest momentarily increases, inhibiting the blood flow in the major veins returning to the heart. The venous system momentarily "backs up" in response, causing a pressure increase in the major veins. The venous pressure increase momentarily raises the pressure of cerebrospinal fluids, including perilymph.

If a diver delays equalization, the round window in the ear bulges outward in response to the pressure transmitted to the cochlea. If the diver at the same time equalizes using a forceful or lengthy Valsalva, the perilymph pressure increase combines with the pressure transmitted from the eardrum and can rupture the round window.

A round-window rupture causes the diver's ears to feel blocked, and diver may experience a hearing reduction, often accompanied by ringing sounds and vertigo. Round-window rupture is a serious injury, and failure to have it medically treated by an otolaryngologist can lead to permanent hearing reduction or deafness in the affected ear. Round-window rupture may affect balance.

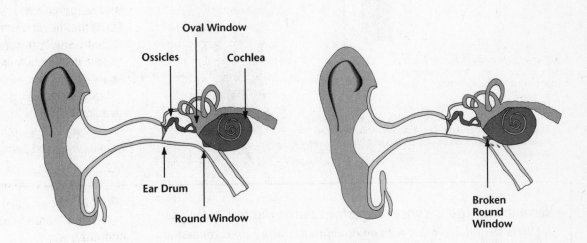

Rupture of the round window on the cochlea takes place if a diver delays equalization during descent and then attempts a forceful or lengthy Valsalva maneuver. In an unequalized ear, the inward flex of the eardrum amplifies as it travels through the ossicles into the cochlea via the oval window. The oval window exerts pressure on the perilymph, and the compensating round window flexes outward. If the diver at the same time equalizes using a forceful or lengthy Valsalva, the perilymph pressure increases and combines with the pressure transmitted from the eardrum and can rupture the round window.

The Sinuses

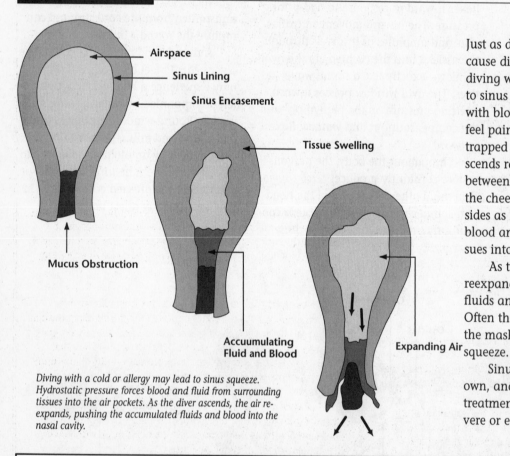

Airspace

Sinus Lining

Sinus Encasement

Tissue Swelling

Mucus Obstruction

Accuumulating Fluid and Blood

Expanding Air

Diving with a cold or allergy may lead to sinus squeeze. Hydrostatic pressure forces blood and fluid from surrounding tissues into the air pockets. As the diver ascends, the air reexpands, pushing the accumulated fluids and blood into the nasal cavity.

Just as diving with a cold or allergy can cause difficulties equalizing the ears, diving with a cold or allergy may lead to sinus squeeze. A diver who descends with blocked sinuses may or may not feel pain as pressure pushes in on trapped air pockets. If the diver descends rapidly, sinus pain may occur between the eyes, over the teeth or in the cheekbones. The pain usually subsides as hydrostatic pressure forces blood and fluid from surrounding tissues into the air pockets.

As the diver ascends, the air reexpands, pushing the accumulated fluids and blood into the nasal cavity. Often the diver surfaces with blood in the mask, a definite indication of sinus squeeze.

Sinus squeeze usually heals on its own, and requires little or no medical treatment, unless accompanied by severe or extended pain.

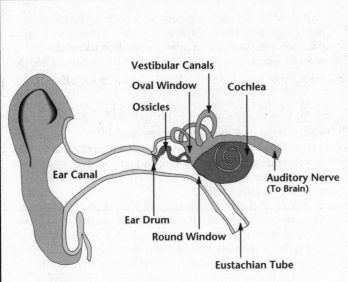

Vestibular Canals
Oval Window
Cochlea
Ossicles
Ear Canal
Auditory Nerve
(To Brain)
Ear Drum
Round Window
Eustachian Tube

Summary of Ear and Sinus Barotrauma Treatment

Blame it all on Robert Boyle. He never put on scuba gear, but he did explain why a diver's ears might hurt when diving or why there may be blood in the mask after surfacing.

As discussed in section two, The Chemistry and Physics of Diving, Boyle determined gas volume varies inversely with pressure. That's just fine for balloons being taken underwater, but a diver is human and may have a cold, allergy, deviated septum, large adenoids or may simply have poorly functioning eustachian tubes. If one attempts to dive, Boyle's law becomes a real pain when the diver can't equalize ear or sinus pressure. Something has to give. The bottom line: a diver can't fight Boyle's law.

Barotitis and Barosinusitis

If higher pressure in the tissues and blood vessels "squeezes" fluid and blood from them into the middle ear and sinus cavities, the result is pain in the ears and sinuses, hearing loss and possibly dizziness. This is called *barotitis* (ears) and *barosinusitis* (sinuses).

Barotitis can lead to middle ear infection. Treatment by otolaryngologists usually consists of oral antibiotics, decongestants and, in persistent cases, steroids. It may take up to six weeks for all the fluid behind the eardrum to either be reabsorbed by the tissues or to go down the eustachian tube. On rare occasions, a small ventilating tube may have to be placed in the eardrum to prevent fluid recurrence. Obviously, the patient can't dive until the tube is removed and the eardrum heals, but in any case, a diver with barotitis should avoid flying and diving until the ear is functioning normally.

Barosinusitis is indicated by pain in the cheeks, between the eyes, alongside the nose and in the upper teeth. The diver should discontinue diving. Treatment by an otolaryngologist usually consists of oral antibiotics and decongestants. Sometimes relief with nasal spray and alternating hot washcloths and ice packs on the cheeks to open drainage pathways help the diver obtain relief. The physician may also recommend pain medicine.

Perforated or Ruptured Eardrums

Perforated or ruptured eardrums are usually caused by continuing descent in spite of pain, repeated ear infections as a child that may make the eardrum easier to break; or extreme force when a diver equalizes, particularly with a cold.

Cold water entering the middle ear space may cause dizziness. The best action is for the diver to alert his buddy, slowly ascend to the surface, and obtain medical care for the affected ear. Blood in the ear canal usually means a perforation.

The diver should see an otolaryngologist, keep water out of the ear and not dive. A ruptured eardrum causes temporary hearing loss, but hearing returns when the eardrum heals. Small perforations heal in one to six weeks. Often, the physician won't need to prescribe ear drops or antibiotics, since these ear injuries may not be infected. However, a physician needs to determine this.

Perforations that don't heal require an operation called a *tympanoplasty*. In tympanoplasty, a tissue graft is placed over or under the hole to repair it.

Inner-Ear Barotrauma

Round-window rupture, or inner-ear barotrauma, is usually associated with delayed equalizing and a forceful Valsalva. The ear may feel full, and hearing may be affected. Deafness may occur immediately or with a slight delay.

A diver who suspects inner-ear barotrauma should see an otolaryngologist immediately. The physician may prescribe immediate bed rest, avoiding any exercise and loud noises. If hearing does not improve, reconstructive surgery may be necessary. Following the injury, the diver should not dive or fly for several months.

Vertigo

Dizziness (vertigo) is a symptom of many types of ear barotrauma and should not be ignored. Causes of dizziness due to diving can range from a minor ear squeeze or eardrum perforation to inner-ear barotrauma. The symptom should be taken seriously, and the diver should consult a physician qualified in dive medicine. Usually, the dive history helps make the diagnosis.

Diagnostic ear testing may be needed to tell whether there has been a tear of the round or oval window. Vertigo may be associated with decompression sickness, but often other symptoms present aid in the diagnosis.

Otitus Externa (Swimmer's Ear)

Although not actually a form of barotrauma, swimmer's ear is probably the most common ear problem of divers. This troublesome condition results from pH of the ear canal becoming alkaline instead of acid due to repeated exposure to water and humidity. Symptoms can range from a troublesome itch to complete closure of the external ear canal, swelling, fever and severe pain.

The best treatment is prevention by flushing the ears with one of the various over-the-counter solutions for this purpose routinely after diving or, if a diver is prone to this problem, flush each time water gets into the ear canals. If a diver finds a lot of wax in his ears, it should be removed periodically by an otolaryngologist.

Exostoses are bony bumps in a diver's ear canals resulting from repeated cold-water exposures. Exostoses can trap debris in the ear canal. A diver with this condition should have the ears cleaned by an otolaryngologist at least twice a year.

Severe swimmer's ear requires attention by a physician. Treatment usually includes cleaning, placing a wick in the ear canal, oral antibiotics, ear drops, heat lamp and pain medication. The diver shouldn't dive or get water in the ear until it has completely healed.

Sometimes a fungus infection will "hide" in the ear canal and an otolaryngologist may be the only physician to recognize it.

General Preventive Measures

Divers should equalize early and often while descending. It helps to use a line to control ascent and descent whenever possible. It also helps if divers ascend and descend feet-down (feet below head level) to decrease venous pressure in the head and neck, making equalizing easier.

A diver should never, ever dive with a cold, allergy or even mild congestion. The slightest swelling of the membranes lining the middle ear, eustachian tube and sinus openings may be enough to prohibit equalizing. A diver with allergies should get them treated.

When divers are finished diving, they should flush their ear canals to prevent swimmer's ear and turn their ears to the sun to allow drying of the ear canal. There are over-the-counter ear wash systems available from pharmacies.

If a diver has frequent trouble equalizing, a physician may be able to help. Often, using nasal spray ten minutes before a dive may help. However, this practice should never be used to allow diving with a cold.

A badly deviated nasal septum (the cartilage and bony partition separating the nostril openings) can cause poor function of the eustachian tube and sinus openings. Before giving up diving due to inability to equalize, a diver should check with an otolaryngologist. Straightening the septums or opening the nose may improve the ability to equalize and allow diving.

By never diving when unable to equalize, remembering to equalize frequently, and by avoiding forceful equalization, a diver should be able to avoid ear or sinus barotrauma.

The Lungs

The lungs generally experience no complications from volume reduction during breath-hold dives because they change volume during normal function.

Potential problems for the lungs differ depending on whether the diver is breath-hold diving or scuba diving. Problems in breath-hold diving are rare, though possible, but problems in scuba diving are potentially the most serious injuries possible in diving. Fortunately, these are also the easiest injuries to avoid.

Lung (Thoracic) Squeeze — As mentioned previously, the lungs generally experience no complications from volume reduction during breath-hold dives because they change volume during normal function. Lungs only naturally reduce volume, however, down to the residual volume. If the pressure compresses the lungs below residual volume, it can produce injury, but this requires a breath-hold dive to extreme depths, *provided* the diver descends with full lungs.

If the diver descends with the lungs empty or nearly empty (in an attempt to

Residual Volume

Lung squeeze occurs when the lungs are compressed smaller than residual volume.

reduce buoyancy, for example), they can be compressed below residual volume in as little as one or two metres/five or six feet of water. Compression below residual volume causes the pulmonary capillaries to swell, filling the reduced volume by slowly leaking fluid into the lungs.

If the squeeze duration remains short and the compression slight, there's little effect because very little fluid accumulates in the lungs. If the squeeze is extended or significant, fluid can accumulate in the alveoli, interfering with gas exchange and causing shortness of breath. A lung squeeze can be life-threatening and can require emergency medical attention.

Despite the potential for lung squeeze, the depth record for breath hold diving exceeds 150 metres/500 feet. Although this is many times deeper than necessary to cause the squeeze, physiologists theorize that the brief duration limits significant problems.

Lung-Expansion Injuries — Most body air spaces respond to pressure decrease with neither complications nor voluntary action by the diver. The lungs, in a scuba diver, also respond easily— provided the diver breathes continuously to keep them equalized to the declining pressure. If the diver holds his breath or air traps within a section of the lung, as hydrostatic pressure declines expanding air will almost always cause lung-expansion injuries.

The "golden rule" of scuba — never hold your breath — originated from the danger of lung expansion. Panic and ignorance have historically been the causes of scuba divers holding their

breath, but nausea, choking and even carelessness are also causes.

Obstruction within the respiratory system may also trap air within a section of the lung, making that portion of the lung effectively "hold its breath." A chest cold or respiratory infection can stimulate the mucus accumulation, causing obstructions. Smoking has been implicated in lung-expansion injuries also.

Following forced expiration, a percentage of the lung bronchioles may collapse, causing a momentary internal lung blockage. The inner surfaces of the bronchioles and alveoli are coated with *surfactant*, which keeps the collapsed air passages from adhering shut. Smoking destroys lung surfactant, inhibiting reopening of the bronchioles, which can lead to sectional conditions in the lung identical to breath holding.

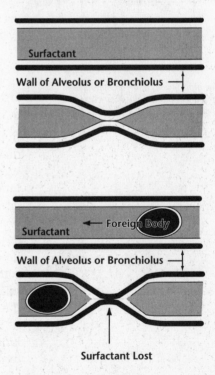

Following forced expiration, a percentage of the lung bronchioles may collapse, causing a momentary internal lung blockage. The inner surfaces of the bronchioles and alveoli are coated with surfactant, which keeps the collapsed air passages from adhering shut. Smoking and other inhaled matter can destroy lung surfactant, inhibiting reopening of the bronchioles, which can lead to sectional conditions in the lung identical to breath holding.

Lung injuries can result from even a small amount of over pressurization. Research has shown that a scuba diver, starting with full lungs, can over expand the lungs by holding the breath and surfacing in as little as one to one and half metres/three to four feet of water. Additionally, lung-expansion injury risk becomes greater with proximity to the surface where the ratio of gas-volume increase per metre/foot rises in accordance with Boyle's law.

Rather than bursting like a balloon, an over pressurized lung tears. The severity of lung-expansion injury arises not from the tear, but from air escaping and entering the tissues and/or bloodstream. Lung rupture can cause any of four distinct injuries: air embolism, pneumothorax, mediastinal emphysema and subcutaneous emphysema. Any lung over pressurization causes pulmonary capillaries and alveoli to rupture, mixing blood and air in the lungs. Often, this causes the victim to cough up blood.

Air Embolism — The most serious injury from lung over pressurization develops if air enters the bloodstream through ruptured alveoli into the pulmonary capillaries, causing an *air embolism*, or *arterial gas embolism* (abbreviated "AGE"). To be precise, an embolism is any foreign body in the bloodstream that can block its flow; an air embolism is such a body composed of air (i.e., a gas bubble), and an arterial gas embolism is a bubble on the arterial side of the circulatory system.

Air entering the bloodstream in the lungs flows through the pulmonary vein to the heart, through the left side of the heart into the aorta and the arterial system. The air bubbles can lodge virtually anywhere in the body's circulatory system, and can — in a manner similar to Type II decompression sickness — cause severe damage by stopping blood flow to tissue.

The first main arterial branches off the aorta are found in the aortic arch above the heart. These include the carotid arteries, which supply the brain. If bubbles travel into the carotids, which is likely, they will go to the brain and cause *cerebral air embolism*.

In much the same manner as with cerebral decompression sickness, the bubbles deny the brain tissue oxygenated blood, which causes a stroke. The symptoms include dizziness, confusion, shock, personality change, paralysis, unconsciousness and death. Compared to decompression sickness, the effects of cerebral air embolism and other lung-expansion injuries tend to be rapid and dramatic. Decompression sickness tends to be somewhat delayed.

If an air embolism victim should be fortunate enough to have bubbles miss the carotid arteries, the emboli can still cause damage and symptoms in other areas of the body. If bubbles were to block the coronary artery, for example, the restricted blood flow could result in heart attack.

Detail of alveolus expanding air is forced into the bloodstream

The most serious injury from lung over pressurization develops if air enters the bloodstream through ruptured alveoli into the pulmonary capillaries, causing an air embolism.

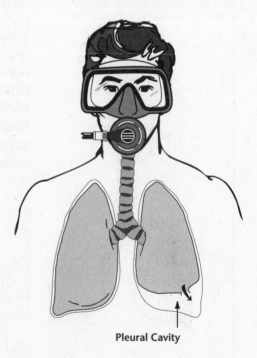

Pleural Cavity

If an over pressurized lung tears at its surface, the expanding air leaks between the lung and the pleural lining, collapsing the lung either partially or entirely. A collapsed lung is called pneumothorax.

Pneumothorax — If an over pressurized lung tears at its surface, the expanding air leaks between the lung and the *pleural lining* (chest wall), collapsing the lung either partially or entirely. A collapsed lung is called *pneumothorax.*

Pneumothorax alone is generally not as immediately life-threatening as an air embolism because the victim still has another functioning lung. The collapsed lung causes severe chest pain and may cause the victim to cough up frothy blood.

Spontaneous pneumothorax occurs without an expansion injury, through a weakness in the lung suddenly tearing and leading to lung collapse. Although uncommon, spontaneous pneumothorax can happen without warning to any individual who has this lung condition. If spontaneous pneumothorax occurs in a diver underwater, it can be more serious than a pneumothorax caused by lung-expansion injury. If a spontaneous pneumothorax takes place underwater, it can be aggravated during ascent, when the air pressing against the collapsed lung expands, increasing pressure on the injured lung. Since spontaneous pneumothorax tends to recur, it precludes further diving unless surgery can correct the problem. This is usually determined by a physician who specializes in pulmonary dive medicine.

Mediastinal Emphysema — Another possibility in a lung overexpansion accident is that the air accumulates in the *mediastinum* (center of the chest). *Mediastinal emphysema* (sometimes called *pneumomediastinum*) is far less serious than either pneumothorax or air embolism.

With mediastinal emphysema, air accumulating in the mediastinum presses on the heart and major blood vessels, interfering with circulation. A victim may feel faint and short of breath due to this impaired circulation.

Subcutaneous Emphysema — *Subcutaneous emphysema* occurs frequently with mediastinal emphysema as air seeks its way from the mediastinum, following the path of least resistance into the soft tissues at the base of the neck. Air accumulates directly under the skin in this area and causes the victim to feel a fullness in the neck and to experience a voice change. The skin may crackle if touched.

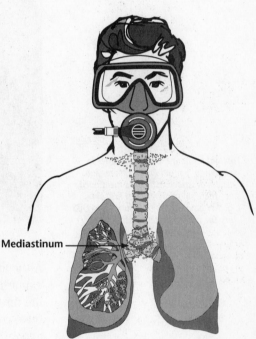

Mediastinum

Subcutaneous emphysema occurs frequently with mediastinal emphysema as air seeks its way from the mediastinum, following the path of least resistance into the soft tissues at the base of the neck.

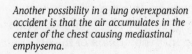

Another possibility in a lung overexpansion accident is that the air accumulates in the center of the chest causing mediastinal emphysema.

Physiological Rationale of First Aid and Treatment for Lung Overexpansion Injury

📖 *PADI Rescue Diver Manual,*   📼 *Rescue Diver Video*

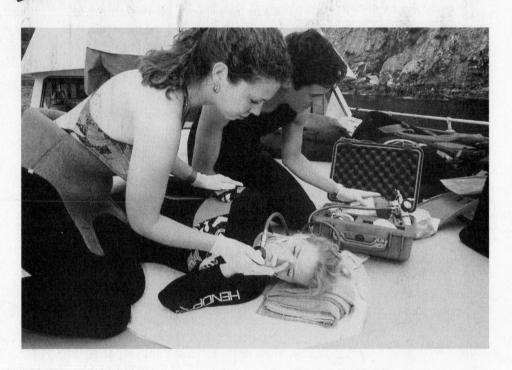

First aid for lung expansion injuries is identical to first aid for decompression sickness described earlier. As mentioned, since there's no difference in first aid, together lung expansion injuries and DCS carry the name "decompression illness."

Although three of the four possible lung-expansion injuries are not immediately life-threatening, the presence of any of these conditions demonstrates that lung-expansion injury has occurred, and air embolism is possible simultaneously. For this reason, rescuers treat a patient with any of these symptoms as though an air embolism is present, leaving the final diagnosis to physicians who specialize in pulmonary medicine.

First aid for lung expansion injuries is identical to first aid for decompression sickness described earlier. As mentioned, since there's no difference in first aid, together lung expansion injuries and DCS carry the name "decompression illness."

Once in medical care, treatment for different lung expansion injuries differs. Air embolism requires immediate recompression to diminish bubbles in the bloodstream and force them into solu-

tion. This effectively restores blood flow to the tissues. None of the other injuries require recompression, provided there's no air embolism.

Pneumothorax requires surgical removal of air from between the collapsed lung and the pleural lining, followed by lung reinflation. Recompression of a pneumothorax patient who is suffering a simultaneous air embolism can be complicated by the reexpansion of air against the lung during recompression. Medical treatment for the pneumothorax must be performed in the chamber before the patient can be brought back to surface pressure.

Mediastinal emphysema and subcutaneous emphysema will dissipate on their own as the blood slowly reabsorbs the trapped air. In extreme cases, oxygen breathing may be administered to speed up the reabsorbtion of the air.

Recommendations Concerning Lung Problems:

1. *When a diver makes breath-held descents, such as during free diving, the diver should always start with the lungs full to prevent lung squeeze.*

2. *A diver should take great care to never hold the breath while using scuba, to avoid lung overexpansion injury.*

3. *Divers should be aware that smoking and lung congestion can create obstructions within the lung that cause conditions identical to holding the breath. Diving should be avoided until any condition causing congestion is completely healed, and divers should not smoke for several hours before a dive. Smokers should consult a pulmonary physician before engaging in diving.*

4. *The best way to be prepared for a lung-expansion accident is to be trained in a rescue diver course or taught by a professional instructor and to carry the emergency equipment recommended by that course.*

Equipment Squeeze

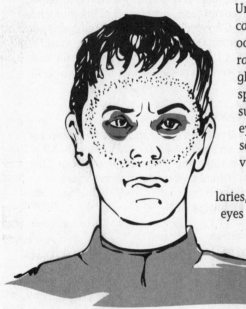

Unequalized equipment air spaces can create problems. Mask squeeze occurs most commonly on very rapid descents when a diver neglects to equalize the mask air space. Increasing hydrostatic pressure forces tissues surrounding the eye to swell into the uncompensated air space to fill the reduced volume.

This swelling damages capillaries, bruising the skin around the eyes and cheeks, sometimes rupturing surface capillaries on the eye as well. Mask squeeze looks dramatic and severe, though sometimes the diver doesn't even

Mask squeeze looks dramatic and severe, though sometimes the diver doesn't even know it happened until looking into the mirror. Mask squeeze generally clears without complications.

know it happened until looking into the mirror. Mask squeeze generally clears without complications, but a victim may want to consult a physician as a precaution.

An unequalized dry suit, (or rarely, air trapped in a wet suit) can pinch the skin and bruise. If the diver disregards the pinching and continues to descend, a dry suit squeeze can raise welts and cause injury.

During ascent, the diver must release expanding air from a dry suit or risk a runaway ascent. A rapid ascent isn't directly hazardous with respect to the suit, but it can cause decompression illness, or injury if the diver strikes something.

Other Air Spaces

Any place air or gas may be trapped in the body has the potential for barotrauma. Air spaces under tooth fillings have, on rare occasion, caused problems, and gas accumulating in the

intestines during a dive may expand on ascent and cause discomfort until passed. Although these barotraumas are possible, they are relatively rare.

Divers Alert Network The Role in Studying Dive-Physiology Problems

As recreational diving's safety and health association since 1981, Divers Alert Network (DAN) provides a wide range of health and safety services for the dive community. These services include a 24-hour dive medical emergency hotline for dive injuries, a medical information line, financial support and training program for recompression chambers, and a variety of dive safety research projects at Duke University Medical Center. DAN also has international DAN offices in areas including Japan, Australia, Europe and New Zealand. DAN has developed a line of affordable oxygen first aid units for dive emergency first aid, and developed programs in their use.

Among DAN's public service to the dive industry is its collection and analysis of dive accident and fatality data. Since DAN is involved in the treatment of most recreational dive injuries in the United States, DAN monitors hyperbaric recompression facilities throughout the U.S. and its territories to determine the number of treated cases of decompression illness (both arterial gas embolism and DCS) and other diving-related accidents, as well as evaluates the factors contributing to each accident. This important information is used to educate the dive community, from the recreational diver to the dive researcher and medical doctor. This information assists physicians in determining changes or trends in the types of diving injuries and symptomatology that occur, as well as how treatment affects outcome. A complete analysis of this information is available to the public in DAN's annual "Report on Diving Accidents and Fatalities."

DAN Flying After Diving Study

The DAN Flying After Diving studies are helping to establish empirical data regarding the necessary surface intervals after diving before traveling by aircraft or otherwise ascending to altitude. This is a critical issue among divers who travel by plane to diving destinations, and the dive operations that serve them. The study has involved numerous chamber tests that simulate diving and flying to altitude, using volunteer recreational divers as test subjects. The project received its original funding from a PADI Foundation grant, and continued with funding by the DAN membership.

Dive Accident and Fatality Trends

According to DAN statistics, the number of U.S. diving fatalities and accidents have remained relatively stable in the past 10 years.

Annual U.S. Recreational Diving Fatalities

Year	1986	1987	1988	1989	1990	1991	1992	1993	1994
	94	87	66	114	91	67	96	92	97

Total Reported Cases of DCI by Type and Year

Type	1986	1987	1988	1989	Year 1990	1991	1992	1993	1994
DCS-I	77	127	137	181	226	233	232	218	227
DCS-II	274	340	288	328	342	437	555	642	644
AGE	81	97	82	111	96	87	76	88	91

While the overall number of dive emergencies has increased slightly over the past 10 years, the number of information requests to DAN's Information Line increases significantly each year. The DAN Medical Department received more than 14,000 information calls in 1995. Increased DAN membership and awareness of this service is responsible for the increased call volume.

DAN Incident Reporting

DAN encourages divers who have experienced a problem or "near miss" while diving to report the event using the DAN Diving Incident Report Form. This program helps DAN and the dive industry understand the reasons why divers get into trouble. Divers can receive a copy of the DAN Diving Incident Report Form by contacting DAN.

For More Information

Information on DAN and its services, is available at 800-446-2671 or http://www.dan.ycg.org.

The Effects of Diving on Pregnancy

A diver could take many diving classes, read dive publications, attend special programs and still never learn much about the effects of diving while pregnant. This topic tends not to interest or concern many divers, at least until they become pregnant or have a diving spouse become pregnant.

For example, a diver returns from a wonderful diving holiday and, sometime later, learns she was pregnant during her vacation. Or, a female instructor, whose income depends on diving, learns she's pregnant. Should she consider scuba diving while pregnant?

Discussing diving while pregnant virtually always focus on one central concern—whether doing so will affect the fetus. By examining the conditions in the underwater environment and how these *may* affect a fetus, a diver can become more aware of the effects of diving during pregnancy.

Squeeze

Squeezes only affect air spaces in or on the diver. Since amniotic fluid completely encloses the fetus, there are no air spaces and a fetus cannot suffer from squeeze.

Lung-Expansion Injuries

Since a fetus doesn't breathe air, but absorbs oxygen directly from the mother's blood, the fetus cannot have a lung-expansion injury. A pregnant diver who suffers from an air embolism, however, endangers her own and the fetus' life. If the embolism requires treatment in a hyperbaric (recompression) chamber, which is likely, the treatment may be risky for the fetus because of gas toxicity (discussed next). On the other hand, considering that lung-expansion injury is an easily avoided malady, and that the fetus itself cannot over expand its lungs, lung-expansion injuries aren't a major concern because it's improbable in a healthy diver who follows appropriate dive practices.

Gas Toxicity

Divers experience increased oxygen and nitrogen absorption. Breathing air at very great depths, or enriched air beyond safe limits, can result in oxygen toxicity (see Oxygen Toxicity). Also, the nitrogen in breathing air can cause nitrogen narcosis at depth. Of these two problems, only increased oxygen has been considered a potential problem to the fetus.

Oxygen toxicity can occur rapidly if a diver reaches extreme depths below 40 metres/130 feet. Experiments on pregnant sheep investigated the safety of the fetus in a high-pressure environment. In studies on increased oxygen pressures, the fetus experienced no significant increase in oxygen content when the mother was exposed to oxygen partial pressures as high as 2.1 ata — well beyond the 1.4 ata limit for recreational diving with enriched air and the contingency maximum of 1.6 ata. At 3.15 ata, fetal oxygen content increased, but this is significantly greater than a diver would face (a PO_2

3.15 ata is equivalent to diving to 141 metres/462 feet using air, or 69 metres/226 feet using EANx40), increased oxygen content should not be a problem for the fetus. This is good news to a diver who discovers after a deep dive that she was pregnant during the dive.

There is one circumstance in which a diver can be exposed to extremely high oxygen partial pressure. A diver treated in a recompression chamber for decompression illness is usually exposed to oxygen at high pressures for a limited time as part of treatment. A fetus exposed to very high oxygen pressures, especially late in gestation, may theoretically be at risk of an eye condition, *retrolental fibroplasia*. This is speculated because premature infants who in the past were given high concentrations of oxygen developed this eye condition, which can result in blindness. However, some chamber operators have observed that babies born to pregnant women treated with hyperbaric oxygen for nondiving-related medical problems did not develop this eye condition.

Another question is whether a fetus may be at risk of getting too little oxygen. The placenta regulates oxygen fluctuations for the fetus. Also, there are natural physiological mechanisms that provide adequate oxygen to the fetus, even if the maternal supply is low. Only in cases of severe oxygen deprivation, such as the mother drowning, would the fetus be likely to lack oxygen.

Decompression Sickness

Can a fetus suffer from decompression sickness or the formation of nitrogen bubbles? This question raises the most complicated issue for physiologists, and many intricacies of the question are unclear. There are three main questions:

1. If a pregnant diver gets decompression sickness, will the fetus be harmed? Studies on pregnant sheep that were exposed late in gestation to high pressures, but not high enough to cause decompression sickness, delivered normal lambs. However, if pregnant sheep developed decompression sickness late in gestation and were untreated, the lambs were stillborn. In theory, then, the onset of decompression sickness in a pregnant diver late in gestation may also result in fetal death. What's not known, however, is the effect on a fetus if a pregnant woman diver develops decompression sickness early in her pregnancy, receives treatment and suffers no apparent lasting effects. Data from hyperbaric facilities who treat medical problems (not necessarily related to diving) may one day be able to answer this based on their collective observations, but presently there's little known.

2. Do bubbles form in the fetus at the same rate as in the mother? This is a serious concern for the diver who discovers she was pregnant after a no decompression dive that is considered safe for her. Early experiments on dogs and rats showed fetal resistance to bubble formation, but more current research on sheep and goats produced conflicting results. In one experi-

ment, sheep were taken to the equivalent depth of 50 metres/ 165 feet, and bubbles were detected in the mothers but not the fetuses. In a similar experiment with sheep and goats, bubbles were detected in both the mothers and the fetuses. However, the lambs and kids were normal upon delivery. Because of this data, many researchers believe that there is some protection for the fetus, and bubbles are less likely to form in the fetus than in the mother. However, there's still little data, so no one has formulated specifications as to the risks associated with a dive depth and duration.

3. Will bubbles cause birth defects? It's speculated that any bubble formed in a fetus could result in a birth defect since a bubble could interfere with the normal development. However, when nitrogen bubbles form in a diver, the lungs usually filter out the bubbles, so the bubbles do not reach the arterial side of the circulatory system where they cause damage. Since the fetus' lungs don't function, it has no system of bubble entrapment, but bubbles formed in the mother will be filtered by the placenta and will not reach the fetus.

Two surveys of women divers have been made in an attempt to learn more about this issue. In one survey, a group diving to 30 metres/100 feet or more during pregnancy had a higher birth defect rate than the nondiving control group. However, the incidence rate did not vary much from the normal range of all birth defects. In the other survey, no increased incidence of birth defects was found.

No conclusive evidence for birth defects has been shown from animal studies. For example, in one experiment, preg-

nant sheep were exposed in early gestation to very high pressures during peak embryonic development. Later, no abnormalities were found in the fetuses. These are encouraging results for women who dived deep before knowing they were pregnant.

Recommendations

The simplest and therefore most common recommendation to pregnant divers is: Don't dive while pregnant. This is the recommendation of the Undersea and Hyperbaric Medical Society and most national training organizations. This recommendation is based more upon what is not known, than upon what is. The data found so far is less pessimistic than this general recommendation implies, but to not dive while pregnant is the safest and easiest recommendation.

For the woman who has made a deep dive prior to knowing about her pregnancy, the information known so far is encouraging. Before anyone questioned diving during pregnancy, several prominent women scientists, such as Dr. Eugenie Clark, dived during pregnancy without problems to the fetus.

If a woman diver is planning a family, she can discontinue diving during the time of the month when she could be pregnant. After a pregnancy, a woman diver can resume diving usually six weeks after the baby is born, but she should check with her doctor before beginning her diving activities.

The Physiology of Color: Perception: How Divers See Colors Underwater

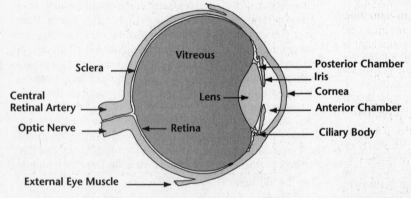

Schematic presentation of the human eye. The image of the world is projected by the cornea and lens onto the retina, the photoreceptors of which abut the wall of the globe (sclera). The optic nerve transmits encoded information of the perceived image to the brain for further analysis.

The environment is filled with electromagnetic radiation covering a spectrum of wavelengths from nanometers (nm) to kilometers (km) (one billion nm equals one metre). Humans are blind to nearly all of this radiation, except a very small band between 400 and 800nm — light. It is roughly this same fraction of the whole electromagnetic spectrum that can travel through water.

Here's a brief review of how the human visual system works: An image is projected by the cornea and lens to the inner surface in the back of the eyeball. This inner surface is covered by a thin sheet of nerve tissue, the *retina*, which actually is part of the brain. About 200 million tiny light detectors densely cover the surface of the retina, facing the wall of the globe. These *photoreceptors* consist of two types: the *rods* and the *cones*. Each of these independently measures the light it absorbs and reacts by generating nerve impulses.

The nerve impulse intensity depends on the amount of light

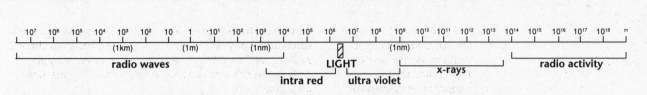

The spectrum of electromagnetic radiation visible to the human eye is only a minute fraction between 400-800nm: light.

absorbed. Bright light causes a strong reaction, and dim light triggers a weak response. The pattern of the light responses across the retina photoreceptors corresponds to the projected image. Nerve cells of the retina encode this pattern into nerve signals and transmits it to the higher brain centers, which "reconstructs" the visual world. During this complicated and still largely unknown data processing, something special is created — color.

Color is merely a sensation that our retina and the brain visual centers produce as an interpretation of the outside world. Natural light is a random mixture of wavelengths in the 400 to 800nm range. Molecules called pigments absorb certain wavelengths and reflect the remaining ones. In this way, reflected light differs from the ambient light in that it lacks the absorbed wavelengths. The ambient light perceived as colorless—white, and light perceived as colored, differ in their spectral composition.

In the retina, the cone photoreceptors are used for color vision. There are three types of these cones, which differ in the light absorbing pigment they contain. Each of the cone types has a typical action spectrum that describes its sensitivity for light of a different wavelength. As shown on the graph, the action spectra of the three cone types of the human retina. The blue, green and red curves show the response intensity to light of constant energy, but varying wavelength. For example: At light of a wavelength of 450nm, the receptor *B* is maximally sensitive, whereas the other two just begin to react. Cone type *G* has its peak sensitivity at 550, and cone *R* at 560nm.

There is an important conclusion to be drawn from this: A given response level in a single cone can either be produced by a relatively low level of light at peak sensitivity or by higher intensities of light with shorter or longer wavelengths than that. Thus, a single receptor does not know if it "sees" low intensity light at its peak sensitivity, or if it "sees" high intensity light at where its sensitivity is low. A single cone is color blind, but the three cones together elicit relative response levels to a given light and enable our visual system, by processing these responses, to make the distinction between intensity and color.

For example: All three cone types respond to light with a wavelength of 500nm; the *G* cone most and the *R* and *B* cones less, but both to the same level. Light that produces exactly this ratio of response levels in the three cones is seen as green. It does not matter if it was light of only one strictly defined wavelength (monochromatic light) or if it was a random mixture of wavelengths and intensities. The only factor that matters is the ratio of the response levels of the three cone types. If lights of defined wavelength are used (monochromatic lights) the visual system experiences light around 400nm as violet, around 450 as blue, around 500 as green, around 550 as yellow, around 600 as orange and around 650 as red. Regardless, the very

same colors are produced by countless mixtures of wavelengths and intensities.

The visual process gets somewhat more complicated by a property of the visual system called *selective adaptation*, a mechanism that tunes color perception so prevailing ambient light is perceived as white. Selective adaptation makes the human eye see the same colors in the living room, regardless of whether it were illuminated by daylight through the windows, or by an incandescent light at night. Taking photographs with daylight color film demonstrates the difference in the spectral composition of the prevailing light in both situations. Pictures taken at night turn out to be unnaturally reddish. The same phenomenon occurs watching a landscape through tinted glass: after a short while, the eye sees the same colors as though looking through clear glass.

Although blue light predominates in deep water, even at 50 metres/165 feet, traces of light with wavelength of 650nm (red) could be measured. In the diver, selective adaptation underwater leads to an increased sensitivity to longer wavelength (red) light and a decreased sensitivity to short ones (blue). The diver perceives ambient light as being rather colorless (white), even on relatively deep dives, and still sees the colors. Under these same conditions, the photographic daylight color film cannot adapt, and becomes "color blind." Photographs taken with natural light in the deep inevitably turn out unnaturally bluish.

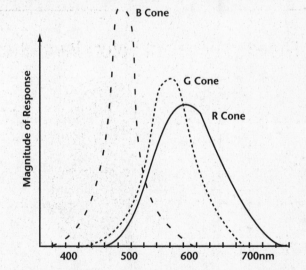

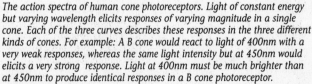

The action spectra of human cone photoreceptors. Light of constant energy but varying wavelength elicits responses of varying magnitude in a single cone. Each of the three curves describes these responses in the three different kinds of cones. For example: A B cone would react to light of 400nm with a very weak responses, whereas the same light intensity but at 450nm would elicits a very strong response. Light at 400nm must be much brighter than at 450nm to produce identical responses in a B cone photoreceptor.

Dive Equipment

Three

The Principles of Equipment Selection and Care

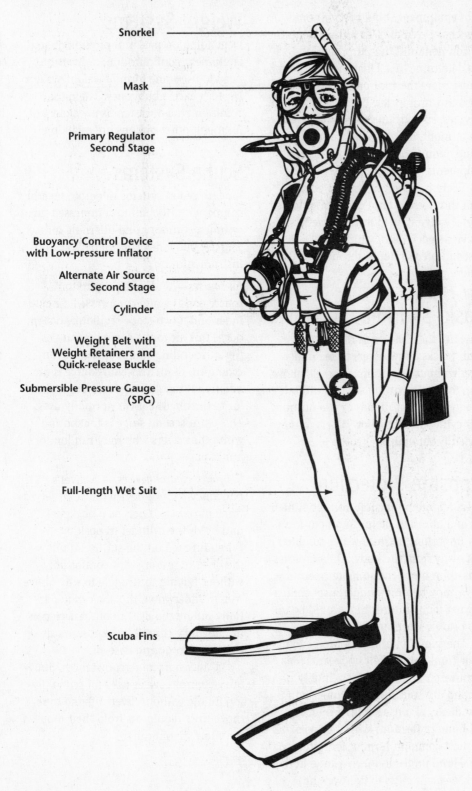

Snorkel

Mask

Primary Regulator
Second Stage

Buoyancy Control Device
with Low-pressure Inflator

Alternate Air Source
Second Stage

Cylinder

Weight Belt with
Weight Retainers and
Quick-release Buckle

Submersible Pressure Gauge
(SPG)

Full-length Wet Suit

Scuba Fins

Recreational divers need equipment. Dive equipment allows people to see and breathe easily for an extended time underwater. Divers move freely underwater and stay warm and comfortable with the appropriate equipment. Human physiology and diving's physics and chemistry impose limitations on people underwater, but equipment minimizes these limitations.

Equipment also affects dive enjoyment. In the early days of diving participation was limited to those willing to endure the shortcomings of primitive equipment. This tended to exclude smaller people, women, children, the elderly and people with disabilities. Today's recreational dive equipment allows nearly everyone to participate in diving at some level. Equipment has become lighter, more attractive and easier to use than ever before.

This section examines nearly all commonly used dive equipment. It moves from the basics — masks, snorkels and fins — to the equipment used for specialized dive activities such as night diving and underwater photography. Different sections discuss why divers need each item, how the item works and considerations for selection, use and care. A number of sidebars present additional information designed to give the reader a greater understanding of the role equipment plays in recreational diving.

The Completely Equipped Diver

What equipment should recreational divers have and use? To some extent, the environment and the purpose of the dive determine this. Divers in cold water require more thermal protection than divers in warm water. Divers engaged in activities, such as underwater photography or night, deep, wreck, ice or cavern diving, require additional specialized equipment.

There is, however, certain equipment that recreational divers should use on every dive. The following briefly overviews each item, which will be discussed in greater depth throughout this section.

Mask, Snorkel and Fins

These are the most basic dive equipment. Masks allow divers to see underwater without distortion. Snorkels allow them to breathe at the surface without having to lift their heads or use air from their cylinders. Fins allow divers to move efficiently through the water.

Exposure Protection

Divers require protection from both heat loss and abrasion. Retarding heat loss is very important because water conducts heat away from the body 20 to 25 times faster than air at the same temperature. Divers may become dangerously chilled in water temperatures that would be uncomfortably warm in air.

Thermal and abrasion protection range from lightweight body suits for warm-water diving, to thick, highly insulating dry suits for cold-water diving. Most divers also use some form of foot and hand protection. Wet suit boots are the most common form of foot protection. Hand protection may range from thick, wet suit mitts to lightweight gloves.

Weight Systems

Depending on personal physiology and equipment configuration, a diver may need to use some form of weight system to offset excess buoyancy. The most common type of system is a weight belt, although other options are available.

Scuba Systems

Modern scuba systems integrate several components, including compressed air cylinders, primary and alternate air sources, buoyancy control devices and instrumentation.

Air sources — A diver's primary air source consists of a compressed air cylinder and a two-stage regulator that reduces this air to the same pressure as the surrounding water. The most common form of alternate air source is an additional regulator second stage, similar to the one the diver normally uses. This extra second stage is for sharing with other divers who may run low, or out of air.

Buoyancy-control devices — A diver's buoyancy-control device (or BCD) serves three purposes. It acts as a backpack and holds the cylinder in position. When inflated on the surface, it allows the diver to rest or swim comfortably without having to struggle to stay above water. Underwater, the diver may partially inflate the BCD to offset decreases in buoyancy caused by exposure suit compression during descent.

Under normal circumstances, buoyancy control devices used for scuba diving inflate without divers having to remove their regulators from their mouths to inflate them orally.

Instrumentation — Divers need:

- a means of monitoring air supply
- a means of determining depth
- a means of measuring time underwater

Divers may also use an underwater compass. This makes it easier to navigate and consequently helps eliminate long surface swims at the end of the dive.

Knife or Tool

Although there is normally only a slight risk of becoming entangled underwater, divers may use some form of a cutting tool. Depending on its design, divers can use a knife to pry and measure.

Dive Tables or Planners

Recreational divers stay within depth and time constraints known as no-decompression limits. Staying within these limits minimizes the risk of decompression sickness and eliminates the need to make decompression stops at the end of a dive.

The no-decompression limits for any particular dive vary depending on depth and time spent underwater, the profile of previous dives and the time that has passed since these dives. To determine these limits, divers use dive tables or dive planners or use a computer.

Log Book

Certification cards only establish that a diver met the minimum requirements for certification at that level. Divers record their dives in log books to provide a tangible record of the diver's experience. Most dive resorts and charter operations require that divers present both a certification card and a log book before they provide dive services.

Equipment Selection

Comfort and fit are among the most important factors in equipment selection. Professional advice may help with selection.

When divers invest in dive equipment, they invest in both safety and enjoyment. By choosing wisely, divers save money for education, dive travel and participating in local dive activities.

Specific criteria apply to individual equipment selection. In addition, however, there are four general principles that apply to the purchase of almost all equipment:

1. Never compromise safety. New divers need equipment that is every bit as appropriate as that used by more experienced divers. Equipment is either right, or it isn't — there is seldom any middle ground.

Fortunately, there is almost no such thing as unsafe dive equipment. However, one must avoid using equipment improperly or buying old equipment that hasn't been checked or serviced properly by a professional.

Wise divers never go without important pieces of equipment simply for the sake of saving money. They know that carefully selected equipment can provide years of service.

2. Comfort is the most important selection criterion next to safety. Usually, the most comfortable equipment is the safest. Comfortable divers can relax and enjoy the underwater environment, al-

lowing them to remain more alert. Uncomfortable divers, on the other hand, are more susceptible to stress and to making mistakes.

A primary factor in comfort is fit. Proper fit makes items such as masks, fins, exposure suits and BCDs perform better. It allows divers to stay warmer or helps them avoid annoying water leaks or muscle cramps.

3. Several items, like regulators, cylinders, BCDs and instrumentation, require regular professional service. The ability to obtain this service on a regular basis may be an important factor.

Before investing in service-dependent equipment items, a diver should ask:

• Is the dealer selling these items authorized to perform the necessary service?

• Does the dealer have the parts, the tools and the training to provide this service on the premises — and within reasonable time?

• Is comparable service readily available anywhere or at popular dive destinations?

If the answer to each of these questions is "yes," a diver can invest in this equipment with confidence.

4. Divers make the best decisions regarding equipment in an environment in which they can try on or test each item, compare similar items side by side and receive advice from knowledgeable professionals. The advice divers receive from a professional diving facility may save money and increase the enjoyment and satisfaction they receive from diving.

Preparing New Equipment for Use

When buying equipment, ensure that professional service is readily available. This is particularly important with regulators.

Brand new items, such as masks, snorkels and fins aren't ready to use right out of the box. Divers need to adjust the straps for proper fit. In addition, most manufacturers coat their new silicone and rubber products with a silicone-impregnated wax preservative. Unless removed, this preservative may cause the straps to slip out of adjustment and prevent mask-defogging solutions from working.

The first step in new equipment preparation is removing the wax preservative. Divers can scrub both sides of the mask lens and all the mask surfaces and fin straps with a nonabrasive cleanser or toothpaste. A toothbrush works well when applying the cleanser or toothpaste to the straps.

After removing the wax, the diver adjusts the mask and fin straps. Preferably, they do this in a relaxed setting, not immediately prior to entering the water.

Although it's a good idea to mark personal equipment items as soon as possible, it's nevertheless best to avoid applying marking paint to masks, snorkels or fins until they have been used at least once. This way, if they prove unsatisfactory, they often may still be exchanged. In addition, one or two uses wear off more of the wax preservative, allowing the paint to adhere better.

When the time comes to apply marking paint, the owner can clean the target area with a small amount of acetone or nail-polish remover. After the paint dries thoroughly, the entire area may be sprayed with silicone to restore the protective coating.

Equipment Care and Storage

Equipment care ensures reliability and longevity. Divers follow basic care and storage procedures, which generally involve three simple steps:

1. Rinsing.

2. Drying.

3. Storage.

Certain equipment, such as cylinders and regulators, may require additional maintenance procedures. Many of these procedures are discussed elsewhere in this section.

Rinsing equipment after every use is important.

pressure stream of water at regulators, valves or gauges, where it could force a sediment particle between an O-ring and metal, thus breaking the seal. With most equipment, if it can't be rinsed immediately, it's best to keep it wet to prevent salt from crystallizing. If divers can't rinse equipment while it's still moist, they should allow it to soak overnight in fresh water before rinsing it under a hose or a stream of fresh water.

Drying

Divers can let equipment air-dry thoroughly, particularly before storing it in areas with poor air circulation since this helps prevent mildew. A closed gear bag isn't the best place to store freshly rinsed equipment.

The ideal equipment drying environment is out of direct sunlight but where air can circulate freely. Exposure suits can hang to dry, and other equipment can dry out in the open where any remaining water can easily drain. Plastic hangers prevent rust stains on exposure suits, which is a risk with wire hangers.

Rinsing

Except on rare occasions when dives take place in perfectly clean spring water, divers must always rinse their equipment with fresh water after use. Rinsing removes dirt, sediments and salt. These substances not only make equipment unpleasant to use again, they can impair performance and promote corrosion by trapping moisture next to metal. Salt is a particular enemy of dive equipment. Not only does it expand as it crystallizes, acting as a catalyst for steel, aluminum and brass corrosion, but the crystals are sharp enough to puncture BCD bladders.

Fortunately, a thorough rinsing with plain fresh water is sufficient to remove most of these substances. Warm water is more effective than cold water, and special sprays effectively dissolve salt. Divers should avoid aiming a high-

Storage

Once dry, many manufacturers have some specific recommendations regarding the storage of certain items. Otherwise, these general recommendations apply:

• The storage area should be out of direct sunlight (preferably completely dark) and away from car exhaust, electric motors and other sources of ozone.

• Rubber products should be stored unbent and unfolded.

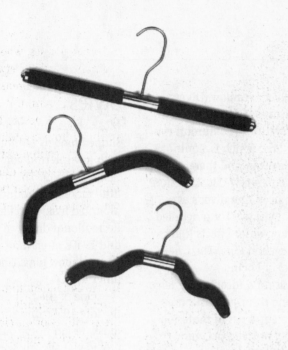

These exposure-suit hangers may be shaped to conform to almost any diving exposure suit.

• Clear silicone items should be stored where they don't come in direct contact with black rubber items, to prevent silicone discoloration.

• Exposure suits are best stored on special broad hangers intended for this purpose.

• If rubber products are stored for a long period, they should be sealed inside plastic bags to help prevent ozone damage. Even if equipment receives proper rinsing, drying and storage, it should still be inspected and tested for damage prior to its next use.

Corrosion and Deterioration: The Natural Enemies of Dive Equipment

The Chemistry and Physics of Diving section describes how readily oxygen combines with a variety of elements. This process is known as *oxidation*.

Most materials, in their natural state, already combine with oxygen (oxidization) and are called oxides. Pure metals, for example, are extremely rare in nature. Iron and aluminum ores are actually iron oxide and aluminum oxide. They reduce to their pure state only through the refining process.

Once pure, most materials seek to oxidize — to return to their more natural state. Steel (which is made from iron), aluminum, brass and rubber will all oxidize, given sufficient time and conditions. Some materials, however, resist oxidation more than others.

Steel, when alloyed with metals such as nickel, has greater resistance to most forms of oxidation. Such steel is commonly known as "stainless" steel; although even stainless oxidizes, given the right conditions.

Aluminum will oxidize, yet has a property in which a surface layer of oxidation can actually prevent the oxidation of the metal beneath. Aluminum, however, is more susceptible to a form of corrosion known as *galvanic action*. This type of corrosion may occur when two dissimilar metals touch one another. The electron flow that results may transfer metal from one surface to another.

Brass, which is among the most corrosion resistant metals, will also oxidize given sufficient time. Catalysts speed up oxidation. Because oxidation involves the transfer of electrons, highly conductive fluids often speed up the process.

Water is a fair conductor of electricity. This is why many metals oxidize faster when exposed to moisture. Salt water is an excellent conductor. Iron-based compounds, such as steel, oxidize (rust) rapidly when exposed to salt water.

Air, on the other hand, conducts electricity poorly. Metals stored in a dry-air environment oxidize very slowly.

Just as conductive fluids speed oxidation of metals in water, exposure to ultraviolet radiation and ozone act as catalysts for the oxidation of rubber. In rubber compounds derived from natural gum latex, ultraviolet radiation from sunlight and exposure to ozone cause the chemical bonds within the material to break down. This allows the material to combine more readily with oxygen and deteriorate.

Conversely, silicone rubber, which is not really a rubber at all but a synthetic substance derived from silicone, generally resists oxidation and deterioration.

Steel, aluminum, brass and rubber are among the most common materials used to make scuba equipment. The basic equipment-maintenance procedures — rinsing, drying and storing in dry air away from sunlight — all help inhibit oxidation and deterioration.

Masks

1940s-1960s
High Volume
Narrow Field of Vision

1970s
High Volume
Wide Field of Vision

1980s
Reduced Volume
Wide Field of Vision

1990s
Very Low Volume
Wide Field of Vision

A mask is the diver's window. Divers wear masks because of the differences between air and water. The human eye can't focus in water, which is significantly denser than air, and therefore, transmits light differently. Masks restore the air space in front of a diver's eyes, allowing normal vision. (For a detailed description of how water affects light and vision, see section One, The Chemistry and Physics of Diving.)

Masks consist of a faceplate or lens, a rubber skirt and a strap. Masks are made from different types of material, come in a variety of styles and may have a number of different features.

Materials

Neoprene rubber, sometimes used in less expensive masks, is usually black: the same color as the carbon that is a major component of this material. Coloring agents may be added to create different colors. Until the mid 1980s, most masks were made from neoprene.

Today, most dive masks are made from silicone. Silicone is usually clear or translucent — although, as with neoprene rubber, coloring agents can be used. Interestingly, the most common coloring agent used in silicone masks is black, to make it resemble the "traditional" neoprene mask.

Masks made from silicone usually cost more than their neoprene counterparts but offer several advantages that offset the price difference. The first is durability since silicone is virtually impervious to ozone or ultraviolet damage. Silicone masks may last three to four times longer than their neoprene counterparts.

Other advantages include comfort, since silicone is softer than neoprene, and photographic appeal, since most silicone masks allow more light to reach the model's eyes and face.

Styles

Mask styles range from simple oval-shaped models to more exotic models with low internal volumes and wider fields of vision. The first masks were little more than round pieces of glass mounted inside circular rubber skirts. Recreational divers in the late 1930s and 1940s often made their own masks from window glass and cutup pieces of inner tube.

One of the first innovations during the late 1950s and early 1960s changed mask design from round to oval. This provided a slightly wider field of vision and a better fit. Oval masks remain popular today among casual snorkelers due to low cost and the ability to fit a wide variety of faces.

The next major step in mask evolution took place during the 1960s. This was the introduction of wraparound and low-profile masks.

Wraparound masks feature two additional panes of glass along the side of the mask to improve peripheral vision. Early wraparound masks had a high internal volume, which meant that divers had to exhale more to keep the mask equalized during descent or to clear it when flooded.

Low-profile masks have a notched faceplate and a nose pocket that allow the diver's nose to protrude past the lens plane. This design puts the lens closer to the face and lowers mask volume. Low-profile masks are easier to equalize and easier to clear. They also offer a wide field of vision, but not quite as wide as that provided by wraparound masks.

Wraparound and low-profile masks remained popular throughout the 1970s. During this time, many active divers owned two masks: a low-profile mask for breath-hold diving and a wraparound mask for scuba diving. The mid-1970s, however, saw the introduction of a number of masks that combined features of both. This style became dominant in the early 1980s and new variations on this theme remain popular today.

The early 1990s saw further innovation. Masks incorporated prisms and extra lenses to improve a diver's view of the chest and simplify the use of buckles and straps.

Features

In addition to a choice of materials and styles, there are other mask features that divers may find desirable. These include:

Feathered skirt edges — On high-quality masks, the rubber skirt gradually thins as it approaches the edge of the mask. This makes the portion of the skirt in contact with a diver's face more flexible, thus ensuring a better fit.

Double skirt — Most better-quality masks have a second, inner skirt that provides a double seal, and a more comfortable fit. This second skirt usually extends around the entire edge, with the exception of the very bottom. This open portion allows water to drain more easily during mask clearing.

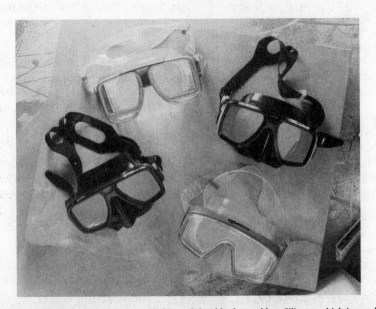

Most masks use silicone because it is more pliable and durable than rubber. Silicone, which is usually translucent, is often dyed black.

Strap adjustment — Divers may need to adjust the mask strap to find the best fit, and later to readjust when switching back and forth between wearing and not wearing a hood.

This is much simpler when masks have buckle systems that allow divers to adjust the strap quickly and eliminate frustration.

Tempered glass — Tempered-glass lenses resist scratches and, to a degree, breakage. If broken, tempered glass generally crumbles into a number of small pieces that are less dangerous than larger, sharper pieces.

Masks equipped with tempered glass may have the notation Tempered Glass stenciled on the lens or on the mask packaging.

Noncorrosive frame — The lenses of early masks were usually secured to the skirt with stainless-steel bands. Today most lenses are mounted in plastic frames comprised of several pieces.

Purge valves — Purge valves are one-way valves that allow divers to expel water from their masks without having to look up or break the skirt-to-skin seal at any point. Purge valves make mask clearing easier; however, most divers agree that mask clearing without a purge valve isn't significantly more difficult. These valves help divers with limited hand use clear their masks, and many divers prefer the convenience.

Choosing the Right Mask

Selecting the right mask is relatively easy. As with many other pieces of equipment, proper fit is the primary consideration. A mask that doesn't fit properly may be uncomfortable and leak — both of which are constant distractions during a dive.

To determine whether or not a mask fits, divers take the following steps:

1. Remove the strap or place it in front of the lens out of the way.

Broad Head Strap

Soft, Flexible Skirt

Noncorroding Frames

Tempered Glass Lens

Quick-release Strap Adjustment

Nose Pocket

Many divers prefer low volume masks because they are easy to clear.

2. Place the mask lightly against the face while looking up. The skirt should rest evenly along all of its edges.

3. Inhale slightly through the nose; the mask should now remain firmly in place, despite gentle tugging or head shaking.

Having determined which masks fit properly, the next step is to compare other features. While a number of masks may fit, some may fit better than others. If so, divers choose the masks that fit best and avoid selecting poorly fitting masks solely for other features.

Underwater Vision for Those with Less-than-Perfect Eyesight

New divers who lack perfect vision may have concerns about how well they can see underwater.

Underwater, divers with impaired vision can see as well as they can above water, thanks to a number of corrective measures. These include purchasing masks with pre-ground lenses to the diver's approximate prescription, having an optician bond lenses with the diver's precise prescription to the inside of the mask lens, or simply wearing contact lenses in an unaltered mask.

Visually impaired divers may be nearsighted (*myopic*) or farsighted (*hyperopic*), and they may even have *astigmatism*. Astigmatism means that the degree of correction required isn't consistent throughout the diver's entire field of vision.

Mildly myopic divers may need no correction at all. The magnifying property of water may provide all the correction necessary.

Many myopic divers can obtain satisfactory results from "optical" masks offered by many manufacturers. These masks have separate lenses for the left and right eyes. For each eye, the dealer stocks a number of lenses in half-diopter increments. By matching these lenses as closely as possible to the diver's actual prescription, divers may obtain highly satisfactory results.

The best possible solution for any diver — and often the only solution for divers who are hyperopic, but without astigmatism, or who have myopia with severe astigmatism — is to have an optician bond lenses ground to the diver's exact prescription to the inside of the mask faceplate. This provides precise correction and allows the diver to select a mask based

solely on fit — not on the fact that it is an "optical" model. Divers should be aware, however, that some low-volume masks don't provide sufficient space between the face and the lens in which to put prescription lenses.

There are many opticians who specialize in making prescription masks. Most dive centers can help divers arrange this service. The total cost is usually no more than a pair of good-quality glasses — often less — plus the price of the mask.

In some locations, selling pre-ground corrective lenses, whether in reading glasses or dive masks, is restricted to licensed opticians or ophthalmologists. In these areas, pre-ground dive mask lenses are probably unavailable through dive retailers. If divers live in such an area, dealing with an optician or ophthalmologist may be the only way to obtain a prescription mask, although local dive centers can undoubtedly provide divers with a referral.

A final option for contact lens wearers is to simply wear their contacts underwater. To do so, the lenses must be gas-permeable, so that changes in pressure won't cause bubbles to form between the contact lenses and the eyes. There is some disagreement as to whether divers who wear contacts underwater run a risk to their eyes, even when wearing gas-permeable contact lenses.

Divers who wear their contacts underwater also risk losing them if their masks flood. To minimize this possibility, contact wearers can close their eyes when flooding their masks, and sometimes they use purge-valve masks. This way, a loose contact may become lodged in the purge valve and won't simply wash away when the diver clears the mask.

Snorkels

Snorkels allow divers to breathe at the surface without having to lift their heads from the water. Scuba divers may use snorkels while swimming or resting at the surface to conserve the air in their cylinders.

To better understand the importance and value of snorkels, consider the following: The typical human head weighs 7-9kg/15-20lb. Imagine a diver trying to tread water while holding this much weight out of the water. Even with fins, this isn't an easy task. Divers who constantly lift their heads from the water or who try to keep them above water are essentially doing the same thing. Snorkels allow divers to breathe with relative ease while keeping their heads almost completely submerged.

The typical snorkel is a curved tube with an opening at one end and a mouthpiece at the other. As with masks and other equipment, however, snorkel materials and features vary. Which combination of materials and features is best for any individual diver depends on factors ranging from how the snorkel will be used to body size.

Materials

Most snorkels sold today are made from a combination of silicone and plastic. The upper portion of the snorkel, or barrel, is usually constructed of semirigid plastic tubing. The lower portion and mouthpiece are usually made from silicone.

Less common today are snorkels made from neoprene rubber. These declined in popularity at the same time as neoprene-rubber masks — and for much the same reasons. An additional reason for the decline in popularity of neoprene snorkels is that when used with silicone masks, the coloring agents in the neoprene tend to discolor any silicone with which they came in contact.

This discoloration is caused by the neoprene rubber compounds which slowly release volatile materials, including carbon (a coloring and preservative agent), into the atmosphere. Silicone, a comparatively porous material, will absorb some of the volatile material and black carbon released by the neoprene.

Features

Today's more popular snorkels incorporate a number of features. The desirability of these features depends on who will use the snorkel and the conditions in which it will be used.

Size — Most snorkels range from about

Modern snorkels feature vent systems to assist clearing and prevent surface chop from entering.

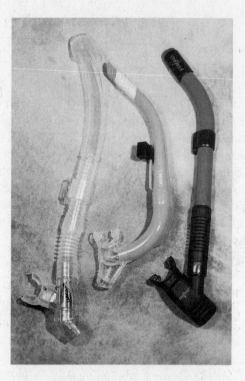

A flexible section near the mouthpiece can help keep the snorkel from interfering with the regulator.

35-45cm/15-17in in length (measured from the center of the mouthpiece to the tip) and from 19-22mm/0.75-0.875in in internal diameter. This contrasts with the snorkels of the 1950s and 1960s, which were typically longer and narrower.

Today's larger but shorter snorkels offer reduced breathing resistance. The larger a snorkel's internal diameter (or bore), the less effort a diver must exert to breathe. The shorter a snorkel is, the less exhaled (or "dead") air a diver will breathe at the beginning of the next inhalation. There are, however, practical limits to the length and internal diameter of a snorkel.

If a snorkel's internal diameter is too large, it may be difficult to clear water from the snorkel prior to breathing through it. Instead of being able to blow trapped water out with one sharp exhalation, a diver may find that exhaled air simply bubbles up through the trapped water. If a snorkel is too short, the tip may be close to — and often under — the surface, allowing water to enter.

Today's most popular snorkels are often referred to as large-bore models. These feature internal diameters of approximately 25mm/1in. Smaller divers, however, may want to consider snorkels with a slightly smaller bore. Due to the difference in body size, these reduced-bore models may not adversely affect breathing resistance. They will certainly be easier to clear. Smaller diameter snorkels may also have narrower mouthpieces.

Shape — Today's most popular snorkels usually fit closely to the contours of a diver's face. Again, this contrasts with the snorkels of the 1950s and 1960s, which typically had a deep, U-shaped bend at the base. Today's more contoured snorkels offer lower breathing resistance, less dead-air space and less tendency to trap water than older snorkels with deeper bends.

The barrels of most modern snorkels curve around the back of a diver's head. This has almost no detrimental effect on breathing resistance and offers a modest reduction in drag. It also reduces the likelihood of the snorkel bumping into an object or becoming entangled.

Comfortable mouthpiece — Few things in diving are as unpleasant as an uncomfortable snorkel or regulator mouthpiece. Fortunately, most high quality snorkels have anatomically designed mouthpieces that increase comfort and minimize jaw fatigue. In addition, the silicone mouthpieces on most quality snorkels are softer and more comfortable than those made of harder, less pliable neoprene rubber.

Offset mouthpiece — The angle at which a snorkel rests against the side of a diver's head is not the same as the angle required for the snorkel mouthpiece to rest comfortably inside the

THE EVOLUTION OF SNORKEL DESIGN

1940s
The first snorkels often had long, small barrels that increased breathing resistance and deep bends that trapped water.

1950s
The ball-in-a-cage kept water out – and sometimes air, too. Corrugated tubes trapped water and further increased breathing resistance.

1960s
The first modern snorkels had larger, shorter barrels and smooth contours for easier breathing and cleaning.

1970s
Adjustable mouth pieces and extra-large diameter barrels appear. Barrels are often contoured to fit closer to the head.

1980s
These snorkels often incorporated purge valves and flexible tubes with smooth internal bores.

1990s
Impulse Snorkel
Dual vent design aids clearing and limits surface chop entering the snorkel.

Snorkel evolution: from simple J-shaped tube to wide bore dual vent models. The vents on top of modern snorkels do not interfere with clearing, as did the earlier ping-pong ball designs.

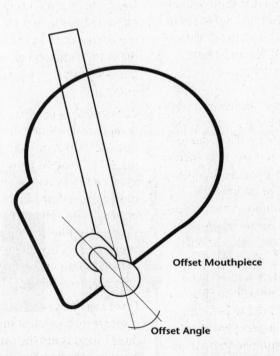

Offset Mouthpiece

Offset Angle

Appropriate snorkel offset ensures the top of the snorkel stays out of the water while the diver is face down.

diver's mouth. For this reason, the mouthpieces of many snorkels are slightly offset. Some mouthpieces even swivel, so the diver may adjust it precisely for comfort. The upper portion of the snorkel may swivel also.

Flexible tube — Depending on body shape and size, some snorkels interfere when a diver breathes from the regulator second stage. In this case, a diver might prefer a snorkel with a flexible section near the base. This allows the snorkel mouthpiece to drop out of the way when not in use.

Self-draining barrel or mouthpiece and other valves — Self-draining barrels or mouthpieces are now common. Snorkels with this feature have a one-way valve either below the mouthpiece or at the base of a separate tube that runs parallel to the main barrel. This valve allows gravity to drain the portion of the snorkel barrel that is out of the water.

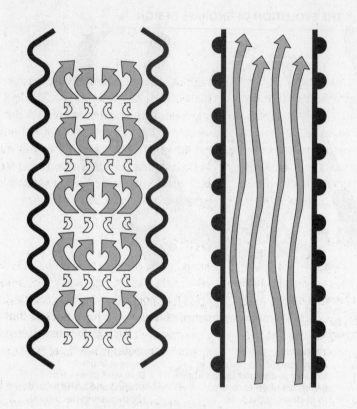

FLEXIBLE TUBE CROSS SECTIONS

Flexible snorkel tubes with internal corrugations can increase breathing resistance and trap unwanted water. Flexible tubes with no internal corrugations help avoid these problems, yet maintain the advantages of flexibility.

Some snorkels also incorporate an additional valve near or on the top of the barrel, which prevents water from splashing down the barrel in choppy conditions. This design allows water to enter when the snorkel is submerged, but doesn't interfere with clearing. Self-draining models account for the majority of snorkels sold today.

Colors — As with masks, fins and other equipment, divers may purchase a snorkel in a variety of colors. This makes it possible to color coordinate masks, snorkels, fins and other accessories.

Typically, the snorkel barrel and plastic fittings are colored. The mouthpiece and other silicone portions of the snorkel may remain clear or translucent.

Attachment systems — Virtually all snorkels come with some means of attaching them to mask straps. This may be a simple rubber or silicone snorkel-keeper that resembles a figure eight with an elongated midsection or a proprietary clip. Divers check the attachment system for security when purchasing and before each use of the snorkel.

Standard or "Figure-of-Eight" Snorkel Keeper

Various Proprietary Plastic Snorkel Clips

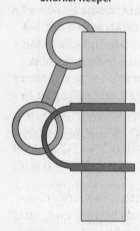
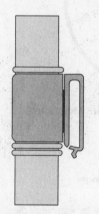
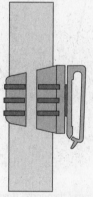
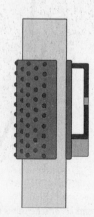

Snorkel keepers vary greatly. Durability and security are among the most important considerations when choosing a snorkel attachment method.

Fins

Fins allow divers to move through the water more efficiently than swimming with their hands and feet. While there is wide variety of fin materials, styles and features, all fins have two things in common: 1) foot pockets and 2) blades attached to those pockets, which provide thrust when moved at an angle to the direction of travel.

Materials

Most modern fins use composite construction. The foot pocket and the heel strap (if there is one) are usually made from neoprene rubber or a similar material. The blade is usually comprised of compounds called thermoplastics.

A less expensive method of construction is to injection-mold the entire fin in thermoplastic or neoprene. A more expensive variation is to mold graphite fibers, which provide maximum efficiency and performance, into the blade.

Composite construction contrasts with the norm in the 1970s when fins were usually made entirely from injection-molded neoprene rubber. While a few solid-neoprene fins remain on the market today, most diving professionals consider the composite fins superior due to their lighter weight, kicking efficiency, and positive buoyancy for most models (which makes them harder to lose).

Styles

Modern fins come in two styles: adjustable and full-foot. Adjustable fins have open foot pockets and adjustable heel straps. Full-foot fins have pockets that enclose the heel. Each style is best suited to specific applications but there is some overlap.

Adjustable fins are most commonly worn by scuba divers. They are generally larger and provide greater thrust. This is valuable when overcoming the drag created by scuba equipment and exposure suits — or when having to swim against strong currents.

Divers usually wear adjustable fins with wet suit boots, and full-foot fins with bare feet. When skin or scuba diving in water below 21°C/70°F (the temperature at which wet suit boots are generally required for adequate thermal protection), adjustable fins are the usual choice.

Adjustable fins have some drawbacks. They require greater kicking effort and are more expensive than full-foot models. They also require wet suit boots — something the casual snorkeler in warmer water doesn't necessarily require. Full-foot fins usually perform better than adjustable fins while swimming at the surface. This is because they are more flexible and have less tendency to break the surface of the water at the top of a diver's upstroke.

For these reasons, full-foot fins remain the preferred choice of most warm-water snorkelers and skin divers. Some warm-water scuba divers choose high

Composite fins with rubber footpockets and thermoplastic blades.

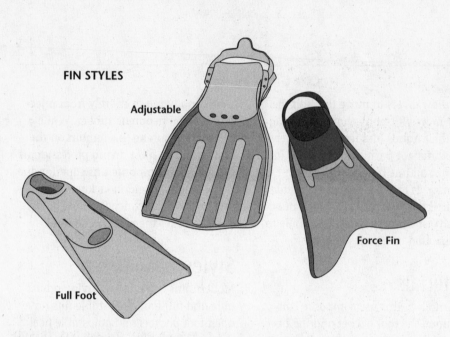

FIN STYLES

Adjustable

Force Fin

Full Foot

Divers may choose full-foot or adjustable fins. Full-foot fins are popular for snorkeling and warm-water scuba diving. Adjustable fins are used almost exclusively for scuba diving — especially in water cold enough to require wet-suit boots. The Force Fin is an unusual design popular with some divers.

performance full-foot fins over adjustable fins. Large composite full-foot fins — especially those with graphite-reinforced blades — provide adequate performance for most warm-water scuba divers.

In addition to the more familiar ad-

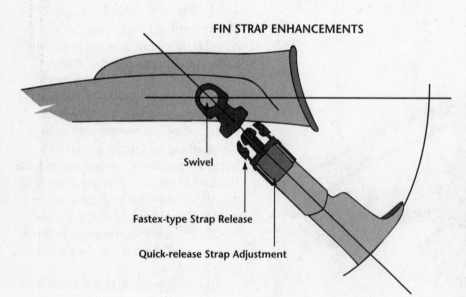

FIN STRAP ENHANCEMENTS

Swivel

Fastex-type Strap Release

Quick-release Strap Adjustment

A buckle assembly that swivels makes donning fins easier and reduces strap wear. Fastex-type releases allow quick fin removal. Ratchet style strap adjustments can make lengthening or shortening straps easy. Heel tabs give divers something to hold on to when pulling straps into position.

justable and full-foot fins, there are also a number of special purpose fins. Some of these aren't really designed for diving, but for activities such as bodysurfing. Other special purpose fins are designed for a particular kind of diving activity, such as competitive fin swimming or spearfishing. These fins typically have extremely long and narrow blades. Monofins, where both foot pockets are attached to one large blade, are also popular with competitive fin swimmers.

Features

In addition to materials, colors and styles, divers can choose from a variety of features. The choices include the type of strap adjustment and performance features such as venting or channeling.

Strap adjustment — For many years, adjustable fins were equipped with a basic metal buckle similar to that found on older masks. This arrangement, although reliable, made adjusting the strap difficult. Many new divers, in particular, turned to their instructors for help in getting their fins adjusted for the first time. Adjusting these fins correctly required powerful hands.

Today, many adjustable fins are equipped with buckles that make adjusting strap length quick and easy. Some of these mechanisms can even be retrofitted to older fins.

Some buckles not only adjust, but swivel. This makes it easier to move the strap out of the way while donning fins, and then move it back into position once the fins are in place.

Strap options — Some divers have difficulty gripping their heel straps when they try to pull them into position. For this reason, some manufacturers include special pull tabs on their straps. Replacement straps with this feature are also available, as are separate tabs that can be added to conventional heel straps.

When replacing straps, be sure that the strap matches the buckle. Straps may slip or become difficult to adjust if the

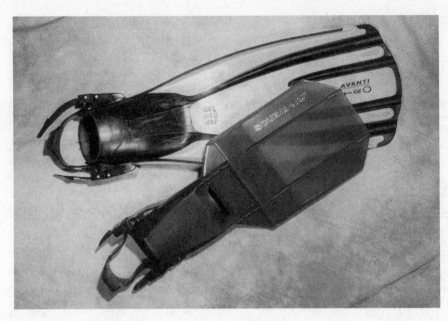
Vented and non-vented fins.

along the sides of the blade. Some fins have additional ribs running from the end of the foot pocket to the tip of the blade.

Some fins have additional blade area outside the ribs, running straight down from the foot pocket sides. This design allows this portion of the blade to contact water that has been undisturbed by the main ribs.

Vents — Vented fins first appeared in the early 1960s. Vents work on either the upstroke or down stroke. Their purpose is to reduce resistance to fin movement while increasing blade efficiency.

Vents designed to move water from the front of the fin to the back seem to work best on more flexible fins. This approach moves water out of the fin's dead space during the down stroke.

Vents that move water from the back of the fin to the front may be more appropriate for stiffer fins. They reduce the effort needed to lift the fin during the upstroke, in which less-powerful leg muscles are used.

strap molding does not suit the buckle ratchets.

Blade design — One of the areas of greatest variation in fins is blade design.

Ribs — Virtually all blades incorporate two or more ribs. Ribs add rigidity to the blade and act as vertical stabilizers to prevent the fin shimmying from side to side as it moves up and down through the water.

Most ribs begin along the side of the foot pocket, then flare outward

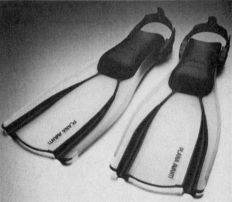
The flexible center section forms a channel on the upstroke and the downstroke to help maximize thrust and efficiency.

Channels — Yet another method of increasing blade efficiency is to design the blade in such a way that it changes shape during the upstroke and down stroke, forming a U-shaped channel in each direction. This helps capture a large quantity of water inside the channel and shoot it out the tip of the fin.

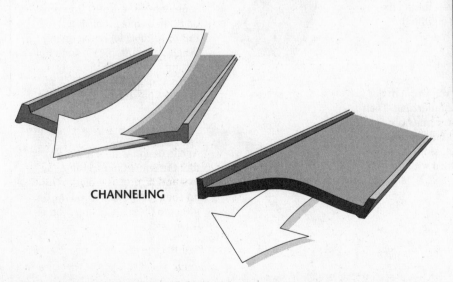

CHANNELING

Channeling causes the fin blade and ribs to form a channel on the upstroke and downstroke that directs thrust straight out of the end of the fin. It is said to greatly increase efficiency.

Milestones in the Evolution of Fin Design

Fins have a long and illustrious history. Man probably first envisioned fins when he looked into the water and wondered how he could emulate the swimming skills of fish. Leonardo Da Vinci, the 15th Century inventor who was far ahead of his time, sketched a diver wearing fins and webbed gloves.

Since then, there have been many milestones in the gradual evolution of the fin. Here are a few of these:

Owen Churchill's Original Duck Feet

Owen Churchill is credited with popularizing the first widely used swim fins in the late 1930s. Churchill's fins improved upon those invented and patented by Frenchman Louis de Corlieu in 1933. When placed next to one another, Churchill's Duck Feet fins resemble a porpoise tail. Even more than 50 years later, Churchill's fins remain popular with body-boarders and bodysurfers.

UDT Duck Feet

During World War II, the US. Navy's Underwater Demolition Team (UDT) members captured the imagination of a nation as combat frogmen. The fins they used were long and rigid with fixed heel straps. The most powerful fins of their time, they required huge kicking effort. More than one user said, "It's like having boards strapped to your feet." UDT Duck Feet fins were widely used by skin and scuba divers during the postwar years and on into the 1960s.

The Voit Viking

At one time, AMF Voit was a major dive equipment manufacturer. Their popular Viking Fins came from the era in which Lloyd Bridges first starred in Sea Hunt. Many present-day divers first started with these fins.

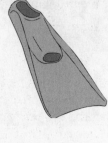

The U.S. Divers Otarie

The Otarie was one of the most popular snorkeling and warm-water scuba diving fins of all times. Hundreds of thousands of divers got their first taste of the underwater environment when they went snorkeling for the first time in these fins.

The Jet Fin

The Jet Fin was the first popular vented fin. When first introduced by Beauchat in France, it had a full-foot pocket *and* an adjustable heel strap. It was later popularized in open-heel form by Scubapro, who helped make the adjustable, vented fin a standard piece of equipment for scuba diving in the late 1960s and early '70s.

The Plana

The AMF Mares Plana was the first widely used thermoplastic-composite fin in North America and it helped reestablish full-foot fins as suitable for scuba diving. When an adjustable version of this fin appeared in the early 1980s, it quickly become one of the most popular fins of all times.

The Apollo Prestige

Apollo designed the Prestige so that the entire fin, including the foot pocket, acts as a blade. This fin channels water behind the fin, rather to the sides, giving it an efficient kick.

Choosing the Right Fins

Divers planning to purchase a pair of fins should first consider the conditions in which they intend to dive. These include:

- water temperatures
- currents
- special activities, such as underwater photography
- sharp objects or other potentially hazardous surfaces (e.g., lava bottoms, wrecks)

While full-foot fins may work well in calm and warm-water conditions, adjustable fins are better-suited for most diving conditions. Divers, however, must assess their strength — particularly in their legs. If divers have strong leg muscles, and if they dive often enough to exercise the specific muscles used while swimming with fins, then they may consider extra-large, graphite-reinforced fins. If divers' leg muscles

aren't that strong and they don't dive often, smaller fins may be more appropriate.

Divers should next compare features and fit, which are critical long-term factors in owning and enjoying fins. Comfort and fit take priority over features.

If divers plan to buy adjustable fins, they should purchase their wet suit boots first and wear them while trying on fins. This is the only way to ensure the best fit.

Here are some points that divers should keep in mind:

- Fins shouldn't be so tight that they pinch or cramp, nor so loose that they wobble when wiggling the feet.

- Easily operated strap-adjusting mechanisms are useful.

- Divers should have no difficulty getting the fin straps up over the heels of their wet suit boots.

Mask, Snorkel and Fin Accessories

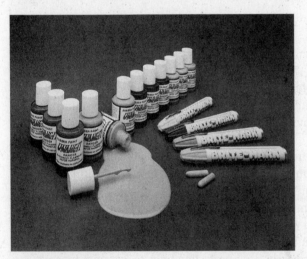

Marking paint, available in many forms and colors, helps distinguish similar equipment.

Many items enhance the use of masks, snorkels and fins. Among these are defogging solution, marking paint, silicone spray and spare-parts kits.

Defogging Solution

The interior surface of a mask lens may fog up due to moisture from a diver's exhaled breath or perspiration. To prevent this, divers have two choices. They may either coat the interior of the lens with a natural defogging solution (such as saliva), or

they may use a manufactured defogging solution.

Most divers find using an artificial solution more pleasing and more effective than saliva. Most defogging solutions work best when applied to a dry lens-surface and rinsed only slightly afterward. Divers should take care not to get undiluted defogging solution in their eyes.

Marking Paint

It is common for a number of divers in a class, on a boat or at a dive site, to have highly similar — if not identical — masks, snorkels and fins. To quickly identify equipment, divers label their own equipment with marking paint.

Special marking paint, which needs to be durable, is available specifically for dive equipment. It comes either in small bottles or in marking pens and works best when applied to clean, dry surfaces.

Preservative Sprays

Neoprene rubber and — to a lesser degree — silicone or plastic deteriorate due to exposure to elements such as ozone and ultraviolet radiation. Special preservative coatings inhibit this deterioration. Among the most popular of these are silicone-based preservatives and lubricants (commonly available as an aerosol spray) and polymer-based preservatives (usually sold as pump-action sprays). The polymer-based preservatives are similar to those marketed for use on automotive vinyl and rubber.

These products may be applied to items such as masks, snorkels and fins, prior to storage.

Divers should not use preservative sprays on regulators or dry suit zippers. Also, once rubber products start to break down, these sprays actually accelerate deterioration rather than inhibit it. It's therefore best to read the manufacturer's instructions regarding the use of preservative sprays. If in doubt, do not use these products.

Spare-Parts Kits

Small items such as mask and fin straps, snorkel keepers and cylinder-valve O-rings may break at any time. Therefore, it makes sense to carry a kit containing one or more of each of these items. Divers assemble these kits piece by piece, or buy them prepackaged from most dive stores.

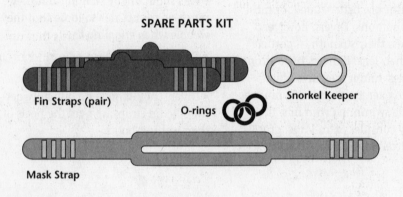

SPARE PARTS KIT

Fin Straps (pair)

O-rings

Snorkel Keeper

Mask Strap

An inexpensive collection of spare parts can save a dive.

Exposure Suits

Divers use exposure suits to protect themselves against heat loss and abrasion. These risks exist almost any time divers enter the water.

Water conducts heat away from the human body 20 times faster than air. Consequently, water has a far greater cooling effect than air at the same temperature. Prolonged exposure to water as warm as 27-30°C/81-86°F can be uncomfortable. Sufficient exposure to water below 24°C/75°F can be fatal to some people.

The underwater environment contains a number of items that can cut, puncture, scrape or sting and bare skin exposed to water becomes soft. Additionally, divers' lack of familiarity with some aspects of the underwater environment may prevent them from knowing what to avoid. Consequently, some contact with potentially harmful objects is inevitable.

This section examines exposure suits, which range from lightweight nylon or Lycra body suits, for abrasion protection only, to wet and dry suits, which combine abrasion and thermal protection. Divers use accessories such as hoods, boots and gloves with these suits to protect the head, feet and hands.

Body Suits

Lightweight, one-piece bodysuits provide sunburn and abrasion protection in warm water and may be worn under wet suits for additional insulation and ease of donning.

Before the advent of body suits, divers sometimes wore long-sleeve shirts and pants for abrasion protection when diving in water too warm for full-length wet suits. Others went without abrasion protection, or just used shorty wet suits. Body suits allow divers to wear full-length abrasion protection that is effective, streamlined and stylish. Even though body suits provide only marginal insulation by themselves, many divers wear them under conventional wet suits to make the suits easier to don. Another benefit of body suits is that, out of the water, they provide comfortable protection against sunburn. Body suits take up minimal space when packed — a definite advantage for travel- ing divers.

Materials

Most body suits are made from lycra, a nylon derivative known for its tremendous elasticity and resistance to abrasion. Lycra is commonly used in swim suits and other athletic wear. Some body suits use lightweight neoprene in the torso area — the area most critical for thermal protection. These materials come in a wide variety of colors so that body suits can coordinate with other equipment.

Body suits may use other materials, such as Polartech®, a fleece-like insulator, which adds significant thermal properties. Polartech suits are thicker than conventional lycra suits, but thinner and lighter than wet suits.

Styles

Body suits usually come in one of two styles: models that have a front zipper to make donning and doffing the suit easier, and zipperless models that usually have crossing panels in the front that allow divers to stretch the suit opening wide enough to allow entry. Some body suits come with short sleeves; though most provide full-length protection from wrist to ankle.

Features

Most body suits have stirrups at the ankles that the divers slip under their heels to stop the suit legs from riding up. Thumb loops make slipping into the sleeves easier. Both of these features are especially valuable to divers who wear body suits under their wet suits, because the stirrups and thumb loops prevent the body suit from bunching up when the wet suit is pulled on.

Wet Suits

Wet suits are the most common form of thermal and abrasion protection used by divers. Depending on style and thickness, wet suits may be comfortable in water as cold as 10°C/50°F and as warm as 32°C/90°F.

How Wet Suits Work

Wet suits prevent heat loss in two distinct ways:

Insulation — By placing a layer of low-density neoprene next to a diver's skin, wet suits greatly reduce heat loss. Neoprene is an excellent insulator, though with depth pressure compresses the foam's gas bubbles, reducing the insulation. The thicker the neoprene — and the shallower the depth — the greater its insulating ability.

Retarded water circulation — Wet suits get their name from the fact that water enters the space between a diver's skin and the foam neoprene. Because this water is usually colder than the diver's skin, it absorbs body heat until water temperature and skin temperature become equal.

As long as this warm layer of water remains in place, maintaining thermal equilibrium needs little heat energy. If water circulates freely in and out of the suit, however, the body uses additional energy to warm the new cold water. This is why snug fit is so important.

Materials

Wet suits are made from closed cell foam neoprene. The term "closed cell" refers to the fact that the bubbles inside the neoprene are not interconnected. This means that water cannot flow through wet suit materials as is it can through porous, water-absorbing materials such as a sponge.

The neoprene used to make wet suits varies in construction, thickness and linings.

Construction — There are two types of neoprene:

Chemically blown foam neoprene is made by adding chemicals to the raw material during the curing process. A chemical reaction creates gas bubbles, which remain trapped within the neoprene as it solidifies. Done properly, this process creates large, uniform bubbles with good insulating qualities.

Nitrogen-blown (or gas-blown) foam neoprene is made by special machines that force nitrogen into sheets of raw neoprene under pressure. When the

pressure is released, bubbles form. This also creates large, uniform bubbles with good insulating qualities.

Recently, new manufacturing techniques and the addition of special softening agents produced lighter, more flexible and warmer neoprene materials than ever. The only drawback is that these new materials are more buoyant, requiring divers to wear more weight.

Thickness — Neoprene comes in various thicknesses, ranging from 2.5mm/1/16in to 7mm/3/8in.

Thinner neoprene is appropriate for warm-water diving — 24°C/75°F and above, and for additional layers under thicker suits. Lightweight wet suits, such as shorties or one-piece jumpsuits, are usually made from this thinner material.

Thicker neoprene is for cold water suits — suits used in temperatures ranging from 10°C/50°F to 26°C/79°F. Most two-piece wet suits are made from neoprene about 6mm/1/4in thick.

Lining — Most wet suits have interior linings that range from simple nylon fabric to plush, synthetic pile. Titanium, which has excellent thermal retention characteristics, is also used as a lining on some wet suits. Titanium and plush-lined wet suits cost more than tradiional wet suits. Unlined suits, which fit very snugly to the skin and are consequently very warm, are now rare because they're difficult to don and tear easily, unless the diver uses lots of talcum powder or shampoo to lubricate the suit before putting it on.

Styles

There is a vast array of wet suit styles. This allows divers to select suits that are best for extremely cold water, extremely warm water and virtually any point in between. The more body surface a wet suit covers, and the more area in which a suit provides a double layer of insulation, the warmer it feels.

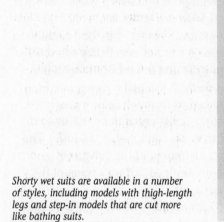

Shorty wet suits are available in a number of styles, including models with thigh-length legs and step-in models that are cut more like bathing suits.

Shorties — Shorties are one-piece wet suits that generally have short sleeves and legs. Shorties provide thermal protection for the torso area, which is the most important area for maintaining body heat. They are best suited for water above 27°C/81°F.

Of the various shorties, those with thigh-length legs are the warmest. These provide insulation in the groin area, which in addition to the arm pits, are important areas for heat loss (because major arteries pass close to the skin's surface here).

Other popular shorty styles include those with beaver-tail closures, similar to full-length wet suit jackets, and step-in models that look more like one-piece swim suits.

A variation on shorty design, that was mentioned earlier, is a hybrid suit that combines a shorty with Lycra sleeves and legs. This provides some thermal protection and full-length abrasion protection. Divers may also wear a shorty over a full-length Lycra body suit.

One-piece jumpsuits — One-piece jumpsuits are warmer than shorties. They provide both thermal and abra-

sion protection from wrist to ankle. Thin, 2.5mm /1/16in, one-piece jumpsuits work well for water from 24°C/75°F through 30°C/86°F.

Two-piece wet suits — Two-piece wet suits are the most popular of all dive suits, due to their flexibility.

Depending on thickness, two-piece wet suits may be used in water as cold as 10°C/50°F and as warm as 27°C/81°F. The jacket of a two-piece wet suit may be used alone as a shorty in water as warm as 32°C/90°F.

The most popular style of two-piece suit is the farmer john (or long john) and jacket combination. Waist-high bottoms were once prevalent, but have largely disappeared from the market. Another two-piece option is a jump suit worn over a hooded or unhooded vest. This and the farmer john combination both provide divers with a double layer of insulation in the critical torso area. Divers can shed part of the combination to dive in warmer waters.

Some jackets extend partially down a diver's legs — much like a shorty wet

Cold-water suits may be either one-piece or two-piece. Most two-piece wet suits consist of farmer-john-style bottoms worn under thigh- or hip-length jackets.

One-piece-jumpsuit style wet suits provide full-length exposure and abrasion protection in water of moderate to warm temperatures.

suit. As with shorty wet suits that use this design, this increases insulation in the groin area. It also minimizes the amount of water that may enter the inner layers of the suit.

Features

In addition to the broad range of styles, there are many features to consider when purchasing a wet suit. Some of these increase a suit's warmth, others increase its durability, convenience or appearance.

Increasing warmth — Among the features and options designed to increase wet suit warmth are attached hoods, wrist and ankle seals, spine pads and customizing.

Attached hoods — Because divers move through the water head-first, cold water may literally be scooped up by a loose-fitting collar and forced inside the suit, where it chills the diver.

One way to help prevent this from happening is to attach the wet suit hood directly to the suit jacket. With this modification, there is no longer a neck opening through which water can enter.

Wrist and ankle seals — Another way to minimize water entry and circulation inside a wet suit is to fit dry suit seals at the wrist and ankles. These seals are made from unlined neoprene and are tapered to fit snugly. Because unlined neoprene fits much more tightly to the skin, water cannot enter as easily. This provides many of the benefits of using a totally unlined suit with fewer of the drawbacks.

Spine pads — Due to natural spine curvature, a channel through which cold water can easily flow forms when a diver dons a wet suit. For this reason, a spine pad is a popular feature — an additional strip of neoprene mounted either on the inside of the wet suit jacket or farmer john. This extra strip fills the hollow space near the spine and minimizes water flow.

Custom fit — Because fit is such a critical factor in a wet suit's ability to provide adequate thermal protection, customizing a suit to a diver's exact measurements is probably the best way to ensure proper fit and maximum warmth. Although most people can find a stock wet suit to fit them adequately, custom wet suits offer the best fit, particularly for unusually shaped individuals. An added benefit of custom-made suits is that they allow divers to select color combinations and optional features that may not be available on stock suits.

Increasing durability — Wet suit features that increase a suit's durability include knee pads, bent knees and elbow pads.

Knee pads — The knee area on wet suits is subject to abrasion and stretching. This is usually the first area to wear out. When divers bend their knees, they not only put an additional strain on the area, they also cause the neoprene in this vicinity to become thinner as the material stretches, which reduces its insulating ability.

Knee pads solve these problems by taking much of the damage that the suit itself might have suffered. Knee pads also help reduce the damage caused by stretching and provide a double layer of insulation.

Bent knees — Another way to overcome the problems associated with knee-area stretching is cutting a suit in such a way that the suit's legs actually bend at the knees. When this is done, the act of bending the leg doesn't stretch the wet suit material as much. This, in turn, reduces wear and helps the neoprene maintain its original insulation.

Elbow pads — The elbows of most suits are subject to the same type of bending and stretching as the knees. For this reason, some divers elect to have elbow pads installed on their suits as well. Like knee pads, elbow pads help reduce stretching and increase insulation but reduce mobility a little.

Bottom pads — Since some divers dive off of rocky beaches by sliding into the water on their buttocks and because others spend significant time sitting, bottom pads can also help a suit's durability.

Increasing convenience
— Items that increase a wet suit's convenience include pockets and zippers.

Pockets — Many divers like to carry a variety of items with them underwater. For this reason, some divers elect to have utility pockets installed on their wet suit's thighs or arms. Such pockets may close with a flap, or they may not

have one. These pockets store items such as dive tables and slates, which divers may use frequently.

Special pockets for storing dive knives and tools may fit on the calves, thighs or upper arms. These pockets are generally designed to accommodate the knife or tool sheath, which remains in place while the diver removes only the knife or tool itself.

Some wet suit manufacturers recommend against installing pockets, as the sewing and gluing involved — as well and the continual tugging on surrounding material — may interfere with the suit's fit and durability. Many divers believe that the added convenience, however, outweighs these drawbacks.

Zippers — Zippers on wet suit jackets provide divers with a convenient means of entry and exit. Zippers on the wrists and ankles to make donning and removing the suit easier were once common; now this feature has almost disappeared. The newer, more-flexible neoprene used in today's wet suits has all but eliminated any need for additional zippers. These zippers also increase cost, inconvenience and water leakage.

Improving appearance — Many divers consider their wet suits a fashion statement as much as they consider them a means to stay warm. Features that may improve a wet suit's appearance include the creative use of color and finished seams and edges.

Use of color — Because wet suits are assembled from a number of individual panels, it's easy to make the panels from two or more different colors. At times, these panels may be cut in such as way that they deliberately improve the final appearance of the suit. Examples of this approach include pieces cut specifically to form contrasting accent panels or stripes.

Finished seams and edges — Finished edges are not structurally important, nevertheless, most divers prefer finished edges to bare, exposed neoprene.

ZIPPER MOUNTING

Interior Zipper with Backing

Exterior Zipper without Backing

When zippers are sewn inside a wet suit, both the zipper and backing material tend to form channels through which water may flow. Sewing a zipper outside a suit may not be as cosmetically appealing, but may reduce water entry and circulation.

The Advantages of a Custom Wet Suit

Custom-made wet suits fit a diver's exact measurements, tastes and colors. For many divers, these suits are a necessity, not a luxury.

Custom suits aren't that much more expensive than stock suits. Nevertheless, divers often end up paying significantly more for their custom suits because they order features, such as custom color combinations or special pockets that may not be available on stock models.

Taking measurements for custom suits requires trained professionals. Most wet suit manufacturers make this training available to their authorized dealers.

When getting themselves measured for a custom suit, divers should wear the bathing suit or undergarment they intend to wear under the suit. This ensures the most accurate fit.

Some custom suit measurements may seem highly personal, but are required to ensure the best fit. Fortunately, most diving professionals can take these measurements while minimizing customer embarrassment.

It's important that customers try their suits on in the store, and that they and one of the salespeople check its fit carefully.

Dry Suits

Representative neoprene dry suit with shoulder entry zip.

The first exposure suits used for scuba diving were dry suits — latex rubber suits that were difficult to put on and were easily damaged. The high-tech undergarments that make today's dry suits work so well did not exist yet, so these suits were colder, and because they weren't fitted with valves, often subjected wearers to serious suit squeeze.

During the 1950s and '60s, wet suits replaced dry suits for recreational diving almost exclusively. At the beginning of the 1970s, the first practical neoprene dry suits appeared. The early '80s saw the introduction of ultralight dry suits made from urethane-coated nylon.

Materials

There are three basic types of dry suit materials: 1) neoprene 2) lightweight shell fabric and 3) "crushed" neoprene.

Neoprene — Neoprene dry suits are made from the same material as wet suits. With these suits, the material itself

Lightweight shell fabric dry suits. The BCD compliments the dry suit design and provides clear access to critical dry-suit controls.

some of the characteristics of neoprene yet is more resistant to tearing, abrasion and compression at depth. Suits made from this material look and perform much like lightweight fabric suits in that they need separate insulation, but have more stretch and comfort. They're very durable, but heavy and slow to dry.

Styles

Unlike wet suits, which come in many styles, dry suits are available in only one version — a suit with long arms and legs. The differences in individual dry-suit models, therefore, tend to be in materials and features such as zipper placement or hood and boot attachment.

Features

Features such as proper fit and water-tight zippers are important on all dry suits. Other features may reflect diver preferences.

provides some of the necessary insulation. As a result, divers wear thinner undergarments with neoprene suits than they would with coated-fabric suits. The neoprene also provides reserve buoyancy in case the suit floods; a diver would still have the ability to become positively buoyant by dropping weights and or inflating the BCD. Their built-in insulation makes these suits popular for extremely cold water.

Lightweight shell fabric — These suits have no built-in insulation or buoyancy of their own. By using appropriate undergarments, divers can remain comfortable in temperatures ranging from 24°C /75°F to water's freezing point. Lightweight fabric dry suits, provided they aren't too tight, generally allow greater freedom of movement than neoprene suits. Some types, such as vulcanized rubber, are very tough, and they dry quickly, making them popular with traveling divers.

Crushed neoprene — This material was developed for commercial diving. It has

Crushed-neoprene dry suits tend to be durable. Their insulation and flexibility qualities lie somewhere between neoprene and lightweight shell dry suits.

Rubber-coated fabric dry suits are functionally similar to lightweight shell dry suits but offer greater flexibility and repair speed.

Fit — An important feature of any dry suit is fit. Although a dry suit should not fit as snugly as a wet suit, it shouldn't be excessively bulky or restrict a diver's movements while bending or stretching. There are specific methods divers can use when trying on a dry suit for fit. Dry suit dealers can show divers how to conduct these tests.

Most neoprene and some lightweight fabric dry suits are available in custom models. These are ideal for divers with abnormally long or short torsos, or whose height-to-weight ratio is outside the norm.

Modified Torso — At least one manufacturer makes dry suits with an overlapping torso. The intent of this design is to allow greater freedom of movement and make it possible for a diver to don the suit without assistance. The suit lengthens for donning, then folds over itself and secures to take up the slack.

Zippers — Zippers in virtually all dry suits are essentially the same: a special waterproof closure that was originally designed for used in space suits. The introduction of this zipper in the early 1970s brought about the resurgence of dry suits in the recreational dive community.

The greatest variable in zipper use is positioning. The most common zipper position is on the back, across the shoulders. This position puts very little stress on the zipper and causes it to rest against flat body surfaces. Due to its location, a diver needs assistance to close the zipper.

Alternate zipper positions include those that run up the front, around the back of the neck and back down the front, and those that run diagonally down the front. These approaches may allow divers to close their zippers without assistance. One suit has a zipper that begins in the center of the back, passes between the legs and ends up in the lower portion of the chest. This facilitates using the bathroom without removing the suit entirely, as well as self donning.

Seals — Dry suits use two different types of neck and wrist seals. Neoprene suits typically use seals made from neoprene. Lightweight fabric suits generally use seals made from a latex material. However, either type may be used, and it's a matter of personal preference.

Proponents of latex seals claim that they're softer and more comfortable, and allow less water leakage. They do not generally last as long as neoprene seals, but they can be easily replaced.

Neoprene seal users claim that such seals can be every bit as watertight as latex seal without being as tight or constricting. These seals generally last longer than latex seals but are more difficult to replace.

Divers should understand that regardless of the type of seal used, no dry suit is totally dry. Dry suit users can expect minor leakage, particularly around the wrists. If a fist is clenched, grooves and channels appear by the tendons on the inside of the wrist; this makes a perfect seal under all conditions impossible.

Dry suit boots — Most dry suits come with attached boots. Neoprene suits typically have built-in neoprene hard-sole boots. Lightweight fabric suits usually have hard-sole latex boots.

Some lightweight fabric suits come with latex socks. Divers wear conventional wet suit booties over these to protect them from tearing. This may require booties one size larger than divers would wear with wet suits, to allow the use of undergarment socks for added warmth.

Regardless of boot type, divers may need to purchase larger fins to fit over dry-suit boots.

Hoods — Most dry suits come with separate, wet suit-type hoods that fit over the neck seal. A few suits have attached hoods. These allow the head to remain somewhat warmer and drier; however, they may make it more difficult to don the suit and establish a proper neck seal.

Synthetic-pile dry suit undergarments, with and without windproof outer layers.

Thinsulate undergarments offer effective insulation with little bulk.

Undergarments — Among the most critical dry suit accessories are undergarments. These provide much or all of the insulation, depending on suit type.

Lightweight polypropylene undergarments may be worn under dry suits for warmer water diving or as liners for thicker undergarments. For moderately cold water, these garments may be all that some divers need under neoprene suits.

Synthetic-pile dry suit undergarments are designed to draw perspiration away from the body. This is an important feature, because moisture cannot escape an airtight suit.

Among the most thermally efficient dry suit undergarments are those made from DuPont Thinsulate® or similar synthetics. Such materials are not only warm, they are also relatively thin and so provide effective insulation without excessive increase in buoyancy.

Layering lightweight undergarments or using extra undergarments, like a sleeveless vest, over others provides the greatest flexibility in dealing with a broad range of water temperatures.

Inflation/deflation mechanisms — Specialized dry suit inflation/deflation hardware is designed for easy use with gloves and to eliminate water entry. The inflation valve usually fits on the chest. The deflation valve may also mount on the chest, or it may fit on the upper or lower arm.

Inflation valves use quick disconnect fittings, similar to those used on BCD inflators, though the actual valve is specific to dry suits. The inflator hose may pass over or under the diver's left or right shoulder. The best position depends on equipment configuration and diver preference.

There are two common types of deflation valve, the variable volume exhaust valve that divers can adjust, or a simple one-way valve that is usually worn on the arm. Raising the forearm vents air, keeping the forearm lower than the suit retains air.

The Pros and Cons of Dry Suits

The primary reason for choosing a dry suit is warmth in cooler water temperatures. Divers who are warm and dry throughout a dive tend to enjoy diving more, tend to remain alert and responsive throughout the dive, and feel like diving more often.

The key to dry suit warmth is an insulating layer of air. Undergarments trap air and create this air space, and without them these suits would be uncomfortably cold.

In wet suits, air or nitrogen gas is trapped inside the neoprene. However, even though this trapped gas provides insulation, a layer of water — one of nature's most effective absorbers of heat — still forms between a diver's skin and the neoprene.

Additionally, neoprene compresses with depth. This means that as divers descend, their wet suits lose the ability to insulate. With dry suits, however, divers can maintain a constant volume of air in their suits throughout the dive. Dry suits, therefore, provide roughly the same degree of insulation at depth as they do on the surface.

Another factor divers consider when choosing between wet and dry suits is air temperature. For example, if a diver is preparing for a boat dive in waters that are 18°C/65°F, given moderate bottom times and depths, a diver could be comfortable in either a wet or dry suit.

In certain conditions, however, dry suits and appropriate undergarments offer significant protection from the elements while divers change before and between dives. Some undergarments with windproof nylon linings serve this purpose.

Even though dry suits are desirable in some instances and vital in others, they aren't without drawbacks. Dry suits are the most expensive form of exposure protection, but the greatest drawback, though, may simply be the attention that they demand.

To begin with, dry suits require greater pre- and post-dive care and maintenance. No matter how tired divers may be after a day's diving, they still need to properly clean, dry, lubricate and store their dry suits.

Dry suits are bulkier than wet suits. This may make certain entries and long surface swims difficult and uncomfortable. Excessive movement may also pull on the wrist and neck seals and cause them to lose some of their watertight integrity.

A dry suit may become uncomfortably hot on the surface on a warm day. Because the air volume inside a dry suit is greater than that of a wet suit, divers may need to adjust their buoyancy under water more frequently when wearing dry suits.

If divers seldom dive in water below 21°C/70°F and don't make exceptionally long or deep dives, there is probably no reason for them to own a dry suit. On the other hand, if divers never dive in water warmer than 15°C/60°F, a dry suit may be the only suit they need.

Dry Suit Diving Techniques

Dealers and qualified instructors can provide dry suit owners with proper dry suit use instruction. The procedures included in such instruction include the proper steps for donning the suit, which vary from suit to suit and generally requires the assistance of a buddy.

Dry suits require more weight than any other type of exposure suit. The standard buoyancy check works well with dry suits, but it is important to ensure that both the BCD and the dry suit are fully vented at the surface. The exact procedure varies depending on suit type. Ankle weights may help keep a dry suit diver's legs from floating up due to air movement within the suit and reduce the amount of weight on the belt. BCDs with integrated weight systems are also popular with dry suit divers who may put all or part of the required weight into the system.

Feet first descents are mandatory in dry suits to ensure complete venting. Underwater, divers add air to their suits during descent to maintain neutral buoyancy and to provide adequate insulation. Virtually all recreational dry suit manufacturers recommend against using a dry suit for buoyancy control at the surface and encourage users to wear separate BCDs for that purpose.

Generally, divers use their suits to maintain desired buoyancy during a dive. If they elect to add air to their BCDs underwater, they must remember to vent both their BCD and their suit during the ascent. Divers should also avoid putting too much air in their suits (due to overweighting), because a large air bubble flowing back and forth through a suit is annoying and may lead to an accidental, feet-first ascent should too much air become trapped in the suit's legs.

Venting a dry suit underwater requires making the deflation valve the highest point (raising the shoulder),

and if using a variable volume exhaust, depressing the exhaust valve button. Because of the air volume in dry suits, divers make larger and more frequent buoyancy adjustments than with a wet suit. It is also important to ensure that undergarments don't bunch up and block exhaust valves. In an emergency, a diver can vent the suit through the wrist or neck seals.

After the dive, divers should follow the manufacturer's instructions for care and maintenance. This involves carefully cleaning the suit (rinsing prior to taking the suit off is a good idea) thoroughly drying both the inside and outside, and lubricating the seals and zipper. Be careful not to get sand or grit on the zipper while taking off the suit. Dry suits must hang up away from sunlight and pollution; the zipper should be left open and there should be no unnecessary creases or folds.

Dry suits aren't for every diver. If they're what a diver needs to remain warm and comfortable on cold water dives, they make a worthwhile investment.

Exposure Suit Accessories

Cold-water, bibbed hoods for use with wet suits. Dry suit hoods usually have no bib.

The whole body needs exposure protection, not just the area between the wrists, neck and ankles. A diver's head, hands and feet also need protection from heat loss and abrasion. Hoods, gloves and boots provide this protection.

Hoods

When left unprotected, as much as 75 percent of a diver's total heat loss takes place through the head. This is why hoods provide important thermal protection in water below 21°C/70°F. Hoods also provide abrasion protection for the

head and neck area.

Hoods come in many styles, thicknesses and lengths. Hoods designed for use with most dry suits are usually wet suit hoods. Most dry suit hoods, however, have no fit and end at the neck.

Cold-water or bibbed hoods are commonly recommended for use with wet suits. This type of hood has a broad flange that usually goes over the farmer-john and under the wet suit jacket. This way, any water that enters around the neck is directed away from bare skin and into the space between the diver's jacket and bottoms.

General-purpose, lightweight diving gloves.

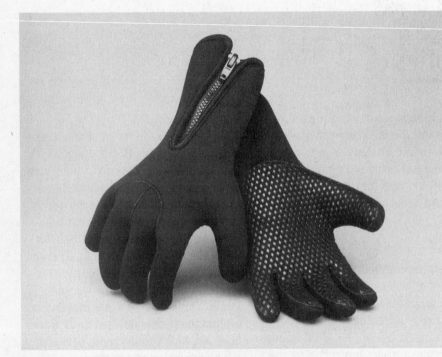

Five-finger wet-suit gloves with zip, suitable for temperate waters.

For extremely cold water or for use under a one-piece wet suit, divers may use hoods that attach to a sleeveless vest.

Hoods come in a variety of thicknesses. Individuals who dive in warm water may be content with a lightweight hood. A common practice is to use thicker material in the hood itself and thinner material in the bib or any portion of the hood that will go under a diver's wet suit jacket. Yet another approach is to use thinner material under the chin and around the neck for greater flexibility and ease of movement in these areas.

Many cold-water hoods have a ring of thinner, unlined neoprene around the facial opening. This softer, more flexible material allows a better seal.

There are even cold-water hoods with tiny cutouts around the eyes and nose and another opening for the regulator mouthpiece. This area is unlined and the mask seals on the outside of the hood. This approach minimizes the amount of cold water coming in contact with the face.

Gloves

Because the hands aren't very well insulated by nature and have numerous blood vessels running close to the skin, they are highly susceptible to heat loss. Heat loss is serious in hands, especially if it leads to a severe loss of dexterity. Divers with cold hands may have difficulty performing important safety-related tasks underwater.

For these reasons protecting the hands underwater is important. Depending on water temperature, divers may use lightweight, non-insulated gloves, wet suit gloves or thick wet suit mitts.

Lightweight gloves — In water above 21°C/70°F, divers may find that lightweight gloves provide adequate protection. Today there is a wide variety of lightweight gloves designed specifically

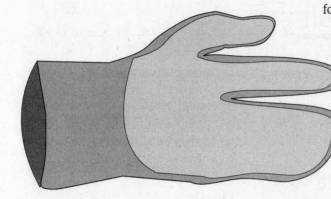

Three-finger wet-suit mitts are among the warmest hand wear available.

for diving. These specialized gloves, unlike many garden gloves, are highly resistant to rotting.

Lightweight gloves may come in a variety of colors that go well with other equipment. Many diving professionals prefer to use bright orange gloves, as students and divers can easily see them when looking for directions. Day-glo orange is particularly effective.

Neoprene gloves — As water temperatures drop below 21°C/70°F, divers may switch to thin neoprene wet suit gloves for additional thermal protection. Such gloves generally have five fingers for greater flexibility and dexterity. A variation on this design for moderately cold water uses wet-suit material on top and thinner, more flexible material on the palms. Many wet suit gloves fit easily over wet suit sleeves. Some even have Velcro straps that allow the wrist opening to fit snugly to minimize water circulation.

Neoprene mitts — For very cold water, divers use thick neoprene mitts. Normally, the index finger and thumb are covered separately, these are usually referred to as three-finger mitts. This design is effective for three reasons:

1. It contains less surface area than five-finger glove designs, resulting in less area through which heat can escape.

2. The less-used fingers can help warm each other.

3. The thicker material used to construct three-finger mitts makes separate finger appendages impractical.

Many divers don't like three-finger mitts, because they may lose too much dexterity. Nevertheless, such mitts provide almost the only practical way of keeping a diver's hands warm in water below 10°C/50°F.

Boots

Divers wear boots for three reasons:

1. For warmth in water below 21°C/70°F.

2. For protection against cuts, scrapes and bruises while walking to, from and around their entry/exit point, or while standing or walking in shallow water prior to donning fins.

3. To guard against abrasion and to ensure a better fit while wearing fins.

Most modern wet suit boots today have molded soles. These soles have a textured surface for better traction and to protect the sides of the boot as well as the bottom. Many provide additional coverage for the heel and toe of the boot and are contoured separately for the left and right feet.

Most boots have side-entry zippers. These greatly increase the ease of donning boots, and add to its longevity by decreasing wear and tear from donning and removing it.

Wet-suit boot. The side-entry zipper design makes putting the boot on easy.

Choosing the Right Exposure Suit

Divers tend to find themselves too cold underwater far more often than they find themselves too hot. The solution is to use adequate thermal protection for the conditions.

Water Temperature

The first factor for divers to consider when selecting an exposure suit is water temperature. Colder water dictates exposure protection that provides greater body coverage and insulation.

Divers should also consider depth, activity level, bottom time and weather.

For many temperatures, two or more suits may provide adequate protection. In general, it's best to select the warmest suit possible. Other factors, though, like air temperature and activity level, may require a lighter, less bulky suit.

Depth

Water temperatures often drop as divers descend, due primarily to thermoclines. Yet, even in environments where this isn't a major factor, divers must consider that depth affects neoprene's insulating ability. As pressure increases, the gas bubbles inside the neoprene compress, which reduces insulation.

At a depth of 30m/100ft, neoprene may provide about one quarter the insulation it does on the surface. This means that divers who go this deep may find that wet suits — no matter how thick they are at the surface — aren't adequate to maintain body heat at these depths.

This isn't a problem in very warm water, as only minimal insulation works well. Once water temperatures dip substantially below 24°C/75°F, however, dry suits may be the only practical means of providing adequate insulation at depths of 18-30m/60-100ft for an extended period.

Activity Level

Activity level influences body heat. Therefore, divers who work hard generate more body heat — and thus require less insulation — than divers who work less underwater.

Expenditure of effort prior to descent affects how comfortable divers feel under water may. Divers who have a difficult time suiting up, who must carry heavy equipment long distances to the water, who enter through surf or who must make long surface swims often welcome the opportunity to descend and cool off.

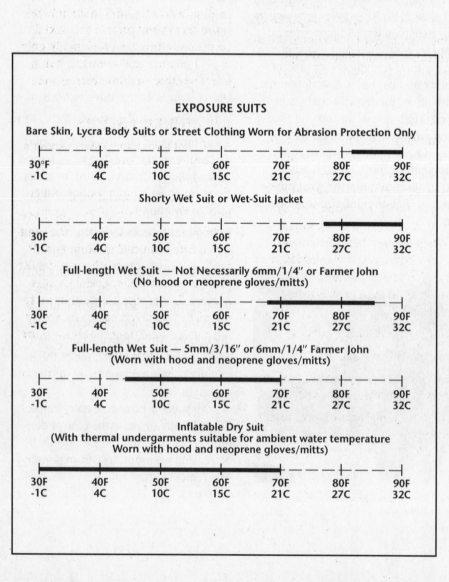

EXPOSURE SUITS

Bare Skin, Lycra Body Suits or Street Clothing Worn for Abrasion Protection Only

30°F	40F	50F	60F	70F	80F	90F
-1C	4C	10C	15C	21C	27C	32C

Shorty Wet Suit or Wet-Suit Jacket

30F	40F	50F	60F	70F	80F	90F
-1C	4C	10C	15C	21C	27C	32C

Full-length Wet Suit — Not Necessarily 6mm/1/4" or Farmer John
(No hood or neoprene gloves/mitts)

30F	40F	50F	60F	70F	80F	90F
-1C	4C	10C	15C	21C	27C	32C

Full-length Wet Suit — 5mm/3/16" or 6mm/1/4" Farmer John
(Worn with hood and neoprene gloves/mitts)

30F	40F	50F	60F	70F	80F	90F
-1C	4C	10C	15C	21C	27C	32C

Inflatable Dry Suit
(With thermal undergarments suitable for ambient water temperature
Worn with hood and neoprene gloves/mitts)

30F	40F	50F	60F	70F	80F	90F
-1C	4C	10C	15C	21C	27C	32C

Dive Duration

When deciding on exposure protection, divers must consider planned dive duration, the total number of dives they intend to make each day and surface temperature between dives.

To a limited degree, bottom time can be a mitigating factor when considering what effect depth has on exposure protection. For example, a wet suit that provides minimal insulation at a depth of 30m/100 ft may be offset by the fact that divers plan to remain there for only a few minutes to stay well within the no-decompression limits.

In general, however, extended dive time or repetitive diving demand greater thermal protection. Most surface intervals don't provide adequate opportunity for the body to thoroughly rewarm itself. This means that during a series of dives of identical duration, divers become colder with each successive exposure.

Weather

The weather is often the least predictable factor when divers decide what type of exposure suit to wear. Nevertheless, the weather may have a tremendous bearing on how comfortable divers remain, both in and out of the water.

When the weather is hot, divers must take into account the possibility of overheating prior to descent. Overheating becomes an even greater factor when divers:

- use full wet suits or dry suits.

- have difficulty suiting up.

- must carry heavy equipment long distances before entering the water.

- must make long surface swims prior to descending.

The possibility of overheating prompts divers to choose a wet suit over a dry suit or a lighter-weight suit over a thicker one.

When the air is cold, divers must consider the effect of both the air temperature and the wind chill factor. In very cold air, divers may become chilled before they even enter the water — especially if suiting up requires standing around in bare skin while donning one piece of exposure garment at a time.

One of the greatest problems with cold weather diving is what takes place between dives. Divers who remain out of the water in damp suits are subject to additional cooling due to the wind chill factor and evaporative cooling. This may cause them to lose even more body heat rather than allowing them to rewarm themselves prior to the next dive. Surprisingly, this is a problem not only in cold weather environments, but in warm weather environments as well.

Additional Factors

Additional factors that affect exposure suit selection are acclimation and frequency of use.

To divers who spend most of their time in 10°C/50°F water, 26°C/80°F water may seem bathtub warm. The same water may seem cool to Caribbean or South Pacific residents who spend most of their time in water several degrees warmer. This is why it isn't unusual to see cold water divers opting for shorty wet suits in conditions that have warm water divers reaching for their full-length suits.

Scuba Systems

For a long time, divers wore and used buoyancy control devices, cylinders and instrumentation separately. Many systems weren't even physically connected.

Today these items are most often part of a unified, multicomponent system that divers put on or take off as a single unit. Each component in the system relies to some degree on its physical connection with other system components to attain the maximum possible efficiency or convenience. Most common scuba systems include:

1 a single high-pressure air cylinder.

2 a two-stage regulator with an alternate air source second stage.

3 a buoyancy control device (BCD) that also doubles as a cylinder harness and may include an integrated weight system.

4 an instrument panel or console attached to the regulator's submersible pressure gauge hose.

Standardization among equipment manufacturers means that divers can assemble systems comprised of any components that meet their needs. With a few exceptions (that adapters can usually fix), components from different manufacturers work together.

Buoyancy Control Devices

Buoyancy control devices (BCDs) have long been considered mandatory equipment for divers. They serve two functions:

• They provide support for resting and swimming on the surface.

• They allow divers to compensate for changes in buoyancy underwater.

In theory, properly weighted divers shouldn't need BCDs to stay on the surface. They should be able to rest at eye level while continuing to breathe through their snorkels.

However, it's difficult to see or to converse comfortably with others from this position. Additionally, if divers miscalculate their weight or carry heavy objects, they have to expend energy to remain at the surface unless they have external support.

By using their BCDs for surface flotation, divers may swim or rest at the surface with little or no effort. They can also see what is going on around them more clearly and converse easily with other divers.

Underwater, neoprene wet suits change volume as divers descend and ascend. Consequently, buoyancy changes and must be adjusted.

By adding or removing air from their BCDs, divers compensate for this change in suit volume. They can remain neutrally buoyant at any depth they choose. When neutrally buoyant, divers move easily underwater and avoid harmful contact with reef animals.

BCD designed specifically for women incorporating expanding material below the shoulder straps.

Materials and Construction

Manufacturers make two types of BCD: those with separate, inner bladders and those with no inner bladders. Most current BCDs are bladderless, as new, tougher materials allow this design, which tends to be more streamlined.

Styles

There are four distinct BCD styles representing five different generations of design.

1. Front mounted BCDs

2. Back mounted BCDs

3. "Advanced design" BCDs

4. Integrated weight BCDs

The latter two styles account for the vast majority of BCDs sold today for scuba diving.

Back mounted BCD with integrated weight system.

Front mounted BCDs — Front mounted or "horse collar" BCDs were the first true BCDs for divers. They are direct descendants of smaller, inflatable dive vests designed primarily for surface flotation. The addition of large-diameter inflation/deflation hoses to such vests enabled divers to add or remove air underwater, thus compensating for exposure suit compression and expansion during descent and ascent.

Front mounted BCDs are convenient to use independently of cylinders, regulators and other scuba equipment, making them well-suited for snorkeling.

Back mounted BCDs — Back mounted BCDs were the first style to integrate the scuba system and buoyancy control device into a single unit and represented a major departure from front mounted styles. They remain popular among such groups as underwater photographers and models (since the BCD doesn't cover up the body as much as other styles), cave and cavern divers, and divers who regularly swim long distances on the surface.

Most early back mounted BCDs were designed for use with traditional backpacks. Some current models integrate the BCD with a padded, non-inflating jacket that distributes the load more evenly. Such jackets are usually equipped with accessory pockets and attachments. Many back inflation BCDs also come with an integrated weight system.

Jacket style BCDs — Jacket style BCDs were the first to combine the buoyancy characteristics of front-mounted BCDs with the comfort and convenience of back-inflation units. The first units appeared in early 1977. By 1980, virtually all manufacturers offered a jacket style BCD. From that point on, dive consumers accepted them willingly.

Jacket-style BCDs have either a single or a double bladder. Early single bladder jackets were similar to modern "advanced design" models in that most

Advanced design BCD.

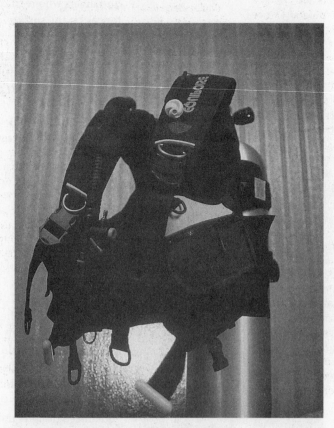

Advanced design BCD with integrated weight system.

of the buoyancy was concentrated under the user's arms. These early models, however, tended to ride high above the diver's shoulders, especially if the BCD was a size too large.

"Advanced design" BCDs — "Advanced design" BCDs got their name from the registered trademark (ADV) of the manufacturer that first introduced them. Generically speaking, these BCDs place most of the buoyancy underneath a diver's shoulders and have quick and comfortable cummerbund releases. Unlike earlier jacket designs, these BCDs don't tend to ride high above the diver's shoulders. This design allows the BCD to handle well on the surface and underwater, adding comfort and convenience.

Integrated weight BCDs — While the basic design has existed for a while, improved weight integrated BCDs enjoy greater popularity than their predecessors. Features include pockets with simple, yet secure systems for holding and jettisoning weights.

The Evolution of the BCD

Since their debut in the late 1960s and early 1970s, BCDs have changed dramatically. Along the way, several units became milestones in the evolution of the BCD.

The Waverly UDT Vest

This vest was not a true buoyancy control device, but it was typical of the surface flotation devices worn by many divers during the 1960s and early 1970s. Of all the vests produced during this period, the Waverly was among the most popular.

For many divers, the Waverly was the first buoyancy device they ever used. It helped educate divers about the value of inflatable buoyancy devices — but also highlighted the shortcomings that future designs would solve.

The Fenzy

The Fenzy was one of the first true buoyancy control devices. Its large-diameter inflation/deflation hose allowed divers to use it both at the surface and underwater. Made of heavy duty vulcanized rubber, Fenzys soon earned a reputation for being nearly indestructible.

The Fenzy introduced many divers to buoyancy adjustment underwater. The French, who made the Fenzy, even coined one of the most widely used terms for these devices: buoyancy compensator.

Soon after the Fenzy's introduction to North America, other manufacturers began producing functionally similar BCDs using less costly methods and materials. This hastened the acceptance of BCDs by the diving community. For some time though, the Fenzy maintained a reputation as the prestige BCD.

The At-Pack

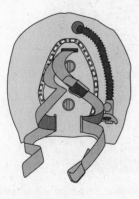

When first introduced in 1972, the At-Pack had some revolutionary features. It was the first unit to integrate a back pack, cylinder, regulator, buoyancy control device and weights. It was also the first BCD to come with a standard low-pressure inflator. Most modern BCDs incorporate a number of concepts that first appeared on the At-Pack.

The US Divers BCII

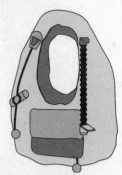

The BCII was one of the first widely used double-bag BCDs. Introduced in 1973, it helped establish the popularity of large, front-mounted BCDs with low-pressure inflation. Interestingly enough, the BCII was virtually the only widely used BCD that didn't use a combined oral/power inflation device.

The Scubapro Stabilizing Jacket

Scubapro invented jacket-style BCDs with the introduction of the Stabilizing Jacket in 1977. The Stabilizing Jacket combined the comfort and convenience of back-inflation units with many of the performance characteristics of front-mounted BCDs.

The durable, single bladder Stabilizing Jacket remains popular with many divers. As testament to this device's importance, the term "stab jacket" is still widely used to describe any jacket style BCD.

The Seatec Bluefin

The Bluefin was the first popular, double-bag, jacket-style BCD and was widely imitated by other manufacturers. Like the Scubapro Stabilizing Jacket, it helped popularize jacket-style BCDs during the late 1970s and early 1980s.

The SeaQuest ADV

The ADV succeeded in revolutionizing buoyancy control device design in a matter of months. The ADV first appeared on the market in December of 1984. By January 1985, other manufacturers started introducing similar designs. Within six months, a number of BCD makers reported that this type of design accounted for most of their sales.

The Sea Quest Quick Draw (not shown)

Introduced in 1990, Sea Quest's Quick Draw was one of the first advanced design BCDs to carry integrated weights of up to 13kg/30lb. By pulling on a handle, the user could jettison up to 9 kilograms/20 pounds of weights. This design, allows many divers to dive without a separate weight belt.

Features

Despite the wide range of BCDs, there are a number of common features. Some of these are simply "nice to have;" others are vital to comfort and performance.

Large diameter inflation/ deflation hose — A large-diameter inflation/deflation hose is essential and accomplishes two objectives:

The large internal diameter allows a diver to easily inflate a BCD orally, without the breathing resistance created by the smaller inflation hoses found on earlier vests.

Because it is mounted on the upper portion of the BCD, air vents from the BCD in common swimming and resting positions.

Low pressure/oral inflation mechanism — Virtually all BCDs sold are equipped with a mechanism that allows both oral and mechanical inflation using air supplied through a low pressure hose from the diver's regulator first stage. These devices usually have two buttons: one for either oral inflation or manual deflation and one which, when depressed, feeds air from the diver's cylinder directly into the BCD.

The "power" inflator buttons on some early mechanisms required considerable strength to use. They also operated in only two positions: all the way on and all the way off. Modern inflators typically require less effort to use. Also, by partially depressing these inflation buttons, divers can inflate their BCDs slowly.

Some low pressure inflators may be integrated or connected to an alternate air source second stage. Still others have special mouthpieces that enable divers

to breathe air from inside the BCD in an out-of-air situation. This is a difficult procedure and is generally *not* recommended except when no other reasonable alternative exists.

Manual deflation valve — To vent air easily at the surface and underwater, most BCDs are equipped with a manual deflation valve — also known as a "rapid-exhaust" or "dump" valve. To activate such a valve, divers either pull down on their inflation hose (which is reinforced with an internal stainless steel wire) or on a separate cord. This usually requires less effort and arm movement than holding the inflation hose overhead to vent the BCD. Divers who wish to vent their BCDs very quickly may sometimes use both deflation valves simultaneously.

Auxiliary inflation — In addition to oral and low-pressure inflation mechanisms, some older BCDs were equipped with auxiliary inflation devices. In North America, this consisted of a disposable

Cummerbund
Waistband

Utility Rings

Low-pressure Inflation
Mechanism

Manual Deflation Valve

Large, Roomy Pockets

Jacket style BCD, or "stab" jacket, with cord operated rapid dump.

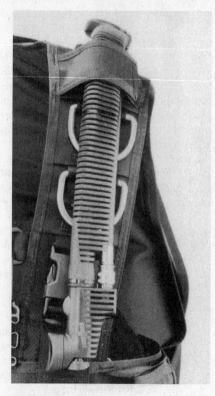

Slimline inflator/deflator mechanism with integral rapid dump.

CO_2 cartridge activated by a pull cord. These systems are extremely rare nowadays and their effectiveness at depth is doubtful due to ambient pressure, which upon release reduces the gas volume inside these cartridges dramatically.

European divers use a small high pressure air cylinder with a variable-rate valve. This system can inflate BCDs rapidly at depth and must be used cautiously to minimize the risk of a buoyant ascent.

Overpressure relief valve — These valves prevent BCDs from rupturing due to overinflation on the surface or underwater. They also prevent leaking low pressure inflators from filling and rupturing an unattended BCD.

Some overpressure relief valves integrate into manual deflation valves. In this case, the valve is usually located where the inflation/deflation hose attaches to the BCD. If BCDs have separate overpressure relief valves, they're generally placed at the lowest point on the BCD. This allows a BCD with a leaking overpressure relief valve to still hold considerable air.

Overpressure relief valves are generally set to open when the pressure inside the BCD exceeds the ambient pressure by approximately 2psi/0.14bar.

Integral backpack and cylinder band — With front-mounted BCDs, divers use plastic backpacks with waist and shoulder straps and quick-release buckles. These backpacks are attached to cylinders with either fixed or quick-release bands.

Some older BCDs are designed to be used in conjunction with these traditional backpacks. With modern BCDs the backpack is a permanent part of the BCD. In some BCDs, there is no backpack — the cylinder bands are sewn directly to the BCD fabric.

Use of quick-release cylinder bands on BCDs is virtually universal, as is the use of nylon — as opposed to metal — bands. Nylon cylinder bands fit a wider range of cylinders and occupy less space when packed in gear bags. When wet, however, they tend to stretch, making a once-secure cylinder loose. For this reason, divers dunk their cylinder bands in water before adjusting them or attaching them to cylinders. This helps reduce the stretching problem and is particularly important when the cylinder band is new.

The quick-release mechanisms on nylon cylinder bands vary from manufacturer to manufacturer. Most manufacturers include a diagram, either stitched to the band itself or molded into the buckle, to assist with rethreading. It is a good idea to avoid unthreading a cylinder band completely unless absolutely necessary.

Cummerbund waistband — Most BCDs use cummerbund-style waistbands, which have several advantages over standard nylon webbing and buckle setups:

Out of the water, they distribute the scuba system's weight more comfortably across a diver's hips. In the water, they hold the BCD more securely in place, and minimize the tendency for inflated BCDs to ride up. Velcro® closure allows divers to don and remove most cummerbund-style waistbands more quickly than conventional waistbands.

Because their size and feel differs from conventional waist straps, there is less confusion between the BCD waist strap and the weight belt.

Cummerbund waistbands are usually sized in proportion to the BCD. Some BCDs allow cummerbunds to be

Cummerbund Waistband

Hose Retainers

Built-in Backpack

Large, Roomy Pockets

Quick-release Buckles and Fastenings

Typical advanced design BCD, rapid dump is often opened by pulling on the inflation mechanism.

interchanged and some cummerbunds may be extended with extra sections. A correctly sized cummerbund should work equally well with or without exposure suits.

Pockets — Most divers carry slates, dive tables and other loose items. BCD pockets are often the most convenient place to put these items. Most BCDs have at least one pocket and some even have multiple pockets designed for specific items such as slates, tools and alternate air source second stages.

When selecting a BCD, divers note the pockets' location and assess the ease of using them in the water.

Hose retainers — When items such as alternate air source second stages and in-strument consoles dangle, they may become damaged or difficult to retrieve. They may also cause damage to delicate aquatic life. Most modern BCDs come with hose-retaining straps that help divers keep these items under control to protect the underwater environment. When purchasing a BCD, divers often compare the placement of hose retainers with their regulator configuration.

Accessory rings — Accessory rings allow divers to attach underwater lights, tools, slates and other items to their BCDs. This helps divers streamline themselves and keep their hands free. Generally, large accessory rings close to the BCD's front are the easiest to use.

Weight Systems

Most people are positively buoyant in fresh water, and even more so in salt water. In addition to this natural buoyancy, divers gain additional buoyancy when they don equipment such as exposure suits and masks. To offset this natural and equipment-produced buoyancy, divers wear weight belts or use integrated weight systems.

The primary component of such systems is lead — an element that is heavy and dense enough for a small quantity to offset the buoyancy of an air space several times its size. Even though all weight systems share this common component, they differ in design.

The primary difference is whether weights are integrated with the scuba system or worn separately on a weight belt. Integrated weight systems vary widely from manufacturer to manufacturer. The only feature such systems appear to have in common is that they provide some means for divers to release the weight to achieve positive buoyancy. As with most equipment, divers should consult individual manufacturers' printed materials and recommendations before selecting or using integrated weight systems.

Materials and Construction

The primary component of most weight belts — apart from the lead weight itself — is a 5cm/2in wide piece of nylon webbing or neoprene rubber. Nylon weight belts are by far the most common, although a few divers prefer neoprene weight belts due to their depth-compensating abilities.

Some weight belts also have compartments made from neoprene or other material to hold lead shot or solid weights. The quick-release buckles or mechanisms on most weight belts are made from metal or plastic.

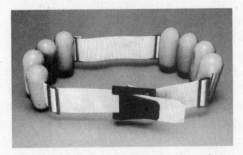

A standard weight belt, equipped with bullet weights and weight retainers.

Styles

Weight belts are available in at least three styles: 1) standard, 2) shot-filled and 3) belts with pockets. There are also variations in the style of weights that can be used with these belts.

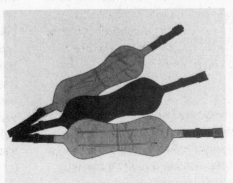

Shot-filled weight belts.

Standard weight belts — The most common weight belt is a simple 5cm/2in nylon or neoprene strap with a quick-release buckle or mechanism. This strap is threaded through the individual weights, which may be held place with metal or plastic retainers.

Standard weight belts have the advantages of simplicity and low cost. Their drawbacks are that changing weights is time-consuming and that some divers find them uncomfortable.

Shot-filled — Shot-filled weight belts have special compartments designed to accept lead shot, usually in small measured sacks. These belts conform well to the body and are relatively comfortable. If accidentally dropped, a shot-filled belt, being softer, may cause less damage than one with solid weights. They are not as durable as standard weight belts, and changing the weight is more difficult than on other styles.

Weight pockets — Some weight belts have pockets in which divers can place individual weights. The pockets can also accept bags of lead shot. It's quick and

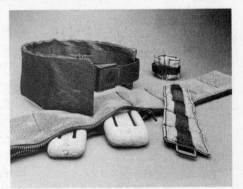

Weight belt with weight pockets.

easy to adjust these belts, and they have the comfort of a shot filled belt. Some versions of this belt are made from neoprene for increased comfort.

Weight styles — Lead weights for diving are available in several shapes and styles.

Rectangular block weights are the most common. The belt threads through these weights in such a way that it holds the weights in place (provided the webbing is thick enough). Retainers, however, ensure that the weights don't slip. Small block weights can be stacked one on top of the other or on top of hip weights. This allows for additional weight without using too much space along the belt. Some block weights are rounded for comfort.

Hip weights are elongated block weights that curve to fit the body. They provide a relatively comfortable way to wear significant weight and they help avoid stacking block weights several layers deep. Hip weights generally use less belt space than a comparable amount of block weights. However, many BCD weight systems can't accommodate them.

Bullet weights are cylindrical weights with rounded ends. Some people find them extremely comfortable. The belt passes straight through the center of these weights, so retainers are mandatory. Bullet weights usually come in 1kg/2lb size and matching block weights are also available.

Block, hip and bullet weights are available with or without a heavy vinyl coating which improves appearance, makes weight belts easier to see, helps prevent damage if the weights accidentally drop and helps reduce exposure-suit abrasion. Coated weights are becoming increasingly popular.

Features

Features common to different weight belts include the type of quick-release buckle or mechanism and the inclusion of depth-compensating devices.

Quick-release buckle — Most weight belts have a standard quick-release buckle similar to those found on older BCDs. Some manufacturers make a special version of this buckle designed especially for weight belts. These buckles may have some distinguishing characteristic that allow divers to differentiate between their weight-belt buckle and similar buckles (i.e., color).

Another type of weight belt buckle — and one of the only types that works

Quick-release buckle.

with neoprene belts — is the wire buckle. These buckles are easy to fasten and release, and eliminate excess strap. They complicate the process of changing weights, however, and some divers feel that they are more prone to becoming caught on unseen objects. Wire buckles aren't as readily available as standard quick-release buckles. For these reasons, a relatively small number of divers use them.

Other types of weight belt buckles are unique to particular manufacturers and at least one of these may be adjusted while fastened around the divers waist.

Depth compensation — As a diver's exposure suit compresses during descent, a belt that was snug at the surface may become loose. For this reason, some weight belts include a portion of elastic material or a special spring buckle designed to take up this slack as the suit compresses. Due to the inherent stretchability, neoprene weight belts provide this function automatically if they are fastened tightly enough on the surface.

Weight-Belt System Use

There is, perhaps, no equipment that divers take for granted more than weight belts or weight systems. Yet, how much weight divers wear, and how they wear it, has a tremendous bearing on their diving comfort and safety.

Properly weighted, a diver should rest on the surface at eye level while holding a normal breath of air.

How much is enough? — Properly weighted, and with no air in their BCDs (or dry suits), divers should float at eye level while holding a normal breath with a near empty cylinder. Weight also has a direct bearing on how often buoyancy adjustments one must make underwater. If divers carry extra weight that they don't really need "to help make it easier to get down," they also have to carry additional air in their BCDs to offset it. The volume of this extra air changes with depth, just as exposure suit volume changes. This causes greater changes in buoyancy, which causes divers to adjust their BCDs more often.

After suiting up, overweighted divers must carry the extra weight on the boat or beach. At the surface, they find their BCDs pulling up and their heavy weight belt pulling down. Underwater, they cannot streamline effectively and they encounter unnecessary drag.

Proper weight system setup — If the weight system integrates with the BCD (or dedicated cylinder-mounted unit) all a diver has to do is select the proper amount of weight and install it according to the manufacturer's directions. Divers must familiarize themselves and their buddies with the release mechanism of any integrated weight system.

Setting up a conventional weight belt involves a little more effort. The free end of a properly adjusted weight belt usually protrudes 15-20cm/6-8in from the buckle when fastened. A new weight belt will most likely need cutting to the proper length. When measuring where to cut, allow for the exposure suit; it's best to measure with the suit on. An additional 5-10cm/2-4in (or more, if the belt is heavy) allows for the webbing that runs through the weights and retaining clips. An additional 15-20cm/6-8in on the end attaches to the buckle. This extra length allows the user to lengthen the belt in the future, if necessary. If the belt has a depth-compensating device, trim each side of the belt evenly. Even trimming keeps the device centered behind the back.

Cutting the weight belt webbing with a hot knife prevents the ends from unraveling. If the webbing is cut at an angle, or the corners are rounded slightly, it is easier to pass through the buckle. A butane lighter (or other flame) may be used to singe the webbing if a hot knife is not available.

Once the belt is the proper length, the next task is determining where — and where not — to put the weights. The center of the back, where weights may catch on or interfere with the cylinder, and 10cm/4in on either side of the

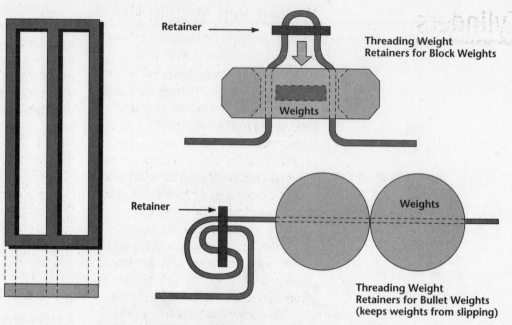

Retainer → **Threading Weight Retainers for Block Weights**

Weights

Retainer → **Weights**

Threading Weight Retainers for Bullet Weights (keeps weights from slipping)

WEIGHT RETAINERS

Two possible applications for weight retainers: holding a block weight in position and preventing bullet weights from moving about.

buckle, where they may interfere with its operation should be kept free. Anyplace else is fine.

Divers should divide their weights evenly on both sides of the belt. Each side should be a mirror image of the other. Nothing is more uncomfortable than a lopsided weight belt. Buying additional weights to get this mirror-image configuration is well-worth it.

Positioning the weights as far forward as possible (without interfering with the quick-release buckle) stabilizes the diver while swimming facedown and helps balance the weight of the cylinder when resting vertically at the surface. This may place weights squarely on the hip bones, which can be uncomfortable, particularly if using block weights. Women, especially, seem to

prefer their weight positioned farther back. If diving regularly in fresh water and marine environments, it is useful to determine the required weight change and design the belt to facilitate adjustment.

Once the weight belt has been set up correctly, liberal use of retainers helps to keep the weights in place.

Donning the weight belt — At one time, divers donned weight belts last, after the BCD and other equipment. This prevented weight belts from becoming trapped beneath the crotch strap of front-mounted BCDs. With jacket style or back mounted BCDs that lack crotch straps, it's easier to don the weight belt first, checking afterward to make certain the diver can ditch it easily.

Cylinders

High pressure cylinders form the heart of any scuba system. They contain large volumes of compressed, dried and filtered gas in a relatively small container. Scuba cylinders — sometimes referred to as "tanks" or "bottles" — enable divers to remain underwater for up to an hour or more, depending on factors like cylinder size, respiration rate and depth.

All scuba cylinders have valves — on/off mechanisms that mate the cylinder and scuba regulator and that may perform other functions such as warning divers that they're running low on air.

When selecting cylinders, divers may choose between two common materials, from among several different sizes and configurations and from a list of optional features.

Materials

The vast majority of scuba cylinders currently available are made from either steel or aluminum. Experimental or prototype cylinders made from stainless steel or fiber-wound composites have appeared from time to time; however, these aren't readily available to recreational divers.

Steel — The first recreational scuba cylinders were made from chrome-molybdenum steel and this material remains popular with many divers today. Steel cylinders are hard (and, therefore, resistant to external damage), and have good buoyancy characteristics. The primary drawback of steel cylinders is that without proper care, they may rust (a chemical reaction that forms iron oxide).

Aluminum — Aluminum is a softer metal than steel, making it more susceptible to damage from impact or improper handling. In addition, because it isn't inherently as strong as steel, the walls of an aluminum cylinder must be thicker. This makes these cylinders larger, heavier and more positively buoyant than comparable steel cylinders.

Like steel, aluminum corrodes; however, a thin coating of this corrosion (aluminum oxide) on the interior or exterior of a cylinder will, unlike iron oxide, actually inhibit further corrosion.

Stainless steel — In theory, stainless steel is a highly desirable material for scuba cylinders, offering the weight, size and ruggedness of steel, combined with the corrosion resistance of aluminum. Unfortunately, manufacturers haven't offered stainless-steel diving cylinders to large segments of the dive community, largely due to the high cost of materials and production.

Fiber-reinforced — The typical fiber-reinforced cylinder is a composite design, consisting of a metal cylinder wrapped in fiberglass, graphite or other fibers. The fiber reinforcement is usually confined to the cylinder walls, the neck and base of the metal cylinder (the strongest sections) aren't wrapped. This results in a compact, lightweight cylinder with a high working pressure.

Fiber-reinforced cylinders are currently used in nondiving applications. If economic, regulatory and other factors allow them to be used for recreational diving, these cylinders may offer the advantage of large gas volumes in relatively small cylinders.

Enriched Air (Nitrox) Equipment Considerations

Thanks to having more oxygen than air (which has approximately 21 percent), enriched air raises equipment concerns that don't exist for air diving. The concern is that as oxygen content rises, substances combust or burn more readily. This means that materials such as neoprene rubber, lubricants such as silicone grease, and contaminants such as dirt particles, may theoretically pose a hazard with enriched air, even though they don't with air.

There's been some debate as to how much oxygen it takes to create a potential hazard; some experts say that if a piece of equipment won't be exposed to more than 40 percent oxygen, standard air equipment is fine. Other experts recommend the gas industry's more conservative stance that any gas blend with more than approximately 22 percent to 25 percent oxygen should be made of special oxygen compatible materials, employ oxygen compatible lubricants and be cleaned for oxygen use. (This is called *oxygen service* equipment.) When enriched air has more than 40 percent oxygen, there's uniform agreement that oxygen service equipment must be used.

The cylinder used with enriched air can affect equipment compatibility. One method of blending enriched air requires putting pure oxygen in the cylinder, then adding air until ending up with the desired proportion of oxygen and nitrogen. Although the final enriched air blend may have less than 40 percent oxygen, the fact that the cylinder will be exposed to 100 percent oxygen during blending means that the cylinder must meet oxygen service standards.

In addition to oxygen fire/explosion concerns, it's also important that no diver accidentally use enriched air thinking that it's air, or use one blend of enriched air thinking it's a different blend. To handle this concern, enriched air cylinders must be specially marked and labeled. In some areas, there are special valves and regulators that prevent an air regulator being used on an enriched air cylinder.

The generally accepted markings for an enriched air cylinder are:

• The cylinder should have a 15cm/6in. wide band on the cylinder. The top and bottom 2.5cm/1in. of the band are yellow, with the center area green. The green area contains "Enriched Air," "Enriched Air Nitrox," or "Nitrox" in yellow or white letters.

• A yellow cylinder requires only the green portion of the band, with "Enriched Air," "Enriched Air Nitrox," or "Nitrox" in yellow or white letters.

• The cylinder has a label or tag that states the cylinder's oxygen content, the fill date, the analyzer's name, the diver's name and maximum depth at which the blend can be used.

• The cylinder has a special visual inspection sticker noting that the cylinder has been serviced specifically for use with enriched air.

Since enriched air has unique concerns that don't apply to air diving, these recommendations apply:

1. Only divers trained and certified to use enriched air should dive with enriched air (except under supervision of an enriched air instructor). Enriched air diving requires special procedures to manage potential risks not present in air diving.

2. Manufacturers have differing recommendations with respect to using their equipment with enriched air. These recommendations should be followed.

3. Enriched air should be put only in properly marked and serviced cylinders. Pure oxygen should never be put in a standard air cylinder, or one that doesn't meet oxygen service standards, because doing so poses a high risk of explosion or fire.

4. Air from a conventional air system should not be put into an enriched air cylinder because it can render the cylinder unsuitable for enriched air use until reserviced.

5. Using a regulator serviced and dedicated for enriched air on a conventional air cylinder may render the regulator unsuitable for use with enriched air until reserviced (consult the manufacturer).

Scuba cylinders are available in steel or aluminium and in a variety of sizes.

Styles and Sizes

The range of scuba cylinders currently available should make finding a size to suit an individual's physical dimensions and dive activities straightforward. Some cylinders even come in "short-and-fat" and "long-and-thin" models, so that divers may select a cylinder with the ca-

pacity they need, but which is proportional to their height.

In North America, cylinder capacity refers to the volume of air stored in the cylinder at its working pressure. The most common sizes are 50- and 80-cubic-foot aluminum cylinders and 71.2-cubic-foot steel cylinders. Aluminum cylinders in the 65- to 67-cubic-foot range have also become increasingly popular in the past few years. The capacity of European and other cylinders is measured in liters when the cylinder is empty. By multiplying this volume by the cylinder pressure in bars, a diver can quickly determine the exact quantity of air available.

When a standard-size single cylinder can't provide sufficient air for a particular dive activity, such as deep diving, divers can choose either extremely large single cylinders or double (twin) cylinders.

A variation on the multiple-cylinder approach is a system that encloses two or three smaller cylinders in a compact plastic or fiberglass housing. Such systems typically provide the capacity of an extremely large single cylinder, but with a lower profile.

Technical comparison of some commonly available steel and aluminium cylinders.

Capacity				Material	Working Pressure		Length		Diameter		Weight		Buoyancy			
Full		Empty											Full		Empty	
Cu. ft.	Liters	Cu. Ft.	Liters		p.s.i	Bar	In.	Cm	In.	Cm	Lbs.	Kg	Lbs.	Kg	Lbs.	Kg
13.3	377	0.065	1.85	Aluminum	3000	203	12.75	32.69	4.37	11.21	4.20	1.91	-1.60	-0.73	-0.60	-0.27
50.0	1,416	0.246	6.97	Aluminum	3000	203	19.00	48.72	6.90	17.69	21.50	9.77	-2.70	-1.23	+1.00	+0.45
60.6	1,716	0.271	7.68	Steel	3300	223	22.00	56.41	6.00	15.38	22.70	10.32	-7.10	-3.23	-0.25	-0.11
65.0	1,841	0.320	9.06	Aluminum	3000	203	18.75	48.08	7.25	18.59	25.10	11.41	-1.80	-0.82	+4.10	+1.86
67.0	1,897	0.330	9.34	Aluminum	3000	203	19.70	50.51	8.00	20.51	26.00	11.82	-1.90	-0.86	+4.00	+1.82
71.2	2,016	0.425	12.03	Steel	2475	168	25.00	64.10	6.90	17.69	30.00	13.64	-4.15	-1.89	+3.50	+1.59
71.4	2,022	0.320	9.05	Steel	3300	223	25.39	65.10	6.00	15.38	26.00	11.82	-7.60	-3.45	-2.30	-1.05
71.4	2,022	0.320	9.05	Steel	3300	223	20.47	52.49	6.84	17.54	29.40	13.36	-11.10	-5.05	-5.70	-2.59
75.8	2,147	0.424	12.01	Steel	2640	179	26.18	67.13	6.76	17.33	31.00	14.09	-5.50	-2.50	-0.13	-0.06
80.0	2,265	0.394	11.15	Aluminum	3000	203	26.00	66.67	7.25	18.59	31.70	14.41	-1.80	-0.82	+4.00	+1.82
80.0	2,265	0.394	11.15	Aluminum	3000	203	22.75	58.33	8.00	20.51	35.20	16.00	-3.30	-1.50	+2.70	+1.23
92.0	2,605	0.453	12.83	Aluminum	3000	203	24.75	63.46	8.00	20.51	37.50	17.05	-3.70	-1.68	+3.10	+1.4
94.6	2,679	0.466	13.19	Steel	3000	203	25.00	64.10	7.00	17.95	39.00	17.73	-14.00	-6.36	-6.00	-2.73
103.5	2,931	0.637	18.04	Steel	2400	162	26.50	67.95	7.80	20.00	44.00	20.00	-7.76	-3.53	+3.50	+1.59

Cylinder Capacity in Metric and Imperial

It's easy to calculate cylinder capacity and the volume of gas that a cylinder contains at any time, even though differences in cylinder markings and nomenclature appear to complicate international comparison.

To determine the cylinder maximum capacity and the amount of air it has at a given pressure, one must first know the internal volume (also called "water capacity," since this is how much water the cylinder would hold). Multiplying the internal volume by the actual cylinder pressure gives how much gas the cylinder has at that pressure. Multiplying the internal volume by the maximum working pressure gives the volume of the cylinder when full (sometimes called "free air").

Countries using the metric system usually refer to a cylinder by its internal capacity in litres, and its working pressure in bar. This information is stamped on to the cylinder neck. For example, a cylinder may be described as "12 litre, 232 bar" or "10 litre, 200 bar."

Countries using the imperial system traditionally refer to cylinders by their air capacity when full in cubic feet. For example 50ft³, 71.2ft³ or 80ft³. Newer cylinders have this stamped on them, though older cylinders often didn't. With some cylinders, it's not always obvious. The "71.2" cylinder, for example, only holds this volume if overfilled by 10 percent, an acceptable practice if there is a "+" sign stamped next to the working pressure or hydrostatic test date. Imperial system cylinders don't have their internal capacity marked on them, but this can be determined by dividing the maximum capacity in cubic feet by the working pressure (stamped on the cylinder neck or shoulder) in atmospheres.

To compare cylinder capacity, use the following equivalent:

$$1 \text{ ft}^3 = 28.3 \text{ litres}$$

Sample Calculations:

metric

A 12 lt cylinder, filled to 232 bar, contains 12 x 232 = 2784 lt of free air.

To convert to imperial:

Given 28.3 lt = 1 ft³

2784 ÷ 28.3 = 98.4 ft³

Therefore, a 12 lt, 232 bar cylinder (a common size in Europe) holds 2784 lt or 98.4 ft³ of air when full (at its maximum working pressure.)

imperial

An 80 ft³ (from manufacturer) cylinder has a working pressure of 3000 psi (from cylinder neck)

3000 psi ÷ 14.7 = 204.1 atm

80 ft³ ÷ 204.1 atm = .4 ft³ internal capacity

converting to metric:

Given 28.3 lt = 1 ft³

4 ft³ x 28.3 = 11.3 lt internal capacity

Features

Scuba cylinders may offer a number of features, ranging from a choice of exterior coatings to a particular type of valve.

Coatings — Scuba cylinders, either steel or aluminum, require coatings for different reasons.

Left uncoated, the exterior of a steel cylinder corrodes rapidly, due to exposure to fresh and salt water, and even to atmospheric moisture. To prevent this, most steel cylinders are galvanized — a process in which the bare cylinder is immersed in a bath of molten zinc which bonds with the steel, creating a corrosion proof barrier.

Newly galvanized cylinders have a shiny silver, metallic appearance — similar to that of new metal refuse containers. With age, the color changes to a duller, more uniform gray.

It is also possible to coat steel cylinders with a cold zinc spray. When freshly coated, such cylinders still lack the distinctive shiny, mottled appearance of newly galvanized cylinders. This nongalvanized zinc coating doesn't last as long.

For appearance, galvanized steel cylinders may require an additional coating of paint or vinyl. This in no way harms the cylinder, however, it's important to make a distinction between this process and that used on certain older steel cylinders, which were simply painted or coated, but never galvanized. On a coated, but nongalvanized cylinder, water may enter through a scratch, nick or pinprick in the coating and become trapped. This may lead to rapid corrosion in an unseen and undetectable area. Such cylinders are best stripped of their coatings, cleaned of any corrosion and galvanized.

For similar reasons, steel cylinders that have any type of paint or coating on the interior should have it removed. Coating the interior of steel cylinders was common between the early 1950s and 1974. These cylinders, however, cannot be visually inspected effectively because extensive interior corrosion could be trapped out of sight. Surviving cylinders from this era have usually had their interior coating removed through tumbling or sandblasting.

Strictly speaking, aluminum diving cylinders need no coating. Uncoated aluminum quickly acquires a thin layer of aluminum oxide. As mentioned previously, this effectively blocks further corrosion.

Nevertheless, most aluminum cylinders are painted or epoxied for cosmetic reasons. This external coating may become partially worn, and the result is a cylinder that looks used and worn. If this isn't acceptable, either strip the remaining coating or have the cylinder recoated.

An uncoated aluminum cylinder turns a dull gray — a color remarkably similar to that of a well used galvanized steel cylinder. A recoated cylinder can be almost any color the owner chooses. It is important, however, not to use heat as part of the recoating process. Temperatures above 82°C/180°F can weaken the aluminum to the point where it no longer safely holds air under pressure.

Boots — The bottoms of steel cylinders are round, therefore they cannot stand upright by themselves. Aluminum cylinders have flat bottoms — but nevertheless can cause damage to the surfaces upon which they stand or, conversely, receive damage from those surfaces. For these reasons, cylinders usually come equipped with a plastic, vinyl or rubber cylinder boot.

The best boots allow easy drainage, so that water won't become trapped between the boot and the cylinder and cause corrosion or salt buildup. Some boots also have a rim that isn't perfectly round. This helps keep the cylinder from rolling when stored on its side.

Valve types — Although most divers buy cylinders that come with appropriate valves, some divers may have reason to change. For example, divers may choose valves for single or double-cylinder setups that allow the use of more that one regulator.

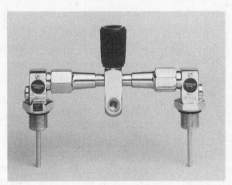

A dual-tank manifold connects two scuba cylinders.

Single-cylinder and double-cylinder valves — Single-cylinder valves are fairly straightforward. They have a threaded end that screws into the cylinder neck and which seals with a large O-ring.

At this end of the valve there is also a narrow pipe — sometimes called a snorkel or a dip tube— that extends down into the cylinder. This tube is designed to prevent moisture or contaminants in the cylinder from restricting or blocking airflow through the valve when its user is inverted.

The balance of the valve is comprised of a simple on/off valve assembly and handwheel, and either an o-ring sealed yoke mount or a five or seven thread female DIN fitting. Yoke mounts and five thread DIN fittings may be used at up to 200 bar/3000 psi. Seven thread DIN fittings should be used at higher working pressures.

The preferred system for a double

A standard cylinder valve with a five thread DIN fitting.

or twin cylinder system is a dual-cylinder manifold. The ends of this manifold are similar to single cylinder valves. These ends join by a fairly heavy duty crosspiece that has a valve outlet in the center.

The greatest advantage of these manifolds is their strength, which adds to the overall rigidity of the double-cylinder system.

Dual-regulator valves — Certain dive activities require divers to use two separate regulators that are connected to the same air supply. This is standard practice in cave diving, and is regularly used in technical, wreck and deep diving.

The single-cylinder version of such a valve is known as a Y or slingshot valve, or H valve. With these valves, two separate stems emerge from a single neck, each topped with a pillar valve similar to those found on the early scuba cylinders.

The dual-cylinder version, known as a dual-valve manifold, looks very much like a standard dual-cylinder manifold, except that there is an extra valve outlet on top of the right-hand cylinder.

With both versions, divers may turn off the air supply to a free-flowing regulator without affecting the airflow to the alternate unit.

A Y-valve is the equivalent of a dual-valve manifold for single cylinders.

Reserve and nonreserve valves — Until recently, most cylinder valves, with the exception of the single-cylinder Y or slingshot valve, were available in reserve and nonreserve versions.

A K-valve is a simple on/off valve. A J-valve contains a spring-loaded reserve mechanism that, if activated, restricts a diver's air supply when the

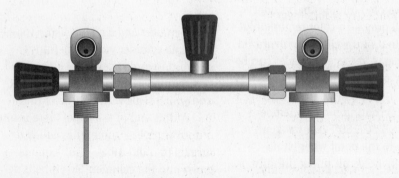

A dual-valve manifold allows fitting two separate regulators to twin scuba cylinders.

K-valve (left) and J-valve with reserve mechanism.

diver reaches a certain cylinder pressure — usually 20 bar/300 psi. Pulling down on the lever that activates the mechanism restarts the airflow. The purpose of a J-valve is to provide divers with a warning that they are running low on air.

Reserve valves were common before submersible pressure gauges became widely available. Today few recreational divers use them, but J-valves still exist in rental inventories. Some of the existing J-valves still work as designed, others have been deactivated to become simple on-off valves. Check with the rental facility to learn whether a J-valve works as a reserve valve or not.

Burst disk — All scuba cylinders have a maximum working pressure past which they shouldn't be filled during normal use. To help make certain that the pressure inside a cylinder doesn't accidentally go beyond this, some cylinder valves have a device known as a burst disk. This device is an industry requirement in North America.

A burst-disk assembly consists of a thin copper disk held in place with a gasket and a vented plug. If cylinder pressure rises to approximately 140 percent of the working pressure, the disk ruptures, and the air escapes through the vented plug.

Burst disks protect against damage

that may occur when a cylinder is over filled. While many compressors incorporate over pressure release devices that prevent filling over a particular pressure, others may continue to run until the pressure becomes so great that damage to either the compressor or the cylinder occurs. Some filling systems incorporate high pressure air banks and are capable of over filling scuba cylinders very quickly. These systems rely on operator efficiency to prevent burst disk rupture.

Burst disks usually rupture when full cylinders sit in a very hot area for long periods. As mentioned in The Chemistry and Physics of Diving section, heat causes the pressure inside a cylinder to rise several hundred psi or several dozen bar. If the burst disk is old — or if a burst disk has the wrong pressure rating — this rise in pressure may be sufficient to cause rupture.

In newer burst disk assemblies the vented plug directs the escaping air to both sides of the valve instead of straight out. This is safer because the escaping air won't cause the cylinder to spin.

O-rings — Cylinder valves rely on small O-rings at the orifice to form an airtight seal with the regulator. Cylinder valves manufactured during the 1960s and early 1970s use smaller, more rounded O-rings. The newest cylinder valves use even smaller O-rings. Cylinder valve O-rings seals rely more on air pressure than the pressure created by tightening the regulator yoke screw or DIN fitting to make a seal.

O-rings wear out or become lost on a regular basis. Spare O-rings can prevent dive cancellation due to the lack of an inexpensive and easily replaced part. Do not damage the sealing surfaces when removing old O-rings.

Cylinder valves also have a large O-ring around the stem that threads into the cylinder neck. This is a dealer-serviceable item that seldom causes problems in the field. Divers generally don't concern themselves with this O-ring.

Deciphering Cylinder-Neck Hieroglyphics

For many divers, the markings stamped on the necks of their cylinders are simply a mysterious code. Fortunately, divers usually only need to know that their cylinders will require the annual inspections and periodic pressure testing indicated on their cylinders' inspection decals. The professionals at a local dive store will be able to interpret all other markings, fill the cylinder to the proper pressure and alert the cylinder owner to anything else of importance that the markings could indicate.

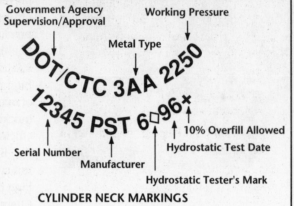

CYLINDER NECK MARKINGS

Government Agency Supervision/Approval
Working Pressure
Metal Type
DOT/CTC 3AA 2250
12345 PST 6◻96✦
Serial Number
Manufacturer
10% Overfill Allowed
Hydrostatic Test Date
Hydrostatic Tester's Mark

Divers who are interested in exactly what the markings mean will find that they are not that difficult to decipher.

Imperial information

The information that follows pertains to cylinders manufactured or distributed in North America. Similar information on cylinders made or sold in other parts of the world should be readily obtainable in those areas.

The First Row

The first row of cylinder markings will contain the following information:

• Government Approval — The first set of characters will usually be either DOT or DOT/CTC. These initials stand for the US Department of Transportation and the Canadian Transportation Commission. Older cylinders may bear the notation ICC for Interstate Commerce Commission.

The authority of the Department of Transportation to regulate the manufacture, sale and use of scuba cylinders in the United States comes primarily from its responsibility to oversee the transportation of high-pressure cylinders across state lines on common carriers. There are many areas in which the sale and use of scuba cylinders doesn't technically fall under the jurisdiction of DOT. Nevertheless, it has become an effective standard of practice in the United States to only sell and use scuba cylinders that meet DOT specifications.

Metal Type — The next set of characters in the first row denotes the type of metal used in the cylinder.

The designation 3A denotes carbon steel. This was used in very early scuba cylinders. It isn't considered desirable in that it is more prone to corrosion than chrome-molybdenum steel or aluminum.

3AA is the designation for chrome-molybdenum steel. It appears on virtually all steel scuba cylinders in use today.

Aluminum cylinders may bear the designations SP6498, E6498 or 3AL. The first two designations identify the special permit numbers under which aluminum scuba cylinders were originally manufactured. 3AL is the permanent designation for the DOT-approved alloy used in aluminum cylinder manufacture. All scuba cylinders manufactured or hydro-tested in the

United States after July 1, 1982 bear this designation.

• Working Pressure — The third set of characters in the first row indicate the maximum pressure, in pounds-per-square-inch, to which a cylinder may be filled for normal use or transportation across jurisdictional lines. A cylinder shouldn't be filled beyond this point.

The single exception to this rule occurs with steel cylinders that bear a plus (+) sign after the date of the last hydrostatic test. These may be filled to 10% above the listed pressure. This notation commonly appears on newly manufactured cylinders but seldom is given on subsequent hydrostatic tests.

Most aluminum cylinders can take air fills up to 3000 psi. A few may be filled to 3300 psi and some even to 4000 psi. The rated pressure of steel scuba cylinders may range from 1800 to 3500 psi. The most common steel cylinder, the 71.2-cubic-foot size, is rated for 2250 psi — 2475 psi with the 10% overfill approval. It is interesting to note that only with the 10% overfill approval does this cylinder reach its advertised capacity of 71.2 cubic feet. At its normal working pressure of 2,250 psi it has a capacity of 64.7 cubic feet.

Subsequent Rows

All scuba cylinders contain a second, and sometimes even a third and fourth, row of information. The sequence in which information may appear in these rows varies. Among that information, however, will be:

• Serial Number — Most scuba cylinders carry a unique serial number that may also identify information such as its size and lot number. This is usually the first information that appears on the second row.

• Manufacturer Identification — This usually appears following the serial number. Because most cylinders are manufactured by large, compressed-gas cylinder companies and not the scuba-equipment manufacturer that ultimately sells the cylinder to the dealer, this name might not be familiar. Luxfer, Kidde and PST (Pressed Steel Company) are among the most common manufacturer notations. The newest cylinders will have no name at all, but a manufacturer identification number instead.

• Hydrostatic Test Date — A cylinder's initial hydrostatic test date will usually appear as the last or only item in the last row of information originally stamped on the cylinder. Subsequent hydrostatic test dates may appear anywhere on the cylinder's neck.

The hydrostatic test date consists of numbers representing the month and year in which the cylinder was tested.

These numbers will be separated by either the hydrostatic tester's initials or by a special symbol that the tester has registered with the Department of Transportation.

Scuba Cylinder Care and Maintenance

Scuba cylinders require additional care and maintenance over and above simply rinsing, drying and storing them between dives. These maintenance procedures include:

- preventing damage to the cylinder exterior and valve.
- preventing moisture from entering the cylinder.
- having the cylinder inspected and tested on a regular basis.

Proper handling — Proper scuba cylinder handling helps prevent exterior scratches, dents and gouges, and valve damage that could render the cylinder inoperable.

Exterior damage can weaken the cylinder structurally to the point that it can no longer hold pressure safely. Aluminum cylinders, which have a softer metal, are particularly susceptible to such damage. Any cylinder that has sustained such damage should be taken out of service.

Although it takes a significant impact to knock a modern valve completely off a cylinder, a modest blow can easily deform the valve which is usually made of soft brass. This is irreparable and can render the cylinder valve inoperable.

To prevent damage, divers should handle scuba cylinders with care. This obviously means not dropping them. Also, when transporting cylinders in motor vehicles or boats, store cylinders in special racks or lay them on their sides and prevent them from rolling. In high traffic areas, such as pool decks, place cylinders on their sides. When laying cylinders down, ensure that they don't damage more fragile equipment, such as BCDs and regulators.

Preventing moisture from entering — Because air under pressure contains oxygen, moisture on the inside of a steel scuba cylinder can be especially harmful. Moisture acts as a catalyst in the oxi-dation (rust-forming) process. Salt-laden moisture is even more devastating than moisture from fresh water.

Inside a damp pressurized cylinder, oxidation that takes weeks to occur at normal atmospheric pressure can take place in a matter of days or even hours. Conversely, it's extremely difficult for oxidation to occur in perfectly dry environments — despite the presence of oxygen.

Aluminum cylinders are, of course, nowhere near as prone to damage from moisture. However, moisture in aluminum cylinders can aid in the formation of a scale (aluminum oxide) on the inside of the cylinder. This scale, if it comes loose, can clog valves and regulators.

For these reasons it's important to keep the inside of a cylinder completely free of moisture. It is important to make certain that any compressor used to fill scuba cylinders has an adequate and operable moisture-removal system. It's also important to never totally empty a scuba cylinder. If the valve on an empty cylinder is left open, water may enter.

Many cylinders are filled in water. Under these conditions, it's easy for water droplets to splash onto the filling whip or valve orifice. These can subsequently enter the cylinder during the filling process. One should take care to prevent this from happening.

For similar reasons, divers should avoid allowing water droplets to become trapped between their cylinder-valve orifice and regulator. This can take place between dives when cylinders and regulators are often dripping wet.

Opening the cylinder valve *momentarily*, to expel water or debris from the valve orifice, is recommended before connecting either filling whips or regulators. In many settings, it's important to do this quietly to avoid disturbing others. Draping a towel over the valve helps reduce noise.

When storing cylinders for an extended period, it's best to have no more than 10 or 20 bar/a few hundred psi of pressure. This reduces the concentration of oxygen, and consequently, any oxygen-related corrosion. The best way to store cylinders is upright so that any moisture damage occurs on the bottom, where the metal is thick and damage is easily seen, evaluated and treated.

Regular inspection and testing — In North America, scuba cylinders are visually inspected every year and pressure tested every five years. These intervals may vary in other countries, and may take place more frequently depending on the cylinder use.

Trained and experienced professionals, usually at retail dive centers, perform visual inspections. The inspection process begins with removal of the cylinder boot, back pack bands, if any, and valve. The inspector then checks the exterior of the cylinder for impact damage and corrosion. Next, the inspector examines the interior of the cylinder using a special light. Dental mirrors may enable the inspector to examine the area around the inside of the cylinder neck.

Finally, the inspector checks the valve for smooth operation and lubricates its threads to help prevent galvanic action between the dissimilar metals of the cylinder and valve. Valves, like regulators, also require periodic overhauls.

If the inspector doesn't detect corrosion or damage, he reassembles, fills, and places a visual inspection sticker on the cylinder. This identifies the facility that provided the inspection and the month and year in which it took place.

If the inspector detects damage or corrosion, he decides upon an appropriate course of action. Rinsing with distilled water and drying with warm air usually removes minor scale or contaminants from the inside of an aluminum cylinder. Minor oxidation on the inside of a steel cylinder may be best left untreated due to the fact that the removal process might actually weaken the cylinder more than the oxidation itself.

Technicians treat extensive oxidation or deep pitting by either tumbling or sand blasting. Tumbling involves putting an abrasive material inside the cylinder, then placing it on rollers where it turns over and over until clean. Sand blasting forces a stream of abrasive material into the cylinder under pressure to remove oxidation.

Because these methods also remove a portion of the cylinder wall, any cylinder that has undergone tumbling or sand blasting, or any cylinder that has suffered impact damage should undergo pressure testing before use.

Pressure testing is also known as *hydrostatic* testing, since water is used during the testing process. The tester fills the cylinder with water and then places it inside a water-filled jacket. The water pressure inside the cylinder is then increased to five thirds of its maximum working pressure (or to the test pressure, if this is included in the cylinder hieroglyphics). This is sufficient to cause the cylinder to expand slightly. This expansion displaces the water in the jacket outside the cylinder. The displaced water flows into a marked collection tube that allows expansion measurement. The pressure in the cylinder is then reduced to ambient and the cylinder contracts. If this expansion and contraction is within acceptable limits, the cylinder passes the test. If not, the cylinder may not be refilled.

After pressure testing, technicians clean and dry cylinders that pass, then stamp them with the current month and year and the tester's initials. In the U.S., only individuals who have met certain requirements and registered with the federal government may conduct such tests. Again, this procedure varies in other countries.

Scuba cylinders should undergo visual inspection at least once a year and pressure tests every five years. Cylinders should also undergo visual inspection whenever divers believe they hear loose material rolling around inside the cylinders or see a red or greenish accumulation appear on the regulator inlet filter. A cylinder should undergo pressure testing any time:

- it is physically damaged or structurally weakened by tumbling or sandblasting

- it is filled to beyond its maximum working pressure.

- it is exposed to heat in excess of 82°C/180°F.

- it is left unused for more than two years.

The Differences Between Steel and Aluminum Cylinders

Steel and aluminum cylinders both have advantages and disadvantages, neither is clearly superior. Which type of cylinder is more desirable depends on several factors, including diver preference.

Resistance to Corrosion Damage

Although steel and aluminum cylinders are both susceptible to corrosion damage, the likelihood of a steel cylinder succumbing to rust far outweighs the likelihood of an aluminum cylinder getting seriously damaged by aluminum oxide. This, perhaps more than any other factor, accounts for the fact that aluminum cylinders currently outsell steel cylinders by a wide margin. Surprisingly, however, this is one of the few areas in which aluminum cylinders offer a clear advantage over steel.

With proper care, a steel cylinder can go many, many years before succumbing to rust. In fact, a number of adult divers today use steel cylinders that were manufactured before they were born.

Nevertheless, a certain percentage of the steel scuba cylinders currently in use are condemned each year due to corrosion damage. This seldom happens to aluminum cylinders.

Another possibility, although remote, is that extensive corrosion inside a steel cylinder could consume a significant portion of the oxygen in the cylinder. This would make the air inside dangerous to use. The possibility of this occurring, however, is virtually nonexistent if the cylinder receives proper care.

Divers who think that they may not be able to keep moisture out of their cylinders may be better off with aluminum cylinders. A number of divers, however, should be able to give steel cylinders equal consideration in their cylinder selection process.

Size and Weight

Aluminum weighs less than steel. Nevertheless, because it is not as strong, aluminum cylinders must be bigger and heavier than comparable steel cylinders. This may concern smaller divers who might find larger aluminum cylinders uncomfortable.

Buoyancy

Because aluminum cylinders must be bigger, they also displace more water and are often more buoyant. This usually means that divers using aluminum cylinders may require more weight on their weight belt or in their weight systems than divers using steel cylinders.

Out of the water, these divers must cope with both the minimal additional weight of their cylinders and their weight systems. This total difference can be from 2 to 4kg/4 to 8lbs.

Hardness

Aluminum is a softer metal than steel. While divers seldom bang their cylinders around intentionally, a certain amount of banging and scraping is sometimes unavoidable.

Divers in certain types of specialty diving activities — most notably cavern, wreck and ice diving — regularly bang their cylinders against solid, overhead surfaces. Steel cylinders undoubtedly take this abuse better than aluminum cylinders, though neither cylinder should show much effect, except paint scratches. Cylinder mesh may also be used to prevent this damage.

Galvanic Action

Dissimilar metals in a moist environment react with one another, ultimately dissolving one of the two metals. Cylinder valves are most often made from brass. This means that the potential for damage from galvanic action always exists in cylinders which are usually made, as mentioned, from steel or aluminum. This is why it is so important to remove and lubricate the valve threads on cylinders at least once a year.

Availability

The availability of cylinders is another major factor in cylinder selection. As one would suspect, aluminum cylinders are usually more readily available than steel cylinders. This has been a major contributing factor to their popularity. For the same reason, steel cylinders are much more common in Europe.

A limited selection may also determine which cylinder a diver uses. If a large adult diver can only choose between an aluminum 11 litre/80ft^3 and a steel 12 litre/72ft^3, he may, understandably, choose the larger cylinder. (Who wants to be the person who had to end the dive because he ran low on air first?)

Under the same circumstances, a smaller adult diver may opt for the steel 12 litre/72. Lower air consumption might mean that this diver could last as long on the 12 litre/72 as larger divers do on their 11 litre/80s.

In recent years, there has been a trend toward making a broader range of cylinder sizes available to divers. Given this situation, more and more divers may make their cylinder selections based primarily on size, with the material as a secondary factor.

Regulators

Large quantities of compressed air are of little value to divers unless they have a means of reducing this air to ambient pressure as it's needed. The human respiratory system can tolerate a differential of no more than 0.14 bar/2 psi between breathing air pressure and the pressure surrounding the lungs. Breathing is, in fact, difficult if the pressure differential is only a small fraction of this amount.

This explains why divers cannot simply breathe from a hose or pipe running to the surface. To breathe comfortably underwater divers require an air supply at ambient pressure.

Therefore, the function of a scuba regulator is to reduce air pressure, on demand, from the scuba cylinder to ambient pressure.

Scuba regulators are also called *de-mand regulators* or *demand valves*. This means that inhaling and exhaling activate them automatically. This contrasts with some commercial dive helmets in which the air flow is constant. Scuba regulators only provide the air needed for each inhalation. This approach uses considerably less air than free-flowing units, which need large compressors on the surface to keep up with the great demand for air. It also prevents carbon dioxide buildup in dead-air spaces — a problem that can occur with some types of commercial and military dive equipment.

Modern regulators form part of an *open-circuit* scuba — meaning that once a diver breathes air, he exhales it into the water rather than back into the system. This is much simpler and less-expensive than closed-circuit, rebreather scuba used primarily by military and commercial divers. Because scuba cylinders contain sufficient air for divers to remain submerged up to and beyond the no-decompression limits at most recreational diving depths, there's only limited benefit, at present, to using more expensive and more complex closed-circuit systems.

Modern regulators are the foundation of a multicomponent scuba system, with direct connections to instrumentation, buoyancy control, exposure suit and alternate air source subsystems. A typical modern regulator system may have four or more hoses emanating from a single first stage, carrying high- and low-pressure air to these various subsystems.

Materials

Modern regulators are constructed from a variety of materials. Virtually all first stages and many second stages are made from cast and machined brass — although critical internal parts may be

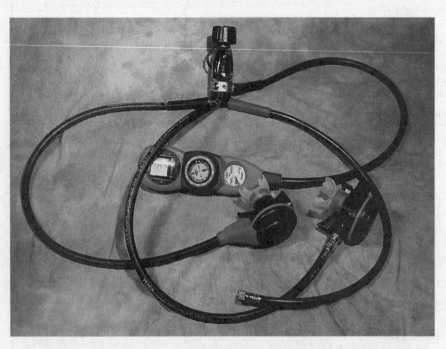

A typical regulator could have four hoses radiating from the first stage. Three intermediate pressure hoses will connect to a primary second-stage, a secondary second-stage and a BCD low-pressure inflator. A high-pressure hose connects to a submersible pressure gauge in the instrument console. Some systems combine the secondary second-stage and BCD low-pressure inflator in a single unit. There could also be additional low-pressure hoses for dry suits.

How Manufacturers Make Regulators

Due to diversity in regulator design, it's not possible to detail a single set of manufacturing processes that would accurately describe how all regulators are made. There are, however, several interesting procedures commonly used in regulator manufacture.

Distributed Manufacturing

Rarely does a manufacturing company construct all of its regulator components in its own plants. In some cases, all of the manufacturing processes are farmed out to other companies that specialize in areas such as foundry work, machining and injection molding. In other cases, manufacturers only farm out certain specialized parts.

Regardless of how much of the manufacturing process a company distributes among specialty companies, the goal is the same: to lower the cost of production and pass these savings on to the customers.

Design

Most larger equipment companies do most or all of their own regulator design and testing. Regulator design consumes a considerable amount of research and development time, meaning that it may take several years from new concept in regulator design to marketable product.

As with all dive equipment, it isn't enough to simply develop a regulator that works better. The design must also be economical to manufacture, easy to repair and stand up to the type of abuse regulators receive in real-life diving.

Ensuring that a design meets these criteria involves extensive testing. For this reason, many equipment companies have sophisticated hyperbaric chambers, sensitive flow-metering instruments and mechanical devices capable of simulating the type of stress a regulator encounters over a number of years. These latter devices often go through a process known as TTD (test to destruct). This gives the design engineers an accurate estimate of how long a particular part should last in normal use.

As a result of the testing process, some designs never make it to the market. Others change radically from their first handmade prototypes to the final production version.

Brass Foundry and Machining

Most regulators make extensive use of brass. Brass is an ideal regulator component. It doesn't oxidize as readily as steel or aluminum and withstands high pressures. Experts can cast, forge and machine brass. In fact, it is far easier to machine than steel because it is softer.

Companies that produce many of their own brass regulator components in-house typically purchase precast brass that has been stamped or forged into the approximate shape of the required component. They then machine it to its final shape and, if necessary, join it to other brass components using a process similar to welding steel. The end result is then chrome plated to provide more complete resistance to corrosion.

Injection Molding

Modern regulators — and, in particular, second stages — commonly use plastics and other synthetic materials. Doing so offers savings in weight and expense. It's also possible to mold plastics into shapes that are either impractical or unattainable in brass or other metals.

Plastic parts are created through injection molding. In this process, the manufacturer first commissions the construction of a mold in the shape of the final part. (Companies specializing in tool and die construction usually make these shapes.) The machinist places the completed mold in an injection-molding machine. Raw plastic is heated and forced into the mold, and when the plastic cools, it may be removed from the mold and trimmed to its final shape.

If a large manufacturer molds its own regulator parts in-house, then it probably also uses the same machinery to make injection-molded parts for masks, fins and other equipment.

Assembly and Testing

Again, most equipment companies perform their own final assembly and testing. This is similar to the process used by repair technicians who perform the last stages of a regulator overhaul, but on a larger scale. Technicians assemble first and second stages using components made either in house or by outside suppliers. Low-pressure hoses may also be made in house, or purchased ready-made on the outside. The fully assembled regulators undergo their battery of tests, then are packaged for shipment to dealers.

made from stainless steel, Teflon® or other materials.

Rubber is a prominent material in all regulator systems. As with many other diving products, silicone is frequently used for parts such as mouthpieces, exhaust tees and valves.

Plastic, nylon and other synthetic materials are also used in regulator systems. The use of these materials offers benefits such as lighter weight, lower cost and increased resistance to corrosion.

Styles

Unlike many other types of dive equipment, there is really only one "style" of regulator used by recreational divers today. This is a two-stage, single-hose model.

The earliest regulators were single-stage, two-hose models. The designation "single stage" refers to the fact that these regulators had single valve assemblies that reduced cylinder pressure directly to ambient pressure. Because these valves had to work with such a wide range of pressures, they had small valve orifices to give the demand levers in the regulators a sufficient mechanical advantage. Not only did this make early regulators harder to breathe from, it also meant that regulator performance could vary widely, depending on cylinder pressure.

The next step in regulator evolution was the advent of two-stage valves. In these, the first stage reduced cylinder pressure to the ambient pressure plus a preset intermediate pressure. The second stage reduced this ambient-plus-intermediate pressure to simply ambient pressure. This allowed larger valve orifices, greater airflow and — because the second stage worked with air at a more constant pressure — more consistent performance throughout the dive.

Double-hose regulators remained popular into the 1960s. In these models, both regulator stages fit in a large housing behind the diver's head. This offered some benefits:

- Lightweight mouthpieces (although double-hose mouthpieces may be buoyant enough to pull upward uncomfortably).

- Excellent resistance to freezing in extremely cold water.

- No bubbles next to a diver's face.

However, this design had drawbacks as well:

- The valves were usually high enough above the level of a diver's chest to unnecessarily increase breathing resistance, which made these regulators hard to breathe from.

- The hoses were an excellent environment for bacteria growth.

- It was difficult to remove water from the mouthpiece without exhaling forcefully or removing the mouthpiece from a diver's mouth.

The first single-hose regulators appeared in 1961. Because a single-hose regulator puts the second stage at virtually the same depth as the user's chest while in a normal swimming position, the air the second stage delivers is at the same pressure as the diver's lungs. Single-hose regulators were also easier to clean and had purge buttons — a feature that greatly simplified regulator clearing. If a diver using a single-hose regulator lacked sufficient breath to clear water from inside the second stage, he could simply press the purge button and air from the cylinder would do it for him.

By the early 1970s, use of double-hose regulators among recreational divers became rare. Hastening their decline was the fact that very few double-

Modern regulator systems are based on a two-stage, single-hose, demand-valve design.

hose regulators could accommodate submersible pressure gauges. Once these became a mandatory safety item, use of double-hose regulators virtually disappeared.

Features

Single-hose regulators may combine a variety of features, including various options on the first and second stages.

First-stage options — Regulator first-stage options include how the valve senses changes in pressure, the type of valve, how the first stage attaches to a cylinder, and the positioning and size of high- and low-pressure ports.

Pressure-sensing mechanism — First-stage pressure-sensing mechanisms fall into two categories: piston and diaphragm. In piston regulators, external water pressure acts on a piston, which is the main moving part in this type of first stage. In diaphragm first stages, the pressure acts on a flexible diaphragm. A push rod on the inside of this diaphragm transmits the diaphragm's movement to the valve mechanism.

Piston and diaphragm first stages each have their advantages and disadvantages — most of which are of little consequence to the owner. A further discussion of these differences appears in the sidebar, The Differences Between Piston and Diaphragm First Stages.

Valve type — Both piston and diaphragm first stages may use either balanced or unbalanced valves. Cylinder pressure affects unbalanced valves to some degree, while it doesn't affect balanced valves. For this reason, balanced valves can use larger openings and deliver more air. This is why balanced first-stages, or ones with specially designed unbalanced valves offering comparable performance have become popular today.

Connector type — Every regulator first stage must have a means to connect to a cylinder valve.

All current North American and Asian regulators, and many European regulators use a yoke. This is an A-clamp shaped device that fits over the top of the cylinder valve and has a threaded orifice for the yoke screw, which tightens the regulator air inlet to the opening on the cylinder valve. There are some slight differences in the size of the openings used on North American and European cylinders and regulators, but adapters may easily compensate for these slight differences.

Some European regulators and cylinders use DIN connectors. With these, the regulator screws directly into the cylinder valve. This is a more secure arrangement and allows the use of higher cylinder pressures. Most regulators with DIN connectors have optional yokes that screw right onto the first stage and allow them to be used with conventional cylinder valves. There are two types of DIN connector: the five-thread version is used for cylinder pressures up to about 200 bar/3000 psi and the seven-thread version is used above that.

High and low pressure port options — Most regulator first stages have one or two high pressure ports and three or more low pressure ports.

Older North American and Asian regulators have high and low pressure ports that are the same size; new models have somewhat larger low pressure ports and much larger high pressure ports. This helps eliminate confusion between the high and low pressure port and allows use of higher capacity hoses. Ports on European regulators follow yet another set of size standards; however, there are adapters that allow interconnection of hoses and accessories on all these units. Divers can avoid confusion by checking with their local dive professional and obtaining expert advice on connectors and adapters if necessary.

Many regulator first stages have their low pressure ports on a swivel at the end of the first stage opposite the yoke. On some of these regulators, there

The Differences Between Piston and Diaphragm First Stages

There are some fundamental differences between piston and diaphragm first stages and these are addressed in this sidebar. These differences shouldn't, however, have a major bearing on which regulator most divers select.

The accompanying diagrams depict how piston and diaphragm regulators work. There are a few variations on these approaches; however, most piston and diaphragm regulators operate like the units described.

As with virtually all equipment, there are advantages and disadvantages to each approach. Here is a summary of these benefits and drawbacks:

- Piston regulators usually have fewer moving parts than diaphragm models, which may lower costs and may make servicing such regulators faster and easier.

- Diaphragm first-stage design inherently prevents water from entering the first-stage mechanism itself. This helps prevent internal corrosion and contaminant buildup, which may lead to more consistent performance between service intervals. Environmental sealing allows piston regulators to achieve these same benefits, but makes them more difficult (and considerably messier) to work on.

- It's often easier to design piston regulators with larger valve orifices than diaphragm first stages.

- Piston first stages may be designed with a swivel arrangement for the low pressure ports, diaphragm first stages cannot.

- Properly qualified technicians with relatively simple tools can adjust the intermediate pressure on diaphragm first stages in the field.

Most piston designs must be completely stripped before adjustment.

Obviously, the benefits and drawbacks of each design are about evenly mixed. In addition, these advantages and disadvantages appear to apply primarily to designers and repair technicians, and not to end users.

To divers who purchase their regulators where they can obtain convenient, factory-authorized service, and who have these regulators serviced on a regular basis, it shouldn't matter much what type of design their first stages use.

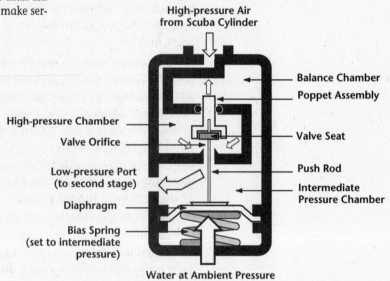

BALANCED DIAPHRAGM FIRST STAGE (OPEN)

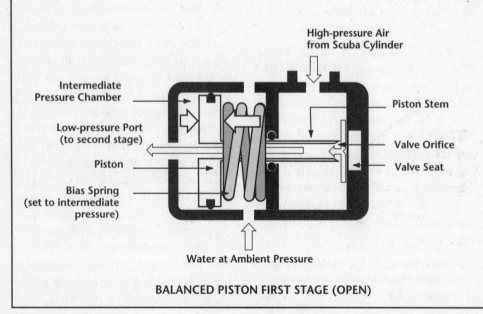

BALANCED PISTON FIRST STAGE (OPEN)

are high pressure ports on opposite sides of the first stage. This allows a user to mount the first stage on the cylinder with the low pressure ports either up or down (depending on personal preference) and still have the high pressure hose come over or under the desired shoulder (usually the left).

Environmental sealing — Some first stages offer environmental sealing. In these first stages, water pressure doesn't act directly on the piston or diaphragm. Instead, it acts on a silicone or alcohol based fluid that seals inside a watertight, yet pressure-sensitive, barrier. This fluid then transmits the pressure to the piston or diaphragm.

Environmental sealing offers two primary benefits. First, it prevents salt, sediment and other contaminants from entering the first stage, thus reducing internal corrosion or contaminant buildup. Second, it helps isolate the valve mechanism from freezing temperatures. This is important in cold-water environments, where excessively low temperatures may actually cause the first-stage mechanism to freeze up.

Second stage options — Second stage options generally include the style, the valve type and whether or not the second stage may be user adjustable.

Style — The most popular second-stage

design is one in which the low-pressure hose comes over the user's right shoulder, the diaphragm and purge button are on the front of the second stage, and the mouthpiece is in the rear, on the top. Such second stages generally have the exhaust valve on the back, at the bottom, with an exhaust tee directing bubbles to either side.

A few regulators using this design have a combined exhaust valve and diaphragm. This places the purge button at the back, behind the exhaust tee.

Any regulator that uses this design has a definite top and bottom. If used while inverted, these second stages may allow water to leak in through the exhaust valve during each exhalation. Also, if used upside down, they interfere with a diver's mask.

Some North American and European regulators have their diaphragm and exhaust valve at the *side* opposite the low-pressure hose. Such second stages are usually smaller and lighter than more conventional ones.

Another advantage of these designs is that they can be used with the hose coming over either shoulder. This makes them especially well-suited for use as alternate air source second stages, as it is impossible for divers under stress to put such a second stage in their mouths upside down.

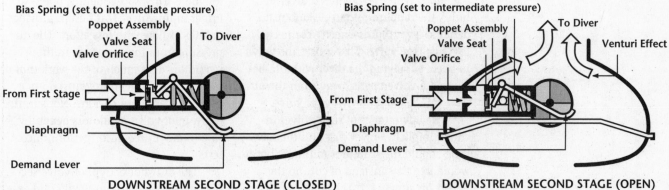

DOWNSTREAM SECOND STAGE (CLOSED)

When a diver is not inhaling from his downstream second-stage, the bias-spring pressure will equal the intermediate pressure and the second-stage valve will remain closed.

DOWNSTREAM SECOND STAGE (OPEN)

When the diver inhales, the second-stage diaphragm pushes on the demand lever which, in turn, opens the second-stage valve. The suction of the flowing air creates a venturi effect that helps the diaphragm remain depressed until the diver stops inhaling. This makes breathing easier.

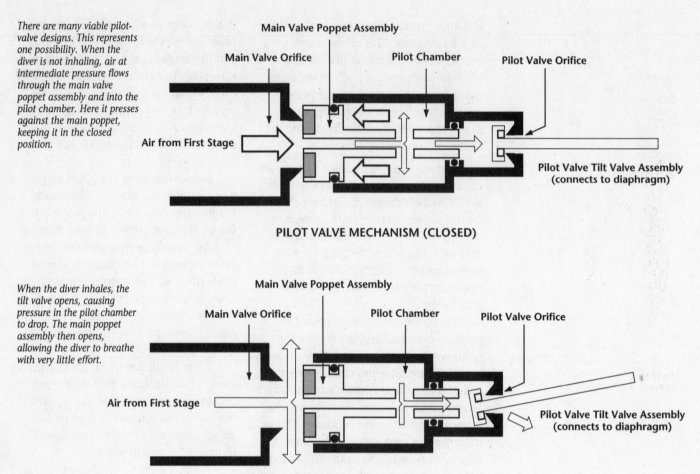

There are many viable pilot-valve designs. This represents one possibility. When the diver is not inhaling, air at intermediate pressure flows through the main valve poppet assembly and into the pilot chamber. Here it presses against the main poppet, keeping it in the closed position.

Main Valve Poppet Assembly

Main Valve Orifice

Pilot Chamber

Pilot Valve Orifice

Air from First Stage

Pilot Valve Tilt Valve Assembly
(connects to diaphragm)

PILOT VALVE MECHANISM (CLOSED)

When the diver inhales, the tilt valve opens, causing pressure in the pilot chamber to drop. The main poppet assembly then opens, allowing the diver to breathe with very little effort.

Main Valve Poppet Assembly

Main Valve Orifice

Pilot Chamber

Pilot Valve Orifice

Air from First Stage

Pilot Valve Tilt Valve Assembly
(connects to diaphragm)

Air Enters Second Stage
and is Breathed by Diver

PILOT VALVE MECHANISM (OPEN)

Type — Second-stage valves fall into two general categories: downstream and pilot valves.

Downstream valves are the most common. With these, when a diver inhales, the diaphragm pushes against a demand lever that is directly connected to a one-way valve. This causes the valve to open, supplying the diver with air. Because the valve opens away from the airflow, it is called a downstream valve.

The advantages of such valves include simplicity, lower cost and the fact that, should the regulator malfunction, it would free flow instead of cutting the diver's air supply off. The diver could breathe from the free-flowing airstream; the rest would escape harmlessly through the exhaust valve as the diver

ascends safely. This is known as fail-safe design.

In some regulators, the demand lever opens a small valve known as a pilot valve. This, subsequently, opens a larger main valve. This design provides greater airflow with less effort. The air pressure from the first stage in these regulators does much of the work that a diver's inhalation efforts must do in more conventional designs. Not surprisingly, pilot-valve regulators generally rate highly in regulator performance tests.

The drawbacks to pilot-valve second stages include complexity and expense. They cost more and may be more difficult for service technicians to repair. Some users also complain of a shallow-water phenomenon known as *flutter*. This is actually an awareness of the slight delay between when the pilot valve opens and when the main valve opens. Flutter usually disappears in deeper water, or if the user simply bites down less forcibly on the mouthpiece, thus increasing the airway size.

Adjustment — All second stages have a built-in internal adjustment feature. This allows precise tuning during servicing. A few second stages have additional adjustments that the user can manipulate. These include adjustments to the spring pressure holding the downstream valve closed and to the venturi effect built into some second-stages. Some models allow the user to turn auxiliary exhaust valves on or off.

Manufacturers that offer these options include instructions that fully explain how each works. Under normal circumstances, however, divers set regulators to breathe as easily as possible. Divers may want to temporarily increase breathing resistance on their regulators in the few situations in which the regulator may be especially prone to accidental free-flowing. These also permit divers to fine-tune their regulators for the best breathing during the entire maintenance cycle.

Under no circumstances, however, should a diver increase breathing resistance in an attempt to conserve air. In the long run, attempts to increase breathing resistance also increase air consumption. A diver's lungs must work harder to overcome any increased resistance; this only serves to increase the growing oxygen debt. Eventually the diver will have to breathe harder and faster in an attempt to pay off this debt.

Increased breathing resistance may also contribute to stress and diving accidents. This makes safety an important reason not to increase regulator breathing resistance without reason.

Other features — Among the other features divers may find on regulator second stages include:

- rollers or Teflon® contact points on the tips of demand levers to reduce internal friction.
- designs or devices intended to release pressure on the second stage valve seat when storing the regulator.

The latter feature can help maintain regulator second stage performance between service intervals.

Choosing the Right Regulator

There are some important criteria divers should consider when selecting a regulator.

Breathing ease and serviceability are perhaps the most important factors in regulator selection. Lack of proper service has a far greater effect on regulator performance than design features.

Divers should consider fast and convenient service when buying a regulator, and buy regulators from a local, authorized dealer that stocks replacement parts and can service the regulator promptly.

This dealer can also make specific suggestions as to a regulator's suitability for specific types of diving. For example, some high-performance regulators have internal parts that are prone to clogging with sand. This is an important consideration if divers do a lot of beach diving.

Another selection criterion is performance. Any regulator a diver chooses should also perform precisely the way the diver wants it to. All modern balanced first-stage regulators breathe easily. Some, however, breathe differently from others.

Before investing, divers try a regulator. Breathing from the regulator in the showroom tells the diver how the regulator performs when it is brand-new.

How much attention should divers pay to comparative performance tests such as those performed by various navies and other agencies? These tests are accurate within the scope of what they evaluate. Recreational divers, however, should bear in mind factors such as:

- The test results aren't published as often as new regulators reach the market or improve. Therefore, a newer regulator may not appear on the test results. Similarly, the test results for a given regulator that does appear on the list may not reflect the performance of newer, improved models.

- The U.S. Navy, for example, tests regulators according to criteria that determines their suitability for military, not recreational, use. For example, some of the test depths are beyond the recommended depth limits for recreational divers. This doesn't necessarily reflect their performance at recreational divers depths and workloads.

- Simply because a regulator can deliver large quantities of air at extreme depths doesn't mean it breathes in a manner that recreational divers find comfortable. Nor does it mean that

The Differences Between Balanced and Unbalanced First Stages

Recreational divers should either purchase regulators with balanced first stages, or models that offer comparable performance. Balanced first stage regulators are unaffected by changes in cylinder pressure and don't gradually become more difficult to breathe from as the cylinder empties.

Balanced first stage regulators usually provide greater airflow and therefore:

- breathe easier at greater depths.
- can easily supply air to accessories such as low-pressure BCD and dry-suit inflators.

- can meet the demands of two divers who may have to breathe simultaneously from a single first stage, if one diver must use the other's alternate air source second stage.

The accompanying diagrams depict how balanced and unbalanced piston first stages function. In studying these illustrations, one notices that:

- In unbalanced first stages, cylinder pressure works to force the piston open. For the piston to overcome this force, the valve orifice must be smaller (than in a balanced first stage). This limits the maximum flow rate.

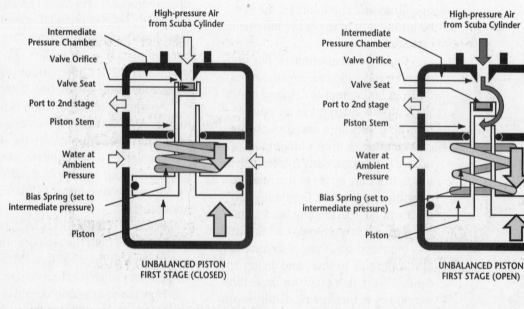

UNBALANCED PISTON FIRST STAGE (CLOSED)

UNBALANCED PISTON FIRST STAGE (OPEN)

When the diver is not inhaling, the air inside the intermediate pressure chamber applies a force to the piston that is equal to the force of the bias spring plus ambient pressure. The piston does not move and the valve stays closed.

When the diver inhales, air pressure in the intermediate pressure chamber drops, the valve opens and air flows. When the cylinder is full, opening force on the valve seat is greatest and breathing effort at its lowest. As cylinder pressure drops, breathing resistance will increase.

competent, professional service for that regulator is readily available in all areas.

When available, comparative test results are a factor in the regulator selection. They shouldn't, however, form the sole criterion.

Divers should bear in mind that:

- Most regulators on the market have proven that they are safe.

- All regulators with balanced first stages (or regulators that offer comparable performance) should meet the needs of most divers within the recommended recreational diving limits.

- Because regular, professional maintenance has more effect on regulator performance than any other factor, the availability of such service may be the single most important factor in regulator selection.

Also, as the pressure inside the cylinder diminishes, it will be easier for air in the intermediate pressure chamber to force the piston to close. This makes it increasingly harder to breathe from this first stage as cylinder pressure drops.

- The operation of the balanced first stage isn't affected by cylinder pressure. Cylinder pressure acts all around the piston stem, but not in the direction needed to force the piston into the open position. This allows the valve orifice to be much larger.

A few manufacturers have found ways around the inherent deficiencies of unbalanced first stage designs. Oversize pistons or special balance chambers result in first stages that offer performance comparable to balanced models, but are easier to service. Simple unbalanced first stages have largely vanished from the marketplace, but may still exist as rental or used stock. With a few exceptions, divers shouldn't be overly concerned about getting a regulator with less than desirable performance characteristics.

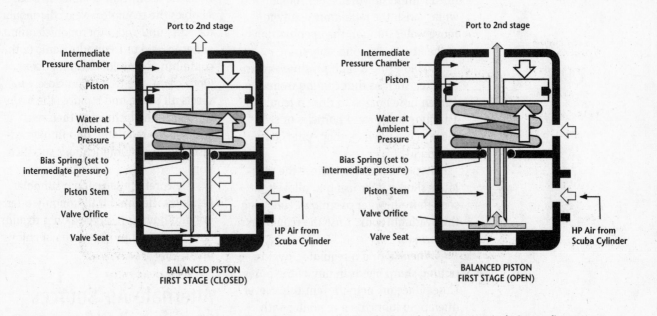

BALANCED PISTON FIRST STAGE (CLOSED)

BALANCED PISTON FIRST STAGE (OPEN)

When the diver is not inhaling, the air inside the intermediate pressure chamber applies a force to the piston that is equal to the force of the bias spring plus ambient pressure. The piston does not move and the valve stays closed.

When the diver inhales, air pressure in the intermediate pressure chamber drops, the valve opens and air flows. Because air from the cylinder never exerts pressure on the piston stem base, cylinder pressure has little bearing on breathing resistance.

Regulator Care and Maintenance

Regulators require more care and maintenance than items such as masks, snorkels and fins. These include special procedures for rinsing and storage, and the need for periodic service by trained professionals.

Maintenance — Failure to rinse a regulator thoroughly — as soon as possible after use — causes its performance to diminish faster than any other factor.

If possible, rinse a regulator while it is still attached to the cylinder and while the air is still on. This reduces the possibility of water accidentally entering the first stage.

If this isn't practical, dry and replace the dust cap securely and keep the second stage lower than the first stage while rinsing. The purge button should not be pressed during rinsing without it being pressurized.

The best way to rinse a regulator is with a gentle stream of fresh water. Alternatively, soak the regulator in a large container, such as a washtub or sink, filled with fresh water. After soaking it a while, swish the regulators gently to move water through the open portions of the first and second stages.

Avoid using a high pressure stream of water, such as that coming from a garden hose nozzle, to rinse a regulator. This may lodge sand particles or sediment in areas where they could cause damage.

If it is impossible to rinse the regulators shortly after using it, allow it to soak in fresh water overnight. Following the overnight soak, rinse the regulators as normal.

When storing a regulator, avoid putting sharp bends in any of the hoses. Hose protectors help prevent this. Never attempt to lubricate a regulator with any substance, and remember that only manufacturer-trained and authorized technicians should disassemble and service regulators.

Service — Have the regulator serviced when:

- One year passes since the last overhaul.

- A regulator has had six months or more of extremely heavy use since its last overhaul.

- There is visible damage to the regulator, such as cracked hoses or mouthpieces, or a discolored inlet filter.

- It doesn't breathe as easily as it should.

- The owner suspects, for any reason, that the regulator is malfunctioning.

Although there are many reasons for regulator service, the solution is usually a complete overhaul. A complete overhaul takes little more time and money than a partial fix. Furthermore, a complete overhaul ensures that the regulator is free from sediment or corrosion, that all worn parts have been replaced, and that it performs as it did when it was new.

An overhaul involves several steps. First, the technician completely disassembles the regulator. Next, the regulator parts undergo a thorough cleaning, either in acid or in an ultrasonic bath containing a special cleaning agent. Once clean, the technician closely inspects all parts, and replaces the worn elements. The technician then reassembles the regulator, and finally, adjusts it to the manufacturer's specifications.

By carefully selecting a suitable regulator, cleaning it thoroughly after use and having it serviced on a regular basis, it should provide years of enjoyment.

Alternate Air Sources

Divers who run very low on, or totally out of, air can use one of several procedures to reach the surface safely. Among

The most common alternate air source is an additional second-stage attached to the regulator's first stage.

An alternate-air-source inflator combines the functions of a BCD low-pressure inflator and an additional regulator second-stage.

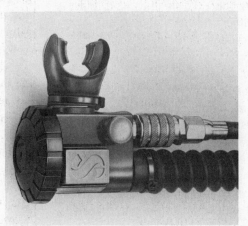

One variation on the alternate-air-source inflator is a conventional second stage that connects, in line, with the low-pressure inflator hose.

the most desirable of these procedures is an alternate air source ascent. Training organizations that certify the majority of divers throughout the world have made the use of alternate air sources by divers in entry-level training mandatory. Most divers consider alternate air sources mandatory equipment.

An alternate air source is any device used — other than a primary second stage — to make an ascent while breathing normally. The use of some alternate air sources requires the help and cooperation of another diver. Other alternate air sources may be used independently and do not require the assistance of another diver.

The following describes the types of alternate air source systems currently available. This includes a listing of the advantages and disadvantages of each system, a description of how each is used and whether it allows out-of-air/low-on-air divers to make independent ascents.

Alternate Air Source Second Stages

An alternate air source second stage — most commonly called an "octopus" — is simply an additional second stage and hose that attaches to the regulator first stage. This gives the diver a primary second stage (the one a diver normally breathes from) and a secondary second stage (which a buddy uses in a low-on-air/out-of-air situation).

Alternate Air Source Inflators

Alternate air source inflators combine the functions of a low-pressure BCD inflator and an octopus second stage in a single unit. A variation on this approach puts a conventional second stage in proximity to a normal inflator and both share the same second-stage hose. These are often called *alternate inflator regulators*.

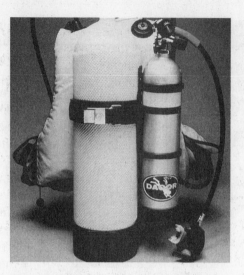

The "pony" bottle is an example of a truly redundant back up system.

Pony Bottles

A pony bottle is a small scuba cylinder that either attaches alongside a diver's main cylinder or between double cylinders. It has its own separate first and second stages.

Pony-bottle systems may be used in the same manner as conventional octopus systems to provide air to an out-of-air/low-on-air diver. In addition, if pony bottle equipped divers experience difficulty with their main air supply, they may switch over to their pony bottles for ascent without having to gain the attention and assistance of other divers. This makes the pony bottle a truly independent alternate air source system.

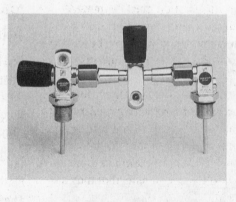

First successful and popular dual-valve manifold.

Pony bottles are especially popular among divers who spend considerable time in deeper water, such as many wreck divers. A pony-bottle's capacity — usually 2-3 liters water capacity/12-20 cubic feet — ensures not only enough air for a safe ascent, but also enough to perform a safety or emergency decompression stop near the surface.

Dual-Regulator Manifolds and Valves

Dual-valve manifolds for double cylinders and slingshot or Y valves for single cylinders, allow the use of two regulators on a single air supply. Cave and cavern divers (notably, Cousteau's colleague and blue-hole explorer, Dr. Richard Benjamin) developed and popularized the first version of these valves. They developed these systems because of concern about the consequences of a regulator free-flowing in a cave or cavern.

Such an occurrence could drain a divers air supply in a matter of minutes, leaving no air to exit the cave with. With a dual regulator manifold or valve, the diver can turn off a free flowing regulator without affecting airflow to the remaining regulator. This leaves a diver with sufficient air to turn around and exit.

Dual-regulator systems have attracted the interest of ice and wreck penetration divers for the same reasons that they appeal to cave and cavern divers. Given careful air supply management, this system ensures that a malfunctioning regulator won't lose the air needed to exit from under the ice or inside a wreck.

The value of a dual-regulator system depends largely upon careful air management. Using such systems requires adhering to the rule of thirds: using one third of the air supply for going into a cavern, cave or wreck, and keeping two thirds in reserve for the trip out. Following this rule conscientiously leaves more reserve air at any given time than that in a pony bottle — and thus achieves virtually all the benefits of a totally independent alternate air source. Failure to adhere to this system, however, could conceivably find someone no better off than an octopus-equipped diver who is out of air.

Self-Contained Ascent Bottles

A self-contained ascent bottle is a miniature scuba cylinder that has a complete regulator assembly built into the valve. It is a totally independent alternate air source system and may even be passed from one diver to another.

A self-contained ascent bottle attached neatly to a BCD.

Buoyancy Control Devices with High Pressure Cylinders

In an out-of-air/low-on-air situation, it is — *theoretically* — possible to breathe from a buoyancy control device provided it is fitted with a small high pressure cylinder and a special oral inflation/deflation unit. The high pressure cylinder also provides a means of backup inflation and a valve fitted to the cylinder allows air transfer to the BCD.

This system cannot be considered a substitute for more conventional alternate air source systems. This is due primarily to the complexity of making a successful ascent using air from a BCD — particularly while attempting to share air with another diver. Additionally, there is a risk of pulmonary infection from breathing through the BCD and the potential for an unexpected buoyant ascent is greater when a BCD can be inflated rapidly with high pressure air.

Instrumentation

Certain information must be immediately available on every dive. Lack of such information may simply be inconvenient or it may lead to unnecessary risk.

In addition, supplementary information can increase the convenience or enjoyment associated with a dive. Instrumentation can supply this information and this section examines these needs and the instruments that may satisfy them.

Need-to-Have Information

The minimum information divers must have during every dive they make consists of:

- maximum depth reached during the dive.
- current depth.
- actual bottom time (time spent underwater).
- current cylinder pressure.

There are some specific reasons why divers need this information.

Depth and time — Accurate depth and time information helps ensure adherence to the no-decompression limits for a particular dive. Consider the depth and duration of previous dives and the time spent on the surface between dives to obtain appropriate no-decompression limits.

Exceeding these limits may lead to decompression sickness (described in The Physiology of Diving section) or force a diver to make a series of emergency decompression stops during ascents. Decompression stops also need to be accurately timed.

If divers have a means of determining their current depth, they may consult this source of information regularly and then simply remember the deepest depth reached during the dive. The only drawback is that unless divers are conscientious about monitoring their depth on a regular basis, they may reach the deepest point in their dive (and possibly exceed the no-decompression limits) at a time when they were not monitoring their depth. This is why some gauges contain a feature known as a maximum-depth indicator.

Individual members of a buddy team may not always remain at the same depth during a dive. Therefore, each member of the team needs an independent means of monitoring depth.

Because any dive entails the risk of separation, it's also desirable that each buddy have an independent means of monitoring time. Should the divers accidentally exceed the depth and time limits, this also enables them to accurately measure any emergency decompression stops or safety stops.

Cylinder pressure —Recreational divers should usually arrive on the surface with a safety margin of at least 35 bar/500 psi remaining in their cylinders. Divers also want to know when they have used half of that portion of their air supply that they don't want to keep in reserve. This enables them to return to the entry/exit point underwater and avoid long surface swims. Divers who penetrate caverns, ice and wrecks have no option; they must know at all times that they have sufficient air to exit the overhead environment.

For these reasons, a means of determining cylinder pressure while underwater is mandatory equipment for all divers.

Nice-to-Have Information

While not absolutely essential, there is a variety of information that may make a dive more convenient or more enjoyable. This information may include:

- direction.

- water temperature.

- approximate dive time remaining, based on current depth and air-consumption rate.

Some instrumentation systems may automatically provide divers with information related to depth and time that they may otherwise have to determine on their own. Such information may include:

- maximum depth reached.

- number of dives made in the past 12 hours.

- current bottom time or bottom time of the last dive.

- current surface interval or length of the last surface interval.

- whether it is acceptable to fly in pressurized commercial aircraft.

- dive time remaining based on current no-decompression limits.

- length of any emergency decompression stops.

Information regarding direction deserves special mention. Although it's theoretically not "need-to-have" information, it is important for divers to find their way underwater. Without this ability, divers may be reluctant to go beyond the immediate vicinity of their entry/exit point. If they do, they risk having to return to that point on the surface. It's usually easier and more enjoyable to do so underwater; however, this requires divers to maintain orientation underwater so that they know the direction back to their entry/exit point.

Instrumentation Systems Design and Construction

There's great diversity in the design and construction of instrumentation systems. Nevertheless, many pressure-sensing instruments share design features. Depth or cylinder pressure monitoring instruments must have a means of sensing changes in pressure. Appropriate mechanisms range from bourdon tubes to electronic transducers.

The *bourdon tube* is among the most common pressure-sensing mechanisms. It's a curved tube — usually made from copper — that tends to straighten if the pressure inside the tube is greater than ambient pressure. The tip of such a tube can connect with rods and levers to an

eccentric gear that, in turn, connects to a gauge needle. Thus, by increasing or decreasing the pressure inside the tube, the needle moves around the dial.

A variation on bourdon-tube design is the spiral tube. In this design, the tube winds around several times in a spiral. The gauge needle subsequently connects directly to the tip of the tube. Because the tube is spiral-shaped, it uncoils only as much as the needle must move for accurate readings. This design is uncommon in submersible pressure gauges, but common in depth gauges.

One concern with bourdon-tube design is keeping the mechanism free from corrosion or sediment buildup. This isn't a problem with the bourdon tubes inside submersible pressure gauges. These tubes only fill with air, and the balance of the mechanism can stay inside a watertight housing.

Depth-monitoring devices are another matter. In the past, depth gauges that allowed water to enter the bourdon tube directly often failed when the tube clogged with salt crystals and dried sediment. Today, such designs usually use nonstick-plastic-coated tubes, which largely overcome this problem.

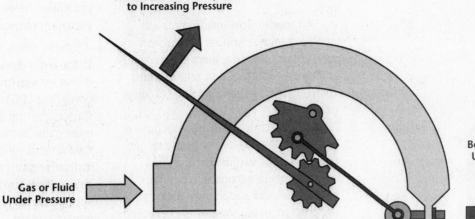

Needle Moves in Response to Increasing Pressure

Gas or Fluid Under Pressure

Bourdon Tube Uncurls with Increasing Pressure

BOURDON TUBE MECHANISM

Bourdon, or spiral-wound, tube mechanisms form the heart of many analog pressure gauges.

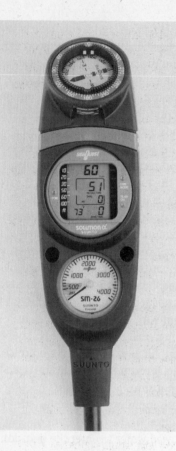

Some consoles combine both digital and analog gauges. In this model, the lower unit contains a submersible pressure gauge, the center unit is a dive computer and the upper unit is a compass.

A more common design is placing a sealed tube and the surrounding mechanism in an oil-filled housing; external pressure on a flexible portion of the housing causes the tube to curl more tightly and move. Thus, the gauge mechanism can function without exposure to contamination.

Electronic pressure-sensing instruments use a device known as a transducer. A typical transducer may consist of a ceramic element whose electrical conductivity increases in direct proportion to increasing pressure. By measuring current flow, the circuitry in such a gauge can monitor pressure, and therefore depth or cylinder pressure. These instruments have become very popular due to their accuracy.

Styles

As mentioned previously, instrumentation is an area of nearly infinite variation. Diving instruments may be:

• digital or analog

• wrist or console-mounted

• integrated or separate

Analog and digital instruments — The terms analog and digital refer to whether instruments have a needle or hand that moves around a dial or give simply a numeric display of information.

All mechanical instruments use analog displays. Analog instruments, long a part of diving, have proven to be sufficiently accurate and reliable, and sometimes have the advantage of lower price.

Most electronic instruments have a digital display. Digital instruments generally equal or surpass their analog counterparts in accuracy. Where an analog pressure gauge may show cylinder pressure being somewhere between 110 bar/1600 psi and 120 bar/1700 psi, a digital gauge may, for example, read precisely 113 bar/1643 psi.

The microchip circuitry that enables digital electronic instruments to give important need-to-know information also makes it easy to provide additional information. For example, where an analog dive timer may provide only time spent underwater, its digital counterpart may give bottom time, surface interval and dive number information.

Some digital instruments provide both a digital and an analog readout. An example is a submersible pressure gauge that shows both the cylinder pressure in psi or bar and provides a graphic representation in the form of a bar graph.

Digital instrumentation generally costs more than an analog counterpart, but the gap is lessening as digital gauges become more popular. Also, while mechanical analog gauges may have luminous dials, divers usually read digital gauges with an artificial light source on night and extremely low-visibility dives.

Most modern digital dive instruments use long-life lithium batteries. Unlike analog instruments, however, that have no batteries to wear out, divers must eventually replace these batteries. This often involves shipping the instrument to the manufacturer — although the interval between battery replacements may be as much as five years, and more manufacturers are switching to user changeable batteries.

Wrist and console-mounted instruments — In the early days of recreational diving, divers wore instruments, with the exception of the SPG, on their wrists. As divers started wearing more and more instruments, this became a problem. Divers tried several solutions: mounting several instruments on a single strap or fastening multiple instruments to homemade, wrist-mounted "dashboards" often improved matters. It didn't, however, totally alleviate many of the other problems associated with wrist-mounted instruments. These included:

- Attaching one or more instruments to a diver's wrist added additional steps to the suiting up process.

- Divers could don wrist-mounted gauges only after their exposure suits. On a hot day or on a rolling boat deck, this was uncomfortable and inconvenient.

- Once in place, large, wrist-mounted gauges could easily snag on cylinder harnesses. For this reason, many divers donned their wrist-mounted gauges after donning their cylinders. Again, on a hot day or a rolling boat, this proved uncomfortable.

Given the inherent drawbacks of wearing multiple, wrist-mounted gauges, it was no surprise that many divers welcomed the introduction of instrument consoles in the early 1970s. These consoles attached several instruments to a diver's submersible pressure gauge, thus leaving the diver's wrists free and speeding up the equipment donning process.

The first consoles were large plastic housings designed to accommodate several separate gauges. A diver would specify which gauges he already owned (or planned to purchase), and the console maker would modify the console to

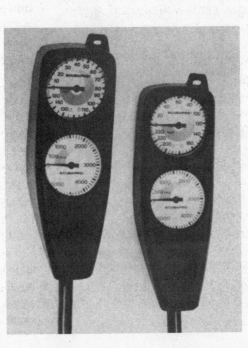

Two-unit consoles are among the most popular designs. Additional instruments may come in add-on or plug-in modules.

accommodate those specific gauges. This type of console is still available and is a good choice for divers who want to use instruments from several manufacturers in a single console.

Shortly after the introduction of custom-made consoles, several manufacturers introduced ready-made consoles with either a submersible pressure gauge and a depth gauge, or those two instruments plus a compass. Ready-made consoles were (and are) generally more compact and less expensive than custom-made models.

Today, compact pressure/depth models are perhaps the most popular of all console designs. Better-quality consoles often integrate dive timers and even thermometers into this design. With some models, knives and compasses are available as add-on modules. Other models may simply be available in larger versions that have built-in compasses.

While instrument consoles have achieved a high level of popularity and may greatly enhance diving convenience, they aren't without their drawbacks. They can be big and bulky and, when allowed to dangle freely, may cause entanglement or allow sensitive instruments to be banged along the bottom. Dangling consoles may also be difficult to see when divers need to look at them.

For this reason, many manufacturers include gauge-retaining straps on their BCDs and consoles. Using these straps helps keep consoles from dangling freely and is highly recommended.

Some divers prefer to keep the size of their console down by wearing one gauge, such as a dive timer or low-profile compass, on their wrists.

Integrated instruments — There has been a trend in the past few years to integrate several functions into a single gauge. For example, a few manufacturers have a miniature thermometer built into the face of some of its console-mounted submersible pressure gauges.

Submersible pressure gauge.

Capillary depth gauge.

Several manufacturers have analog depth gauges with digital dive timers built into the face.

The best example of integration is with digital instruments. The space in an instrument console that used to hold a single analog depth gauge can easily house a digital instrument that reports maximum depth, current depth, bottom time, surface interval, dive number and other information. Some manufacturer's consoles and dive computers have a single, integrated display. All the information they provide appears on this one screen.

Instrument Types

A description of the different instruments, their specific functions and the various ways they may be available follows.

Submersible pressure gauge — Submersible pressure gauges (SPGs) let divers monitor their air supply throughout the course of a dive. Such gauges connect by a flexible hose to the high-pressure port on a regulator's first stage.

The most common form of a submersible pressure gauge is an analog model with a spiral-wound bourdon tube. European SPGs typically go to 300 bar. North American SPGs typically read up to 3500-4000 psi. From 0-35-70 bar/500-000 psi is color-coded (usually red) to warn of a dwindling air supply.

This section may not be calibrated in the same increments as the rest of the dial because the gauge may not be as accurate here as it is at higher pressures. In addition, the precise 0 point may vary from gauge to gauge among the same make and model. It is important to note that even though a gauge reads, say approximately 20 bar/250 psi, the cylinder may be close to empty.

Most SPGs have a plug similar in function to a cylinder valve burst disk. If the bourdon or spiral tube develops a leak, this plug ruptures long before the gauge housing explodes. Nevertheless,

turning the face of an SPG away from any nearby divers is recommended when opening a cylinder valve, in case the plug is nonfunctional (it is a good idea to ensure that the plug is not pointing at someone either).

Most SPGs attach to the high-pressure hose with a special swivel connection. Without regular maintenance, these connections may develop minor leaks. While annoying, such leaks are seldom substantial enough to place a diver in any immediate danger. Nevertheless, they indicate that the hose connection requires immediate, professional care.

Depth gauge — Recreational divers may choose from a wide variety of depth gauges. Among those available are:

Capillary — These gauges consist of a small-diameter, clear plastic tube that is wrapped around a circular dial. The tube is open at one end and closed at the other.

As its wearer descends, a water column rises inside the tube as the air is compressed in accordance with Boyle's law. At a depth of 10m/33ft in salt water, the dividing point between the air and the water inside the tube moves halfway around the dial. The dial is calibrated in depth increments that match this rate of compression. Thus, by matching the water column in the tube with the corresponding depth calibration, a diver determines the depth.

While a properly calibrated capillary depth gauge is inexpensive and can theoretically be accurate, these gauges also have some drawbacks, which make them less popular as primary depth gauges. These include susceptibility to inaccuracy due to sand and other particles, difficulty to read (especially at depths deeper than 9m/30ft) and air bubbles that may hinder performance.

Open bourdon tube — An open bourdon tube depth gauge is one in which the bourdon tube is open to the surrounding water. This is a less expensive approach than that used by sealed, oil-filled depth gauges.

In the past, there were problems with these gauges becoming clogged with salt or sediment. This problem has been largely solved by coating the inside of the tube with nonstick plastic, but open bourdon tube depth gauges aren't particularly popular.

Oil-filled — Oil-filled depth gauges are widely used. They are commonly found in ready-made instrument consoles. Their function was previously described in the section on gauge design and construction.

While these gauges deliver among the best all-around performance for most divers, their users should be aware that nearly every analog gauge has a small error factor associated with it.

Diaphragm depth gauges — Diaphragm depth gauges aren't as common as oil-filled gauges. They are generally more expensive and are highly accurate. With these gauges, a flexible diaphragm connects to the gauge needle through a series of connecting rods, levers or gears. Diaphragm gauges often have an adjustment mechanism that allows the user to reset the needle to 0 at altitude.

Digital — Digital depth-monitoring devices are becoming increasingly popular. They may be an integrated part of an all-electronic console or they may come as a wrist model.

Virtually all digital depth gauges automatically provide a readout of both current and maximum depth. Advertised accuracy for these gauges is generally 15cm/6in, making them extremely accurate.

Depth gauge features — There are a number of features common to different depth gauges. These include:

Maximum-depth indicators: The majority of analog depth gauges and virtually all digital ones automatically provide an indication of the maximum depth reached during the dive.

The max-depth indicator on analog gauges consists of a second, separate needle that the main needle pushes ahead of itself as the diver descends. As the wearer ascends, this max-depth needle remains at the deepest depth reached. Max-depth needles must be manually reset to 0 at the beginning of each dive.

Altitude adjustment: Most depth gauges are calibrated for sea-level pressure. This renders them inaccurate at altitude. Some gauges can actually get damaged when taken to altitude, be-

Analog depth gauge with maximum-depth-indicator needle.

cause their needle bends backwards against the 0 post.

To overcome this difficulty, some gauges — most notably diaphragm models — are equipped with an altitude-adjustment feature. This may be a dial that allows the user to reset the needle to 0. Or, it may be a plug that the diver may remove to equalize pressure inside the gauge with ambient pressure. Most digital depth gauges automatically adjust for altitude.

Accuracy — All gauge manufacturers test their depth gauges for accuracy. Digital depth gauges and dive computers are typically accurate to within 15 cm/6 in of the indicated depth. This means that, while divers shouldn't place blind faith in any instrument, mechanical or electronic, a properly func-

make the cost of mechanical depth gauges prohibitive.

Recreational divers should also be aware that, because the recommended limit for recreational diving is 30m/100ft under most conditions and 40m/130ft with special training or supervision, there is little value in depth gauges that read much beyond 45m/150ft. Not only do such depth gauges have calibrations that are closer together and harder to read, they may also be less accurate at the depths most frequently encoun-

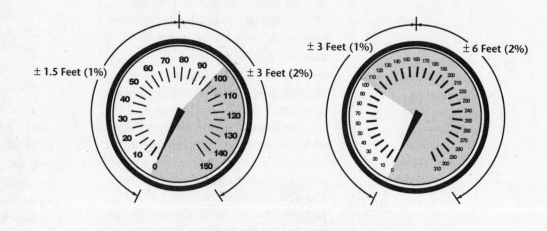

GAUGE ACCURACY

Typical depth-gauge accuracy scales. The unshaded areas represent the recommended range for recreational divers.

tioning digital depth gauge or computer won't give or act on a substantially inaccurate depth reading.

The situation for mechanical/analog depth gauges is somewhat different. A typical range might be one percent of the full scale for the first half of the depths listed on the dial and two percent for the second half. In other words, a newly manufactured 50m/150ft depth gauge is acceptable if it gave a reading of 26m/80ft for an actual depth that might be anywhere between 25-27m/77-83ft. Greater accuracy than this would

tered during recreational diving.

Factors such as age or mishandling affect gauge accuracy. For this reason, divers should check the accuracy of their depth gauges — both mechanical and electronic — on a regular basis.

One way of doing this is to compare the depth gauge against a functioning capillary gauge in shallow water. While this won't tell a diver what a gauge's error factor is in deeper water, it at least alerts that a gauge is giving inaccurate readings.

The best test, however, is taking the

gauge to a diving retailer who has appropriate testing equipment. This allows comparison of actual to indicated depth over the full range of the gauge's scale.

If the degree of discrepancy is significant, the owner should have a technician repair the damage, if possible, or replace the gauge.

Underwater timepieces — Underwater timepieces fall into two categories: watches and timers. Underwater watches have the advantage of multiple use above and underwater; however, divers must remember to set or consult them at the beginning and end of each dive or surface interval. Dive timers function automatically — but can only be used for diving. Here is more detailed information on each:

Analog and digital watches — Dive watches are available in analog or digital models, and models that combine the features of each.

The original underwater watches — for a long time the only practical means

Dive watches with rotating bezels.

of timing dives — were water-resistant analog models with rotating bezels. To time dives or surface intervals with these watches, divers align the zero on the bezel with the watch's minute hand. Then, at the end of either a dive or a surface interval, the diver consults the watch to see how far along the bezel the minute hand has moved. This gives the length of the dive or surface interval in minutes. If more than one hour has elapsed, consult the hour hand also.

High-quality dive watches may include many of the features found on quality watches of any type, plus:

- a ratcheted bezel that only rotates counterclockwise. (If accidentally moved during a dive, it will yield a longer, more conservative bottom time.)

- a flat or recessed crystal that is less prone to scratching.

- exaggerated serrations on the bezel that make it easier to set while wearing gloves.

- a depth rating of at least 200m/660ft. (Recreational divers, of course, seldom go beyond one sixth this depth; however, most high-quality watches have this extra margin in common.)

Digital dive watches usually have a stopwatch function that divers may use to time dives or surface intervals. This yields a precise, digital readout of exactly how much time has passed, without the need to add or subtract hours or minutes.

Digital dive watches generally cost less than their analog counterparts (and many consider them less prestigious). The drawback to digital watches, however, is that the stopwatch-activating buttons are usually extremely small. This may make them extremely difficult or impossible to use when wearing gloves.

There are also special dive watches that combine the features of both digital and analog models. They afford their users the prestige associated with owning and wearing a fine analog watch — and the practical advantages of both types.

A final word about underwater watches: divers may choose from a wide variety of watch straps. The most practical of these may well be a continuous loop of fabric with either a Velcro type or buckle closure. Such straps pass through both of the pins that hold the watch to the strap. If one pin breaks, the strap — and the watch — still remain in place. The Velcro type of such straps generally have the added advantage of being able to fit over either a diver's bare skin or the exposure suit.

Despite the practical advantage of fabric straps, some divers prefer metal or rubber straps for reasons of appearance. It's best to wear watches equipped with such straps underneath a wet-suit sleeve. This helps protect against accidental loss. A few watches have specially designed metal straps that help prevent accidental loss and expand to fit over exposure suits.

Mechanical and electronic timers — The primary drawback of underwater watches is that divers must remember to set or consult them at the beginning and end of each dive or surface interval. In contrast, mechanical and electronic dive timers are activated automatically by the change in pressure just below the surface.

The first automatic dive timers were mechanical models. These were essentially pressure-activated stopwatches. Divers who used them had to remember to wind them periodically and to reset them to zero before the start of each dive. Mechanical dive timers can only be used to time dives, not surface intervals. They were generally mounted as an add-on to consoles rather than integrated into them. They could also be worn on a diver's wrist.

Electronic dive timers typically monitor bottom time, surface interval and the number of dives the user has made. Some even let divers know when it is acceptable to fly after diving and many include thermometers and ascent warning devices. These digital dive timers are available as wrist-mounted models, add-on modules to consoles or integrated with depth gauges.

Underwater compasses — An underwater compass is virtually the only dive instrument that isn't currently available in both digital and analog models. "Mechanical" compasses, in which a magnetic needle floats in an oil-filled housing, are simple and reliable.

An underwater compass has a north-pointing needle or card, a center or lubber line that indicates the direction of travel, and a rotating bezel or index marks that can be turned to match the direction in which the needle is pointing. By turning the compass until the needle matches either the zero on the bezel or the index marks, a diver knows that the compass is now pointing in the same direction as it was when this heading was set. The setting of the bezel or index marks also tells the diver this heading as measured in degrees.

Better-quality compasses are easy to read when divers look over them at an angle. Many newer compasses also have a side-reading feature, in which a diver can tell his direction of travel while looking at the compass from the side. Most divers prefer to have their compasses mounted on or in their consoles. This makes it easier to keep the center line of the compass aligned with the center of the diver's body.

Thermometers — Thermometers, while by no means essential diving instruments, can nevertheless provide divers with helpful information. They can help educate divers about the tremendous difference in heat absorption between air and water of comparable temperatures. They can also help divers record what exposure-suit combination works best for them at varying water temperatures.

Underwater thermometers in wrist and console-mounted styles.

Underwater thermometers are available in small, analog models that may attach to a wrist strap or console, or in digital or analog models that integrate with consoles and dive computers.

Dive computers — Dive computers begin by providing much of the information available from digital depth gauges, dive timers and even integrated electronic consoles. They then go one step further by telling their users when they must ascend to stay within the no-decompression limits for a particular dive. If the user exceeds these limits, some computers may calculate how much emergency decompression is required and at what depth. Some computers

The Evolution of Dive Instruments

Before the submersible pressure gauge (SPG) appeared on the market, divers relied on reserve valves to avoid out-of-air situations. This was neither totally reliable, nor comforting. Therefore, manufacturers began developing SPGs in the 1960s, but it took until the 1970s to develop a reliable and safe SPG that attached to a first stage regulator

SPGs remain a diver's most referred to and needed instrument to this day, but in the interest of safety and comfort, the diving "industrial revolution" of the 1970s and 1980s brought with it new instrumentation and configurations.

Integration became the norm in the early and mid-80s. Divers who wore their compasses and depth gauges on one wrist, and their watches and thermometers on the other, took a long time preparing themselves and found the whole experience of multi-instruments a little impractical. Therefore, when manufacturers introduced consoles that integrated SPGs, depth gauges, compasses, and sometimes thermometers, divers naturally embraced this new philosophy.

What followed was a piece-by-piece instrument evolution from time pieces to computers. For example, timers evolved from analog watches to pressure activated stop watches to digital underwater timers and dive computers. Manufacturers made digital readouts for every piece of equipment, including depth gauges and SPGs. Digital instruments are generally more accurate and give more precise readings than their analog counterparts.

Perhaps the greatest revolution in instrument technology is the dive computer. Other than giving divers updated no-decompression information every few seconds, computers became the ultimate integrated instruments by providing other pertinent dive data. This included depth, time, temperature and emergency decompression if needed.

Air-integrated computers include an SPG by connecting to the first stage high pressure port through a hose or by hoseless relay. The data tells divers their existing air supply, and gives them an estimate of the time remaining before running low on air.

While compasses have remained essentially the same for the past few decades, designers added a few features that help divers use them more efficiently. These include easy-to-sight window degree settings, glow in the dark markings for night diving and low profile design.

This instrument revolution has made diving a little easier and more comfortable. Now a diver doesn't have to look over two wrists to find out the depth and direction of travel. Also, small integrated instruments fit better, reduce the possibilities of arm and hose entanglement and look good for photography.

What does the future hold for recreational diving instrumentation? It seems that this is a question of supply and demand more than technology.

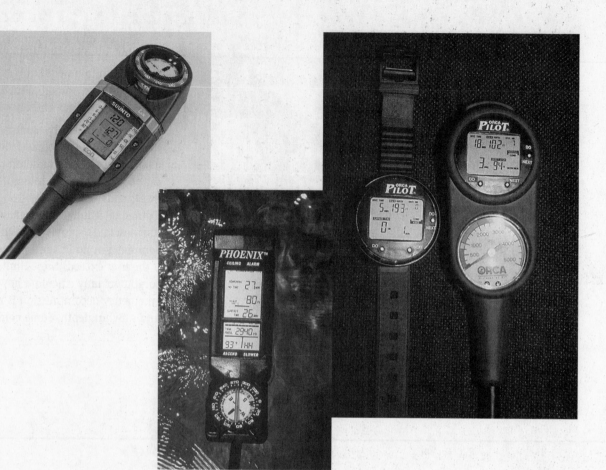

Popular dive computers, some in consoles with other instruments.

also calculate the number of minutes the available air supply will last, based on current depth and air consumption.

Electronic dive computers use their time and depth sensors to calculate the nitrogen absorption of different theoretical body tissues or "compartments" during a dive. If the nitrogen level in any of these compartments approaches acceptable limits, the computer tells the diver to ascend to a shallower depth, where, depending upon the dive, a diver may have more time available thanks to a multilevel profile. Thus, dive computers extend available time beyond the normal table limit based on the no decompression limit of the maximum depth reached.

If the nitrogen level in any com-partment exceeds acceptable limits, the computer tells the diver that emergency decompression is required, and depending on the model, may guide the diver on the depth and duration of emergency decompression stops. The exact information displayed during emergency decompression varies from computer to computer.

Currently, there are several decompression models, or algorithms used by dive computers. The models reflect various approaches to the decompression problem, and may differ in their no decompression limits, the time allowed on repetitive dives and credit for ascending to a shallower depth.

At the moment, dive computers are more expensive than other diving in-

This computer calculates air-use time limits as well as no decompression limits.

strumentation systems, but as time passes, their prices decline and features increase. Considering the convenience and the additional dive time computers provide, many divers find them well worth the investment. (For more information, see *The Recreational Divers Guide to Decompression Theory, Dive Tables and Dive Computers*, published by PADI.)

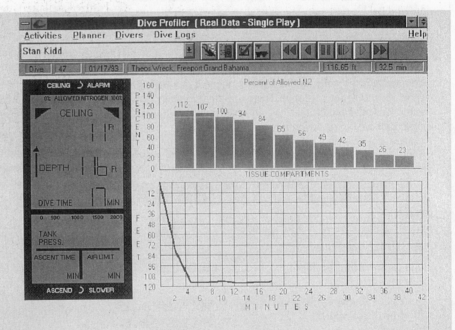

Dive computer data downloaded to a personal computer.

Diving Accessories

In addition to the four main categories of dive equipment discussed previously, there are a number of accessory items that may contribute greatly to the safety and enjoyment of each dive. These are items that all divers should either own or have access to, and use.

Dive Knives and Tools

Because there is a remote, but possible risk of entanglement while diving, divers carry some form of cutting tool. This is usually a dive knife or specialized dive tool. From a more practical

Dive Computer Use, Not Abuse

Recreational Divers Guide to Decompression Theory, Dive Tables and Dive Computers

Diving will remember the 1980s as the "computer revolution" — the period during which the dive computer dawned and shortly after, dominated. The dive computer age has unquestionably been one of the significant changes in diving since the invention of open circuit scuba.

The dive computer offers substantially more dive time than conventional dive tables when making a multilevel dive, but it doesn't change the rules of decompression theory. Dive computers and tables draw upon the same theories, test data and field experience. The difference comes from the fact that dive computers can apply these to fit the dive better, thereby eliminating unnecessary rounding and maximizing no decompression time.

In short, a dive computer is nothing more than a calculator connected to a watch and a depth gauge so it can write a custom dive table for each dive. There's nothing inherently "better" or "safer" about the "custom table" a dive computer writes compared to a conventional printed dive table. There's no *theoretical* difference between using a table and using a computer; the difference is practical in terms of more no stop dive time.

This means that the rules and recommendations that apply to dive table use apply equally to dive computers. These include:

1. Make the deepest dive of the day first, and make repetitive dives successively shallower.

2. Avoid "sawtooth" profiles that have lots of ascents and descents in a single dive.

3. Ascend at 18 metres/60 feet per minute or slower, as prescribed by the computer.

4. Stay well within computer limits, especially if factors predisposing an individual to decompression sickness apply (see the Physiology of Diving section for more about these factors and decompression theory).

5. Divers shouldn't attempt to share a single computer; each diver needs a computer.

Besides additional no decompression time, the newer dive computers have features that give these instruments additional utility.

PC Interface — Perhaps the most important new feature in several computers is the ability to download the actual profile of a dive into a personal computer. The dive computer mates with a computer interface that takes dive data (either by reading code on the LCD face or, most commonly, by reading data through electronic contacts), and brings it into the PC.

A special program (most are in the Windows™ platform) runs the interface and displays the data. Typical displays include a profile, which charts the dive time and depth, and log book displays, which accept manually entered additional information for permanent storage.

More sophisticated PC interfaces permit the diver to modify the dive computer program, such as adjusting ascent rates and maximum nitrogen levels permitted. Generally, the maximums of these computers are within accepted ranges, but the interface option allows the computer to display more conservative figures.

Enriched air dive computers benefit divers trained and certified to use enriched air (nitrox). The diver sets the computer for the enriched air blend used, and the computer tracks the oxygen exposure and no stop dive time. The combination of dive computer and enriched air can provide incredibly long no stop times. Again, however, the computer does not relieve the diver of having to follow the same recommendations, guidelines and procedures that enriched air divers using tables must follow.

standpoint, a dive knife or tool provides divers with a means to measure, pry and accomplish other tasks.

Dive knives come in a variety of styles and sizes. They range from knives that are similar in appearance and size to large hunting knives (Bowie style blades), to compact, stiletto-like knives that are small enough to fit alongside a diver's console. Dive knives differ from other knives primarily in the type of metal used to make them and the handle design and sheath.

Most dive knives are made from No. 440 stainless steel or a similar metal. This grade of stainless steel provides a good compromise between resistance to corrosion and the ability to hold an edge. Some knives are also plated to provide additional corrosion protection.

Most dive knives will rust if not cleaned thoroughly after each dive. This is the price divers pay for having knives that hold an edge longer than if a more corrosion-resistant grade of metal were used. Some knives may also need disassembly during cleaning so the diver can

clean the area inside the handle.

Dive knives must have handles that divers can grip easily while wearing gloves. Most larger dive knives have oversized rubber handles. Many smaller dive knives have handles that are extensions of the blade, but are serrated for a better grip.

In addition to a cutting edge on one or both sides, many dive knives have features such as:

- a serrated edge for sawing or filing.
- a notched section specially designed for grabbing and cutting line.
- distance markings etched into the blade for measuring.

Virtually all dive knives come with a sheath. The sheath generally has two straps so that the diver may attach it to a leg or an arm. Sheaths have straps that stretch to compensate for exposure-suit compression.

A rubber retaining ring or a quick-release mechanism, such as a push button generally secures the dive knife in its sheath. The quick-release mechanism

Diving knives and tool.

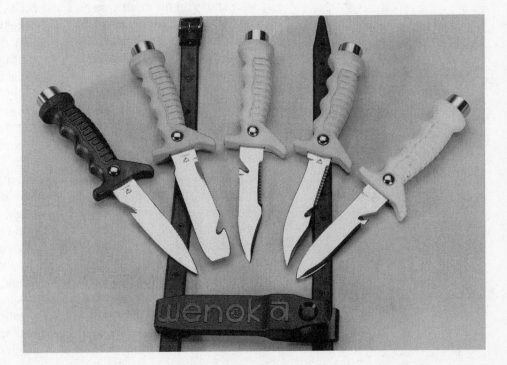

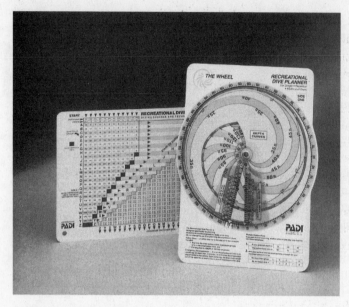

Dive tables and dive planner.

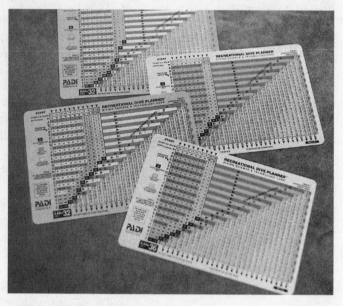

Enriched air (nitrox) dive planners.

appears to have become the more popular approach during the past few years.

Most divers wear larger knives on the inside of their calves for easy access and to avoid entanglement. Divers can also wear knives on the thigh, arm or weight belt. A popular custom wet-suit option is a knife pocket designed to hold the knife sheath and avoid the need for straps. Several instrument consoles may offer a compact dive knife as a built-in feature or an add-on option.

Dive tools are essentially knives with a prying or screwdriver-style tip instead of a point. They are similar to dive knives in most other respects and many divers recognize them as simply another form of dive knife.

Divers who fly and transport their equipment in carry-on luggage may find that a utilitarian-looking diving tool is easier to explain to airport security than a commando-style stiletto. Nonetheless, it's usually simpler to carry dive knives and tools in checked luggage.

Plastic Dive Tables and Dive Planners

Most divers have a paper version of the dive tables in their dive manual or log book, although this is of little value once they go underwater. Because divers may accidentally exceed preplanned depth and time limits, or because their computers may malfunction, they may take with them a set of plastic dive tables or dive planners to help them recalculate their dive profiles. This helps avoid situations in which divers surface to find that they have missed a required, emergency decompression stop — or one in which they surfaced prematurely, missing extra bottom time they could have enjoyed had they had tables at their disposal underwater.

Plastic dive tables or planners should, of course, be easy to read and follow. They should also provide precalculated, adjusted no-decompression limits for different combinations of depth and repetitive group.

Log Books

A diver's certification card only provides evidence that, at one point in time, the diver met the performance standards required for certification at that level. Unless there are current Scuba Review stickers or Discover Local Diving stamps attached to it, there is nothing on the card to indicate the frequency or breadth of experience a diver has had since certification.

This is but one of the many reasons that divers carry and use log books. Additional reasons for using log books include:

- Log books provide an excellent means to relive and share one's diving experiences. They provide a tangible record of an individual's dive history.

- Divers may often include details about a particular dive that they might otherwise forget. This can be helpful information about environmental conditions, the type of equipment used or how to dive the site under the prevailing conditions.

- Log books are required proof-of-experience for many levels of leadership training.

- An increasing number of dive operations requires divers to present both a certification card *and* a log book before they will provide dive services.

The minimum information a log book should provide for each dive is the date, dive-site location, depth, time and a means for a dive buddy, divemaster or instructor to verify the log entry. Most log books provide additional entries for divers to record information on environmental conditions, the type of dive, equipment used and comments or observations.

In addition to the different styles of log books, several companies now offer computer dive logs through specialized software. In addition to allowing for all the information one can include in a regular log book, some of these programs automatically add the dive number, the total bottom time after each dive and even compute the diver's pressure group after each dive and surface interval.

PADI Adventure Log binders and inserts.

Underwater slates.

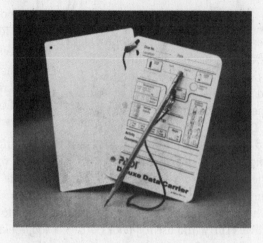

Slates

Unless divers are fluent in sign language, there is a limit to the amount of information they can communicate by simple hand signals. The use of gloves further complicates this process.

Underwater slates enable divers to communicate relatively complex information. Divers can further speed communications by writing down commonly used messages on their slates ahead of time and pointing to the appropriate message when the need arises. Underwater research and similar activities are highly dependent on the ability of divers to record detailed information on underwater slates.

Most underwater slates are approximately the same size as plastic dive tables. Many divers keep these together on a ring with their tables and similar plastic information cards. Some slates are built into the backs of instrument consoles.

To work adequately, slates must have an attached pencil that functions reliably underwater. It also helps to attach an eraser as well, so that the user can erase unneeded or confusing messages underwater.

Other forms of underwater slates include one that allows divers to write on an easily erasable magnetic surface that doubles as a regular slate on the opposite side.

Equipment Bags and Carrying Systems

Until assembled and donned, scuba equipment consists of a number of loose, separate items. To transport and tempo-

Equipment bags come in a variety of styles, materials and sizes.

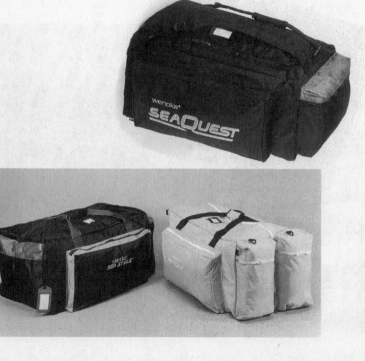

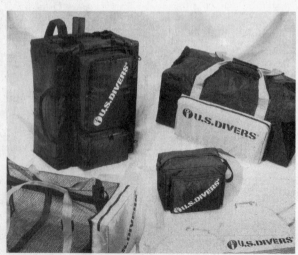

rarily store equipment, divers use a variety of equipment bags and carrying systems.

Equipment or gear bags range from small, lightweight fabric or mesh bags used to carry snorkeling equipment to large, heavy-duty backpack or duffel-style bags that can accommodate all the equipment a diver might need for cold water diving, short of a cylinder and weights. These large, compartmentalized gear bags fit the needs of most divers. Such a bag enables the diver to suit up aboard a crowded dive boat while minimizing the possibility of loss or damage to equipment and occupying the least space.

One of the most popular designs in equipment bags during the past few years has been the backpack-style model. These have shoulder straps and possibly a waistband that allow a diver to comfortably transport the weight and bulk of his equipment on the back. These straps may zipper into special compartments when not in use.

Most backpack-style gear bags have separate compartments for items such as fins, masks and regulators. Some of these compartments may be padded, to minimize the possibility of damage to more delicate items such as masks.

Recent equipment bag innovations include wheeled models that allow divers to tow their heavy bags rather than carry them for long distances. Both duffel- and backpack style equipment bags may come with wheels that make moving these bags much easier for divers.

Dive Flag and Float

Divers often share the water with other people. To let others know where they are — to warn watercraft and skiers to stay away — dive teams may tow or anchor a float and flag. In some jurisdictions or countries, dive flags are required by law.

Depending on where and under what conditions a dive takes place, the appropriate dive flag may be either a red rectangle with a white, diagonal stripe or a blue and white, double-tailed pennant. Some divers fly both flags.

When diving from a boat, the dive

Dive flags and floats.

flag usually flies from the mast or most visible part of the boat. Divers entering from shore, or who travel some distance from the boat fly their flag from a float. Floats can either be smaller models, designed simply to support a flag staff, or they may be larger units that can also store extra weight, or other items that divers may not want to carry with them underwater. Users can usually store the line that runs between the divers and the float on a reel or spool. If divers remain in a single location, they may anchor their float to the bottom and remain in its immediate vicinity.

Local laws may regulate how close divers must remain to their flag and how far watercraft and skiers must stay away. If there are no laws governing these distances, a common recommendation is that divers remain and surface within 15m/50ft of the flag and that boats remain at least 30-60m/100-200ft away.

Submersible flares, a whistle and an inflatable signal tube in a neat package.

Rescue Diver Manual

Signaling and Safety Devices

Divers can use a variety of signaling de-

vices to attract attention for normal or emergency situations. These can be as simple as whistles for surface use. Most divers wear BCDs that are either factory-equipped with whistles, or add them to their ensemble.

There are, however, a number of other signaling and attention-getting devices that divers can use in an emergency. These include power whistles, small emergency strobes, flares, dye markers and inflatable signal tubes. Divers can inflate these tubes, which stand up on the surface, and make divers much more visible from boats. All these items can fit into a BCD jacket for easy access.

Emergency oxygen equipment and first aid kits vary from simple units for personal use to comprehensive sets that a divemaster or instructor may have available while supervising dive groups. Emergency oxygen systems supply medical grade oxygen to treat decompression illness and near drowning. Systems that combine demand and free flow systems are generally preferred. Many divers also carry pocket masks for rescue breathing, in and out of the water. Divers often carry pocket masks in their BCD pockets, and may keep them with first aid kits and emergency oxygen equpment. The PADI *Rescue Diver Manual* lists items recommended for a diving first aid kit.

Specialty Dive Equipment

Specialized dive activities often require using specialized dive equipment. Some of this equipment, such as underwater cameras, is unique to a particular specialty. Divers may use other equipment, such as underwater lights, as part of several activities and specialties.

This subsection provides an overview of many common pieces of specialty dive equipment. It also describes what they are and some of their applications.

Underwater Lights

Underwater lights are a vital part of night, cavern and, in some instances, wreck diving. In addition, divers may use them during daytime sight-seeing dives to look into cracks and crevices and to restore some of the natural color to objects that lose their true colors at depth.

For night, cavern and wreck penetration diving, prudent divers carry at least two battery-powered lights. The

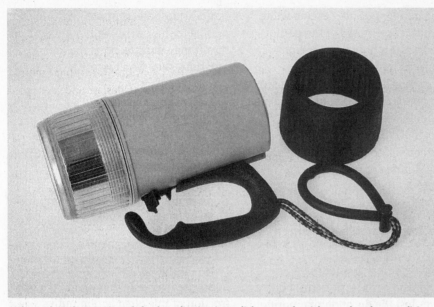

Lights such as these are intended to be a diver's primary light source for night, wreck and cavern diving.

ies. Rechargeable batteries cost more, but are less expensive to use over a long period. Nonrechargeable batteries are less expensive, but once discharged become useless.

Rechargeable batteries generally provide a greater, more consistent level of power — but do so over a shorter period. As their charge drops, the light output fades rapidly. Nonrechargeable batteries burn longer, but — as their charge diminishes, the light output fades gradually .

Recharging a light after use generally takes four to 12 hours — sometimes longer. A nonrechargeable light simply needs new batteries for reuse.

Rechargeable lights — particularly those using dry Ni-cad cells as opposed to gel

larger of these is the diver's primary light — the one that he depends upon for the majority of the dive. Because underwater lights break, divers carry a backup light, which will usually guide them to the exit point should their primary lights fail.

For night diving, divers also use a small marker light, usually a chemical light, attached to their cylinder valve or snorkel. This serves two functions:

1. It helps divers locate each other, even if their light beams point in opposite directions.

2. Should divers suffer a failure of both their primary and backup lights, marker lights help other divers locate them. They may even provide a modest amount of light to see by, so that divers who wear them can have some light while ascending.

Chemical and marker lights may also mark anchors, descent lines and other reference points divers may establish as part of their dive.

Battery Types

Underwater lights may use either rechargeable or nonrechargeable batter-

Small lights make good back-up lights for night, wreck and cavern diving and provide a convenient source of illumination during daylight dives.

cells — are more prone to damage through mishandling. Suddenly jarring some dry Ni-cad-powered rechargeable lights can cause them to discharge rapidly. It can be harmful to allow a rechargeable Ni-cad light to discharge completely.

It's also possible to damage some rechargeable lights through improper recharging procedures. Recharging lights that are partially discharged or charging for too short a period may cause the battery pack to develop what is known as a "memory" of the partial charge. Once this happens, the light won't burn as long as it should.

Nonrechargeable batteries stand up better to abuse. They also appear to be more reliable when a light sits unused for a prolonged period.

For these reasons, rechargeable batteries are suitable only for primary lights that:

- divers use frequently.
- will be properly recharged between dives.
- have owners who care for them properly and who desire a powerful light that can last the duration of a normal dive.

Nonrechargeable, alkaline batteries work better for:

- backup lights.
- primary lights that receive infrequent use.
- any light that won't receive optimum care.

Divers can prolong nonrechargeable battery life by removing them from the light and storing them in a cold environment, such as a refrigerator.

A submersible strobe light.

Primary Lights

Primary dive lights are generally larger and heavier than backup lights. They have a lens that is several centimeters or inches across and they use at least a lantern battery or an equivalent number of D cells.

Some primary lights have separate battery packs that connect to the light by a flexible cord. Bulbs for such lights range from sealed-beam lantern bulbs to powerful quartz-halogen bulbs mounted inside specially designed parabolic reflectors.

Most primary lights have either a pistol grip or a separate, parallel handle. Most divers attach this grip or handle to their wrists with a lanyard, so that if they must let go of the light at any time, they won't lose it.

Backup Lights

The lights that most divers prefer as backup lights are seldom much larger than the diameter of the C-size or smaller batteries they contain. This small diameter allows users to grip the light much like they would a common flashlight.

Many of these lights use three C cells — although special-purpose dive lights are available that are only a tiny fraction of this already diminutive size.

Advances in bulb and reflector technology have made it possible to create small lights that provide substantial illumination. In some cases, the output rivals that provided by larger, more powerful lights. Yet they are compact enough — and inexpensive enough — to make ideal backup lights. Divers may also carry such lights conveniently on daytime dives, enabling them to restore lost colors to underwater objects or peer into dark places.

While most divers use a lanyard in conjunction with their primary lights, they may simply clip backup lights on to a BCD or store them inside the BCD pocket.

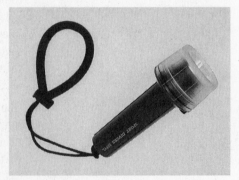
Compact back up light.

Night Diving

Underwater Imaging Systems

A wide variety of equipment enables recreational divers to take still photos, movies and underwater videos. All underwater imaging systems share two special needs: the need for water and pressure protection and, in many cases, the need for an artificial light source to restore lost color.

Rapid technological advancements in still photography, and especially video, make systems obsolete or dated quickly. Therefore, divers should decide on what's best for their needs before purchasing an imaging system, and should consult closely with an underwater photography specialist before investing heavily in a system.

35mm underwater camera systems with self-contained camera and strobes.

Amphibious single lens reflex camera

Photography Systems

Still photo equipment for underwater photography varied in the past from self-contained 110 cameras to housed medium-format cameras. Experience showed that 110 cameras and other cameras that use built-in strobes don't provide the necessary quality desired by those with serious interest in photography.

Cameras that use separate strobes, interchangeable lenses, and variable settings, on the other hand, provide recreational photographers with the same equipment used to take quality magazine photographs.

There are basically two types of underwater still photography systems: amphibious camera systems, and housed camera systems.

More expensive 35mm amphibious cameras use separate underwater strobes. They provide professional-quality photos at nearly any recreational depth, and can use a variety of lenses. A major camera manufacturer, Nikon, markets an amphibious single lens reflex camera (SLR). Due to this camera's high purchase cost, the same manufacturer still offers its viewfinder model, which has dominated the underwater photography market since its inception in the mid-60s. Other companies today also offer a wide range of underwater cameras, strobes lenses and accessories.

Divers can also obtain watertight housings for many land cameras, including most popular 35mm and medium-format cameras. Some serious underwater photographers prefer this approach since it gives them access to a much greater variety of lenses and accessories than is available for amphibious cameras. Housed systems are usually bulkier and more expensive than traditional underwater amphibious cameras, and there are several companies that offer a wide range of housings for most top-of-the-line cameras.

Movie and Video Systems

Underwater housings for 8mm, 16mm and 35mm movie cameras have been available for a number of years. Use of housed movie cameras remains the preferred approach for creating professional underwater wildlife documentaries.

With video becoming increasingly popular, many divers use housed video camcorders of all types. The ability to have both the camera and the recorder in a single compact unit, coupled with video's extreme ease of use and no developing delays, has made this approach irresistible to a great number of divers.

Video cameras and equipment are going through one of the fastest changes in the history of technology. Therefore, divers should pick a system that works for their needs, and not worry about every new break in camcorder technology. Some of the available video chip technology today costs a few thousand U.S. dollars and rivals professional Betacam quality, which costs considerably more. Luckily for divers, this mainstream technology, coupled with underwater housings, creates excellent video images of the underwater world.

Both underwater movie and video systems share a common need for a sustained source of artificial light. Unlike still cameras, whose strobes and flashes need only shine for a tiny fraction of a second, movie and video cameras need a continuous light source.

Although these lighting systems are available, many divers use video cameras without lights, especially in shallow or clear water. These lights are convenient, however, when recording in deeper water, at night or inside crevices.

Search and Recovery Tools

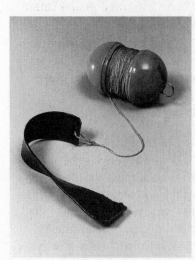

Portable marker buoy.

Search and recovery is a broad area that covers everything from finding objects that accidentally fall overboard to discovering buried treasures. The basic tools for this activity include marker buoys, metal detectors and lift bags.

Marker Buoys

A common means of locating objects underwater is running a boat over the area and monitoring sonar signals. Unfortunately, divers may quickly lose the object if they cannot mark its location within seconds of passing over it. Special marker buoys work well for this purpose, and divers can simply toss the marker overboard and a weighted line unrolls and anchors itself on the bottom near the object. These same markers work equally well when deployed by divers who find objects underwater and send a marker to the surface.

Metal Detectors

Divers can locate many objects underwater by using simple search patterns. However, when the object is metallic — and especially if it has been underwater for some time — it can easily become buried under sand, sediment or coral.

To find such buried objects divers may use special underwater metal detectors. These range from small models that divers can carry and use underwater, to large magnetometers that ships tow.

The type most often used by recreational divers consists of an elctrometal plate mounted on a long handle. The plate passes over the bottom, emitting a magnetic field. Metal disrupts the field pattern, which the detector registers and then emits an audible signal or shows movement on a dial.

Another type sends out electromagnetic pulses, and compares the characteristics of sequential pulses as the detector moves to detect metal.

Lift Bags

Divers have to occasionally bring a lost object to the surface. Unless the object is small enough to fit into a diver's palm or BCD pocket, the best method involves using a lift bag.

Lift bags usually resemble small hot-air balloons. After attaching the object, divers inflate the lift bag using air from the extra second stage or a special air-inflation tool. Better quality lift bags have a venting mechanism so the diver can release expanding air and keep the bag's rate of ascent under control on the way to the surface.

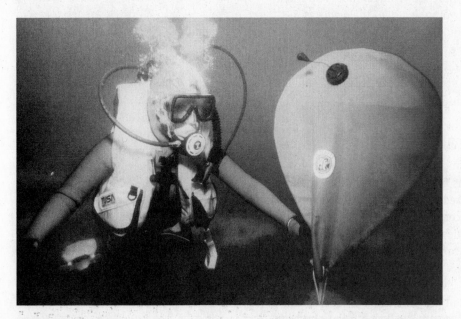

Lift bags may be used to bring objects to the surface. A valve on the lift bag allows the diver to control the ascent rate.

Other Specialty Dive Equipment

The Nav-Finder

There are other pieces of specialty dive equipment that divers may use for a variety of purposes. These include:

The Nav-Finder

The Nav-Finder is an underwater plotting board that divers can use to track a complex underwater course. Its uses include map making, search and recovery and underwater navigation. A particularly valuable use of the device is recording a complex, multileg compass course. The Nav-Finder can quickly provide divers with the compass heading that takes them directly back to their starting point.

Locator Systems

Personal diver locator systems help divers find a boat's anchor line or any marked object by using a transmitter (beacon) and receiver system. Divers can tie the beacon to an anchor line and carry one or more receiver. The receivers point to the beacon so the divers can always find the quickest way to the boat at the conclusion of a dive. The beacon can also be left at a point that divers wish to return to on a later dive.

The various models and styles use different signal readouts and have various ranges and other features. Divers who use these systems benefit from them especially in low visibility and night diving conditions.

Communication Systems

There are several communication systems available to recreational divers today. These include sophisticated full-face mask configurations to simpler mouthpiece microphone systems that may be used with a conventional scuba mask. Optional surface stations allow divers to communicate with the surface and vice versa.

Various models have different ranges, frequencies, operating depths,

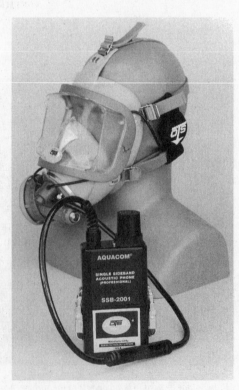

Personal through water communication system

Dive reel

battery types and other features. These systems allow divers to talk underwater, which may be essential in certain conditions, such as film making and commercial operations. Specific models are now available for recreational use. These have less range than commercial units, but are simple to use and much less expensive.

Reels

Reels are an invaluable safety and convenience tool for a number of specialty diving activities. In search-and-recovery diving, they allow divers to quickly establish a circular-sweep search pattern. They are critical to cavern and wreck-penetration diving, where divers must have a continuous guideline back to the surface. For underwater navigation, they're helpful in setting up a course over which divers may measure the time and number of kicks required to go a certain distance. They may also be used in night diving by divers who want to make doubly certain that they can find their way back to their entry and exit point.

Diver Propulsion Vehicles

Diver propulsion vehicles — also known as DPVs or "scooters" — allow divers to cover large distances underwater without having to kick. Because they save energy, they reduce air consumption or allow divers to go farther and see more on a single air cylinder. They also provide some disabled divers with an efficient means of propulsion.

DPVs typically consist of a housing containing a rechargeable battery and headlight with handles and a shrouded propeller. The propeller's speed may be fixed or variable, with the on-off switch that stops the propeller whenever the operator releases the handle. This prevents a DPV from disappearing in the distance because its operator accidentally let go.

Some DPVs come equipped with a towing harness to reduce the strain on a diver's arms. Some models also have "dashboards" on which divers can mount depth gauges, compasses and other instruments. This can:

- reduce the need for DPV operators to stop and look at their instrument consoles while instantly alerting them of their depth (it's easy to descend or ascend very quickly on a scooter without realizing it).

- allow operators to maintain a compass heading while traveling underwater or on the surface.

Prudent DPV Use

Not only can DPVs take divers deep quickly, they can take divers farther in a matter of minutes than they can swim back using their remaining air. This is an important consideration since scooters can malfunction and their batteries can discharge with little warning.

One technique divers can use to keep from going too far is to remain within sight of a single set of reference points at all times. Another technique is to limit scooter use to recognizable terrain they can swim back from with minimum air.

An ideal situation is one in which two divers each have their own scooters and are conscientious about remaining together (It's easy to become separated while using DPVs). By limiting scooter excursions to half the duration of the expected battery charge or less, a diver with a functioning DPV can tow a buddy whose scooter malfunctions. On the other hand, if divers don't plan and monitor their battery consumption, both DPVs could run down within minutes of each other, some distance from the divers' exit point.

It's very common for two or more divers to tow each other using a single DPV. In this situation, divers who head away from their exit point should remember to turn around after using only a fraction of their total air supply. This helps ensure that, if the scooter ceases to function, the divers will have sufficient air to return to their starting point without a long surface swim.

Another important consideration when using DPVs is watching the ascent and descent rates. It's important for divers to remember their training and equalize early and often, while descending. It's also quite important to ascend slowly while using a DPV to avoid lung expansion injuries or other maladies associated with quick ascents. Divers must remain cognizant of their depth and ascent rate anytime they use a DPV, especially when maneuvering in a way that they don't usually do with fins.

It's a good idea for DPV divers to enroll in a specialty course that teaches proper DPV use and to practice using them in a confined water environment before going to open water. It's also important to maintain these expensive pieces of equipment properly according to the manufacturer's recommendations.

Careful dive planning and cautious ascents help prevent long return swims and difficulties due to high ascent rates.

The Aquatic Realm

Four

Introduction to the Aquatic Realm

This section follows the current mainstream scientific approach to the geologic time scale. There are other views. This is not an endorsement of a particular philosophy; the aim is to provide useful information for as many readers as possible.

This view of the Earth was seen by the Apollo 17 crewmen as they traveled toward the moon. Shown in the photograph are the Mediterranean Sea area, the Antarctic ice cap and almost the entire African coastline. Photo courtesy of NASA.

Purpose and Goals

The earth's oceans, seas, rivers and lakes are home to a tremendous number of organisms. This section identifies these species: from the smallest single-celled plants to the largest animal on this planet, the blue whale. It also discusses how people can interact with these creatures in a positive, safe and responsible way.

From kelp beds to coral reefs, each habitat presents unique conditions that shape many characteristics of indigenous species. These diverse organisms have developed a number of successful, and occasionally dramatic, adaptations that reflect the nature of the dense, fluid environment in which they live. This section further overviews the nature of the aquatic realm and these adaptations.

Some of the most rewarding underwater experiences involve aquatic life interaction.

The World's Oceans

The world's oceans cover approximately 71 percent of the earth's surface, with an average depth of 3800 metres/12,500 feet. About 80 percent of the Southern Hemisphere is covered by water, compared to 61 percent of the Northern Hemisphere.

Despite the fact that 84 percent of the seafloor rests at depths below 1825 metres/6000 feet, most of our knowledge of the aquatic realm is confined to depths less than 90 metres/300 feet. Considering that most divers rarely venture below 30 metres/100 feet, our relative ignorance of the earth's aquatic environments is to be expected.

Ocean Basins

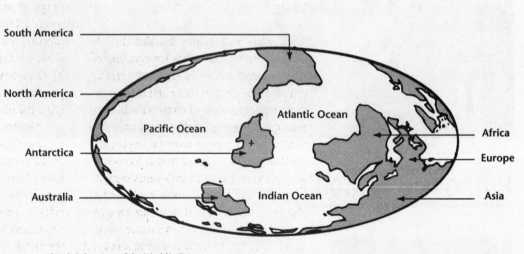

South Polar view of the World's Oceans.

The world's oceans can be separated into four major basins: the 1) Atlantic, 2) Pacific, 3) Indian and 4) Arctic. From a South-Polar view, it is clear how these major bodies of water form one large, interconnected ocean system. The Antarctic continent is surrounded by the Antarctic Ocean, which has three large embayments extending northward. These three oceanic extensions, partially separated by continental barriers, are the Atlantic, Pacific and Indian oceans. Other smaller oceans and seas, such as the Arctic Ocean and the Mediterranean Sea, project from the margins of the larger ocean basins. Connections between the major ocean basins permit exchange of seawater as well as marine plants and animals.

An equatorial view of the earth does not show the significant connections between the world's oceans. However, because man's interest in the world's oceans has centered in the tropical and temperate regions, this view is more practical. The Pacific, Atlantic and Indian ocean basins cover the majority of the earth.

Topographical Features of Ocean Basins

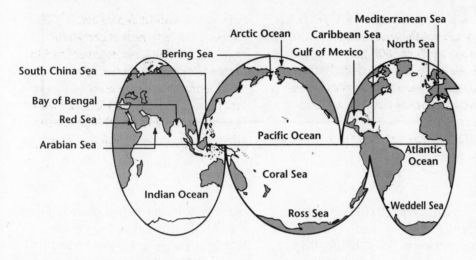

An equatorial view of the World's Oceans. Note the size of the Pacific Ocean alone.

The ocean floor — from the shoreline to its greatest depths — has topographical features that create diverse and varied terrain. The continental shelf is an underwater extension of continental landmasses. If the sea level lowered only five percent of its present average depth, the shelf would be exposed to air. As recently as 10,000 to 15,000 years ago, a large portion of the current continental shelf was land. At that time, an ice age caused much of the ocean's water to become solid ice, thereby lowering sea level and exposing the continental shelf.

The width of the continental shelf varies considerably, from a few kilometres/miles offshore (such as off Miami) to hundreds of kilometres/miles offshore (as in Alaska). In total area, the continental shelf accounts for about eight percent of the total seafloor surface area. However, some of the world's most valuable and sensitive ecosystems are found in this area due to light penetration of the relatively shallow waters. Divers have a particular interest in the continental shelf, because practically all diving takes place in this narrow, coastal band.

The edge of the continental shelf drops off at a significant angle at depths around 110-190 metres/350-600 feet, beginning the continental slope. This slope continues down to depths of 2800-3700 metres/9000-12,000 feet, where the largest surface area of the seafloor begins, the abyssal plains.

Undersea mountain chains called *oceanic ridges* occupy about 30 percent of the ocean-basin area. Seamounts and many islands are formed by the volcanic activity that takes place along these ridges. The tallest peaks of these linear mountain systems occasionally break the surface, creating islands such as Iceland and Ascension Island.

A Comparison of the Major Ocean Basins

Ocean	Area $x10^6$ km²/mile²	Volume, $x10^6$ km³/mile³	Average Depth, m/ft	Maximum Depth m/ft
Pacific	165.2/63.8	707.6/169.8	4282/13,917	11,022/35,822
Atlantic	82.4/31.8	323.6/77.7	3926/12,760	9200/29,900
Indian	73.4/28.3	291.0/69.8	3963/12,880	7460/24,245
Arctic	14.1/5.4	17.0/4.1	1205/3916	4300/13,975
Caribbean	4.3/1.7	9.6/2.3	2216/7202	7200/23,400
Mediterranean	3.0/1.2	4.2/1	1429/4644	4600/14,950
Other	18.7/7.2	17.3/4.2		

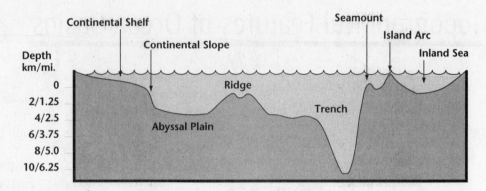

An idealized cross section of the ocean bottom showing the major topographical features. The horizontal scale is greatly compressed.

Finally, deep trenches cut into the deepest parts of the ocean. Usually found at the margins of basins, deep-ocean trenches are especially common in the Pacific. The deepest point in any ocean is the Challenger Deep in the Marianas Trench in the western north Pacific at 11,022 metres/36,250 feet.

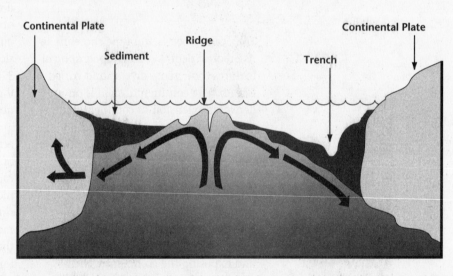

Graphic representation of a cross section of sea floor spreading showing the relative direction of motion of oceanic and continental crust.

Plate Tectonics and Seafloor Spreading

The world's ocean basins have not always been in their current configuration. Beneath the soft sediments covering most of the deep-ocean floor is the earth's crust. This outer covering is made up of a top layer of sediments in varying degrees of consolidation into sedimentary rock and an underlying layer of dense volcanic rock. Evidence indicates that the ocean-basin floors are moving horizontally at the rate of about 2.5 centimetres/1 inch per year. In a process called *seafloor spreading*, new crust forms through volcanic activity at the oceanic ridges. The new material is carried away from the ridge as if it was on a conveyor

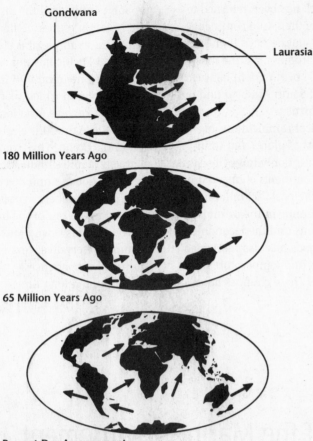

180 Million Years Ago

65 Million Years Ago

Present Day Arrangement

belt until it approaches the continental slope. At this point, one of two things happens. Either the crust is forced down into the earth's mantle, where it melts, or it is pushed up onto a continent to form a coastal mountain-range. The mechanism behind this movement of the earth's crust is probably a convective process where molten rock surfaces by volcanic activity, moves away from eruption sites and is forced back down into the mantle when it reaches a solid boundary.

The earth's crust consists of several major plates whose boundaries are trenches or ridges. On top of these plates and moving with them are the continents. As a result of this coordinated movement, the continents have drifted long distances over geologic time. Seafloor spreading also accounts for many well-known phenomena: the rocks to either side of a ridge increase in age as one moves away from the ridge's center; oceanic sediments more than 200 million years old are relatively rare because

The direction of movement and relative position of the major continental land masses over time. About 200 million years ago, one large land mass, Pangaea, separated into two large continental masses, Laurasia and Gondwana. Since then they have separated into smaller masses which have drifted apart in the directions indicated by arrows.

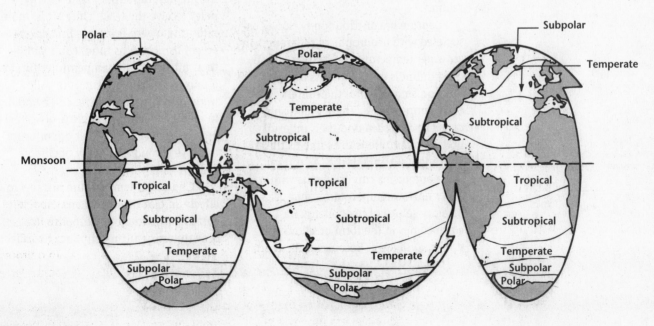

Global marine climatic zones.

most crustal rock has been returned to the mantle since then; and continents exhibit a jigsaw-puzzle fit as if one large block had been fragmented, the most obvious example being the fit between the east coast of South America and the west coast of Africa.

The biological ramifications of these movements of plates and continents are great. Not only have the coastlines of all the continents changed dramatically over the past 200 million years, but the change in the arrangement of continents and the location of island archipelagos has also reoriented oceanic currents and temperature patterns worldwide. These changes have probably influenced the distribution and isolation of marine flora and fauna. For example, it is clear that the Indo-West Pacific has not changed for some time, meaning that the area has been a center in which species have had a chance to evolve for a long period. Some believe that this is where life began in the ocean. This, combined with a relatively stable climate, has allowed species to flourish and diversify, creating a great number of species that have radiated to the rest of the tropical Pacific basin. This is why Micronesia, for example, offers divers extremely varied marine life experiences— it has simply been around a long time.

Physical Characteristics of the Marine Environment

Temperature

Temperature is one of the most influential environmental factors in the aquatic realm.

Marine life distribution is closely associated with geographical differences in seawater temperatures. This is because most animals and all plants lack a mechanism to control their internal body temperatures. These organisms are called *cold-blooded* and their internal body temperature is the same as the environmental temperature. As a result, these organisms can only exist within a fairly narrow temperature range. The primary source of heat energy for the earth comes in the form of solar radiation from the sun. Because of the earth's curvature, the planet and (more specifically) the planet's water heat differentially. The equatorial latitudes receive the greatest amount of solar energy, the poles receive the least. Only birds, mammals and a very few large *pelagic (open ocean)* fish, such as tuna, can regulate their internal body temperatures (up to a point). These organisms are called *warm-blooded (homeothermic)*. The ability to regulate body temperature gives these organisms a much greater opportunity to move through a variety of climate zones.

Change in temperature has several effects on aquatic organisms. First, it can alter the rate of metabolism (cell growth, oxygen consumption, heartbeat

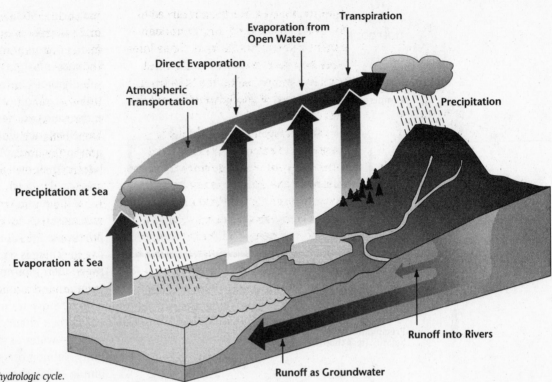

Direct Evaporation

Evaporation from Open Water

Transpiration

Atmospheric Transportation

Precipitation

Precipitation at Sea

Evaporation at Sea

Runoff into Rivers

Runoff as Groundwater

An idealized drawing of the hydrologic cycle. Water enters the atmosphere primarily through evaporation and transpiration by plants. Water returns to the planet surface primarily through precipitation.

and other physiological processes). For cold-blooded organisms, the environmental temperature regulates their metabolism. As a rule, metabolic rates for such animals increase two to three times with every 10°C/50°F rise in temperature. Clearly, seasonal changes in water temperature can profoundly affect aquatic organisms. A cold-blooded species' ability to tolerate temperature fluctuations can be crucial to its survival. Many aquatic organisms use seasonal changes in temperature to trigger the release of sperm and eggs into the water. Species common to Pacific Northwest shores, such as the bay mussel, use this environmental cue to ensure that all the individual mussels within the region spawn at once.

Water Chemistry

The chemical composition of water is another major factor influencing the aquatic realm. Seawater is the accumulated product of the mixing, over mil-lions of years, of particles from air, rocks and soil with rainwater. Compounds from these sources compose about 3.5 percent of seawater. The other 96.5 percent is pure water. Traces of all naturally occurring substances can be found in the world's oceans and generally fall into one of three categories: inorganic substances (usually referred to as salts and nutrients), dissolved gases, and organic compounds (usually originating from living organisms). In recent years another category has emerged: organic and synthetic compounds such as DDT and other pollutants, which can have devastating effects on aquatic life.

The bulk of material dissolved in the oceans' water is salts. The amount of salt in water is referred to as salinity and is measured in parts per thousand ($^{0}/_{00}$). Average sea water salinity is 35 $^{0}/_{00}$. Salinity ranges from 0 $^{0}/_{00}$ in freshwater rivers, streams and lakes to over 40 $^{0}/_{00}$ in regions of the Red Sea. Salinity changes due to precipitation or evaporation and varies greatly where shallow bays or in-

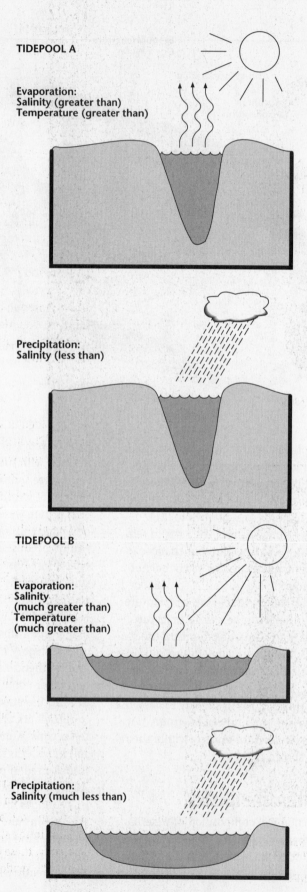

TIDEPOOL A

Evaporation:
Salinity (greater than)
Temperature (greater than)

Precipitation:
Salinity (less than)

TIDEPOOL B

Evaporation:
Salinity
(much greater than)
Temperature
(much greater than)

Precipitation:
Salinity (much less than)

Effects of pool shape and volume on physical factors in a tidepool habitat. Deep and having a small surface area, tidepool A remains stable physically, with less water loss and gain through precipitation and evaporation than in tidepool B, which is unstable physically due to its large surface area and shallowness. Temperature and salinity vary less in tidepool A.

lets enclose bodies of water. On a smaller scale, tide pools can provide an example of an environment subject to dramatic changes in salinity. During a rainstorm, salinity drops as fresh water dilutes salt water, or, on a hot day, salinity rises as evaporation carries away fresh water. The effect such water chemistry changes have on aquatic plants and animals relates to their own internal chemical balance.

All aquatic plants, invertebrates and most fish have body fluids that approximate the salinity of the water they live in. There is a chemical balance between their internal body fluids and the external environment. Most plants or animals have no mechanism that can adjust their chemical balance if they experience water of radically different salinity. Salmon are perhaps the best example of fish that exhibit *osmoregulation*, the mechanism that allows them to migrate between fresh and salt water.

Dissolved Gases

Oxygen, carbon dioxide and nitrogen are the most abundant gases found dissolved in water; the amounts vary with environmental and biological factors. One factor affecting the solubility of gases in water is temperature. Cold water can hold more gas than warm water. The metabolic activity of plants and animals also determines the amounts and kinds of gases in water. Plants produce oxygen and use carbon dioxide during photosynthesis while animals use oxygen and produce carbon dioxide during respiration.

Carbon dioxide is abundant in most regions of the world's oceans. Oxygen dissolves into water either as a by-product of photosynthetic activity or, to a small degree, from the atmosphere. The result is that the surface of the world's oceans is rich in oxygen, while the ocean depths tend to be low in oxygen, demonstrating the critical role plants play in oxygen distribution.

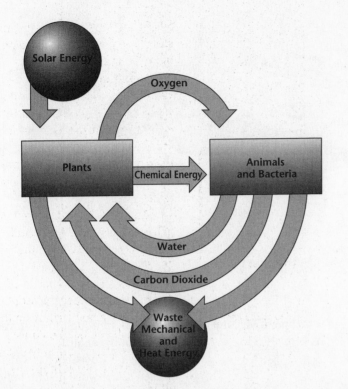

An idealized diagram showing the paths of nutrient and energy flow in a "typical" ecosystem (aquatic or terrestrial).

Nutrients

Sunlight and nutrients are the basic requirements for aquatic plant growth. Animals provide nitrate and phosphate — the major nutrients used in the photosynthetic process — by excreting them into the water as waste products. Nutrient distribution depends partly on depth: plants take up nutrients in shallow water, while animals produce wastes at all depths. Consequently, this depletes nutrients at the surface and concentrates them in deeper water. This is opposite to the vertical distribution of oxygen and reflects an important biological cycle: primary production of plant material; consumption of this material by aquatic animals and finally, excretion of waste products, which releases nutrients.

Light

As described in section one, The Chemistry and Physics of Diving, sunlight is altered greatly when it penetrates water.

Of all factors, turbidity most determines the vertical distribution of aquatic plants. The maximum depth at which aquatic plants can survive (based on the minimum amount of light needed for photosynthesis) increases as turbidity decreases. Aquatic plants do not usually live below 190 metres/600 feet. Certain plants use different portions of the spectrum for photosynthesis, depending upon the type of photosynthetic pigments they use. For example, red algae use the green and blue ends of the spectrum, allowing them to survive at greater depths than the green and brown algae, which use the red end of the spectrum. Red algae appear red because they absorb the greens and blues, and reflect the reds — the color that the eye sees. Ocean life distribution depends, in part, on the need for plants to remain in the shallow sunlit regions. Typically, these areas are along coasts where the seafloor is shallow and can

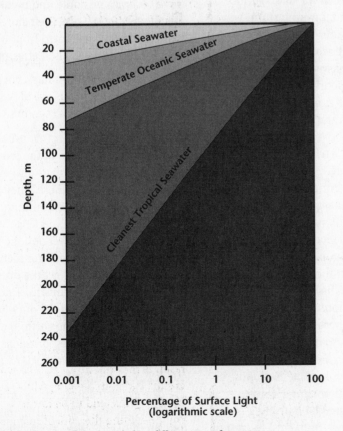

Relative penetration of sunlight through three different types of seawater.

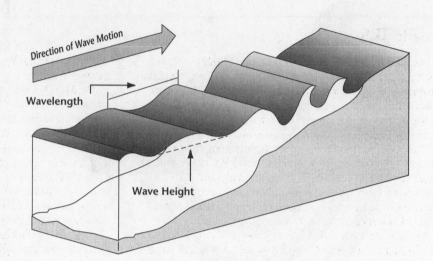

Direction of Wave Motion

Wavelength

Wave Height

Section through a breaking wave. Wind energy acts on the surface of the water to move it horizontally. Energy stored is released when the wave enters progressively shallower water, breaking when the water depth is less than one half the wavelength.

provide a place of attachment for larger plant species such as kelp.

Waves

Water moves in many ways over the earth's surface. Waves range in size from a fraction of an inch for small surface capillary-waves to towering storm waves more than 30 metres/100 feet high. Wind causes most waves.

How wind energy transfers to the water surface is poorly understood. It is known that wave size is related to wind velocity, the duration the wind blows and the extent of the area over which it blows (called the *fetch*).

Once generated, waves move away from their area of origin. It is only the wave shape (or energy) that advances, not the water itself, just as a wave snapped down the length of a rope doesn't move the rope. The farther the wave travels from the energy source, the slower and lower the wave becomes, until it eventually stops.

The wind's energy, transferred to the water's surface, also diminishes with depth. The effects of even the largest wind-driven waves become negligible at depths of about 45 metres/150 feet. Waves are measured by both their length (the distance from crest to crest or trough to trough) and the height (the

distance from trough to crest, perpendicular to the length).

When a wave reaches water about as deep as the wave height, bottom friction begins to slow the forward speed, causing the wave to bunch up and become higher and steeper. Eventually the wave becomes unstable and breaks. Breaking waves release their stored energy, which was generated from wind perhaps hundreds of kilometres/miles away, onto the shore.

Tides

Tides are responsible for the, usually, twice-daily rise and fall of the sea surface that alternately covers and exposes marine life along the shore. They play an important role in determining when certain locations will experience strong currents. Tides also affect aquatic life, principally in marine environments where tidal currents affect the distribution of planktonic organisms. Tidal movement results from the gravitational interaction of the earth, moon and sun. ("Tidal" waves, or *tsunamis*, result from seismic activity such as earthquakes, not from the tides.)

The cyclical nature of the orbits and planetary motion of the earth, moon and sun make the tides predictable. Tide duration, number and range depend on

Tsunamis

On August 27, 1883, Krakatoa, a volcanic island in Indonesia, exploded and two-thirds of it disappeared. This triggered a tsunami, or tidal wave, that rose to more than 30 metres/100 feet and destroyed the coastal regions of the Sunda Strait killing at least 30,000 people. The energy from this wave reached the English Channel, halfway around the world.

Tsunamis, or seismic sea waves, have nothing to do with the tides. They're usually generated by sudden movements of the ocean floor. Tsunamis are extremely large waves and are particularly common in the Pacific. Due to a series of unstable underwater trenches at the margins of crustal plates, fault activity is common in this area.

In the open ocean, where depth has a minimal influence on wave form, one example had a wavelength of 150 kilometers/95 miles, a wave height of .5 meters/20 inches and moved at about 800 kph/500 mph. This wave took over 10 minutes to pass, for example, under a ship in midocean.

Technically, tsunamis are classified as shallow-water waves due to their extreme wavelength and minimal wave height. Because of this, they are almost undetectable in the open ocean, but when they approach shallow water they slow down and pile up with devastating consequences.

On April 1, 1946, the waters of Hilo Bay, Hawaii, rapidly receded seaward. The bay emptied as the trough preceding the first wave crest hit shore. Minutes later a wall of water eight metres/26 feet higher than the usual high tide mark pounded ashore. More than 150 people were killed in Hawaii as a result of this wave, which originated in the Aleutian Trench off Unimak Island in Alaska. A wave from the same source also struck Scotch Cap on Unimak where a lighthouse, whose base was 14 metres/45 feet above sea level, was obliterated by a wave estimated to be over 36 metres /120 feet high.

This wave, which seismographs and tidal monitoring stations recorded throughout the Pacific, prompted the formation of an international warning system to measure water levels at recording stations in the wake of underwater seismic activity and thus detect tsunamis and warn areas likely to be hit. A tsunami that crashed ashore in Hawaii in 1957 confirmed the system's effectiveness when it killed no one even though it was larger than the wave of 1946.

the relative position of these three bodies and the local topographical features. By using this information, people can generate accurate tide and current tables to predict both the times and heights of tides anywhere in the world. Aquatic organisms — particularly those living in the intertidal zone — simply

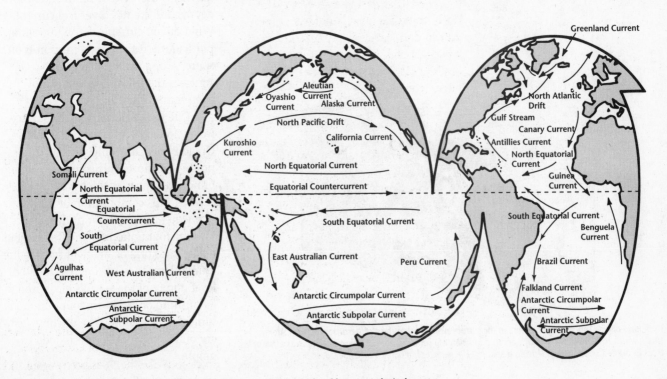

World surface currents. The direction and magnitude of these currents is regulated by meteorological events.

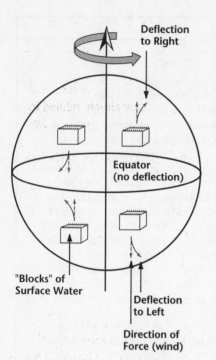

Deflection to Right

Equator (no deflection)

"Blocks" of Surface Water

Deflection to Left

Direction of Force (wind)

Diagram showing the Coriolis Effect on water movement. Surface water can be thought of as "blocks," wind as the force acting on them. Because of the earth's rotation, objects deflect to the right of the direction of force in the Northern Hemisphere, to the left in the Southern Hemisphere.

rely on biological clocks to regulate their activity to the tides.

Surface Currents

When winds blow over large areas with reasonable consistency of direction and strength, significant volumes of water move horizontally across the oceans. In the Northern Hemisphere, the trade winds (near latitude 15°N) blow from northeast to southwest; the westerlies in the midlatitudes blow primarily from the southwest. At very high latitudes, the polar easterlies blow from east to west. A mirror image set of these wind belts exists in the Southern Hemisphere.

The energy from these wind systems drives the major surface ocean-currents. Some of these currents transport more than 100 times the volume of water carried by all of the earth's rivers combined. These, the world's greatest currents, greatly affect aquatic life distribution. As with a wind-driven wave, surface current speed diminishes rapidly with depth, becoming negligible at depths

around 190 metres/600 feet.

The earth's rotation also affects the major ocean currents. This is termed the *Coriolis Effect*, and explains the fact that objects in the Northern Hemisphere deflect to the right of the direction of the force acting on them (in this case, the wind is the force and the object is the water's surface). The opposite is true in the Southern Hemisphere. There, objects deflect to the left of the direction of force. The result is that in the Northern Hemisphere, water tends to pile up in the middle of the Pacific Ocean as the major ocean currents travel from east to west, hit continents and have nowhere else to go. The same is true in the Southern Hemisphere, due to the opposite deflection. These circular water movement patterns are called *gyres* and are of major importance in marine life distribution.

Upwelling

Upwelling occurs when surface water moves offshore in regions where the continental shelf is narrow. Consequently, water rises from the adjacent depths and creates a vertical current. Wind driven currents cause upwelling, particularly if the wind direction is offshore. Along the west coast of North America the prevailing winds move from north to south.

Due to the Coriolis Effect, surface water flowing south past Washington, Oregon and California deflects to the right — offshore. Subsequent upwelling brings cold, nutrient-rich water to the surface. This combination of nutrient-rich water and sunlight at the surface lays the foundation for the tremendous abundance and diversity of marine life found along these shores. On a global level, many of the world's most productive fishing grounds are found in areas subject to upwelling. The anchovy fishery off the coast of Peru is a good example.

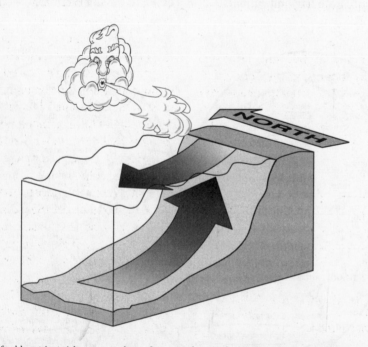

Upwelling of cold, nutrient-rich waters to the surface near shore in the Northern Hemisphere. Along shore, winds blowing north to south act as a force on the surface waters. Surface water moves offshore as a result of the Coriolis Effect, leaving a space at the surface that is filled by colder, deeper water.

Aquatic Plants and Animals

The Taxonomic System

Approximately 1.5 million different kinds of living organisms currently exist on earth. A large percentage of these organisms live in aquatic environments, although the bulk of living species are represented by terrestrial insects. Through the process of evolution and the diversification of life, each of these species exhibits some genetic relationship to all the others. Often, this relationship is not immediately apparent. For example, it is easy to see that sharks and salmon are both fish. However, the fact that seals are more closely related to cats than they are to sea lions is not as clear. To refer specifically to one kind of organism without confusion, scientists have developed the taxonomic system of classification. This system categorizes organisms based on their similarities and differences. In this way, the system reflects evolutionary relationships. Phylogeny is the study of these relationships and helps people understand how life evolved on earth.

Taxonomy arranges organisms into a hierarchy that begins with large, relatively nonspecific groupings and works through a series of increasingly specific layers to get to the species — the fundamental unit of this system. A species is defined as a group of closely related individuals that can and do produce fertile offspring.

Taxonomists created the following categories:

Kingdom
Phylum
Class
Order
Family
Genus
Species

Kingdom is the most general category, an example being the Animal Kingdom — loosely defined as all those organisms that do not make their own food. Each of the following categories gets more specific. Groups that are more closely related, based on form and structure, emerge.

Scientific Names

Those who are not familiar with scientific names may find them awkward. However, while many common names, "seahorse" for example, have become standardized through common use, most of the thousands of aquatic species simply do not have common names. Of the ones that do, at times, serious confusion exists. A classic example is "dolphin." The "dolphin" is a game fish, but the name is more frequently used to describe the familiar marine mammal.

Scientific names are generally derived from Latin or Greek roots and usually refer to some part of the organism's anatomy. Each organism has both a genus and a species name; this is called the binomial. The genus is always capitalized, the species always in lowercase.

Taxonomic Category	Giant Kelp	Purple Sea Urchin	Bottlenose Dolphin
Kingdom	Plantae	Animalia	Animalia
Phylum	Phaeophyta	Echinodermata	Chordata
Class	Phaeophycae	Echinoidea	Mammalia
Order	Laminariales	Echinoida	Odontoceti
Family	Lessoniaceae	Strongylocentrotidae	Delphinidae
Genus	Macrocystis	Strongylocentrotus	Tursiops

Taxonomic classifications of three common marine organisms.

Aquatic Plants

Phylum Cyanophyta: Blue-Green Algae

Most blue-green algae are found as colonies of simple, single-celled plants. There are approximately 200 species of blue-green algae. Blue-green algae commonly form the film that creates slick growths on most rock substrates at the water's edge. The colonies are either composed of single cells scattered randomly through a gelatinous matrix or masses of filaments of cells surrounded by a gelatin mass. When viewed under a microscope, these plants generally appear blue-green since their chief photosynthetic pigments are *chlorophyll* (green) and *phycocyanin* (blue).

Blue-green algae are very simple organisms in terms of their cell structure. Unlike more-complex cells, they do not appear to have nuclei, and for this reason are more closely aligned with bacteria by some scientists. The presence of

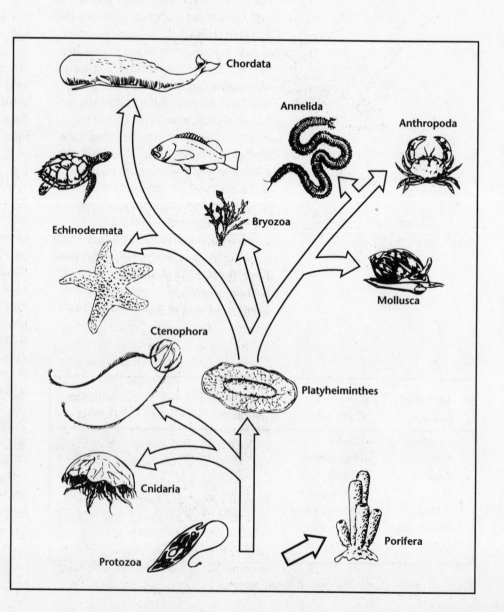

Phylogenetic tree of major animal phyla indicates theorized evolutionary relationships and origins. Note that chordates appear to have evolved from stock having echinoderm ancestors, while groups such as arthropods and molluscs are evolutionary "dead ends."

photosynthetic pigment, though, allows them to produce high-energy compounds, such as sugars, for food.

The blue-green algae are more common in freshwater and damp, wet terrestrial environments than in the ocean. They are abundant along the shore.

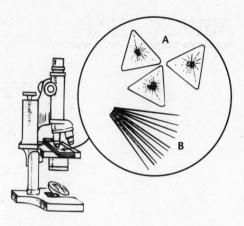

Representative diatoms: A) Triceratium sp.; B) Thalassiothrix sp.

Blue-green algae commonly occurs as a thin, slippery film or tuft on rocks in shallow intertidal marine habitats.

Phylum Bacillariophyta: Diatoms

Diatoms are common in both marine and freshwater environments. There are between 6000 and 10,000 species of marine and freshwater diatoms. They are either free-floating, attached to the substrate as a thin growth or found in filaments similar to the blue-green algae. Because most are microscopic, they generally go unnoticed. But, since they are important as both food for other organisms and as producers of oxygen in aquatic environments, any treatment of the aquatic-realm must include them.

The two outstanding features of diatoms are the presence of a cell wall made mostly of silica and their olive or yellow-brown coloration, caused by their primary photosynthetic pigment — chlorophyll. The silica cell wall takes a variety of shapes, depending on the species. Often these include ribs, pits, pores, tubercles, spines and other features. It is the accumulation of diatom skeletons over millions of years that creates diatomaceous earth.

Phylum Pyrrophyta: Dinoflagellates

The other major microscopic group of aquatic single-celled plants are the dinoflagellates. Of the approximately 1100 species known, the majority are marine (93 percent). This is a particularly interesting group of organisms because they have characteristics common to both plants and animals. Like other true plants, the majority contain photosynthetic pigments and can make their own food. Like animals, however, they can also propel themselves through the water by the use of a long whiplike appendage called a flagellum. Because of this, their place in the taxonomic order is unclear. In some schemes, they are aligned more closely with animals than with plants. It is from their random, whirling motions created by the beating action of this appendage that the name dinoflagellate arose (dino is a Greek root meaning "whirling").

Dinoflagellates reproduce asexually by splitting in two. Under the right environmental conditions, they can reproduce rapidly, doubling their population with each division. The result is that

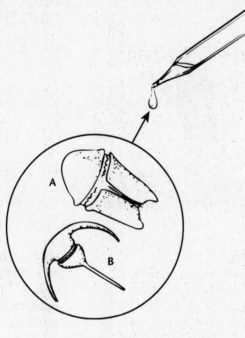

Representative dinoflagellates: A) Gymnodinium, sp.; B) Ceratium sp.

they can become the dominant species in localized plankton assemblages. The phenomenon known as red tide results from a rapid increase (or bloom) in the population of certain dinoflagellate species that have a red tint.

In addition to coloring the water, red tides can cause serious illness and even mortality for other forms of marine and terrestrial life — even people. Species of the dinoflagellate genus *Gonyaulax* produce a toxin called *saxitoxin*. During red tides, this species is so plentiful that filter-feeding organisms, such as clams and oysters, begin to accumulate the toxin in their flesh. When a person eats a clam or other shellfish with these accumulations, illness and even death may occur. This condition is called *paralytic shellfish poisoning* (PSP). During summer months in temperate regions, certain beaches may be closed to clamming if red-tide conditions have been observed.

Another phenomenon caused by population explosions of dinoflagellates is what is commonly (and erroneously) referred to as "phosphorescence" of the water. This is the occurrence of tiny whirling flashes of light seen at night when an oar dips in the water or a powerboat creates a wake. This is, in fact, *bioluminescence* and is caused by a tiny dinoflagellate that can create its own "cold" light when disturbed or agitated, such as by an oar, hand or propeller. Members of the genus *Noctiluca* are generally responsible for this.

Phylum Chlorophyta: Green Algae

Of all the macro-algae, the greens are the most diverse, with approximately 7000 species. The vast majority of these are found in fresh water. Only about 13 percent are marine. As the name implies, the dominant photosynthetic pigment of this group is chlorophyll. This phylum includes many single-celled species, but many can be seen with the naked eye. These larger species generally occur in marine habitats. Perhaps the best known is the sea lettuce, *Ulva sp.*, that can form vast expanses of thin, light-green sheets in the shallows of quiet temperate bays and inlets. Other forms include thin, flexible filaments and even thick, spongy growths such as

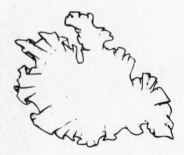

A common intertidal green alga, sea lettuce, Ulva sp.

Codium. Green algae are most common in shallow intertidal habitats where they provide both food and shelter for a number of organisms, such as small snails and shrimp. These organisms are often either transparent or colored a light, matching green. This adaptation indicates the relationship with the algae.

Phylum Phaeophyta: Brown Algae

While there are only about 1500 species of brown alga, this group is almost entirely marine (99.7 percent). These are the most noticeable aquatic plants, primarily due to their size. While some species are a similar size to the green and red algae, many of the browns take on enormous proportions. In fact, the largest aquatic plant — giant kelp — is a brown alga.

In keeping with a name-by-pigment approach to algae classification, this group has (in addition to chlorophyll) *fucoxanthin*, which usually results in a golden brown or olive coloration.

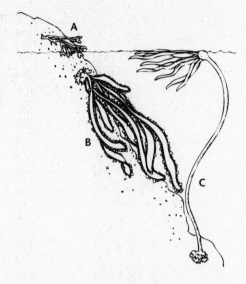

Three common brown algae: A) rockweed (Fucus sp.); B) feather boa (Egregia sp.); C) bull kelp (Nereocystis sp.).

The physical shape of the brown algae varies considerably: some have single, fleshy stalks; others have thin, hollow sacs; some display compact, brain-like masses, feathery growths or other distinctive characteristics. A feature of the kelp group is an enlargement at the base of the plant called the *holdfast*. This feature serves to securely fasten the plant to hard substrates. Holdfasts differ from roots in that they do not absorb nutrients. On larger plants, such as kelp, float bladders (containing carbon monoxide in some species) attached to the fronds ensure that the majority of the plant remains upright and near the sunlit surface.

The life cycle of these plants typifies the reproductive strategies of most algae. Individual mature kelp plants release both eggs and sperm into the water at the end of summer. The eggs immediately settle to the seafloor and wait for a still free-floating sperm to make contact. The likelihood of this happening is poor. Each adult kelp plant, therefore, produces millions of sperms and eggs. As a result, the chances of at least one sperm fertilizing one egg are greatly increased. The fertilized egg remains minute through the winter.

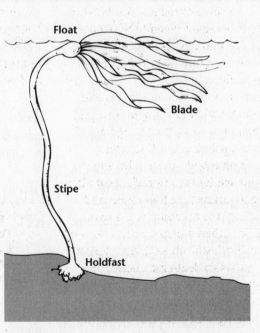

Major morphological features of a common macro-alga, bull kelp, Nereocystis sp.

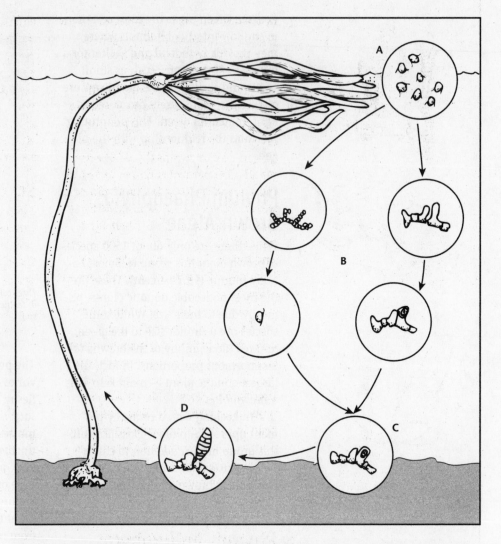

Life cycle of the bull kelp, Nereocystis leutkeana: A) in late summer spores are released from the adult plant; B) these become part of the plankton and develop into either eggs or sperm; C) fertilization takes place externally with the resulting embryo settling to the bottom to attach to the seafloor (at this stage the plant is very small and inconspicuous); D) in the spring the embryo grows into the adult or (sporophyte) stage.

Due to the small size of these newly fertilized plants, the life cycle of many marine plants was not completely known until they could be reproduced in the laboratory. As spring approaches and light levels increase, the fertilized plant grows rapidly, achieving adult size over the summer. The giant kelp *Macrocystis pyrifera* can grow up to 30 centimetres/1 foot per day, forming expansive "beds" in the spring and summer, which thin out in the winter. This type of life cycle (where an individual plant or animal can have more than one physical form in its life) is common in aquatic organisms. Perhaps the most familiar terrestrial example is the metamorphosis of the butterfly.

Phylum Rhodophyta: Red Algae

Red algae are the most diverse and specious of the aquatic macro-algae (of approximately 4000 species, 98 percent are marine). They are not usually as large as the brown algae, but they do occur in many varieties. Some of the delicate species are small and go unnoticed. However, they do become progressively more

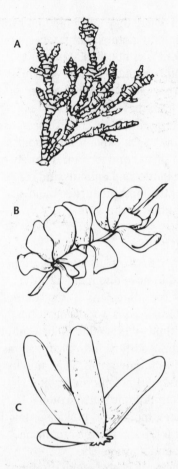

Three common red algae: A) coralline alga (Corallina sp.); B) epiphytic red alga (Smithora sp.); C) finger alga (Halosaccion sp.).

abundant with depth, due mainly to the presence of *phycoerythrin*, a pigment that absorbs the green and blue components of the light spectrum.

Because this short-wavelength light penetrates water more effectively than long-wavelength components (such as reds and oranges), some red algae can live at depths devoid of other plants. This vertical zonation, based on the pigment's ability to absorb different wavelengths of light, is particularly evident in tropical habitats where light penetration is greatest. Here, the green and brown algae dominate the shallows, while the reds are more abundant at depth.

Some red algae exhibit the interesting adaptation of extensive calcification. A few intertidal species have such large quantities of calcium carbonate in their tissues that they become skeletonized, forming either flat, encrusting growths on rocks or retaining an upright branching form with articulating joints along the blades. In both cases, calcification provides a tough outer coating that protects the algae from grazing by herbivorous fish.

Phylum Anthophyta: Flowering Plants

Like marine mammals, the flowering plants in marine habitats are terrestrial species that have returned to the sea. Terrestrial flowering plants (angiosperms) probably originated in aquatic environments and gradually moved onto land to take advantage of a new environment with less competition. Over time, some of these land plants reinvaded aquatic habitats (primarily harsh marine ones) where there was less competition with other land plants. These species had the right set of adaptations to allow them to live in places such as estuaries, mud flats and wave-swept rocky shores.

It is beyond the scope of this publication to describe the many freshwater angiosperms that abound along the shores of lakes, rivers and streams. Of approximately 250,000 species of flowering plants, only two groups have successfully invaded the marine environment: seagrasses and mangroves. These species are so successful that they generally create their own unique habitat wherever they are found.

Sea Grasses

There are about 45 species of sea grasses, the majority occur in tropical and subtropical marine habitats. Of these, three genera are commonly encountered. In the tropics, turtlegrass (*Thalassia sp.*) is found in shallow, quiet water embayments. Along the temperate shores of North America and

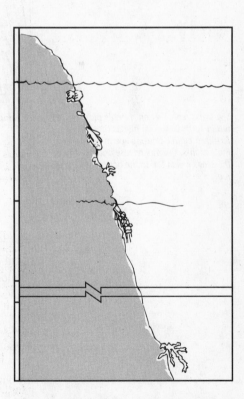

Vertical distribution of marine algae. Different species are found at different depths depending on their ability to photosynthesize using the elements of the light spectrum available. Greens and browns are restricted to shallow depths, while reds are found in deeper water because of their ability to use the blue-green end of the spectrum for photosynthesis.

Sea-grass reproduction. Female plants retain seeds in special blades that are fertilized by free-floating sperm released by male plants. Curents release and distribute the seeds which fall to the bottom and take root.

seafloor where they take hold and begin growing into mature plants. Once a mature plant is established, it begins to send out horizontal rootlike structures called rhizomes. Additional leaves sprout from these, large expanses of plants form and these create a seagrass "meadow." Such expanses of seagrass provide shelter and food for a variety of marine plants and animals and create some of the most productive biological communities in the world.

Mangroves

Mangrove trees are an unusual group of plants that have also reinvaded the shallow coastal regions of tropical and subtropical oceans worldwide. It has been estimated that 60 to 70 percent of the earth's coastline in tropical regions is lined with mangroves. Their importance as a distinct marine habitat is clear from this one statistic alone. Like seagrasses, mangroves provide a unique habitat for many marine organisms, some found nowhere else.

There are twelve major groups (genera) of mangrove trees worldwide. They share a number of characteristics that allow them to live in the marine environment. First, they have shallow "prop" roots that spread widely and hold the plant firmly in the soft mud bottoms where they are found. The roots send up thin vertical extensions called *pneumatophores* that extend above the surface of the mud and allow the plant to obtain oxygen.

Mangroves have a peculiar reproductive strategy that allows them to distribute their species over long distances. The seeds germinate while still on the parent plant. Without an intermediate resting stage, the seedling begins to grow, elongate and become heavier at the bottom. Finally, it drops from the parent into the water below, where it floats upright due to the heavy bottom. Seedlings that are carried by currents into shallow water are stimulated to put out root anchors as soon as the bottom

Europe, eelgrass (*Zostera sp.*) is the dominant genera, forming vast expanses or "fields" in shallow water. Along rocky, wave-swept coasts of the same continents, surfgrass (*Phyllospadix sp.*) survives, in spite of the coastal waves' incessant pounding.

These three major groups reproduce in basically the same way. Sexual reproduction is a cycle: flowers develop and seeds form inside; male plants release sperm and fertilize the seeds; the seeds are then released and distributed by water currents, eventually sinking to the

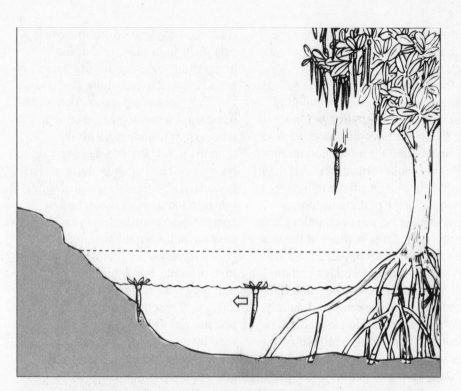

Mangrove-seed distribution. Fertilized seeds drop from mature plants into the water, where they float upright and drift with the tides until they land on a distant or adjacent beach. If the tide is out, they simply stick in the sand surrounding the parent plant.

end strikes the shore. Here they start another mangrove colony or add to a pre-existing one. The advantages of this strategy are obvious for a plant living on the edge of the sea. Seeds that float can be carried great distances by currents. Because the seedlings float upright (vertically), with the majority of the plant below the surface, when they enter shallow water the seedlings will ground themselves and take root.

Aquatic Animals: Invertebrates

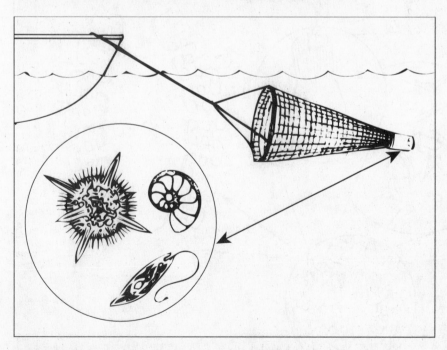

Representative protozoans collected in a plankton net: A) Radiolarian; B) Foraminifera; C) Phytoflagellate.

Phylum Protozoa: Single-Celled Animals

The one characteristic that the approximately 30,000 protozoans share is their unicellular (made up of a single cell) nature. Protozoans are either a single cell or part of a colony of loosely aggregated cells. This is a large and diverse group that functions and behaves like the more familiar large animals, but they do it on a tiny scale. There is some debate among protobiologists (scientists who study protozoans) as to whether these organisms should be considered unicellular or simply very small acellular animals. As their name implies (proto=first; zoan=animals), they have all the necessary features to survive in a microscopic world at a simple level. Protozoans are found in both fresh and salt water as part of the plankton, they are also found attached to the seafloor or to objects on it.

Familiar protozoans include *Amoeba*, *Paramecium* and the malaria protozoan (many are parasitic in nature). All are microscopic. The order *Foraminifera* ("forams") is a common marine group. They make intricately coiled shells (or tests) that resemble those of higher-order snails. Some planktonic forams, such as *Globigerina*, are so abundant that their tests cover large portions of the seafloor. After thousands of years, these deposits may be tens of feet thick and are called globigerina oozes. The chalk cliffs of Dover, England are composed mainly of foram tests that accumulated on the seafloor and were subsequently lifted above sea level.

Other common marine orders include the *Radiolaria*, which make delicate shells from silica, and a ciliate group (those covered with tiny movable hairs called cilia) called the *Tintinnida*.

Protozoans feed on a variety of organic substances. Some feed on diatoms, others absorb nutrients directly from the water. Some feed actively on bacteria or catch other protozoans. Protozoans defend themselves by growing spines or tough outer shells, by fast "swimming," or by timing their activities to avoid potential predators.

It appears that protozoans evolved from a simple, noncellular predecessor that may have resembled a dinoflagellate, possibly some type of half plant/half animal. This hypothesis is strengthened by the success of present-day dinoflagellates that exhibit both plant and animal characteristics.

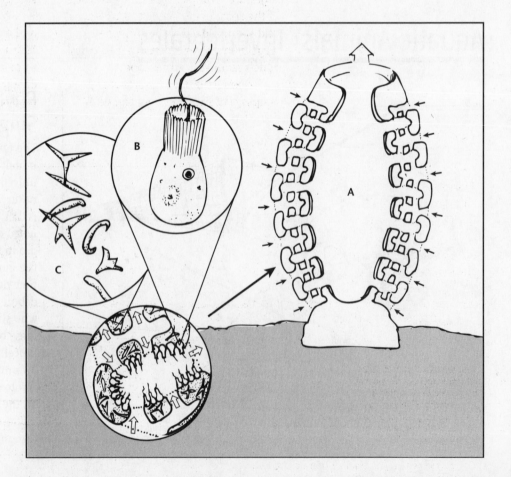

Sponge morphology: A) section through a vase sponge indicating water flow direction through a sponge; B) magnified view of collar cell; C) magnified view showing a variety of spicule types.

Phylum Porifera: Sponges

The sponges are an interesting group of simple invertebrates. Approximately 10,000 species are found worldwide, most of these are marine. They are often a major component in an ecosystem, where their success is probably due to their simplicity.

Sponges display less cellular organization than any other multicellular organism. There are no identifiable organ systems (such as respiratory, circulatory or digestive). Each sponge consists of a group of loosely associated cells, some of which are specialized for different functions. These cells are organized around a system of pores, canals and chambers. The "body" of the sponge is composed of *spicules* made of either calcium carbonate or silica.

These spicules form a framework upon which the cells and water passages are arranged. The shape and size of the spicules are specific to the species and sponge identification is based largely on examination of the spicules, which requires a microscope.

Sponges display a variety of shapes and sizes, but they can be divided into two main groups: those forming vase-like or basket shapes and those that are spread out flat. All attach to a hard surface like rock or a piling. Sponges are filter-feeders, this is evident from their internal arrangement of cells and spicules. The outside of any sponge is covered with small pores that are lined with special cells called collar cells. These cells are flagellated. Their only function is to wave their tiny flagellae continually, for the entire life of the sponge. This activity creates a current that moves water into the body of the sponge. At one end of these cells is a collar-like appendage that catches any potential food — usually organic debris, diatoms, protozoans and bacteria. The water is funneled through an intricate series of canals and, in vase sponges, exits out one large opening called the osculum. In encrusting forms, there are a series of smaller oscula distributed unevenly over the entire sponge.

Sponges reproduce both sexually and asexually. They generally contain both male and female sex cells at the same time, alternately producing sperm or eggs. The quantity of eggs or sperm produced is remarkable, reaching mil-

Sexual reproduction in sponges: A) male and female sponges release millions of eggs and sperm into the water; B) sperm fertilize eggs externally; C) microscopic larvae result, becoming part of the zooplankton; D) larvae settle to seafloor, attach to a hard substrate and begin developing into adult sponges.

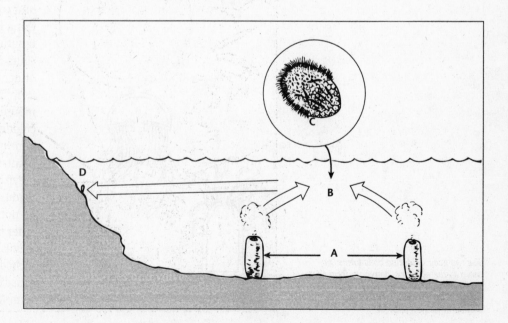

lions. Sperm and eggs are released into the water in great, smoke-like clouds. The need for such vast quantities of reproductive material is due to the random nature of external egg fertilization. When a sperm and an egg meet, a microscopic, wormlike larva results. (The resemblance between flatworms and larval sponges suggests that sponges probably originated from a small, flatworm-like ancestor.) This larva eventually settles to the bottom, attaches to a hard surface and begins growing into a sponge through cell division.

Relatively few animals eat sponges, probably due to the unpalatable spicules. A number of animals do reside in sponges, however. The patient observer may see a variety of brittlestars, worms, shrimp and even small fish living in the canals and channels of large sponges.

Phylum Cnidaria: Hydroids, Sea Anemones, Corals and Jellyfish

About 10,000 species comprise this phylum. These are the first organisms discussed here that can be characterized as complex. Still, the term must be used carefully.

All cnidarians are made up of three distinct body layers: 1) an outside layer or epidermis 2) an inner layer or *gastrodermis* and 3) a middle layer or *mesoglea*. Mesoglea is most pronounced in the jellyfish and is perhaps most familiar as the jellylike mass found washed up on beaches. All cnidarians are radially symmetrical. A ring of tentacles surrounds a central opening that acts as both entrance and exit for food and waste. This opening leads to the saclike gut. The most notable shared characteristic is the presence of stinging cells, called *cnidoblasts* (the origin of the phylum's name), that are located in the tentacles. These cells produce a structure unique to this phylum called a *nematocyst*. These delicate units resemble small capsules, each containing a threadlike organ that, upon stimulation, is shot out and lodges in the source of the stimulus. Hopefully for the cnidarian, the stimulus is a potential prey item such as a small shrimp, worm or fish. Nematocysts are also used for defense, but to a lesser degree. A battery of venom-injecting Nematocysts, venom injecting cells, cause a jellyfish's stings.

Cnidarians come in two basic forms. A polyp form is typified by animals such as hydroids, sea anemones and corals. Each is attached to something hard by a basal disc, with the mouth directed up (depending, of course, upon the attitude in which it is attached). Jellyfish exhibit the medusa form; they are free-swimming, with the mouth generally pointed down. Most cnidarians have a life cycle that incorporates both of these forms at some point. Hydroids have both an attached polyp stage as well as a free-swimming medusa stage. Corals and sea anemones do not usually have a medusa stage; the other major class of cnidarians — the jellyfish — have eliminated the attached polyp form (in most species). Because of this diversity of body forms and complex life cycles, it is best to describe

The two basic cnidarian body forms: A) polyp — the attached, dominant form of hydroids, anemones and corals; B) medusa — the free-swimming, planktonic, dominant form of jellyfish.

the details of the cnidarians on a class by class basis. Each class is fairly distinct and has readily identifiable characteristics.

Class Hydrozoa: Hydroids, Fire Coral, Portuguese Man-of-War

Hydroids are the least familiar cnidarians, with a few exceptions. They are usually small (less than an inch high) and go unnoticed by all but the most careful observer. Hydroids can be found in both individual-polyp and colonial forms. Individual-polyp forms often look like miniature sea anemones on stalks; colonial forms encrust rocks and other hard substrates.

Most hydroid life cycles include a change from polyp to medusa and back again. A typical scenario begins with a colonial hydroid attached to the seafloor in the polyp stage. Specialized individual polyps create tiny medusae that stack up on each other, resembling a pile of dishes. The medusae are released, top one first, and float away from the colony in a free-swimming

stage. These are males and females and they produce eggs and sperm. These "jellyfish" release eggs and sperm into the water, like the sponges, and rely on random sexual encounter for fertilization. Fertilized eggs develop into larvae, called *planulae,* that are similar to sponge larvae. Individual planula settle to the seafloor, attach and begin growing into polyps. The rest of the individuals in the colony are produced asexually by division or budding from the original polyp.

Most hydroids feed on microscopic prey: copepods, small worms, the larvae of other species and other hydroids. The toxicity of the nematocysts varies greatly. Fire coral is a colonial hydroid that has exceedingly powerful nematocysts capable of penetrating human skin and causing pain, itching and swelling. The other unique feature of fire coral is that it builds a skeleton of calcium carbonate in a fashion similar to true corals.

The Portuguese man-of-war, *Physalia physalis,* is also a colonial hydroid, not a true jellyfish. The float, tentacles and other parts of this superorganism are created by specialized individuals of the colony. In this case, the polyps never release the free-swimming medusa, they remain a part of the polyp colony and continue producing eggs and sperm. The Portuguese man-of-war has some of the most toxic nematocysts of all the cnidarians.

Class Scyphozoa: Jellyfish

The jellyfish, and some species that are not as familiar (for example, a few forms of *attached* jellyfish), make up this group of cnidarians. All are marine species ranging in size from a fraction of an inch to several feet in diameter, with trailing tentacles up to 9-12 metres/30-40 feet long in large specimens.

In this class, the medusa stage is the dominant body form. True jellyfish can be distinguished from the medusa stage of hydroids by the lack of a thin

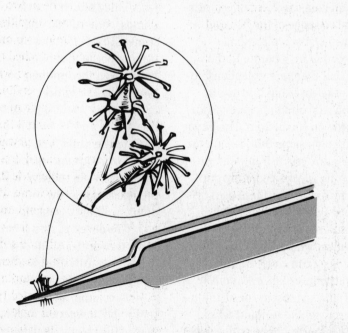

Close-up view of a representative colonial hydroid showing branching structure of polyp development. Note resemblance to coral polyps.

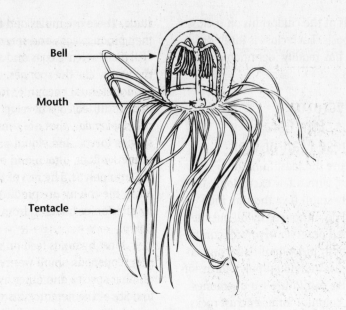

Bell

Mouth

Tentacle

Representative jellyfish showing bell and radial symmetry of tentacle arrangement.

shelf of tissue that is continuous around the margin of the bell in hydroid medusa (called the velum). Being unattached, and with rudimentary nervous and muscle systems, jellyfish are carried through open water by currents. They are generally the largest members of the ocean's plankton. Gentle, rhythmic pulsations help the jellyfish stay near the surface, where it feeds on small fish. A unique organ called a *statocyst* is distributed around the edge of the bell and monitors the jellyfish's direction.

Sexes tend to be separate in the Scyphozoa, but there are exceptions. Inshore species release eggs and sperm into the water, creating microscopic larvae that settle on the bottom. The larvae grow into a polyp stage that, when mature, releases tiny jellyfish into the water. Open-water species generally skip the polyp stage; their fertilized eggs develop directly into juvenile jellyfish.

Jellyfish are perhaps best known for their contact with bathers, swimmers and divers. They can cause injuries ranging from minor skin-irritations to fatalities. The active agents of such injuries are, of course, the stinging cells located in the tentacles. Historically, jelly-

fish have a bad reputation from such incidents, even though encounters are accidental. Most jellyfish injuries occur from people accidentally swimming through the trailing tentacles or from handling a specimen that has been washed up on the shore. While the organism may appear lifeless, the nematocysts remain active. A classic example of self-inflicted injury occurs when a gloved diver handles a toxic species in the water and then touches his face at the end of the dive, stinging himself by transferring intact nematocysts to the face via the glove. The best protection against jellyfish "attacks" is to simply stay aware in the marine environment.

Class Anthozoa: Sea Anemones, Soft and Hard Corals

This group always takes the polyp form as adults and includes such common marine animals as sea anemones, soft corals, sea fans, sea whips and hard corals. All have a saclike gut. The general body plan resembles a paper bag with tentacles arranged around the edge of the bag opening. They are found in all marine environments, but are particularly abundant in shallow coastal areas, where they attach themselves to rocks, pilings, coral rubble and other hard substrates. Their life-styles are almost exactly opposite that of free-swimming jellyfish, even though their body plans are essentially the same.

In most species, the sexes are separate. Some may be both male and female at the same time (*hermaphrodites*), producing eggs and sperm either concurrently or alternately. Eggs and sperm are released into the water where random encounter results in a fertilized egg. This develops into a flatworm-like larva that settles to the sea floor, attaches to a firm substrate and grows into the adult polyp form.

In colonial species, such as corals and some anemones, additional members of the colony are created through

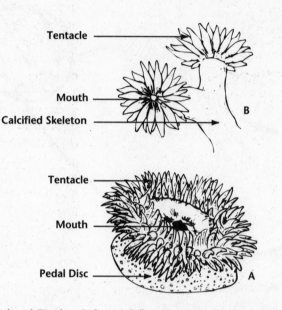

Comparison of sea anemone (A) and coral (B) polyps. Both are radially symmetrical and bear stinging cells (cnidoblasts). Anemones are usually solitary, corals typically colonial. Corals develop hard, calcified internal skeletons, anemones do not.

formation of coral reefs around the world in tropical waters. Reef-building corals are restricted to the tropics; they require warm water to maintain the high metabolic rate necessary for the production of the skeleton. Most reef-building corals also have an abundance of symbiotic, microscopic, single-celled plants (algae), called *zooxanthellae*, in their tissues. These tiny plants appear to aid coral in its ability to build its skeleton by providing oxygen and nutrients directly to the corals' tissues as by-products of photosynthesis. In return, the plants make use of the carbon dioxide given off by the coral during respiration. The intense sunlight characteristic of equatorial latitudes increases the efficiency of photosynthesis in the algae, thereby accelerating the rate of skeleton-building by the coral.

Phylum Ctenophora: Comb Jellies

Approximately 80 species of comb jellies are distributed worldwide in marine environments. The phylum includes spherical pea-sized species and ribbon-like species up to 1 metre/3.28 feet long. All look and act like jellyfish and are radially symmetrical. They differ from jellyfish in two major ways.

First, they lack stinging cells of any kind. While they are carnivorous, most collect their prey with two paired tentacles that have regularly spaced, shorter branches coming off the main stem. These are sticky, and catch small planktonic organisms that are drawn to the mouth and eaten.

Second, on the outside of the body are located several (usually 8 - 12) rows or bands of large cilia that beat continuously. These are called ctenes (the "c" is silent) and are used for locomotion. Most comb jellies are hermaphrodites, producing eggs and sperm. Following a common strategy for invertebrate reproduction, they release eggs and sperm

budding. This kind of asexual reproduction seems remarkable even for an animal as "simple" as a sea anemone. One common temperate-water species, the plumose anemone (*Metridium senile*), creates offspring by spreading out its pedal foot so that it forms a thin edge of tissue at the margin. This part of the foot firmly attaches to the bottom while the anemone contracts the central portion of the foot, tearing the fragile margin into tiny pieces and each piece grows into a new anemone. Pedal laceration is one of the more remarkable forms of reproduction demonstrated by invertebrates and indicates a simple nervous system.

Corals are similar to sea anemones in that they have the same body plan, stinging cells and life-style. The main difference is that they secrete an internal, hard skeletal structure composed of calcium carbonate (absorbed from the surrounding water). This skeleton provides protection and support for an otherwise soft organism.

Most anthozoids are colonial and represent species that contribute to the

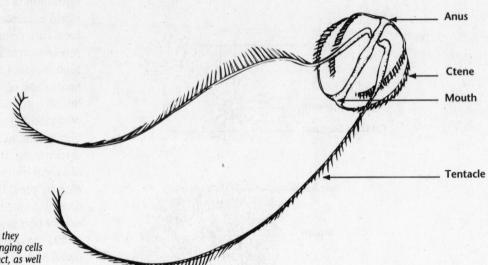

Anus

Ctene

Mouth

Tentacle

Representative ctenophore. While they resemble cnidarians, they lack stinging cells and have a complete digestive tract, as well as the characteristic rows of ctenes.

into the water by the thousands, random fertilization takes place. Microscopic free-swimming larvae become "macroscopic" plankton as adults.

Phylum Platyhelminthes: Flatworms

This phylum includes free-living flatworms and approximately 25,000 species of parasitic tapeworms and flukes. Some of the 4000-odd species of free-living flatworms that make up the class *Turbellaria* may be encountered by divers. Most are about 2.5 centimetres/1 inch long, extremely flat, and appear as a thin, film crawling on rocks and in between barnacles. A few tropical species, on the other hand, may be brilliantly colored, fairly large (15 centimetres/6 inches) and may even swim in rhythmic undulations if disturbed.

The general characteristics of flatworms include bilateral symmetry (having a clearly defined anterior-posterior orientation with the left and right sides of the body forming mirror images of each other), one-way digestive tract and a simple nervous system (they have rudimentary "eyes"). Because they are so flat, the surface-to-volume ratio of a

flatworm is high and metabolic exchange, such as respiration, can occur through the skin. Most flatworms are carnivorous.

Flatworms are also hermaphroditic; there is a physical exchange of sperm between two individuals, one impregnating the other. Fertilized eggs are freely shed into the water to develop into planktonic larvae that eventually settle on the seafloor to begin their life as adults.

Flatworms have remarkable powers of regeneration. Some regenerate as a

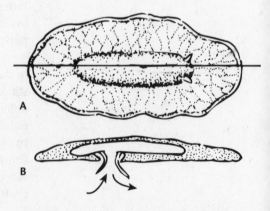

A

B

Representative flatworm: A) view from above showing bilateral symmetry, B) flatworm one-way (incomplete) digestive tract.

form of asexual reproduction. A flatworm that is severed in half may develop into two complete worms. The genus Planaria are commonly used to demonstrate regeneration in high-school biology classes. Given the environment in which many flatworms live (under loose rocks that are occasionally moved about by rough seas, etc.), such an adaptation makes sense.

Phylum Nemertea: Ribbon Worms

Approximately 800 species of ribbon worms are found worldwide. They are bottom dwellers and are common in shallow coastal regions. They are bilaterally symmetrical, unsegmented and long. One species from the Northeast Atlantic is reputed to reach 18 metres/ 60 feet and is aptly named *Lineus longissimus*. Most are significantly shorter, averaging 1.5-3 metres/5-10 feet in length. Ribbon worms are easily broken and

sensitive to touch, consequently, it is difficult to locate intact specimens.

Two major features distinguish ribbon worms from the preceding phyla. First, they have a complete digestive tract with both a mouth and an anus. Secondly, they are carnivorous and actively hunt prey, such as other worms. They attack and subdue their prey with a tonguelike apparatus called a proboscis. The proboscis is a tubular, eversible organ that remains inside the worm when not in use. When potential prey is located, the proboscis is ejected with great force by constriction of the muscles behind it. At its tip are a cluster of sharp, piercing barbs called stylets. These grab the prey and pull it back to the mouth for ingestion.

Sexes are separate in most ribbon worms. They typically release eggs and sperm into the sea for external fertilization, resulting in most cases in a planktonic larva that settles on the bottom and develops into the adult form.

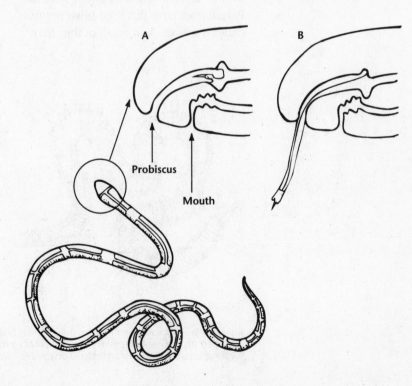

Representative ribbon worm: A) close-up view showing relationship of proboscis to the mouth (note they are separate); B) with proboscis extended.

Phylum Annelida:
Tubeworms,
Bristleworms,
Clamworms

This phylum of approximately 14,000 species includes the common earthworm and parasitic leeches. Most free-living marine species are members of the class *Polychaeta*, of which there are about 8000 species. This group of worms is the most easily observed of all the worm groups. Many species are found crawling on rocks or in reefs, and some build permanent and semipermanent tubes in prominent places in the marine environment. They are all bilaterally symmetrical and have a complete digestive tract. Several major features separate them from the other worm and wormlike organisms found in the sea.

First, they are segmented. Their bodies are arranged longitudinally in distinct segments that, in polychaetes, are all identical (this kind of segmentation is termed *metamerism*). This is important because an organism needs both segmentation and a body cavity to be able to develop complete organ systems. Polychaetes have this fluid-filled cavity, called a *coelom*. As a result of this, they

have complete digestive, respiratory, circulatory, excretory, nervous and sensory organs. These worms are significantly more complex than the phyla previously described.

All characteristics mentioned above apply to the phylum as a whole (including leeches). Polychaetes can be further differentiated by the presence of pairs of flap-like appendages on each segment called *chaetae*. Generally there are spines embedded in these appendages that are either family, genus or even species-specific. Polychaete identification is grounded in the study and description of the kinds and shapes of these spines. Like sponges and their spicules, polychaete identification relies to a large degree on the tremendous diversity of spine characteristics.

Head type also facilitates Polychaete identification. Antennae, tentacles, eyes, eversible jaws, fleshy flaps and *cirri*, reflect the behavior of a particular species. These physical characteristics allow accurate interpretation of the animal's life-style.

Polychaetes can be subdivided into two major groups based on life-style: those that attach to a substrate (sedentary), such as the types living in tubes, and those that do not. The attached

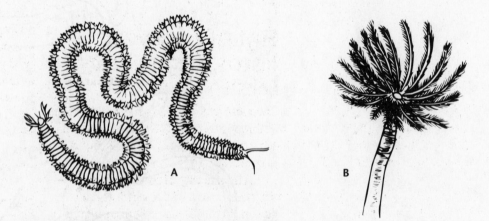

Representative polychaete worms: A) free-living (errant) form (clam worm) characterized by well-developed locomotory appendates and sense organs; B) attached (sessile) form (feather duster worm) characterized by a tubular structure with anterior appendages develped for filter feeding.

forms must wait for food to come to them. As a result, they have developed head appendages designed to trap passing food. Some have complex filtering mechanisms others use long, often sticky, tentacles that can reach beyond the tube. The majority of polychaetes live in mud or silt and simply eat the sediment surrounding them, excreting indigestible, inorganic material such as sand. Those that move about are generally hunters of small prey and are equipped with an array of sensory organs for locating prey and jaws for capturing it. Some graze passively on attached organisms such as sponges.

The sexes are usually separate in polychaetes and individuals simply release their eggs and sperm into the water. Some species increase the chances of random external fertilization by synchronizing the release to occur at the same time for all individuals in the area. Such swarms usually occur at night and may be triggered by seasonal environmental cycles. The fertilized egg develops into a planktonic larva called a *trochophore*, quite different from those of the previously described phyla. Provided it survives a risky planktonic existence, the trochophore metamorphoses into the adult form upon settling to the bottom. Some tube-dwelling species keep their young in brood pouches until they mature.

Phylum Arthropoda: Insects, Spiders, Crabs, Lobsters, Shrimp

There are over a million species of Arthropods. They have penetrated most terrestrial and aquatic habitats that can support life.

The majority of species belong to the class Insecta and few of these are present in the marine environment. Of the marine forms, the class Crustacea is most abundant, represented by some 30,000 species. These include crabs,

shrimp and lobsters, and many more obscure species. Most crustacean species are microscopic; they make up the majority of planktonic organisms. At the other end of the scale, some crustaceans may grow to be quite large: the giant spider crabs of temperate waters can have a leg span of 3.7 metres/12 feet.

Economically, crustaceans are important to man as a food source that has been harvested for centuries. Recently, a good deal of research has gone into the aquaculture of certain species, such as shrimp, crab and lobster, in response to both dwindling wild populations (often a result of overfishing) and increased interest by consumers.

All arthropods are bilaterally symmetrical and segmented. This is perhaps most evident in the jointed legs of both insects and crustaceans, a unique arthropod trait and the origin of the phylum name —"jointed foot." Articulating joints allow movement despite a hard exoskeleton made of *chitin*. This provides a protective outer shell. The disadvantage is that all arthropods go through a molting process. The outer layer is shed to allow growth. This means that growth occurs in spurts, and the frequency of molts decreases with age.

Arthropods display great appendage specialization: claws, antennae, spines, hairs and legs reflect the diverse habitats and behavior arthropods adopt. Because most crustaceans roam in search of food, they have well-developed organs for taste, touch and sight. Internally, crustaceans have distinct organ systems in body spaces. The circulatory system is open (not restricted to vessels) and the organs are bathed in blood that is pumped around the body by several muscular hearts.

The sexes are separate in virtually all crustaceans, and copulation is common. Males impregnate females, who often carry eggs during gestation. In the species that do carry a brood, the numbers of eggs produced is generally in the hundreds, reflecting the advantage these individuals have for survival due to a certain amount of parental care. This is in sharp contrast to the approach taken by sponges and most worms that produce thousands or millions of *gametes* to ensure the minimum fertility rate for species continuation. Crustacean eggs usually have a nutritious yolk to provide a food source for the young. Eggs generally hatch out as part of the plankton and go through a series of rapid molts, adding segments with each spurt of growth. Eventually the adult form is reached, but this may be after 6 to 12 metamorphic stages. As with insects, crustaceans' juvenile forms often look nothing at all like the adults.

The following discussion is not comprehensive; the groups that are described are those most readily encountered and observed by the casual aquatic explorer.

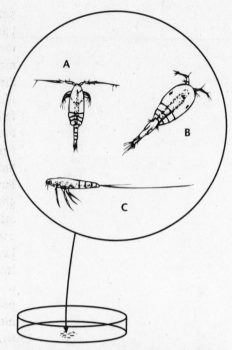

Magnified view of representative copepods: A) calanoid copepod, a common member of the zooplankton; B) cyclopoid copepod, found in both planktonic and bottom-dwelling (benthic) habitats; C) harpacticoid copepod, found primarily buried in soft sediment (infaunal) habitats.

Class Crustacea
Sub-Class Copepoda: Copepods
Copepods are very common and are found in all marine environments. There are approximately 7500 species, most of which are microscopic. They are a major component of plankton and they feed primarily on diatoms. They are an extremely important food source for larger invertebrates and fish. The sexes are separate in copepods and copulation occurs. Some males have modified antennae that allow them to firmly grasp females, a significant adaptation in an aquatic environment. Females carry a batch of eggs for a time before releasing them into the sea.

Sub-Class Cirripedia: Barnacles
While there are approximately 900 species of barnacles, only a few species occur in accessible marine habitats. They are perhaps most familiar to boaters who must regularly have them removed from the hulls of their vessels. As adults,

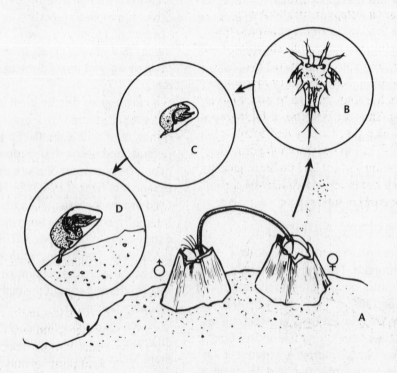

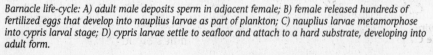

Barnacle life-cycle: A) adult male deposits sperm in adjacent female; B) female released hundreds of fertilized eggs that develop into nauplius larvae as part of plankton; C) nauplius larvae metamorphose into cypris larval stage; D) cypris larvae settle to seafloor and attach to a hard substrate, developing into adult form.

barnacles attach themselves to rocks, pilings, boats and other solid substrates in the marine environment with a cement-like secretion from glands on the first pair of antennae. They wave their "feet" in the water to collect passing food. While most barnacles are hermaphrodites, cross fertilization does occur via a long penis that can be extended from one barnacle to another. Free-swimming barnacle young are programmed to settle in the company of other barnacles, preferably no farther away than one barnacle-penis length. Juvenile barnacles can "taste" the substrate before they attach to it, testing for a site where other barnacles reside. Barnacles are particularly suited to live along wave-battered rocky coastlines where their hard outer shells of fused plates protects them from the pounding surf. Barnacle identification relies on the number and arrangement of these plates, which is , in most cases, species specific.

Sub-Class Malacostraca —
Order Stomatapoda: Mantis Shrimp

Like their terrestrial counterpart, the praying mantis, mantis shrimp are alert, perceptive organisms that display interesting behavior. They range in size from less than an inch to over a foot long. They are best known for the way in which they capture and subdue prey. These shrimp have two long arm-like appendages that fold up like a jackknife when not in use, much like the claws of a praying mantis.

The shape of the end segment of these claws varies by specie and are specialized for certain prey. Those that feed on snails, for example, have stout, hammer-like claws that are rapidly extended, hitting the shell repeatedly until it is broken. Species that feed on soft-bodied organisms, such as worms and even fish, have claws terminating in razor-sharp segments, often with additional spines for holding prey. Large specimens of these species should be regarded with respect as they can inflict serious wounds to divers.

Order Isopoda: Sea Lice

Isopods resemble terrestrial pill bugs in that they are all flattened (dorso-ventrally), have multiple legs and are fairly

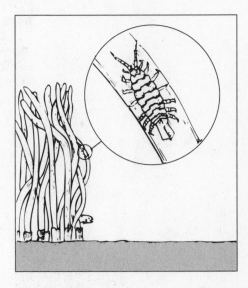

Representative isopod clinging to eel grass. Note the bilateral symmetry and jointed external body-skeleton, which are characteristic of arthropods.

cryptic, living hidden between cracks and crevices in shallow coastal areas. There are some large species (up to a foot in length) that live in the deep sea. They are scavengers and feed on a variety of organisms, but they usually graze on marine plant particles and organic debris. Copulation occurs and the eggs develop into fully formed juveniles in the female's brood pouch.

Representative mantis shrimp. This species has long, sharp, serrated claws for holding and cutting soft-bodied prey, such as fish.

Articulating Sharp-edge Claws

Representative amphipod feeding on kelp float. View does not show the side-to-side (lateral) compression of the body, diagnostic of this group.

Order Amphipoda:
Beach Fleas, Skeleton Shrimp

Amphipods are found everywhere in the marine environment. From tidepools to the deep-ocean trenches, they contribute significantly to any assemblage of marine organisms, particularly as a food source for larger animals. Flea-like in appearance, they are flattened from side to side (laterally) and, like isopods, have numerous legs. They have an obvious head with several pairs of antenna. Amphipods feed primarily on detritus and plant material. One group, the skeleton shrimp (family Caprellidae), is particularly interesting. The body is elongated, and the legs terminate in recurved spines allowing them a firm foothold on the slippery algae upon which they are found. They resemble a praying mantis, with two large claws used for capturing small prey.

Order Decapoda —
Sub-Order Natantia: Shrimp

There are approximately 2000 species of shrimp worldwide, and they form a remarkably diverse and opportunistic group. Mostly scavengers, shrimp can be found in every marine habitat. They are characterized by an elongated body usually divided into two major sections: a fused head and thoracic region, and a segmented tail section. A number of legs are present on the thorax, with the first forelegs specialized into claws and pincers of various shapes and sizes. The tail has a number of fan-shaped appendages on the bottom side (*pleopods*) that are used for swimming.

The shrimps' nervous system allows some fairly complex behavior. The sensory organs are well developed, this indicates a highly mobile creature. Vision and touch are particularly well developed in shrimp, with the eyes located on moveable stalks and long antennae for sensing their environment from a safe distance.

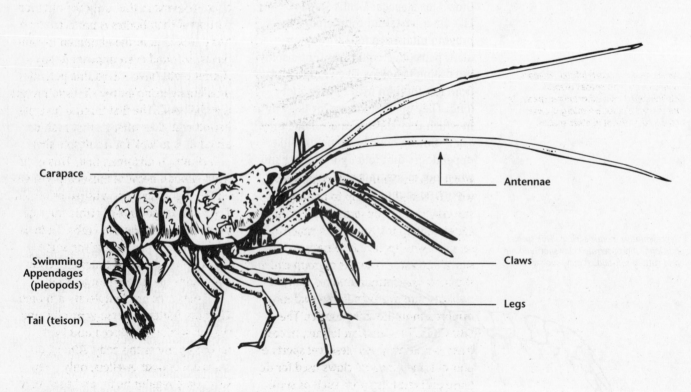

Carapace

Swimming
Appendages
(pleopods)

Tail (teison)

Antennae

Claws

Legs

Representative shrimp species. Note paired appendages: antennae, legs, etc.

Sub-Order Reptantia:
Lobsters, Hermit Crabs, Crabs
Over one third of all crustaceans are members of this large and diverse group. Further, most are large (compared to the microscopic forms) and often conspicuous. There are three distinct groups within this suborder:

1) lobsters

2) hermit crabs and their allies

3) true crabs.

Several species of lobsters are of commercial value as edible invertebrates. In general, lobsters are shy, retiring creatures by day when they hide in caves and depressions in rocky or coral reefs. They actively comb the seafloor at night for food that consists mostly of dead or dying animals, or very slow sea creatures. There are both warm- and cold-

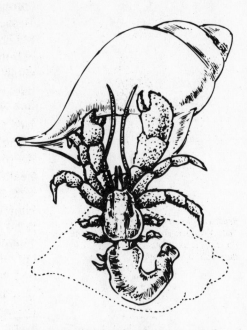

Representative hermit crab exploring a new snail shell. Note soft, coiled abdomen.

American (East Coast) lobster (Homarus americanus). This species is easily differentiated from other lobster species by the presence of its two enlarged claws (chelipeds), absent in other species.

water species. Spiny lobsters are somewhat flattened from top to bottom, shrimp-like in body form and lack large claws, relying instead on a formidable set of forward-pointing spines and stout, sharp antennae. There is a group called slipper lobsters inhabiting tropical reef habitats that are even flatter and more armored than the spiny lobster. The East Coast, or American lobster, in contrast, is relatively spineless, yet sports a pair of large, unequal claws used for defense and crushing prey, such as snails and clams.

Hermit crabs are an unusual group of crustaceans in that only the anterior portion of their bodies is protected by a hard exoskeleton; the abdomen is completely soft and even appears flabby. Hermit crabs have solved this potential problem by using empty shells to protect the abdomen. The first thing a juvenile hermit crab does after its first molt as an adult is to look for a suitable shell and climbs in abdomen first. This is difficult enough because most empty shells on the ocean floor get crushed or buried. The result is that most hermit crabs get shells from other hermit crabs. There is a kind of shell pool where the same shells get used several times as hermit crabs grow and need a larger shell.

True crabs are completely armored. They are flattened dorso-ventrally, and the tail section is reduced and kept tucked up under the body. Almost all crabs are bottom dwellers, only a few swim on a regular basis, and then they use specialized legs, not pleopods like shrimp. Crabs are in the order Decapoda, as they all have 10 leg-appendages, the first 2 of which are usually in the form of claws or pincers. The shape and nature of these first appendages tell a great deal about the life-style of a crab. Those with large, robust claws feed on heavily armored creatures such as clams and snails. Those with small, delicate claws may be herbivores and neatly cut away bits of seaweed for sustenance. The physical or morphological characteristics of all the crustaceans can tell a great deal about their lifestyle if interpreted correctly.

Representative true crab. Bottom dwellers, most crabs have flattened bodies to facilitate moving under and through loose rock habitats.

Phylum Mollusca: Chitons, Clams, Snails, Octopus and Squid

In spite of significant diversity, these animals evolved from a single group and are closely related. All 75,000 species of mollusks have certain common characteristics, and many of these are unique to this phylum.

All mollusks have bodies that are soft and fleshy. Most have a muscular foot that takes a variety of forms. Snails crawl with it, clams dig with it and octopuses "walk" with a foot that has become divided into eight tentacles.

A portion of the mollusk's soft body is a thin flap of flesh called the mantle that extends from its point of origin and surrounds the body. In certain mollusks, a shell is produced by secretions from the mantle. Mollusk shells take one of three forms: 1) as a single shell, (often spiral but not necessarily — some are cap-shaped as well); 2) two shells that are hinged together; or 3) eight overlapping plates arranged in a row. The space between the body and the mantle is called the mantle cavity, in which the gills (if present) are located.

Mollusks are bilaterally symmetrical. This symmetry is easily identified in such forms as the clam, but less so in a snail with a spiral shell. If the animal inside the shell is examined, however, it is apparent that there are two eyes, two antennae and other paired appendages. Except for one rare deep-sea group, mollusks do not display a great deal of segmentation. They do, however, have distinct organ systems, including a complete digestive tract and some sophisticated sensory organs. These are most evident in the octopus and squid.

In most mollusks, the sexes are separate (although some hermaphroditism does occur). Eggs and sperm are released into the water, producing larvae called *veligers*. In those species with planktonic larvae, the veliger eventually settles down to the seafloor to begin life as a juvenile snail, sea slug, clam, etc. Copulation and even egg-laying and brooding occurs in some species. The most complex sexual behavior occurs in the octopus and squid group and is described later.

Mollusks can be found in every marine habitat, yet they have successfully invaded both freshwater and terrestrial habitats as well. Like the arthropods, there are several species that are economically important to man (primarily as a food source). Because of the tremendous diversity of mollusks, they will be described on a class-by-class basis.

Representative chiton: A) dorsal view, chiton crawling over rock (note eight overlapping plates); B) ventral view showing location of mouth and foot (note bilateral symmetry).

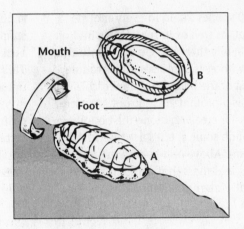

ies usually blend with their backgrounds. Their shells consist of eight overlapping plates that become separated when the chiton dies. These plates are often found washed up on shore and are commonly called angel wings. The shape and arrangement of the plates is a critical identifying characteristic for taxonomists.

Chitons crawl along the seafloor on a large, muscular foot. Almost all are herbivores, scraping thin films of algae off rocks with a tonguelike apparatus called a *radula*. The radula is a unique molluskan organ, consisting of a ribbon of tiny teeth, that is rubbed against an algae-bearing surface. Radulas are also present in many snails.

Class Amphineura: Chitons or Sea Cradles

There are approximately 600 species of chiton, all of which are marine. While most are not more than an inch or two in length, the gumboot chiton of the Pacific Northwest may reach over a foot in length. At first glance, chitons may be overlooked — their oval, flattened bod-

Class Gastropoda: Limpets, Abalone, Snails, Sea Slugs

The gastropods are the most diverse and largest class of mollusks, with over

Side view of representative snail crawling on seafloor. Inset shows action of radula scraping algal growths from rock surface. As the mouth opens, the radula is pushed forward and pulled up, scraping algae off rock with radular teeth.

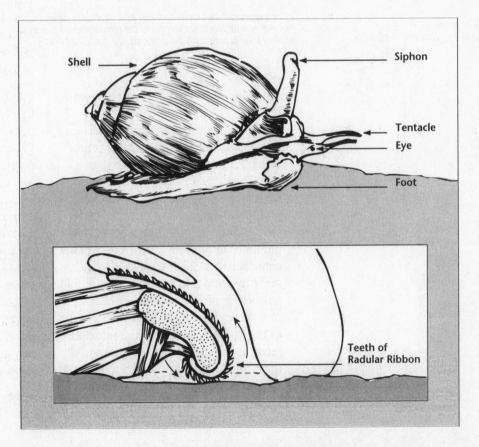

64,000 species found in every marine habitat, as well as in fresh water and on land. While there is a clearly identifiable head with eyes, tentacles and a radula, the rest of the body is asymmetrical. There is a prominent ventral foot, used mostly for creeping along the bottom (although some species use theirs to dig or swim). Above and behind the foot is the visceral mass that contains the animal's internal organs.

snails is twisted 180°, creating a U-shaped passage that brings the anus back out to the shell's single opening. This condition is called *torsion* and is a unique gastropod characteristic.

The sexes are usually separate in gastropods, but as is typical for the invertebrates, there are many exceptions. Copulation generally takes place, resulting in a gelatinous egg mass or hard capsules. Thousands of eggs are

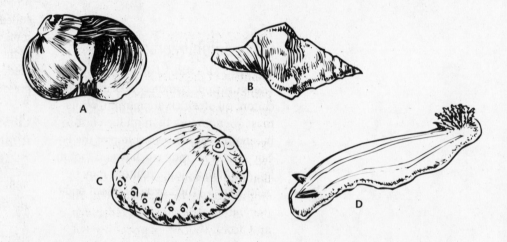

Representative shell types: A) moon snail (globular); B) whelk (high spired); C) abalone (low spired); D) nudibranch (shell absent). Shells are created by the secretion of calcium in layers by the soft, flexible mantle. The shape the shell takes is genetically programmed and species specific.

Most gastropods (meaning "stomach-foot") have a single spiral shell. Shells are created by extracting calcium carbonate from the water and incorporating it in a secretion that is released from the soft, malleable mantle. Some shells display ornate designs which the mantle can build in varying forms and shapes. Each animal is genetically programmed to produce a shell with unique characteristics. Shells provide a hard outer covering that protects the characteristically soft body. Those gastropods that do not have hard outer shells, such as the *nudibranchs,* often exude noxious secretions from body pores, making them taste and smell noxious to potential predators. The gut tract of shelled

eventually released from the mass as either larvae or miniature adult replicates. Slipper-shell snails (*Crepidula fornicata*) are usually found in chains permanently attached to one another and employ one of the more-interesting reproductive strategies. They begin life as males and change to females as they mature. The oldest members of a chain are usually the large females, who are located at the bottom with younger males on top. These young males impregnate the older, larger females before becoming older, larger females themselves who then get impregnated by a new generation of younger males, and so on...

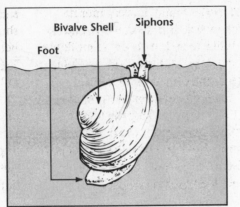

Representative clam (pelecypod). Siphon length, shell shape and digging ability by the foot are all factors in determining the kind of soft substrate clams live in, from dense mud to coarse sand.

Class Pelecypoda: Clams, Mussels, Oysters, Scallops

Members of the class Pelecypoda are perhaps the most reclusive group of marine invertebrates. Most of the 7000 species of clams, scallops, cockles, mussels and oysters spend their entire lives buried in mud or sand, with a brief expedition into the water column as free-swimming larvae prior to settling on the bottom. Adapting to a sedentary and usually buried existence has left the pelecypods with few external characteristics that are normally associated with animals. The body is compressed and enclosed in a pair of symmetrical *calcareous* shells called valves, hence the name bivalves. These are hinged at the margin of the shell and connected with a tough ligament. Two large muscles hold the shell closed.

The mantle cavity in bivalves is large and contains a pair of gills that are used for both respiration and food collection. Water is brought into the cavity and expelled via a double-barreled siphon, created by a fold in the mantle. Small food particles are trapped on the gill filaments and transported to the mouth by thousands of tiny cilia. Since the siphon is located at the posterior end of the clam, they actually bury themselves in a headfirst position.

All pelecypods have a well-developed foot that is generally used for digging. The etymological meaning of the name pelecypod ("hatchet foot") refers to the shape of most clam feet. The shape and level of muscular development of the foot, coupled with the shape of the valves and the length of the siphon, tell a great deal about the life history of a particular species of bivalve.

For example, razor clams are found in the shallows of high-surf beaches, usually near the surf line. In this wave-swept environment, the clams need to be able to move rapidly to avoid being either buried or washed onto the beach. The resulting adaptations include a narrow, thin shell, a well-developed and efficient digging foot, and short siphons (since they live near the surface).

Some pelecypods, such as mussels, do not bury themselves at all. Instead, they attach to a hard substrate by producing thin, tough threads of a sticky material that hardens upon contact with water. These threads are called *byssus* threads.

The sexes are separate in almost all pelecypods and copulation is rare. Sperm and eggs are released for external fertilization. The fertilized eggs develop into free-swimming veliger larvae, then settle permanently to the bottom, where they develop feet and shells.

Class Cephalopoda: Octopus, Squid, Cuttlefish, Nautilus

Included in this class are both the largest invertebrate species, the giant squid, (which can grow to more than 10 metres/35 feet in length) and the most intelligent species of invertebrate on earth, the octopus.

Octopuses, in particular, display behavior that is reminiscent of mammalian behavior including problem solving. Cuttlefish can communicate visually with each other, and female octopuses gently clean and guard their eggs. What this group of mollusks lacks in numbers (600 species), it more than makes up for in behavior and special-

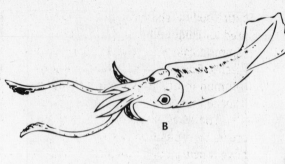

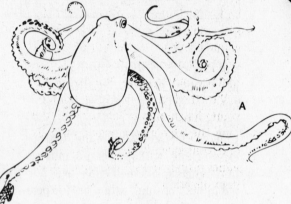

Representative cephalopods: A) bottom-dwelling octopus; B) free-swimming squid; C) free-swimming (yet bottom-oriented) nautilus. All have highly developed sense organs and are efficient predators.

ization of characteristics. Cephalopods are found living both in the water column, as exemplified by the streamlined squid, and among the bottom community organisms, as exemplified by the octopus. Cephalopods are clearly bilaterally symmetrical. There is no real foot, and the shell is either reduced (except in nautiloids), internalized or absent altogether. The prominent head (cephalopod means "head-foot") bears a number of tentacles, each of which has one or more rows of suckers. The mouth is centrally located at the base of the tentacles and is armed with a parrot-like beak used for biting into prey, such as fish or hard-shelled invertebrates like crabs and clams.

One of the most interesting aspects of the cephalopods is the sophistication of their sensory organs. Cephalopods have excellent eyesight. Their visual systems closely resemble in form and function those of higher vertebrates, such as mammals. Their tactile senses are also

extremely effective.

The mantle is extensive and surrounds the visceral mass, creating a rather large mantle cavity that houses gills and an anus. A modification of the foot, called a *funnel*, is located ventrally. When water is sucked into the mantle cavity for respiration, it is forced out through the funnel. In this way, most cephalopods can jet-propel themselves backward through the water. The open-water forms, such as squid, are particularly adept at this type of locomotion.

An ink sac is generally present and the release of its contents via the funnel seems to be a defense mechanism, creating a diversionary smoke screen.

The skin of all cephalopods is laden with pigment cells called *chromatophores*. Some deep-water species have chromatophores that light up (bioluminesce). Chromatophores are controlled by the muscular system, which allows squid and octopus to make remarkably fast color changes over their entire bodies. These color changes are used for camouflage and to visually communicate with other members of its species. Color changes are particularly common in ritualized courtship displays prior to mating.

The sexes are separate and mating occurs by copulation. Males do not have a penis, but a modified tentacle called a *hectocotyle* arm. This tentacle is grooved and smooth (lacking suckers) and is used to insert sperm into the female. Squid lay jelly-filled egg cases; the young are left to hatch on their own. Octopus lay eggs in grape-like strands that are guarded and cleaned continually by the female until fully developed young hatch months later. During this time, the female never leaves the eggs and, consequently, does not eat. Females usually perish after the birth of their offspring.

Phylum Bryozoa: Moss Animals

The 4000 to 5000 species in this phylum are not particularly well known due primarily to their small size. "Bryozoan" comes from two Greek words: bryo ("moss") and zoan ("animal"). Bryozoans are colonial organisms. The colonies grow as flat sheets, plant-like tufts, fleshly lobes or coral-like growths. Colonies range in size from less than an inch across to several feet wide. As with other small and inanimate-appearing organisms, divers do not normally examine bryozoans closely.

Close examination reveals that bryozoans are composed of thousands or even millions of individual animals that are fused together and share one skeletal structure. Each individual animal — called a *zooid* — is fully devel-

Representative bryozoan colony (Membranipora sp.) growing on kelp blade. Inset shows body-structure detail. Note that each individual (zooid) is separated from the rest of the colony by a body wall.

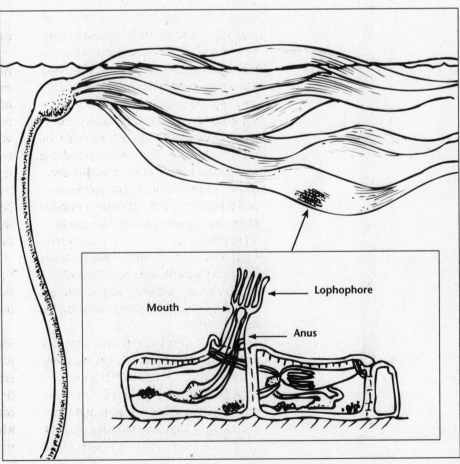

Lophophore

Mouth

Anus

oped and quite advanced. Complete organ systems are present, including digestive, respiratory, circulatory, muscular and nervous systems. Compared to other small colonial organisms, such as hydroids, this group is highly sophisticated.

A unique characteristic of this and just a few other groups (making it a diagnostic trait) is the presence of a *lophophore*. A lophophore is a looped feather-like organ that collects small particles of food by filtering water, in the same way clams filter-feed using their gills. Like hydroids, individuals in the colony are specialized for certain functions. One of the most interesting are the zooids called *avicularia*. These individuals, armed with muscle-operated jaws, defend the colony by pinching intruders.

Bryozoans are hermaphroditic; they produce male and female gametes, either simultaneously or alternately. There are two approaches to reproduction, the first is immediate release of the fertilized egg, which develops into a free-swimming larva. This larva is equipped to feed and spends some time in the plankton before settling down and starting a new colony. This colony grows, asexually, by budding of genetically identical individuals. The second strategy is more complex and more common. In this case, fertilized eggs are kept in a special brood chamber within the colony. These larvae do not feed as part of the plankton, but settle down rapidly, as they are relatively well-developed before release.

Bryozoans are widely distributed. They are found in both fresh and salt water. They are similar to corals and hydroids in that they attach to almost any hard substrate.

Phylum Phoronida: Horseshoe Worms

While this group is small (only 15 species), horseshoe worms are abundant

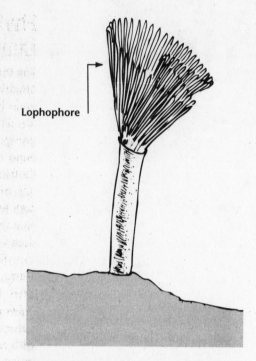

Lophophore

Representative phoronid. Note superficial similarity to sessile polychaete worm except for the horseshoe shape of the lophophore.

and obvious in cold and warm marine environments. Usually, they are mistaken for tube-dwelling polychaete worms. However, despite a superficial resemblance, they are not segmented and they do not have the chaetae (pairs of bristles) associated with the polychaete worms.

Horseshoe worms live in chitonous tubes five to seven inches long. A lophophore, in this case a horseshoe-shaped arrangement of tentacles, is located at the head and is different from any polychaete feeding apparatus.

The presence of this organ closely ties this group (in evolutionary terms) to the bryozoans and brachiopods that also have lophophores. Complete organ systems are also present, with the gut forming a *U*-shape, which places the anus at the head end just outside the perimeter of the lophophore. Phoronids are filter feeders, as are many tube-dwelling polychaetes.

Phylum Brachiopoda: Lamp Shells

The approximately 300 living species of brachiopods are descendants of a large and diverse fossil record that spans the last 600 million years. Historically, this group has been extremely successful in aquatic environments, representing thousands of species. Their numbers began to decline around 250 million years ago, leaving the existing representatives as a mere shadow of what once was a dominant marine group.

Brachiopods superficially resemble clams, having a bivalved calcareous shell that does not get much larger than a few inches across. However, the shell valves are arranged top and bottom with respect to the animal inside (as opposed to clams, whose valves are arranged around the sides of the animal). Additionally, the valves are usually unequal in brachiopods and are generally attached to a hard substrate by a short, fleshy stalk protruding near the hinge.

Their relationship with bryozoans and phoronids is clear given the presence of a large lophophore in the form of two long, coiled tentacles. As with the other lophophorate phyla, this organ is used for filter feeding and collecting plankton and other food particles. Microscopic cilia transport these particles to the mouth.

Unlike the other two lophophorate phyla, however, brachiopods have no anus, and thus a one-way digestive system. The result is that waste material is ingested and excreted through the same orifice (similarly to some members of the Cnidaria).

The sexes are usually separate, with external fertilization the rule. Typically with invertebrates, there are exceptions; some brachiopod females retain their eggs and wait for free-swimming sperm to fertilize them. In these few cases, the eggs are brooded in the shell and larvae released. The larvae then become temporary plankters, eventually settling to the seafloor to become attached adults.

Phylum Echinodermata: Sea Stars, Brittlestars, Featherstars, Sea Urchins, Sea Cucumbers

This exclusively marine group is one of the most perplexing invertebrate phyla due primarily to the unusual appearance of the 5900 species.

All echinoderms are bottom-dwellers, found primarily in rocky, cold-temperate habitats. Most move slowly and they range in size from half-inch sea cucumbers to giant 20-rayed sea stars over three feet across. All show a five-ray (pentameric) radial symmetry as adults.

The key to their placement high on the evolutionary ladder lies in the development of their larvae, which begin life as bilaterally symmetrical organisms, but display radially symmetry as adults. From the adult appearance, it is difficult to imagine that these animals are really

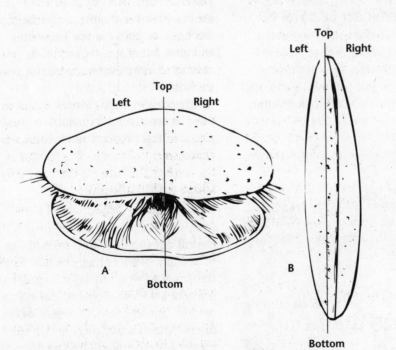

Comparison of shell and body orientation in: A) brachiopod; B) clam.

the closest living relatives to the higher vertebrates, the chordates.

Echinoderms have a skeletal structure composed of spines, loose plates or fused plates (depending upon the class). The phylum name reflects this unique characteristic: echino ("spiny") and derma ("skin"). Definite organ systems are present and one in particular is unique to the phylum. This is the water-vascular system that operates the hundreds of tube feet (found only on echinoderms). Some groups also have small pincerlike organs called *pedecellariae* distributed over their outer surfaces. These are used primarily for defense and in some cases for feeding on small planktonic organisms.

The sexes are separate (usually), and eggs and sperm are shed into the water freely, often being released from pores on the dorsal surface. The bilaterally symmetrical larvae remain in the plankton for a few days to a few weeks before settling down to the bottom and adopting adult-echinoderm habits.

There are five major classes in this phylum that are described individually.

Class Asteroidea: Sea Stars

Sea stars are characterized by having five or more stout arms that radiate from a central body. Tube feet are present and prominent, they are located ventrally in the *ambulacral* grooves that run the length of the arms. The mouth is located ventrally and central, the anus is dorsal. A calcareous sieve plate called the *madreporite* is also found on the top and slightly off-center. This serves as the entry point for water to operate the water-vascular system. Spines and plates are embedded in the skin and flesh, sometimes forming an armored outer shell. In some species, fingerlike gill filaments protrude from the dorsal surface, causing a furry appearance. Two-jawed pedecellariae can also be found on the dorsal surface.

Sea stars have interesting feeding habits. Most are scavengers or predators of slow-moving animals such as clams. For example, when a clam is found, the sea star wraps its arms around the clam and begins pulling the bivalve shell apart using the tube feet. Once the slightest compromise in the tightly clamped shell occurs, the sea star everts its stomach through its mouth and into the clam shell, digesting the prey in its own shell. Once the meal is fully digested, the stomach is pulled back in.

Sea stars also display remarkable powers of regeneration. If an arm is severed and retains at least part of the central body, a complete new individual will grow out of the single arm. In the meantime, a new arm is regenerated on the original star. In some species, this ability is taken to an extreme and applied as an asexual reproductive strategy, arms are dropped and become new stars.

Class Ophiuroidea: Brittle Stars, Basket Stars

In this class, the body is comprised of a central disc that is distinct from five or more long, slender arms. The tube feet are arranged regularly on the arms, but are adapted for feeding and picking up detritus and other organic debris as the animal crawls under rocks and in sediments. Both the mouth and madreporite are located on the ventrally and there is

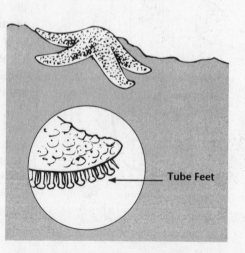

Tube Feet

Representative sea star. Inset shows detail of tube feet, unique structures present only in echinoderms. Tube feet are used primarily for locomotion in sea stars.

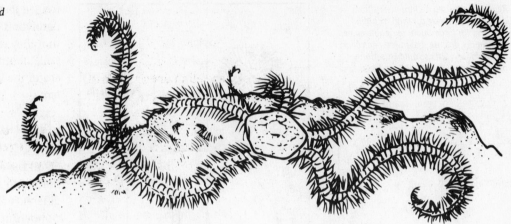

Representative brittlestar. Note five-rayed (pentamerous) radial arrangement of "arms" around the central disc.

no anus. The upper surface is generally covered with interlocking plates, the number, size and arrangement of these plates are used in ophiuroid identification.

As the name implies, this is a fragile group on the whole, with arms breaking regularly upon any kind of disturbance. Consequently, they are capable regenerators, growing arms back rapidly. Brittle and basket stars are active at night when fewer predators are present and the risk of brachial trauma is less.

Class Crinoidea:
Sea Lilies, Feather Stars

There are approximately 600 living species of crinoids. This group, like the brachiopods, has a much richer fossil record, with species numbering in the thousands over the past 400 million years. Most species today are found in shallow tropical habitats, although there are some deep-sea species.

The less-abundant sea lilies have a body cup supported on a jointed stalk attached to the seafloor. The more common feather stars are not attached as adults but are supported by a ring of appendages called *cirri*. Both forms have five arms radiating out from the central cup. These arms fork repeatedly to form many branches. Specimens average about 30 centimetres/1 foot tall. Finger-like tube feet on the branches are used for collecting passing food, such as plankton, that is passed in mucus strings down a ciliated groove in the arm to the mouth. Crinoids are unique among the echinoderms for having both the mouth and anus situated dorsally. No spines or pedecellariae are present. Instead, the body and arms are usually covered with interlocking or even overlapping plates. When disturbed, feather stars can "swim" by a sinuous movement of the branched arms.

Representative crinoid. Sea-star relatives, the tube feet of these organisms are used primarily as feeding structures, distributed over the "arms" and used for collecting planktonic prey.

Representative sea urchin. Inset shows detail of outer-body covering including tube feet for locomotion, moveable spines for primary defense and jawed pedicellaria for secondary defense against settling organisms and soft-bodied predators.

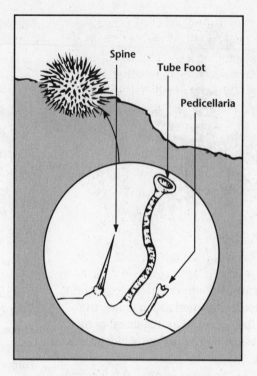

Spine

Tube Foot

Pedicellaria

ranged teeth. Almost all echinoids are herbivores, grazing on marine plants that they snip off with these teeth. The skeletal and muscle apparatus that operates the teeth is called *Aristotle's Lantern.*

Class Holothuroidea: Sea Cucumbers

Of all the echinoderms, this group is hardest to relate to the rest. The main difference is body orientation. Sea cucumbers are worm-shaped, they appear at first glance bilaterally symmetrical. Their radial symmetry is apparent when they are viewed carefully from one end to the other. They are round and elongated. Five rows of tube feet exist on some species, two rows on others and sometimes none at all. This further compounds the confusion.

The holothurian skeleton is not well developed, consisting of randomly distributed calcareous plates in the body wall. The mouth is located at one end, an anus at the other. Around the mouth are a group of specialized feeding tube feet that collect plankton in sedentary species, or pick up detritus and organic debris off the seafloor in species that are more mobile.

As with other echinoderms, holothurians have great powers of regeneration, particularly with respect to the internal organs of their respiratory and digestive systems. When disturbed, sev-

Class Echinoidea: Sea Urchins, Heart Urchins, Sand Dollars

Echinoids, a well-known class with truly spiny skins, have an internal skeleton, called a test, which is comprised of fused plates. Generally roundish in form, the test has five equidistant rows of tube feet protruding and batteries of three-jawed pedecellariae. The spines are attached to the test in ball-and-socket joints that allow them to rotate and track approaching intruders. The mouth is on the bottom and consists of five radially ar-

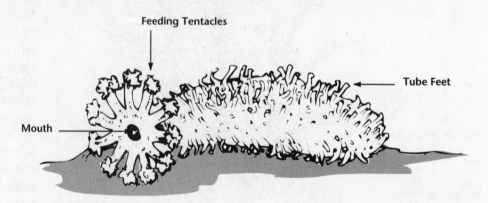

Feeding Tentacles

Tube Feet

Mouth

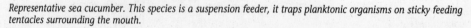

Representative sea cucumber. This species is a suspension feeder, it traps planktonic organisms on sticky feeding tentacles surrounding the mouth.

eral species simply throw up their insides at an attacking predator (called evisceration), fouling any delicate parts such as fish gill-filaments or crab mandibles. The empty shell of a sea cucumber crawls away and begins growing a new set of organs.

Phylum Chordata: Chordates

Sub-Phylum Urochordata: Tunicates (Sea Squirts)

There are approximately 1375 species of sea squirts occurring in most marine environments. They are an important group as they provide a phylogenetic link between the invertebrates and the vertebrates; this is reflected in their

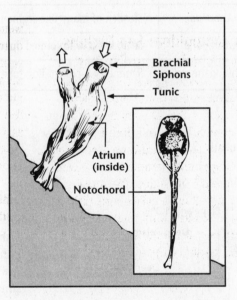

Representative solitary sea-squirt (tunicate). Inset shows planktonic tadpole larva with developed notochord that will be absorbed as larva develops into sessile adult form.

placement as a subphylum in the taxonomic scheme.

Larval tunicates look completely different to the adult form. It is in these larval stages that certain chordate characteristics are seen. Tunicate larvae look like miniature tadpoles with an enlarged head-end that tapers rapidly to form a trailing tail. Within the tail is a stiff supporting rod called a *notochord*. This structure acts like the characteristic invertebrate backbone. Additionally, the larva has a pharynx with gill slits, another characteristic of higher vertebrates.

The free-swimming larva eventually settles to the seafloor, locates a firm substrate and attaches itself by using an adhesive pad on its head. At this point there is a dramatic metamorphosis. The tail is absorbed, the pharynx becomes barrel-shaped (while retaining the gill slits) and two external openings emerge that resemble a clam's siphon. The entire body becomes enclosed within a gelatinous leathery tunic (hence the name). The overall appearance is asymmetrical although generally globular (in solitary species). At this stage, tunicates are often mistaken for sponges in spite of the fact that they have complete organ systems and use the enlarged pharynx for extremely efficient filter feeding. Clearly, the larval forms exhibit the chordate characteristics while the adult is a more typical invertebrate.

Most tunicates are hermaphrodites, eggs or sperm are released to be externally fertilized like many sedentary invertebrates. The larva remains planktonic for a while before settling down to become an adult. Some species remain solitary, others reproduce asexually by budding to form colonies. These may appear as a number of distinct individuals like corals or they may form dense gelatinous masses where identification of specific individuals becomes difficult. Tunicates are fairly abundant and are found in most marine ecosystems.

Major Characteristics of the Principle Invertebrate Phyla

Symmmetry	Digestive tract	Excretory organs	Circulatory system	Respiratory organs	Segmentation	Phylum	Distinctive Features
Asymmetry	N	N	N	N	N	Protozoa	Microscopic; one-celled or colonies of like cells
Asymmetry	N	N	N	N	N	Porifera	Body perforated by pores and canals
Radial / Incomplete		N	N	N	N	Cnidaria	Nematocysts; digestive tract sac-like
Radial / Incomplete		N	N	N	N	Ctenophora	Comb plates for locomotion
Bilateral / Incomplete		Y	N	N	N	Platyhelminthes	Flat, soft; digestive tract branched or none
Bilateral / Complete (with anus)		Y	Y	N	N	Nemertea	Slender, soft, ciliated; soft proboscis
Bilateral / Complete (with anus)		Y	N	N	N	Bryozoa	Grow as moss-like or encrusting colonies
Bilateral / Complete (with anus)		Y	Y	N	N	Brachiopoda	Dorsal and ventral limy shell; a fleshy stalk
Bilateral / Complete (with anus)		Y	Y	Y	N	Mollusca	External limy shell of 1, 2, or 8 parts, or none; body soft
Bilateral / Complete (with anus)		Y	Y	Y	Y	Annelida	Slender, of many like segments; fine setae as appendages
Bilateral / Complete (with anus)		Y	Y	Y	Y	Arthropoda	Segmented, with jointed appendages; exoskeleton containing chitin
Radial / Complete (with anus)		N	Y	Y	N	Echinodermata	Symmetry 5-part radial; tube feet; spiny endoskeleton

Y=Yes   N=No

Percentages of Fish Species Living in Various Habitats

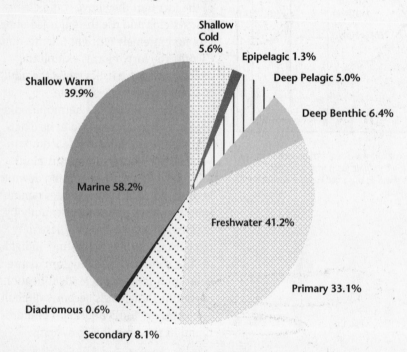

Pelagic refers to open water, benthic refers to fish associated with the seafloor.

Sub-Phylum Vertebrata
Super-Class Gnaphostomata: Fishes

Fishes are the consummate aquatic organism, seemingly perfectly adapted for life in the aquatic realm. Fishes can be simply defined as aquatic *poikilothermic* (coldblooded) vertebrates that have gills throughout life, and have limbs in the shape of fins. While this may seem like a very simple definition, it effectively eliminates all other organisms. This definition does not reflect the enormous diversity of forms fishes take, the habitats they occupy or their biology. Unlike the amphibians, reptiles, birds and mammals, fishes are a heterogeneous group. From lamprey and hagfish to lungfish and flatfish they include a tremendous diversity of species.

There are an estimated 19,000 living fish species compared with 21,000 tetrapod species. In other words, fish make up about half of all known vertebrate species. Further, the number of new fish species described annually usually exceeds the number of all other new vertebrate species combined. It is estimated that the eventual number of living fish species may be 50 percent greater than presently recognized, with close to 28,000 species. In contrast to amphibians, reptiles, and mammals, the known diversity of living fishes exceeds that of known fossil fish species. On the other hand, there is a much richer fossil record of fish than birds, for example, even relative to their numbers. This makes sense, given the nature of the process of fossilization. This process is facilitated in aquatic environments where movement of sediments can effectively bury and preserve species.

Fishes range in size from a 2.5 centimetre/1 inch adult Philippine goby to the 14-metre/45-foot whale shark, the largest cold-blooded animal on earth. The shape of fishes varies greatly. Some are brilliantly colored, such as coral reef fishes, others are quite drab, such as the cryptic flatfish. Some, such as oceanic sharks, are sleek and graceful, moving with little resistance through a medium 800 times denser than air. Others are described as ugly and grotesque. Fins may be missing or greatly modified into holdfast organs like the suction disc on the pacific lumpsucker or as a lure for attracting prey, as with the anglerfish. About 50 species, most of which are cave-dwellers, lack eyes. Scales may be present or absent. Bodies may be inflatable, such as in the pufferfish family or, as in the seahorse family, encased in an

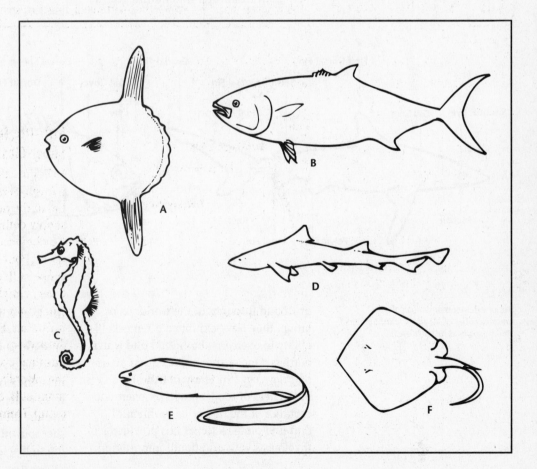

Fish body-shapes: A) ocean sunfish; B) tuna; C) seahorse; D) shark; E) moray eel; F) stingray. Body shape in fish reflects life-style, swimming ability, feeding behavior, sensory development and habitat preference, among other characteristics.

inflexible bony armor of fused scales. Internal anatomical features, both soft and hard, also vary greatly and in some cases take on bizarre specializations.

Fishes live in almost every conceivable kind of aquatic habitat. From South America's Lake Titicaca, the world's highest large lake to Lake Baikal, Russia, the world's deepest, fishes live in every aquatic environment including the deep ocean trenches, perhaps the most physically stressful environment on earth. Some species live in almost pure fresh water, some in very salty lakes, in caves where total darkness occurs and in the most torrential streams. In Africa, a species of Tilapia lives in hot soda lakes with temperatures as high as 44°C/111°F, while under the Antarctic ice sheet, the ice fish Trematomus lives at about -2°C/28°F. Many species have developed air-breathing organs and live in stagnant tropical swamps; others demand well-oxygenated waters to survive.

Both freshwater and marine fishes

on the past dispersal of fishes and where certain groups of fishes originated.

The largest number of both freshwater and saltwater fishes occur in the tropics, with a progressive reduction in the number of species toward the polar regions. The greatest number of species of freshwater fishes occur in Southeast Asia. However, the Amazon River has almost as many species. The marine waters of the Indo-Pacific, including the Red Sea and Indian Ocean to northern Australia and Polynesia, exhibit the greatest diversity of fish species, most occurring in a triangle formed by the Malay Peninsula, New Guinea and the Philippines. The Caribbean region is also rich in fish life, but has not the diversity of the older, more stable Indo-Pacific region. The least diversity of species occurs in the Arctic and Antarctic regions. On a global scale the greatest concentrations of fish species in both fresh and salt waters inhabit Southeastern Asia.

Most species of fishes live their en-

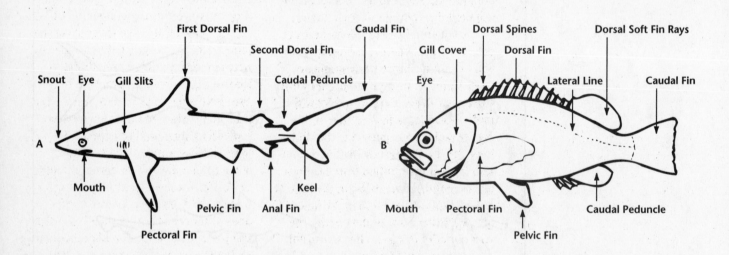

Major external morphological characteristics of: A) shark (elasmobranch); and B) sea bass (osteichthyes).

are found throughout the world. As a group, they have exhibited a remarkable ability to overcome both land and water barriers. One of the most exciting areas of *ichthyology* (the study of fishes) today is in the field of zoogeography. General acceptance of the theory of continental drift and plate tectonics has provided ichthyologists with additional information

tire lives either in fresh or marine waters. A few live part of their lives in each environment, these species are referred to as being diadromous. Among these, most are anadromous, spawning in fresh water but spending most of their lives in the sea. A very few do the opposite, spawning in the oceans but returning to live in freshwater environments.

Such species are catadromous. There are also many cases of species that are capable of spending brief periods of time in water of greatly varying salinities such as fish living in estuaries near the mouths of rivers.

About 6850 fish species (37 percent) normally live in freshwater lakes and rivers. Such water systems cover a mere one percent of the earth's surface and account for only 0.01 percent of the earth's total water volume. About twice this number (11,650 — 63 percent of all species) live their lives in the oceans that cover 70 percent of the earth's surface and account for 97 percent of its water. This seems like a disproportionate number of freshwater species, given the distribution of water based on salinity. One theory explains the disparity by assuming that there has been a greater tendency for *speciation* in freshwater forms because freshwater fishes are more easily isolated when river systems become lakes. In general, isolation leads to the development of different species as populations adapt to the different environmental conditions of each habitat.

A variety of environmental factors determine just where a certain species will live. In freshwater environments, species may show a preference for lakes, streams or rivers. Certain species will prefer warm lakes to cool ones, or the deeper regions as opposed to the shallows. Stream fishes may exhibit a zonation in their distribution from headwaters to mouth, some living in the riffle or quiet areas, others living in the areas of greatest water flow. In the oceans, the vast majority of species live in coastal areas (around 9100 species). Most fishes living beyond the average 180 metre/ 600 foot deep-sea continental shelf are deep sea species, numbering around 2300. Only about 250 species are found in the shallow sunlit waters of the open ocean.

Many species have limited ranges of distribution. One small minnow, for example, lives only in one spring in Nevada. Many other species are found in only one place in the world. Nearly one third of Hawaiian reef fishes, for example, are endemic to those islands. Some species, on the other hand, have broad ranges, demonstrating their ability to tolerate extreme environmental conditions. The best examples of such fishes are the approximately 107 species that are found worldwide in both tropical and subtropical waters. Of these, about 14 are shore species, 90 are oceanic in nature and only 3 species live on the seafloor.

Fishes' diversity of behavior is almost as great as their diversity of morphology. Some travel in groups called schools, others fiercely defend specific territories. Some provide parental care, while others scatter eggs and sperm freely into open water. A number of interesting and extremely specialized symbiotic relationships occur between different species of fish and invertebrates. The pearlfish, that lives within the body cavity of sea cucumbers, is a good example of the former; the parasitic male of the deep sea angler fish, permanently attached to his mate, is an example of the latter. Fishes have adapted to a wide variety of foods. Some are specialized to feed on aquatic plants, plankton and even toxic prey such as corals and jellyfish. Some fishes produce venom or poison, electricity, sound or light for defense, offense and mate recognition. Some species are known hermaphrodites or exhibit sex reversal with age. A certain number of fishes migrate tremendous distances as part of their life cycles using a variety of environmental cues to navigate expanses of open water. The larvae and young of some oceanic species live their adolescent lives inshore, moving out to sea as they mature. Species of salmon migrate thousands of miles from the open sea up river systems to spawn in the stream beds where they were born.

Comparison of Major Morphological Features of the Five Vertebrate Classes.

	Skeleton	Body Covering	Respiration	Eggs
Fish	Fins	Scales	Gills	Membrane
Amphibians	Limbs	Moist skin	Gills/skin	Membrane
Reptiles	Limbs	Scales	Lungs	Hard shell
Birds	Limbs	Feathers	Air sacs	Hard shell
Mammals	Limbs	Fur/hair	Lungs	Live-bearing

Class Reptilia: Marine Iguanas, Sea Turtles and Sea Snakes

Of approximately 6000 species of reptiles, about 40 have returned to marine environments. These fall into three groups; one lizard (the marine iguana), seven species of sea turtles and more than 60 species of sea snakes. Additionally, there is a marine crocodile in the Indo-Pacific and freshwater crocodiles, alligators and turtles that will not be discussed here.

The success of this class is primarily due to the development of a hard-shelled egg. This single adaptation has allowed the reptiles to invade terrestrial environments, cutting their ties to the aquatic realm. Amphibians are still tied to water environments because of the lack of a hard shell necessary to keep moist eggs from drying. Aquatic reptiles have evolved from land-based forms. The few species that returned to the sea developed aquatic adaptations while losing their terrestrial ones. However, most still exhibit the major reptilian characteristics.

The reptilian eggshell is porous, allowing for the exchange of atmospheric gasses necessary for respiration of the embryo, yet solid enough to provide physical protection. A large yolk provides food for the developing embryo. The most important adaptation of the reptilian egg is the development of an *amnion*, the thin embryonic membrane between the inside of the shell and the embryo. This structure maintains the integrity of the developing egg.

All reptiles are cold-blooded (poikilothermic). As a result, most marine reptiles are found in warm-temperate and tropical waters. They have complete skeletal systems including a backbone, the diagnostic characteristic of the phylum. Fully developed organ systems are also present. The body is covered with scales or fused plates.

Iguanas — There is only one species of lizard that has successfully invaded the sea, *Amblyrhynchus cristatus*, the marine iguana. Found only in the Galapagos Archipelago, this species barely qualifies as an aquatic reptile. While it feeds on marine algae, such as seaweeds, much of its time is spent lying in the sun on the rocky Galapagos shores. Their black coloration helps them absorb heat from the sun's rays, which warms them after repeated feeding dives. Like most reptiles, the marine iguana regulates its internal body temperature behaviorally by lying out in the sun during the day to warm up. Growing up to 1.5 metres/5 feet long, the marine iguana resembles the more familiar land, or desert, iguana in its body shape. A gregarious species, marine iguanas are generally found in large groups.

Sea Turtles — Of the seven species of sea turtles, six are on threatened- or endangered-species lists, due largely to their commercial value as food, leather, jewelry and other products. Their decline is also due to man's activities on or near beach-nesting sites.

While there are very few species, and declining numbers of individuals within those species, sea turtles are still one of the most familiar and popular of all aquatic animals. They range in size from the giant leatherback (over 1.8 metres/6 feet long and weighing hundreds of pounds) to the petite green sea turtle. They also differ from terrestrial forms in several ways.

First, their shells are streamlined and flattened to facilitate movement through water. Additionally, the shell is not as solid structurally as in terrestrial

Representative sea turtle. Sea turtles are characterized by having a flattened, streamlined shell and flippers for limbs. Additionally, they have well-developed salt excretory glands.

forms. Second, the head cannot be pulled back into the shell, a result of its altered shape for swimming. Third, the forelimbs are modified as rigid flippers and the hind limbs as paddles that aid in steering and, in females, in digging nests on the beach.

While sea turtles live most of their lives in the aquatic realm, they still return to land to bear their young. For example, green sea turtles return approximately every three years to the same beach where they were born. This jour-

ney may be several hundred miles for some individuals. Males and females mate in the water near shore. At night, females laboriously crawl out of the water to a place high up the beach where they excavate a deep hole. There they deposit up to one hundred golf ball-size leathery eggs. These are buried and left to incubate for sixty days, the females return to sea. Each female may, over several months, repeat this process up to five times.

Under the cover of darkness, the eggs finally hatch simultaneously. Digging their way to the surface, the baby turtles make a mad dash for the surf, attempting to evade potential predators such as land crabs, birds and mammals. Those that survive running the gauntlet between nest and surf line must still survive the first year of life at sea before growing to a safe size. They will return to the same beach when they are four to six years old to complete the cycle. In the meantime, they will grow into adulthood, feeding on a variety of marine life such as shellfish and bottom fish. Some species even eat jellyfish.

As mentioned previously, most species of sea turtles are endangered. This is due to the combination of their commercial value and their breeding habits. In particular, eggs and juvenile turtles are particularly vulnerable on beaches that are in close proximity to human activity. In the Caribbean, several major beach nesting sites are located near resort areas. One problem resulting from such proximity is the disorientation of newly hatched turtles caused by street and resort lighting; it is theorized that young turtles use the brightness of the sky reflected over the water to guide them to the surf. Lighting adjacent to nesting areas can throw them off, and infant-turtle deaths have been caused by cars as confused baby turtles intent on heading out to sea crossed the beach onto coastal roads.

Conservation measures include relocating eggs to safer beaches, enclosing nests in predator-proof cages and working to decrease artificial lighting on beaches near nesting grounds. Some hope is also offered for adult turtles that are caught accidentally in the nets of shrimp trawlers through the recent development of TED — the Turtle Exclusion Device. This highly controversial apparatus is a cage-like device that is fitted near the bottom of a shrimp net. Its trap door allows turtles swept up in the net to escape. Shrimpers claim that TED decreases their catch and that it is not very effective. While still being tested, TED appears to provide at least some relief to this problem.

Sea Snakes — All sea snakes are found in the tropical Pacific, primarily in the Indo-Pacific. Growing up to 1.8 metres/6 feet long, these cobra relatives are best known for their extremely toxic venom, which they inject into prey, such as fish, through small fangs. The venom can cause death in humans and these animals should be treated with extreme caution.

Sea snakes exhibit several adaptations specific to life in the sea. Most obvious of these is the paddle-shaped tail that greatly aids their movement through the water, which they never leave. Special salt excretory glands are located near the mouth that cope with salt buildup in the body. Sea snakes can stay submerged for up to 30 minutes on one breath. During the day, they are typically seen resting under coral heads on tropical reefs. They hunt at night, using a keen sense of smell to locate resting fishes. Nearly all sea snakes bear live young that are fully functional at birth.

Class Mammalia: Sea Otters, Seals, Sea Lions, Walrus, Manatees, Dolphins, Whales

Of all the animals that make their home in the aquatic realm, this group — the aquatic mammals — engages and captivates humans more than any other. Perhaps it is man's phylogenetic relationship to these highly specialized mammals that stirs such interest. Part of this fascination lies in their complex behavior and their ability to live, as warm-blooded, air-breathing mammals, in the waters of the earth's oceans.

As with the reptiles, all present-day and extinct species of aquatic mammals evolved from forms that had made the transition from aquatic to terrestrial environments. Reptiles, birds and mammals all produced species that could survive on land to escape increasing competition in the seas and to take advantage of the relatively new land environment. It was only after millions of years of selection and evolution that competition on land, particularly for food, became so great that a few species began the gradual selective process that readapted them for a return to the sea. The abundance of food along the shores of the continents was the major impetus for this return.

While many aquatic mammals appear fishlike (dolphins for example), all

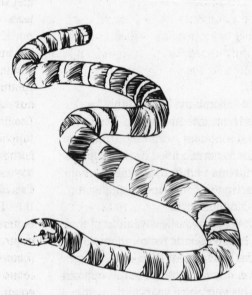

Representative sea snake. Inhabitants of the tropical Pacific, sea snakes have laterally flattened (compressed) tails that assist them in swimming.

Representative marine mammals: A) sea otter; B) seal; C) walrus; D) manatee; E) dolphin; F) baleen whale.

have retained the fundamental, diagnostic traits that make them mammals. They are all warm-blooded (*endothermic*); they all have hair of one type or another at some point in their lives (it may only appear embryonically); and they all bear live young that they suckle.

While these characteristics are found in all mammals, land or sea, those species that have returned to an aquatic existence have had to develop adaptations that allow mammalian characteristics to work in water, under very different conditions than those in which they originally evolved.

Present-day aquatic mammals descended independently from six major mammal lines. Walking seals (sea lions, fur seals and walruses) appear to have developed from a stem bear group. There are approximately 15 species of

walking seals. All can move about on four legs. Because they have visible ears, they are often referred to as "eared" seals.

Sea otters (one species) appear to have evolved from an ancient stem otter group. Crawling seals (harbor seals, elephant seals, monk seals) also seem to have evolved from the stem otter group. The hind limbs of these seals cannot support their bodies out of water. Rather, they crawl when on shore. They have no visible trace of ears, although ears are present.

The *sirenians* include four species of manatees and dugong. They are all tropical and arose from a stem ungulate (hoofed mammals) group. Toothed cetaceans make up the largest group of aquatic mammals, with about 65 species of dolphins, porpoises and whales. They all have distinct, conical teeth. As odd as it may seem, they also appear to have evolved from the same stem ungulate group that gave us cows, horses and elephants.

The ten species of baleen whales, again evolved from the stem ungulate group mentioned above, make up the sixth group. These are the "great" whales, distinguished from the toothed cetaceans by both their size (the blue whale, at close to 30 metres/100 feet long, is the largest living creature on earth) and the presence of baleen instead of distinct teeth. This structure is unique in the animal kingdom and acts as a strainer for feeding on minute planktonic prey.

Evidence for the theory that aquatic mammals developed from terrestrial species is found both in the fossil record and in the embryonic and adult forms of present-day species. Several preaquatic mammal ancestors have been identified from fossil remains. It is the comparison of these fossil forms with present-day species that paleobiologists and taxonomists use to make their best guess at phylogenetic relationships.

Vestigial organs provide additional evidence in living forms. These organs are relics of the past. For example, before a baleen whale is born, it has a tiny set of teeth that never break through the gum. Most cetaceans (whales and dolphins) have a few bristly hairs at birth, some of which may remain throughout the animal's life. Dolphins have hind-leg buds for a few weeks of their fetal life and as adults they have vestigial hips that take the form of a pair of slender bones found in the posterior tail muscles. On a very rare occasion, a dolphin or whale is born with a pair of nonfunctioning, partially formed hind legs.

One can see the chronological move toward an aquatic existence in present-day species by comparing the development of their limb structures. Sea otters, the most recent species to return to an oceanic existence, still have rather ordinary front paws, while their hind limbs have become flippers, which greatly aid swimming. In the walking and crawling seal groups (collectively belonging to the order Pinnipedia — "wing-foot") both forelimbs and hind limbs have become flippers. The manatees have lost their hind limbs completely, but the front limbs have remained articulate and flexible for swimming and walking through seagrass meadows.

The dolphin and whale groups (order Cetacea) are the oldest and best adapted group. Their hind limbs are completely absent and their forelimbs have become rigid flippers from the shoulder. The development of a dorsal fin and tail flukes indicates a complete adaptation for life in the aquatic realm.

Aquatic mammals have had to adapt to the severe physical factors that characterize the aquatic realm described in section One, The Chemistry and Physics of Diving. The overriding physical considerations are loss of body heat due to cold, movement in a fluid environment and the ability to stay submerged for prolonged periods of time without breathing.

Like all mammals, otters, seals, dolphins and whales are warm-blooded, endothermic organisms. One of the first factors these animals had to cope with was cold, particularly because water has a thermal conductivity 20 times that of air. To combat cold, aquatic animals have developed three major adaptations. First, they are generally large animals. Sea otters are the smallest, but, as males average around 45 kilograms/100 pounds, even they aren't small compared to land mammals as a whole. Then there are the whales, the largest animals on earth. A large surface-area to volume ratio means that an animal can have more mass with less surface area from which to radiate heat as it gets larger. On land, large size (and mass) is a disadvantage because of the great structural stress put on a large animal due to gravity. In water this is not a problem, thanks to Archimedes' Principle, immense size is possible and even desirable.

Second, all aquatic mammals have developed efficient outer-body coverings composed of either dense fur, a thick fat layer called blubber, or a combination of both. If fur is dense enough,

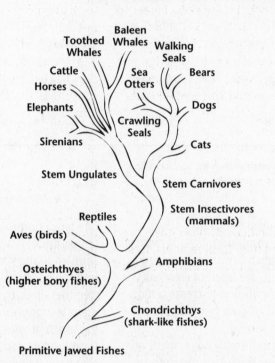

Phylogenetic tree indicating theorized evolution and origins of the chordates, including marine mammals.

it can trap a thin layer of air between the animal's skin and the cold water, acting as an insulator in the same way water trapped in a well-fitting wet suit provides insulation for a diver. How thick does fur have to be for this concept to work? Fur-seal fur has 46,000 hairs per square centimetre or 300,000 hairs per square inch; sea otters (the only marine mammal without a blubber layer) have an incredible 92,000 hairs per square centimetre or 600,000 per square inch. This is why they were hunted almost to extinction for their lush fur coats.

Blubber is a layer of fat richly supplied with blood vessels present in all aquatic mammals except sea otters. In seals it may be only a few inches thick. In a blue whale it is several feet thick

and is one of the main reasons they have been hunted by humans to the brink of extinction. This layer of fat acts as a great insulator of cold, protecting the internal organs from extreme temperature changes due to the surrounding environment.

Third, most aquatic mammals have a circulatory system called a countercurrent exchange system. It is basically a heat exchanger. Blood traveling from the extremities towards the heart is cooler than blood flowing away from the interior. Because the veins (inward flow) lie next to the arteries (away from the heart), there is an exchange of heat; the warmer arterial blood slightly warms the venous blood through conduction before it reaches the body's core. This helps keep the critical core temperature from dropping dramatically.

A second major physical factor that has kept most land mammals from invading the sea is the problem of how to move efficiently through water. This is a particular concern when it comes to catching prey. With the exception of the sirenians, all aquatic mammals are carnivorous, a reflection of the abundance of high-energy food in the sea. It is interesting to look at the efficiency of locomotion of aquatic mammals compared to what they eat. Killer whales, the most highly adapted marine-mammal carnivores, are perhaps the fastest marine mammals, achieving speeds of up to 56 kph/35 mph. Manatees, the only herbivorous aquatic mammals, are extremely slow moving and tend to lie just under the surface without moving. As a result, they are often mortally wounded by propellers from speed boats. Clearly, a manatee that grazes on attached aquatic plants does not need to be a fast swimmer to feed.

Aquatic mammals are, for the most part, streamlined. The cetaceans are tapered at both ends, with the addition of dorsal and tail fins. Legs have become flippers, particularly evident in the pinnipeds. All the sex organs and

	Heat Retention	Locomotion	Diving Ability	Feeding Type
Sea otter	Air in fur	Webbed paws	Poor	Carnivore — fish, invertebrates
Seal	Blubber layer	Primarily hind flippers	Excellent	Carnivore — fish
Sea lion	Blubber layer Air in fur	Primarily front flippers	Good	Carnivore — fish
Walrus	Blubber layer	All flippers	Good	Carnivore — invertebrates
Manatee	Blubber layer	Front flippers hind "fluke"	Good	Herbivore — aquatic plants
Toothed whales (including dolphins)	Blubber layer	Tail fluke	Excellent	Carnivore — fish, squid
Baleen Whales	Blubber layer	Tail fluke	Excellent	Planktivore — large size, krill, small fish

Comparison of the seven primary marine mammal groups and their adaptations to the aquatic realm.

nipples are pulled back into pockets to further the streamlining. Even eyelashes are absent, which further reduces drag. The neck bones are fused in cetaceans (except beluga whales) to create a more rigid vertebral column to which strong muscles are attached.

Aquatic mammals have not developed gills. They have kept their mammalian lungs and breathe air. This means that whenever they want to submerge, they must hold their breath, like a free-diving human. Aquatic mammals have made some significant changes to the mammalian respiratory system to accomplish repeated and lengthy dives to considerable depths. For example, the weddell seal can dive to 600 metres/2000 feet for over an hour. Dolphins dive to 150 metres/500 feet regularly and can achieve depths of 450 metres/1500 feet. The depth record is held by one unfortunate sperm whale that was discovered entangled in a cable at 1130 metres/3720 feet.

The moment any aquatic mammal submerges, a number of physiological and behavioral responses take place. The heart rate may drop to as little as one tenth normal. Metabolic rate and temperature decrease also. Blood is shunted to the vital organs, the brain and the heart, and away from the extremities. Both the blood and muscles of aquatic organisms are capable of carrying much greater quantities of oxygen than land mammals, and the muscles also have a greater tolerance for lactic-acid and carbon-dioxide buildup. Neither the pinnipeds nor the cetaceans ever suffer from decompression sickness (see section Two, The Physiology of Diving) because upon diving, the lungs collapse and air is pushed into nonabsorptive areas of the body, primarily the trachea. To facilitate the beginning of this diving response (called *bradycardia*), the nostrils have moved either to the end and top of the snout, such as in the pinnipeds, or to the top of the head, as in the cetaceans.

As previously mentioned, abundant food and little competition drew land mammals back to the sea. Marine mammals can be set apart from all other mammals because they are the only ones that feed exclusively in the aquatic environment.

Marine mammals store food internally as fat. An adult female gray whale may weigh 24 tons at the peak of her feeding season. This may drop to 16 tons after she has made her winter migration and has had a calf.

Chewing food underwater is difficult because some of the meal may be lost each time the mouth is opened. Consequently, all aquatic mammals swallow their food whole, with little, if any mastication. With the exception of the manatees and dugongs, all marine mammals have grasping, tearing and holding teeth (or baleen plates). To compensate for the lack of predigestive food breakdown in the mouth, marine mammals have very long intestinal tracts. The intestine of a bull elephant seal was once measured to be 201 metres/662 feet long. Dolphins have four stomachs, another reminder of their link with ancient ruminants.

Aquatic mammals can be categorized into four types based on feeding habits. The first type feed on fish, squid and shellfish and generally feed near shore. These include otters, seals, sea lions, walrus and dolphin. Those that specialize on shellfish, such as walrus, have hard crushing molars. Sea otters hammer shellfish on flat rocks until they break. Seals, dolphins and sperm whales eat fast-moving prey, such as fish and squid, and have sharp, conical teeth for capturing and holding prey.

The second type of marine mammals regularly feed on warm-blooded prey. There are only two species in this group: killer whales and leopard seals. The killer whale, the largest member of the dolphin family, eats seals, sea lions and dolphins, as well as fish. One 9 metre/30 foot long killer whale was found to contain 13 porpoises and 14 seals in its alimentary tract. There are no recorded attacks on man by killer whales. Leopard seals of the Antarctic feed almost exclusively on marine birds, particularly penguins, which they skin by firmly grasping them in their recurved teeth and literally shaking them out.

The third feeding type eats plankton. This group is comprised primarily of the baleen whales, which strain the water for their minute food. In the polar regions, which are the feeding grounds for many baleen whales, a small shrimp-like crustacean called krill makes up the major portion of the baleen whale's diet. These five-centimetre/two-inch crustaceans congregate in huge numbers. In fact, they have been investigated as a human food resource. The world's largest animals can feed on one of the smallest due to the efficiency of the baleen as a strainer and the fact that it does not take great amounts of energy for whales to open their mouths and collect food as they swim. Some whales use a reverse-flow approach, sucking in mouthfuls of water that are then forced out through the baleen by the action of the tongue.

The fourth feeding type is the herbivorous sirenians. Manatees and dugongs feed exclusively on aquatic plants. Their lips are very sensitive and flexible, allowing them great mobility as they manipulate a seagrass blade or water hyacinth. As in other herbivorous mammals, their teeth are made for grinding and they must eat enormous quantities to extract the necessary food value to meet their basic metabolic needs (up to 22.5 kilograms/50 pounds of plant material per day).

Sensory organ development in aquatic mammals varies like the other morphological characteristics that have already been discussed. Species that have been living in the aquatic realm the longest appear to have the most finely attuned senses for life in water. The best example is perhaps the echolocating abilities ("sonar") of the toothed cetaceans. Sea otters, on the other hand, perceive the aquatic realm through only slightly altered land-developed senses.

Mechanical receptors, such as

touch and hearing, are well suited to an aquatic existence because of the quality of sound transmission through water. Smell and taste are perhaps the least useful and these have for the most part degenerated in aquatic mammals. Vision is also less useful in water because of turbidity and the scattering and absorptive effects on light as it enters water. Some seals have extremely good eyesight and even hunt at night. River dolphins, on the other hand, have very poor vision, given their life in zero-visibility river water. They have instead developed excellent auditory senses.

Marine mammals use sound for two purposes. The first is communication. Aquatic mammals can make sounds that range from the snarling, coughing barks of seals to the melodic and almost haunting "songs" of the humpback whale. Each species has a defined repertoire of sounds that signify some action or intent. This appears to be most complex in cetaceans, particularly the whales.

The second application of sound is for navigation, orientation and the identification of foreign objects. As far as is known, only the toothed cetaceans use this technique, although it is believed that other marine mammals, such as sea lions, may also use sound in this way. Termed *echolocation*, the theory is that a sound emitted at a particular frequency and in a certain direction travels through water and hits the first thing it comes to, bouncing off the object and back at its source, in this example, a dolphin. A comparison of the time it takes consecutive waves to bounce back indicates how far away the object is. The way in which the sound has been altered upon striking the object provides the dolphin with qualitative information such as the object's density. A similar system is used by bats that are nocturnal, aerial hunters. In this regard, air is an analogous environment to the aquatic realm.

Echolocating sounds are emitted through the *melon* (the forehead) and

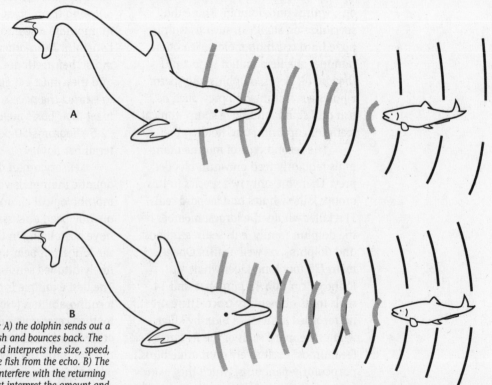

Echolocation in a dolphin: A) the dolphin sends out a short "click" that hits a fish and bounces back. The dolphin hears the echo and interprets the size, speed, texture and location of the fish from the echo. B) The dolphin emits clicks that interfere with the returning echo, in which case it must interpret the amount and kind of distortion in the echo as well.

Giant kelp, *Macrocystis pyrifera,*
Eastern Pacific Region

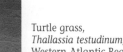

Turtle grass,
Thallassia testudinum,
Western Atlantic Region

Sea palm, *Postelsia palmaeformis,*
Eastern Pacific Region

Coral reef, Indo-West Pacific Region

Elephant-ear sponge, *Demospongiae,*
Indo-West Pacific Region

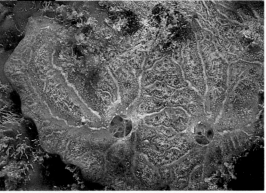

Encrusting sponge, *Demospongiae,*
Western Atlantic Region

Vase sponge, *Niphates digitalis,*
Western Atlantic Region

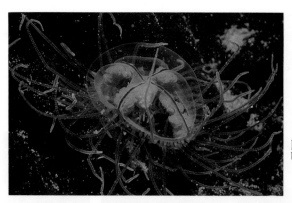

Jellyfish, *Gonionemus vertens,*
Eastern Pacific Region

Jellyfish, *Aurelia aurita,* Western Atlantic Region

Colonial hydroids, *Aglaophenia* sp.,
Eastern Pacific Region

Sea anemone, *Tealia* sp., Eastern Pacific Region

Fire coral, *Millepora alcicornis,* Western
Atlantic Region

Sea anemone, *Condylactis gigantea,* Western
Atlantic Region

Plumose anemone, *Metridium
senile,* Eastern Pacific Region

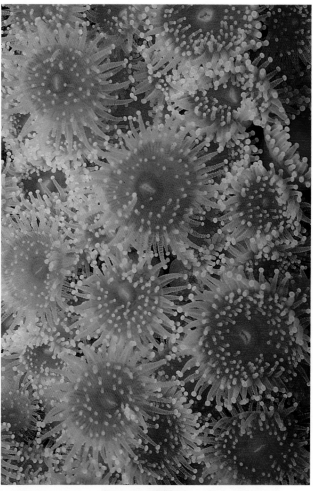

Strawberry anemones, *Corynactis californica,*
Eastern Pacific Region

Octocoral, *Octocorallia,* Indo-West Pacific Region

Sea pen, *Ptilosarcus gurneyi,*
Eastern Pacific Region

Leather coral, *Sarcophyton* sp., Indo-West Pacific Region

Soft coral, *Dendronephthya* sp., Indo-West Pacific Region

Soft coral, *Dendronephthya* sp., Indo-West Pacific Region

Sea fan, *Melithaea* sp., Indo-West Pacific Region

Octocoral, *Octocorallia,* Indo-West Pacific Region

Bubble coral, *Caryophyllidae,* Indo-West Pacific Region

Tube coral, *Dendrophyllia* sp., Indo-West Pacific Region

Coral reef,
Indo-West Pacific Region

Coral reef, Indo-West Pacific Region

Soft coral, *Dendronephthya* sp.,
Indo-West Pacific Region

Star coral, *Montastrea cavernosa*,
Western Atlantic Region

Coral reef, Western
Atlantic Region

Elkhorn coral, *Acropora palmata*,
Western Atlantic Region

Star coral, *Montastrea cavernosa,*
Western Atlantic Region

Flatworm, *Pseudoceros* sp.,
Indo-West Pacific Region

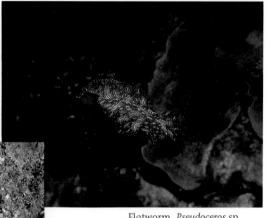

Flatworm, *Pseudoceros* sp.,
Indo-West Pacific Region

Ribbon worm, *Tubulanus
polymorphus,* Eastern
Pacific Region

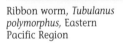

Tube worm, *Serpula vermicularis,*
Eastern Pacific Region

Christmas-tree worm, *Spirobranchus gigantea,*
Western Atlantic Region

Fireworm, *Hermodice carunculata,* Western
Atlantic Region

Kelp crab, *Pugettia producta,*
Eastern Pacific Region

Rock crabs (mating), *Cancer productus,*
Eastern Pacific Region

Anemone shrimp, *Lebbeus grandimanus,*
Eastern Pacific Region

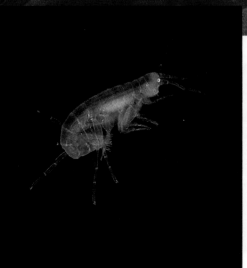

Beach flea, *Gammaridea,*
Eastern Pacific Region

Giant barnacle, *Balanus nubilus,*
Eastern Pacific Region

Arrow crab, *Stenorhynchus seticornis*,
Western Atlantic Region

Anemone shrimp,
Periclimenes yucatanicus,
Western Atlantic Region

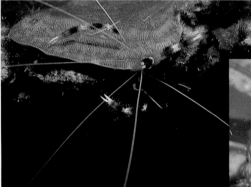

Cleaner shrimp, *Stenopus hispidus*,
Western Atlantic Region

Hermit crab, *Dardanus venosus*, Western Atlantic Region

Horseshoe crab, *Limulus polyphemus*,
Western Atlantic Region

Spiny lobster, *Panulirus argus*, Western Atlantic Region

Coral crab, *Mithra* sp., Western Atlantic Region

Swimming crab, *Portunus* sp., Indo-West Pacific Region

Slipper lobster, *Scyllaridae,* Indo-West Pacific Region

7-11 crab, *Carpilius maculatus,* Indo-West Pacific Region

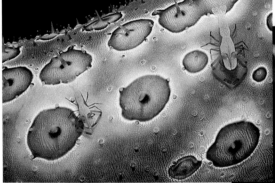

Cucumber shrimp, *Periclimenes imperator,*
Indo-West Pacific Region

Squid, Loligo opalescens, Eastern Pacific Region

Octopus, *Octopus dofleini*,
Eastern Pacific Region

Nudibranch, *Diaulula sandiegensis*,
Eastern Pacific Region

Spanish-shawl nudibranch, *Flabellinopsis iodinea*,
Eastern Pacific Region

Alabaster nudibranch,
Dirona albolineata,
Eastern Pacific Region

Green abalone, *Haliotis fulgens*,
Eastern Pacific Region

Annulated top-shell, *Calliostoma annulatum*,
Eastern Pacific Region

Whelk, *Kelletia kelletii,* Eastern Pacific Region

Heart cockle, *Clinocardium nuttallii,* Eastern
Pacific Region

California cowrie, *Cypraea spadicea,* Eastern
Pacific Region

Scallop, *Chlamys henricia,*
Eastern Pacific Region

Lined chiton, *Tonicella lineata,*
Eastern Pacific Region

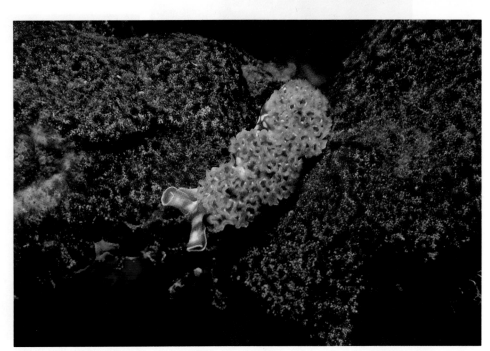

Lettuce slug, *Tridachia crispata,* Western Atlantic Region

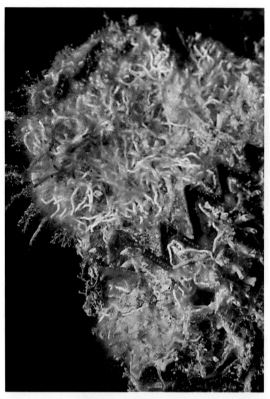

Mangrove scallop, *Lopha* sp., Western Atlantic Region

Flamingo-tongue snail, *Cyphoma gibbosum*, Western Atlantic Region

Tulip shell, *Conus spectrum*, Indo-West Pacific Region

Vermitid snail, *Vermitidae*, Indo-West Pacific Region

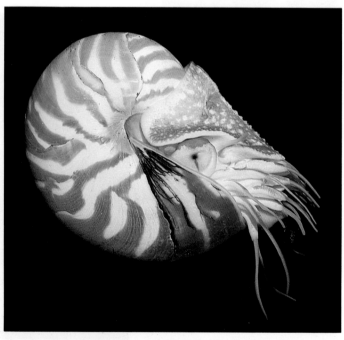

Sea slug, *Phyllidia varicosa*, Indo-West Pacific Region

Chambered nautilus, *Nautilus pompilius*, Indo-West Pacific Region

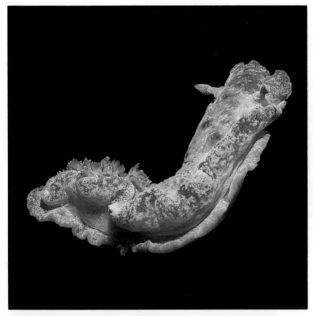

Spanish dancer, *Hexabranchia sanguinensis,* Indo-West
Pacific Region

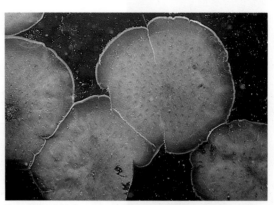

Bryozoan, *Membranipora membranacea,* Eastern
Pacific Region

Bryozoan, *Phidolopora pacifica,* Eastern Pacific Region

Brachiopod, T*erebratalia transversa,* Eastern
Pacific Region

Crinoid, *Florometra serratissima,*
Eastern Pacific Region

Brittlestar, *Ophiuroidea,* Eastern Pacific Region

Sea cucumber, *Cucumaria miniata,* Eastern Pacific Region

Sea urchin, *Strongylocentrotus franciscanus,* Eastern Pacific Region

Sea cucumber, *Parastichopus californicus,* Eastern Pacific Region

Sand dollars, *Dendraster excentricus,* Eastern Pacific Region

Sea star, *Mediaster aequalis,* Eastern Pacific Region

Sun star, *Pycnopodia helianthoides,* Eastern Pacific Region

Leather star, *Dermasterias imbricata,* Eastern Pacific Region

Bat star, *Pateria miniata,* Eastern Pacific Region

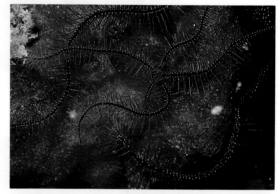

Brittlestars, *Ophiuroidea,* Western Atlantic Region

Long-spined urchins,
Diadema antillarum,
Western Atlantic Region

Sand star, *Astropecten* sp.,
Western Atlantic Region

Crown-of-thorns star, *Acanthaster planci,* Indo-West Pacific Region

Sea cucumber,
Bohadschia sp.,
Indo-West Pacific Region

Sea star, *Linkia laevigata*, Indo-West Pacific Region

Feather star, *Crinoidea,* Indo-West Pacific Region

Sea squirts, *Clavelina* sp., Western Atlantic Region

Sea squirts,
Styela montereyensis,
Eastern Pacific Region

Sea squirts, *Clavelina huntsmani,* Eastern Pacific Region

Stickleback, *Gasterosteus aculeatus*, Eastern Pacific Region

Kelp greenling, *Hexagrammos decagrammus*,
Eastern Pacific Region

Dogfish shark, *Squalus acanthias*,
Eastern Pacific Region

Flounder, *Platichthys stellatus*,
Eastern Pacific Region

Yelloweye rockfish, *Sebastes ruberrimus*, Eastern Pacific Region

Sturgeon poacher, *Agonus acipenserinus*,
Eastern Pacific Region

California sheepshead, *Semicossyphus pulcher,* Eastern Pacific Region

Sailfin sculpin, *Nautichthys oculofasciatus,* Eastern Pacific Region

Sculpin, *Cottidae,* Eastern Pacific Region

Monkey-face eel, *Cebidichthys violaceus,* Eastern Pacific Region

Ratfish, *Hydrolagus colliei,* Eastern Pacific Region

Big skate, *Raja binoculata,* Eastern Pacific Region

Wolf eel, *Anarrichthys ocellatus*, Eastern Pacific Region

Tiger rockfish, *Sebastes nigrocinctus*, Eastern Pacific Region

Plainfin midshipman, *Porichthys notatus*, Eastern Pacific Region

Lingcod, *Ophiodon elongatus*, Eastern Pacific Region

Bay pipefish, *Syngnathus griseolineatus*, Eastern Pacific Region

Porcupinefish, *Diodon hystrix*, Western Atlantic Region

Squirrelfish, *Holocentrus rufus*, Western Atlantic Region

Queen parrotfish, *Scarus vetula*, Western Atlantic Region

Blue parrotfish, *Scarus coeruleus*, Western Atlantic Region

Trunkfish, *Lactophrys bicau-dalis*, Western Atlantic Region

Moray eel, *Gymnothorax* sp., Western Atlantic Region

Porkfish, *Anisotremus virginicus*, Western Atlantic Region

Southern stingray, *Dasyatis americana,* Western
Atlantic Region

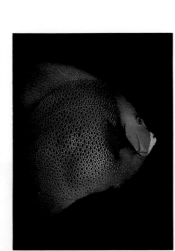

Gray angelfish, *Pomacanthus
arcuatus,* Western Atlantic Region

Queen angelfish, *Holocanthus ciliaris,* Western
Atlantic Region

Blue angelfish, *Holacanthus bermudensis,* Western Atlantic Region

Scorpionfish, *Scorpaenidae,* Indo-West
Pacific Region

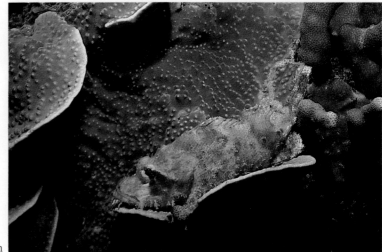

Scorpionfish, *Scorpaenidae,* Indo-West Pacific Region

Lionfish, *Pterois* sp., Indo-West Pacific Region

Clownfish, *Amphiprion ocellaris*, Indo-West Pacific Region

Trunkfish, *Ostraciidae*, Indo-West Pacific Region

Goldfish, *Anthias pleurotaenia*, Indo-West Pacific Region

Black-spotted pufferfish, *Arothron nigro-cinctus*, Indo-West Pacific Region

Sea catfish, *Plotosus* sp., Indo-West Pacific Region

Unicornfish, *Naso brevirostris,* Indo-West Pacific Region

Raccoon butterflyfish, *Chaetodon lunula,*
Indo-West Pacific Region

Convict tangs, Ancanthurus *triostegus,* Indo-West
Pacific Region

Butterflyfish, *Chaetodon* sp., Indo-
West Pacific Region

Trumpetfish, *Aulostromus maculatus,* Western
Atlantic Region

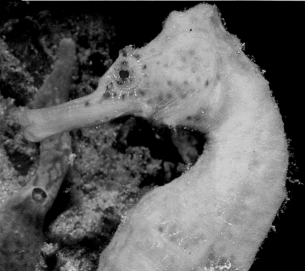
Seahorse, *Syngnathidae,* Western Atlantic Region

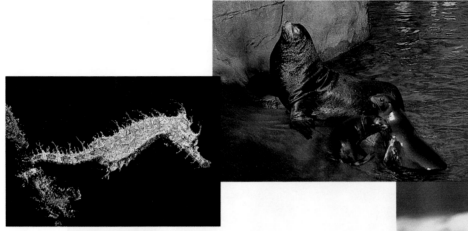

California sea lions, *Zalophus californianus*, Eastern Pacific Region

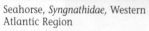

Seahorse, *Syngnathidae*, Western Atlantic Region

Sea otter, *Enhydra lutris*, Eastern Pacific Region

Walrus, *Odobenus rosmarus*, Eastern Pacific Region

Bottlenose dolphin, *Tursiops truncatus*, Eastern Pacific Region

jaw of a dolphin and received through the lower jaw. Vibrations travel through a thin, oily, fatty substance in the lower jaw, past the acoustic window and on to the inner ear. It is a very sophisticated system and the subject of a great deal of research.

Reproduction for mammals living in the aquatic realm is somewhat more complicated than for those on land. Many marine mammals are *polygynous*, that is, a single male will mate with a number of females. Further, to avoid confusion, males and females are often physically different, particularly with respect to size (males generally being larger). This kind of sexual dimorphism also appears in terrestrial mammals. Courtship is often ritualized with a number of different kinds of communication (visual, olfactory, auditory, tactile). In the pinnipeds, males often defend territories and develop a distinct pecking order determined by ritualized displays of strength and stamina. Rarely are such encounters fatal, although some can be physically harmful to one or both combatants.

Once a pair is established, copulation can occur. All aquatic mammals, except seals, mate in the water. Those species that migrate usually breed in warmer waters, traveling to cold, nutrient-rich waters to feed. Pinnipeds mate by the male entering from behind. Cetaceans mate frontally, generally on their sides with respect to the surface of the water.

The gestation period of the fetus follows fertilization. This varies depending on the group. For sea otters gestation lasts 12 to 13 months, seals 9 to 12 months, dolphins 8 months, whales 10 to 16 months. In all seals the fertilized embryo remains inactive for the first several months of its life before attaching to the uterine wall. This process is called delayed implantation and its purpose is to prolong the time of the young in fetal form so that its birth is postponed until the following spring or summer when conditions are optimal.

The next phase is birth. Seals give birth on land, cetaceans in the water. Baby whales and dolphins all emerge tail-first to prevent drowning in the event of a difficult birthing. Generally speaking, all aquatic mammals are born fully developed and operational. Because of the harsh aquatic environment, it is important that the young can function immediately after birth.

Nursing, which occurs in one form or another in all aquatic mammals, is the next step. The milk of most marine mammals is significantly richer in fat content than their terrestrial brethren. Whale milk may be 40 to 50 percent fat, compared to four to five percent in cow milk. Nursing may continue for a long time, and growth during the early stages of marine mammal development is phenomenal. Blue-whale calves nurse for six to seven months, during which time they grow at an average rate of 3.8 kilograms/8.5 pounds per hour. Harp-seal pups double their birth weight in their first five days. Weaning varies considerably in aquatic mammals.

Aquatic mammal reproduction differs from that of land mammals in three ways. First, gestation periods are longer in order to create well-developed young at birth. Second, seasonal reproductive events are not as sharply marked as with land counterparts. This reflects the general events and stability of the physical aspects of the aquatic realm. Third, aquatic mammals often fast during the reproductive season. Sometimes this is the result of a long migration or the need of the adults to spend all of their time guarding and training their young.

Most aquatic mammals perform geographical migrations at some point in their lives. These may be only daily movements from one feeding ground to another, such as in seals, or seasonal migrations such as in the gray whale, which travels the entire west coast of North America over the course of its an-

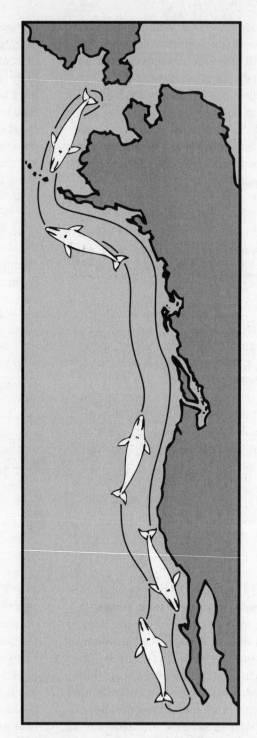

Gray-whale migration. Each year gray whales move from Alaskan waters, where they feed in the spring and summer, down the coast to the Gulf of California to breed and give birth during the fall and winter. By making this annual migration, they can take advantage of the best aspects of both areas; abundant food in Alaska and temperate, safe water conditions in Baja in which to reproduce and bear young.

nual breeding cycle. The question is, why migrate? Apparently, it is more efficient for highly mobile animals such as dolphins and whales to move from one environment to another to take advantage of seasonal changes in those areas.

The abundance of food in the Arctic draws gray whales there in the summer, while the temperate climate of Mexico in the winter makes for good breeding and birthing grounds. Marine mammals use environmental cues such as the length of the day, celestial orientation, water temperature, currents, and shoreline characteristics for navigation and orientation on long migratory trips.

One of the most controversial topics in aquatic mammal research is the degree of their intelligence. It is controversial because it is difficult to measure and observe in these organisms, which leaves room for a good deal of speculation. Animal behaviorists generally measure animal intelligence by observing behavior both under natural and artificial conditions. Demonstrations of problem solving and communication through a distinct and defined language are generally considered measures of high intelligence. Additionally, the size and structure of the central nervous system (brain) can indicate levels of intelligence. When it comes to size, a ratio of brain size to body size must be figured. A dolphin's brain is about the same size as a human's. Certain regions, especially the neocortex area, are extremely well-developed in the dolphin. On the other hand, it is believed that the number of layers (*lamina*) of the cortex determines the degree of abstract thinking and reasoning possible in an animal; in this regard, the dolphin's brain is not very well-developed.

Part of the reason aquatic-animal intelligence is a controversial topic is that it is easy and even tempting to draw conclusions about their intelligence based on subjective observations. Play behavior appears commonly as part of the behavioral repertoire of many marine mammals and is considered an indication of intelligence. However, it is easy to misinterpret such behavior without the benefit of observation both in the field and under controlled circumstances.

Man's intelligence seems to have developed around the spoken language and the ability to grasp objects through the use of a prehensile hand, enabling man to build. Aquatic mammals have no real need to build in their environment. However, they do need to communicate, and it would appear that they have developed a highly sophisticated system of communication with other members of their species.

Human Interactions with Aquatic Life

Since the development of the open circuit scuba by Jacques Yves Cousteau and Emile Gagnan in 1943, man has been able to enter the aquatic realm for extended periods with new found ease and freedom on scuba. With this one technological breakthrough, man gained a direct window to the aquatic realm by periodically and temporarily becoming part of it.

With this relatively new-found capability of entering the aquatic world safely and easily comes the responsibility of interacting with its inhabitants in a thoughtful and responsible manner. Human interactions with aquatic life can be passive or active, depending upon the person's activity and purpose. The first step toward responsible interaction with aquatic life depends on forming an accurate perception of how man's activities will affect these creatures.

Human Perceptions of Aquatic Life

Most aquatic organisms look nothing at all like land plants and animals. For example, there are no land counterparts to organisms such as sea cucumbers, sea anemones, sponges or jellyfish. As in terrestrial species, the physical form of aquatic species reflects their adaptation to the environmental constraints imposed on them. Such constraints are quite different from those of terrestrial environments (see sidebar, The Differences Between Marine and Terrestrial Ecosystems).

To many people, aquatic organisms seem oddly shaped, appear strangely colored and behave in a peculiar manner when compared to animals like dogs and cats. In fact, to some, it is hard to imagine that a sponge, for example, is an animal at all. It would appear that the way aquatic organisms are perceived depends, to a large degree, on what they look like.

In general, people consider animals without fur, complex behavioral patterns or eyes as inanimate objects. Aquatic animals that fit in this category include sponges, corals, sea stars, tubeworms, sea urchins, sea squirts and other slow-moving or attached organ-

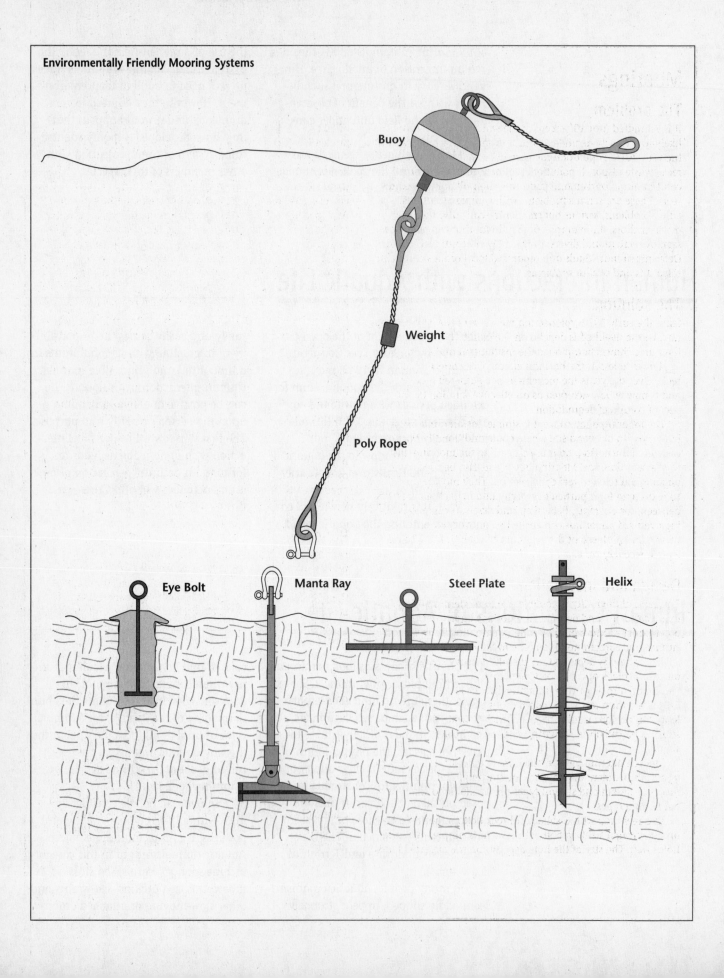

Environmentally Friendly Mooring Systems

Buoy

Weight

Poly Rope

Eye Bolt

Manta Ray

Steel Plate

Helix

Moorings

The problem

It is estimated that 40 percent of the world's coral reefs are likely to seriously degrade, perhaps even beyond recovery, by the year 2015. Population increase in coastal areas adjacent to reefs, waste disposal, pollution, sedimentation, overfishing, coral mining, tourism and curio collection all damage coral reefs. These are serious problems with complex solutions. Other problems, serious but smaller in scale, also face the reefs. Anchors, for example, pose a threat that can easily be seen by recreational divers: they simply rip coral reefs apart. Determined individuals and organized local groups can help solve this and similar problems.

The solution

Since the early 1970s, pioneering members of the dive community, whose livelihoods depend on the quality of the reefs in their area, have championed the installation and use of mooring buoys to lessen the harmful effects of anchors on coral reefs. Over the years the movement has gathered momentum and is now widely accepted as an effective solution to one aspect of coral reef degradation.

The mooring buoy concept is simple: install a mooring buoy close to or over a site where boats traditionally anchor. Instead of anchoring, boat users tie off to the mooring and this lessens damage. Mooring buoys can also be used as an ongoing aid to coral reef conservation. They may be used to zone an area for a particular activity and help avoid conflicts between, for example, fishermen and divers. If an area is being overused, moorings can easily be removed, placed elsewhere, and replaced at the original site when it has had adequate recovery time.

Design and installation

This kind of flexibility is possible due to modern mooring system technology and design. All moorings have three elements: a permanent fixture on the seafloor, a floating buoy on the surface and something to join one to the other.

Traditional systems usually include a heavy weight such as an engine block or a cast concrete block, a length of heavy chain and a rope, or riser, that attaches the chain to the buoy. This is less than ideal. The chain drags easily around the seafloor with obvious results, the block may drag if excessive strain is placed on the mooring and the entire system is unsightly.

Modern alternatives are much more efficient and less damaging. Embedment anchors are the starting point of any mooring system and several types are available to suit different bottom types.

In a reef area with a solid coral rock bottom, boring a hole and securing a steel eyebolt with cement is simple, neat and holds well. The size of the hole depends on the expected loads

and in some cases, multiple holes bored in proximity and bridled together are used to withstand heavy use.

In mixed bottoms of clay, sand, gravel and broken bedrock or coral rubble, a proprietary system called the "Manta Ray" is useful. This device consists of a ray-shaped plate hinged on the end of a steel rod and it is jack-hammered into the substrate. At a specific depth, the device is pulled up, the plate turns flat and holds securely. An eyebolt on top of the steel rod provides an attachment point. These devices are available in many sizes to suit specific applications and have a good track record.

Another option is the helical anchor, which is a square section steel rod with circular plates welded to it in corkscrew fashion. These anchors hold well in softer bottoms and can be made in sizes to suit most applications. They are driven into the bottom with a hydraulic device and can be removed relatively easily if needed.

These three types of anchor hold so well that the chain needed with traditional systems is no longer required. Polypropylene rope (which floats), or other rope with attached floats, can be used and will keep the riser from resting on the bottom eliminating one of the most significant problems with traditional moorings. Top off the system with an appropriate buoy, usually about 50 cm/18 inch diameter, and a short length of high visibility floating polypropylene rope to facilitate pick up by users. Finally, It is important to ensure that the riser is long enough to allow for tidal variation, but short enough to prevent floating rope becoming a hazard to navigation.

Project planning

Installing mooring buoys requires professional expertise at all phases of project planning and implementation. Several factors must be considered and in many situations, the scope of the project will demand cooperative effort between relevant government agencies and interested parties. The anticipated use of the project site determines the number, location and type of moorings deployed. Funding for installation and ongoing maintenance, a crucial element of any mooring buoy system, must be organized. Educational programs must be undertaken to ensure that private users understand what the buoys are for and adequate arrangements for enforcement of the project or site regulations needs to be in place.

Mooring systems also have their problems. They concentrate activity in a particular area. They limit the number of vessels that can use the site, usually one per mooring. Permanent mooring buoys destroy natural landscapes and seascapes. Conflict of interest is not uncommon, shark fishermen, for example, may want to use a buoy over a dive site. Overall, and studies of existing sites confirm this, the benefits far outweigh the disadvantages. Mooring buoy projects are firmly fixed as a healthy element in the future of the world's coral reefs.

isms. Because of their apparent lifelessness, people tend to interact with them as if they were inanimate objects.

At the other end of the spectrum are organisms that display a variety of easily observed, complex behavioral patterns. These animals also usually have eyes. The quintessential animate aquatic organisms are marine mammals. It is easy to see that animals such a sea otters, seals, dolphins and whales are complex creatures.

In-between these extremes are fish. They are confusing to most people because they move and have eyes, yet they appear to lack other characteristics (such as emotion) present in the "higher" animals. While fish are animated, their lack of familiar characteristics puts them somewhere in-between sponges and dolphins.

Occasionally, aquatic life is presented to the public anthropomorphically, that is, an organism is given human characteristics. Examples from circuses and shows include the chimpanzee tea party and the dolphin wearing a hula skirt and a lei. Dressing up animals in human attire makes them appear inferior. This widens the gap between man and the other plants and animals with which he shares this planet.

Some aquatic animals have historically been characterized as being dangerous to humans. While it is true that almost any animal is potentially dangerous when provoked, the incidence of human injuries caused by aquatic animals is extremely low. The reputation of animals such as sharks, jellyfish, and killer whales as bloodthirsty killers is the result of exaggerated reports, which often become myths. In the case of sharks, more people are killed each year through allergic reactions to bee stings than fall victim to shark attacks. Such storytelling hinders the development of human/animal relationships.

Passive Interactions with Aquatic Life

The majority of human interaction with aquatic life is active (see following section). Even mere human presence can be considered an interaction. Most aquatic animals are extremely aware of their environment, particularly with respect to interruptions or changes to the normal routines. The presence of a person wading in a tidepool, snorkeling through a kelp bed or scuba diving on a coral reef is immediately sensed by many of the inhabitants of such environments, particularly those animals that are highly mobile and have advanced sensory organs.

Generally, the greater the commotion created in the aquatic realm, the harder it is to observe aquatic life. Disturbances such as exaggerated movements, sound production (such as the noise of bubbles escaping while scuba diving) or artificial light (an underwater light or camera strobe) are foreign to most aquatic animals. The exception is in areas where humans enter the water on a regular basis, such as in marine parks, where many of the habitat's residents become accustomed to the presence of people.

Passive disturbances immediately alert sensitive aquatic animals to a human's presence. The more mobile organisms, such as fishes, often leave the area before humans even know they were there. Those species that remain within visual range often change their behavior due to human presence. One reason ichthyologists know so little about the reproductive behavior of fishes, for example, is that the presence of a human observer often interrupts any courtship or copulatory behavior. A great deal more is known about the reproductive behavior of territorial fish, because animal behaviorists can habituate such species to their presence through repeated contact. Over time, the fish accept the observer's presence, at which point it may be safely assumed that the behavior of the fish is natural and not affected by the observer simply being there. Quiet, thoughtful movement rewards the observer with a greater number of unique and memorable encounters with aquatic life.

Passive observation has the least effect on aquatic life and can be very rewarding for the patient observer.

Active Interactions with Aquatic Life

Avoiding accidental contact with sessile marine life requires control under water and a little forethought.

Accidental and Careless Contact

It is almost impossible to enter the aquatic realm and not have some physical contact with its inhabitants. Human contact can have serious consequences for aquatic life, particularly the smaller plants and animals. Consider, for example, the deleterious contact of turning over a tidepool rock and crushing or exposing its residents, or walking over a coral reef at low tide. Such contacts with aquatic organisms are almost always careless or accidental, and the resulting injury or death of plants and animals rarely malicious. Rather, it results from little forethought and awareness of the outcome of such activities.

Most marine and freshwater organisms are covered with a protective coating of mucus that aids in their defense against bacterial infections, which are common in aquatic environments. Any kind of physical contact, such as leaning on a coral head, handling a fish (particularly with dry hands) or resting an object (such as a dive light) on a reef, compromises the integrity of these mucus coatings, exposing the animal to potential infection.

However, not all aquatic animals have such coatings and it is safe to handle certain parts of some animals (such as shelled animals like snails and clams) without harming them. In general, it is wise to avoid, as much as possible, physically disturbing aquatic environments and their inhabitants. Accidental contact is just that, and the majority of it can be avoided through forethought.

Marine Bites and Stings

Medical advances are significant since ancient mariners and healers first proposed remedies for marine-acquired envenomations and poisons. Medical researchers have uncovered and reported a great deal about the biological origins of marine toxins, the mechanisms that organisms use to deliver these toxins and their physiological effects upon experimental animals and on humans.

If offensive venoms are associated with the mouth and teeth, and defensive venoms are associated with the tail, stings, barbs and skin secretions, then most marine venoms must be classified as defensive. There is little aggression involved with the majority of animal-inflicted injuries. With the exception of a few species of shark, few aquatic creatures attack humans without provocation.

Generally, marine venoms are composed of numerous ammonia-based chemicals that digest proteins and other compounds produced by the body. The venoms can destroy cell membranes, break down cellular energy sources, induce severe allergic reactions, initiate inflammation, cause abnormal bleeding, disrupt the elimination of waste products, impede nerve impulse transmission and otherwise wreak havoc with normal physiology. Unlike venoms found commonly in terrestrial organisms, many marine venoms do not cause enough immune responses in humans or other animals to allow the development of antitoxins or antivenins.

To list every type of marine animal capable of inflicting a bite or sting would require an entire book. Below are a few examples and a description of their potential effects on the careless diver.

Cnidarians (see Phylum Cnidaria: Hydroids, Sea Anemones, Corals and Jellyfish) are an enormous group with approximately 10,000 species. At least 100 of these are potentially hazardous to humans. The phylum has a unique characteristic — stinging cells called cnidoblasts. The stinging structure within the cnidoblast is called a nematocyst. Included in this group are the Portuguese man-of-war, jellyfish, soft and hard corals, and sea anemones. The stinging cells are located on the outer surfaces of tentacles or near the mouth, and are triggered by contact. A human contacting a large jellyfish, for example, could trigger the release of several million stinging cells that diffuse venom through the skin into general circulation.

Nematocyst venoms contain various chemicals, depending upon the species. The effects upon humans range from annoying to life-threatening.

The fire corals (Millipora sp.), which are hydroids, not true corals, probably account for more cnidarian stings than any other species. Unprotected and unwary recreational divers handle, kneel or lean upon it regularly. Immediately following contact with fire coral, the diver suffers burning or stinging pain. Intense and painful itching follows within seconds, frequently causing the victim to vigorously rub the affected area, worsening the sting. In 5 to 30 minutes, hives develop, marked by redness, warmth and itching. The injuries become swollen and reach maximum size in 30 to 60 minutes. In the case of multiple stings, the lymph glands may become inflamed and painful .

The Atlantic Portuguese man-of-war (Physalia physalis) consists of a floating sail and gas chamber suspending multiple nematocyst-bearing tentacles that may measure up to 30 metres/100 feet in length. As this colonial animal moves through the ocean, the tentacles rhythmically contract, sampling the water below for potential prey. If a tentacle strikes an object, the nematocysts fire. Each tentacle in a large specimen may carry more than 750,000 nematocysts. Such stings may cause serious injury to humans.

Sea nettles (e.g., Chrysaora quinquecirrha and Cyanea capillata), which are found in both temperate and tropical waters, are capable of inducing moderately severe stings. They carry a venom that contains at least seven enzymes, with at least one component that is toxic to the heart, nervous system and skin.

The larger jellyfish include the box jellyfish and the sea wasps (e.g., Chironex, Cyanea and Chirospsalmus spp.) These creatures contain some of the most potent venom in existence. A number of these box-shaped jellyfish inhabit the Indo-Pacific and (less frequently) the Caribbean.

A particular box jellyfish, (Chironex fleckeri), also called the sea wasp, is the most venomous sea creature known. Found primarily in Australian waters, it can cause death by shock, profound muscle spasm, muscular and respiratory paralysis and cardiac arrest in as little as thirty seconds. Most stings are minor; severe reactions or death usually only follow skin contact with tentacles in excess of 7.5 meters/25 feet in length.

The sea wasp's sting is immediately painful and, if severe, the victim usually struggles only a minute or two prior to collapse. The toxic skin reaction may be intense, with rapid formation of hives, blisters and skin marks. More severe reactions in women and small children have been attributed to greater hairless body surface area and less body mass.

Medically, cnidarian stings are similar, with a range in severity. The severity is related to the season and species, the number of nematocysts triggered, the size of the animal, the location and surface area of the sting, the victim's health, and the size and age of the person stung (the very young and old, and smaller people tend to be more severely affected).

Mild stings may result only in annoying skin irritation, whereas severe stings can progress rapidly to involve virtually every organ system. In a severe reaction, the skin injuries are intensified and compounded by other possible symptoms: fatigue, headache and effects on the nervous system, such as paralysis, delirium and cardiac arrest. Exposure suits can minimize or eliminate the probability of a severe injury.

Within the phylum Mollusca, two groups stand out as venomous: octopuses and cone shells. Octopus bites are rare, but some species can administer extremely venomous bites. Fatalities have been reported from the bites of the Australian blue-ringed octopus (Octopus maculosus and Octopus lunulata), which are small and easily handled.

The octopus's salivary glands secrete toxins that are released in the throat of the octopus. This venom, normally released into the water to subdue crabs, can be injected into the diver by a forceful bite. The venom is a paralytic agent that rapidly affects nerve activity, notably the nerve to the diaphragm.

Most victims are bitten on the hand or arm as they handle the octopus. The bite often goes unnoticed or causes only a small amount of discomfort, described as a minor ache, slight stinging or pulsating sensation. Occasionally, the bite is initially numb, followed in 5 to 10 minutes by discomfort that may spread to involve the entire limb and last up to six hours. More serious symptoms are related to the neurotoxic effects of the venom. Within 10 to 15 minutes after the bite, there may be oral and facial numbness, followed by paralysis and respiratory failure.

Cone shells (Conus sp.) are fairly common snails in the tropical Pacific. They are predators of small worms, other snails and even small fish, which they subdue with the injection of venom through a harpoon-like apparatus. Again, the venom acts on the nervous system of the prey. Several species have venoms that, if injected, can prove fatal to humans. Cone shells should be handled with care.

There are several hundred species of scorpion fish, differentiated into groups based on their spine structure. These include zebra fish, lion fish, scorpion fish, sculpin and stone fish. At least 80 species have been known to cause injuries to swimmers and divers.

The venom organs consist of spines along the back and sides of the various species. When any of these fish are removed from the water, handled, stepped on or otherwise threatened, reflexes erect the spine. Venom is injected by a direct puncture wound through the skin by the spine.

Scorpion fish stings vary according to the species. As with cnidarians, the type of sting, species, degree of venom released and the age and health of the victim all affect the severity of the injury.

Pain is immediate and intense. Untreated, the pain reaches its peak in 60 to 90 minutes and persists 6 to 12 hours. In the case of the stone fish, the pain can be severe enough to cause delirium and can persist for days. Stone fish stings can also be fatal.

The wound and immediate area are initially dusky-colored, with surrounding areas of redness. Other symptoms could include fever, hypertension, respiratory and heart effects, and shock.

From the preceding examples, it is apparent that venoms generate diverse effects on the diver. It is interesting that aquatic animal toxins have such an effect on humans, given the fact that most, if not all, are defensive or offensive adaptations developed in response to nonhuman life-forms. The increasing awareness of such adaptations has been primarily a response to the increasing frequency with which human contact is made with such organisms. This increased contact is, in part, a measure of man's relatively recent ability to enter the aquatic realm and interact with its inhabitants. Although the effects of marine bites and stings can be serious, divers who wear exposure suits and are wary of what animals they may touch or handle are unlikely to ever have a serious injury from a marine creature.

Intentional Contact

Direct handling of animals, such as fish, usually puts unnecessary stress on the organism.

The result of intentional contact with aquatic plants and animals is the same as accidental contact; it can compromise the health of the organism. Activities such as capturing, holding, petting and riding larger aquatic animals are often stressful to the animal. Because of the great abundance of life in aquatic environments and the ease in which many aquatic organisms can be approached, the opportunity for such encounters is frequent and often irresistible. Further, the negative effects of such encounters are often not manifested until well after the encounter has occurred. Examples include the development of a bacterial infection or unknowingly interrupting the initiation of a reproductive courtship ritual. As a result, the cause and (negative) effect such contact may have is not seen (or appreciated) at the time of contact.

Riding aquatic animals is rarely, if ever, beneficial to the animal giving the ride.

Feeding Aquatic Animals

Fish feeding has gained a tremendous amount of attention and popularity with recreational snorkelers and scuba divers. If very limited, the results of feeding aquatic organisms are generally not harmful, except when one species is used to feed another. The best example is the use of sea urchins to feed certain fish species. The conclusion one must draw from such an act is that the sea urchin is less important than the fish to which it will be fed. While the removal of a few sea urchins amidst hundreds may not appear to effect the environment, it remains an irresponsible act for two reasons. First, the effect of removing sea urchins from the habitat is not seen immediately. However, this does not mean that such removal is free of long-term effects. Such actions could very well interrupt food chains or in some other way create an imbalance in the ecosystem. Second, such an act promotes the misconception that sea urchins are inanimate objects that are not an integral part of the ecosystem. The idea that any species may be removed from the system without a negative effect is neither acceptable nor correct.

When fish feeding is extensive and frequent, it can significantly alter the natural behavior of aquatic animals. Over time, an entire area may be affected as the animals fail to follow their normal feeding patterns.

Underwater Photography

Photographing aquatic life not only sharpens observational skills, but allows the diver to share his experiences in the aquatic realm with others.

Another activity that has gained a great deal of popularity by recreational divers is photography. Aquatic life makes up a large percentage of subjects for amateur and professional photographers alike. Some of these subjects are more affected by being photographed than others. It can safely be said that the life of a sponge is not greatly changed by having its photograph taken, unless the photographer rests the camera on it. Capturing more active and sensitive organisms on film may have quite different results, particularly if, in the process of making the exposure, the photographer interrupts some kind of behavior such as feeding, defense or reproduction. On the whole, however, the dramatic increase in marine life photography has done a great deal to increase public awareness of such organisms and a careful photographer can take beautiful pictures without disturbing the subject organisms.

Recreational Collection and Consumption of Aquatic Life

Collecting aquatic life for personal consumption or other use is the most direct way an individual can affect aquatic life. Removing species from ecosystems, particularly in large numbers, can have lasting effects. The question is, how many and how often can a species be removed to maintain a sustainable yield (a population that contains enough reproductively mature individuals that can create enough progeny to make up for the loss by removal)? The nature of the aquatic environment makes it extremely difficult to accurately monitor populations of aquatic organisms and hence determine sustainable yields. In turn, it is difficult, at best, to estimate what may be a safe removal rate for most species. Most studies of sustainable yields are done on commercially harvested species such as salmon, tuna, cod and others, where the fate of an industry lies in making accurate annual forecasts. Little work has gone into the same studies for most other species.

For those interested in hunting and collecting marine organisms, adhering to guidelines, such as size and catch limits imposed by the relevant authorities, is the first step toward responsibly interacting with aquatic life. The second is avoiding any behavior that may have a negative effect on an entire species. Perhaps the most responsible way an individual can participate in harvesting is to contribute time, money or both to activities that enhance man's knowledge of the species harvested or in some way helps to maintain a sustainable yield. Examples include direct donations to conservation organizations or participation in organized community-service activities, such as the construction of artificial reefs or beach cleanups. An activity that directly enhances or promotes the continuation of the species that a person removes seems to make the most sense.

The Differences Between Marine and Terrestrial Ecosystems

The differences between terrestrial (land) and marine environments and ecosystems may seem obvious. One is dominated by a gaseous medium (air), the other by a fluid one (water). The morphological and behavioral adaptations of plants and animals living in each are direct reflections of the vastly different environmental conditions that characterize terrestrial and marine environments.

On a general level, it is clear to see why horses have legs and fish have fins. This becomes crystal clear when a horse tries to swim across a river or a salmon jumps onto land. But just what are the differences that characterize land and sea and shape the evolution of organisms? The differences can be divided into two categories: physical characteristics and structural and functional characteristics.

Water is approximately 800 times more dense than air. This single physical characteristic has a more profound effect on the nature of aquatic ecosystems than any other. The extreme density of water (compared to air) means that relatively large organisms and particles can float in water with little, if any, energy expended. This has allowed for the development of an entire community of organisms — plankton. No other community like it exists. Further, all other marine communities are constantly bathed in the medium (water) containing plankton.

The presence of plankton has resulted in the concomitant development of a diverse and abundant array of filter-feeding organisms such as barnacles, tubeworms, clams, sponges, bryozoans, sea cucumbers and even certain fish and whales. This type of feeding mechanism is not found in terrestrial ecosystems.

Organisms can remain in one place because the ocean's waters are perpetually in motion. Filter feeders save energy by staying in one position and catching food as it passes by. This sessile mode of existence is not possible for land animals because a plankton-like community does not exist in air to nourish such an assemblage as it does in the sea. This is an outcome of the ability of water to support (literally) a floating, planktonic community.

Another outcome of the combined effects of water density and motion is the development of motile larvae in many marine organisms, particularly sessile ones. On land, certain groups of plants do distribute their gametes by airborne spores, pollen and seeds, but not animals. The result is that on land, plants get dispersed widely, while animals tend to be distributed in isolated and distinct groups based on geographic location. In the sea it is difficult to maintain distinct, isolated communities because of the planktonic dispersal of young, as well as the general lack of geographical boundaries, particularly in the open ocean.

Light is another environmental factor that shapes ecosystems. The character of light is greatly affected by water (see section One, The Chemistry and Physics of Diving), but is affected relatively little by the atmosphere. Light can only penetrate water to about 185 metres/600 feet, which means that the majority of the world's oceans and its inhabitants exist entirely in darkness. This fact restricts the distribution of plants in the seas to a narrow layer at the surface. In comparison, all land ecosystems (with the exception of caves) are exposed to enough incident light to allow plants to grow and flourish.

In the oceans, some communities exist without the benefit of a plant (autotrophic) component at all, depending upon other sources for a primary energy base. Perhaps one of the most exciting oceanographic discoveries of the century was when the research submarine Alvin stumbled upon deep-sea vent communities in the Galapagos Rift System. There, thousands of feet below the surface and in complete darkness, exist complex communities whose energy base relies on bacteria that can extract chemical elements from the surrounding water to make organic compounds for food (chemosynthesis, as opposed to photosynthesis by plants).

Additionally, light is absorbed deferentially by water, which is not the case on land. The absorption of the red end of the spectrum in the shallows and blues in deeper waters determines to a large degree how marine plants are distributed vertically in the oceans. This is a result of a physical environmental factor (differential absorption of light). Terrestrial plants are vertically distributed primarily in response to competition from other plants for light, a biological factor.

The effects of gravity have greatly shaped the course of land ecosystems, while the lack of gravity in the ocean has affected its inhabitants. Buoyancy of objects in water means that marine plants and animals do not need to develop heavy skeletal structures. On land, for plants to remain erect, significant cellulose structures such as wood and fiber are necessary. For animals, particularly vertebrates, it means the development of cartilage and bone skeletons.

With respect to locomotion, the effects of gravity on land are much greater than in a fluid medium, such as seawater. Land animals must raise their mass against gravity with every step. This form of locomotion requires much more energy than swimming movements that incorporate periods of effortless gliding.

The biochemical makeup of terrestrial and marine organisms reflects their disparate energy needs. The relative percentages of carbohydrates and fats in land animals is high. Such compounds store energy. Marine organisms on the whole are composed primarily of proteins, with little carbohydrate and fat (the exceptions are marine mammals, which have a high fat content specifically for energy storage necessary due to body heat loss). A vivid illustration of the difference in these percentages is the comparison of an average cut of beef with its associated fat and a relatively fat-free halibut fillet.

Oxygen is the last physical component that has a significant effect on organisms. Its availability differs greatly between land and sea environments. Air, which contains approximately 21 percent oxygen, is fairly evenly distributed over the surface of the earth. Further, it is already in a gaseous state. The oxygen content of seawater is not as great and varies widely depending upon other physical factors such as temperature and salinity. Oxygen-rich parts of the ocean include high-surf beaches and wave-swept rocky shores, where air and water meet. Oxygen-poor environments include deep-sea sediments and stagnating mud flats, where little dynamism exists.

When ecologists talk about the structure of an ecosystem, they are referring to how all of the physical and biological components of an ecosystem fit and work together. They are talking about the relationships of the organisms to each other and to the physical world. Often ecological relationships can be characterized by the presence (or absence) of certain important components. For example, plants generally play a key role in any ecosystem. Terrestrial communities are universally dominated by large flowering plants (angiosperms). With the exception of kelps, there are no really large marine plants. The dominant plants in marine communities are microscopic algae (usually either diatoms or dinoflagellates). This is a fundamental difference between land and sea communities that has resounding effects on the structure of each.

Small plants allow for and encourage small animals that can eat them. The major plant-eaters of the sea are the microscopic copepods, which are found everywhere. While there are many species, generally only one or two species are extremely abundant. Copepods are very different than their enormous land counterparts, such as antelope, bison, cattle and others. Both represent the primary link in the food chain — organisms that turn plant energy to animal energy.

As previously mentioned, land plants need a significant support structure with which to fight gravity. This structure is largely inedible (wood, fiber, bark, etc.). The result is that grazing on plants by land herbivores rarely removes the bulk of the plant from the ecosystem. Consequently, land communities tend to be plant-dominated and more stable than marine systems. In the marine communities, the entire plant can be removed quite easily due to its size. The result is that copepods actually regulate phytoplankton populations. Compared,

then, side to side, land communities can be described as being dominated by long-lived plant assemblages with shorter-lived assemblages of animals. Marine communities are dominated by long-lived animal assemblages with generally shorter-lived plant species whose presence may be quite seasonal. Terrestrial communities are referred to as redwood forests, oak forests and grass prairies. Marine communities are referred to as coral reefs, clam beds, oyster reefs and mussel beds.

Lastly, a major element in describing the structure of any ecosystem is how energy moves through it. Food chains chart pathways for energy and provide a vehicle for drawing comparisons. Terrestrial food chains are shorter than those of marine communities, primarily due to the nature of the first level of the chain — plants. They are the organisms that convert solar energy into organic energy, the process upon which most ecosystems are built. In aquatic communities, the microscopic nature of both the plants and the majority of animals (copepods) allows room in the chain for several levels of carnivores that can eat each other. The result is that marine food chains have on average four to five links and that most of the large animals of the sea are carnivores.

For example, a marine food chain may start with phytoplankton that are eaten by copepods that in turn are eaten by filter feeders such as herring. The herring is eaten by squid, which provides a meal for a shark, hence a total of five links in the chain. A terrestrial food chain may start with a plant such as grass, which is grazed on by an antelope that in turn is eaten by a lion, hence three links in the chain.

As members of the assemblage of terrestrial animals, humans tend to take for granted the adaptations that they and all the other land-fixed organisms have developed that allow them to exist. Some of the fascination with marine life stems, perhaps, from the perception that the aquatic realm is like an entirely separate world. Clearly, living in a fluid environment has its own set of rules that its inhabitants must follow to survive. It is no wonder humans can still only enter it as a visitor.

The Aquatic Realm in Peril

There is no question that the planet's aquatic ecosystem is under tremendous stress, and predictions for the future are serious. Worldwide coral reef degradation is well documented. Scientific estimates indicate that *all* of the world's major fishing areas have either reached or exceeded their natural productivity limits. Even worse, over half of them are in serious decline. Similarly, the catch of freshwater fish has reached its maximum sustainable yield. Most of the earth's rivers, lakes and inland seas are fully fished or overfished.

Despite much popular mythology to the contrary, especially as regards coral reef damage, the causes of these problems are clearly not related to the activities of divers. In fact,

scientists estimate that less than one percent of coral reef damage is related in any way to dive activities. Instead, the issues are global in nature.

The basic cause is a simple one: the world's ever-increasing population. This reached three billion in the first half of the 20th century and 4 billion by the 1970s. At the current rate of growth, the world will gain 85 million people per year for at least the next two decades, with global population estimated at over 11 billion people by the middle of the next century. Since fully one-half of the world's people live within 100 km/ 60 miles from the seacoast, the current pressures, and those yet to come, are immense.

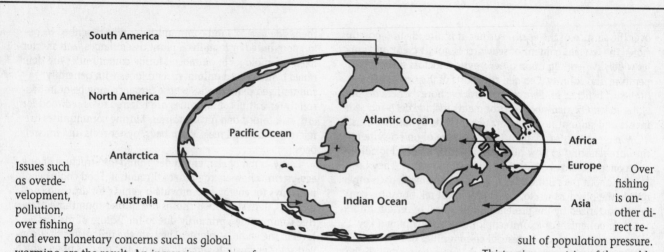

Issues such as overdevelopment, pollution, over fishing and even planetary concerns such as global warming are the result. An increasing number of people and their demands on the world environment are at the root of the peril facing the earth's aquatic ecosystem.

The results of overdevelopment are many and widespread. The growth of coastal cities causes destruction of wetlands through land reclamation (scientists estimate that one half of the continental United States' 220 million acres of wetlands have been destroyed in the last 200 years); dredging of port areas and resultant sedimentation smothers corals and many other sessile marine species. Denuding vegetated areas causes further silting as the earth's natural defenses against erosion are removed; and massive diversion of fresh water can alter the salinity of huge bodies of ocean water (Florida Bay, for example, through loss of too much of its freshwater flow, has become hypersalinic — this has been found to be the chief cause of the well-publicized decline of the coral reefs in the Florida Keys).

Closely related is damage caused by direct pollution. Besides the obvious issues of waste and garbage disposal, there are many other significant destructive pollutants. The effects of oil spills are well-known; less known, but many times more significant is the huge amount of oil — some 11 million gallons annually for each city of 5 million people, mostly from automobiles — that enters the aquatic environment as runoff through sewage systems. Fully one-third of the toxins in the waterways have actually settled out from air pollution. Increased use of fertilizers and pesticides in farming have had significant effect on both fresh water and marine systems, killing aquatic organisms directly, as well as triggering secondary results such as algal blooms.

Another form of pollution involves the introduction of alien species, especially in rivers, streams, and lakes. Whether deliberately released or inadvertently carried, in ships bilges, for example, such species may have no natural enemies and can quickly overtake and kill off native species. Such animals as the zebra mussel in the Great Lakes of the United States and the walking catfish in the U.S. southeast are prime examples. Aquatic plants are also at issue as well. For instance, parts of the eastern Mediterranean are dominated by a specie of algae whose spores were accidentally introduced by ship. In the areas where it has taken hold, it has smothered and replaced virtually every native bottom plant species.

Over fishing is another direct result of population pressure. Thirty-nine countries of the world are defined as "dependant" on fish as a major (more than 10 percent) source of protein. In fact, more than 950 million people in 38 countries depend on fish for more than one-third of their protein intake.

Unfortunately, it is clear that the limits for fishing have been reached. Despite a doubling of the world's fishing fleet since the 1970s and vastly improved technology, the annual fish catch has remained static since 1989. It is estimated that 70 percent of the world's food fish species are either fully exploited, overexploited or rebuilding from past overfishing. The annual catches of key species like Atlantic cod, bluefin tuna, Japanese pilchard, Cape hake, haddock and chub mackerel are less than one-third of what they were in the early 1970s.

Decreasing fish populations have resulted in far more damaging fishing methods, such as long lines and gill nets, which cause massive kills to unwanted species. In fact, scientists estimate that nearly one-fourth of all fish caught — some 25 million tons annually — are discarded as unwanted species.

Additionally, increased use of explosives and cyanide are killing the very reef systems that serve as the spawning and habitat for food fish. Motivated by the aquarium and live food fish trades, the cyanide problem is becoming a major issue in the rich Indo-Pacific region.

Finally, global climatic changes, less predictable and potentially with the greatest future ramifications, may be affected by human-induced causes. Global warming and changes in ocean temperatures, feared to be caused by destruction of the ozone layer, affect species distribution and survivability. Loss of an estimated six to twelve percent of phytoplankton growth and significant reductions in the Antarctic krill, a crucial food source for many fish, bird and marine mammal species, is thought to be directly related to ozone depletion above Antarctica. The long term effects of such planetary change are both unknown and frightening to consider.

The threats to the aquatic environment are widespread and solutions depend upon the human race finding better ways, on a worldwide basis, to live within the planet's environmental resources. The issues faced will require worldwide governmental recognition and cooperation. Otherwise, the potential consequences are simply too dire to contemplate.

Around the World Underwater

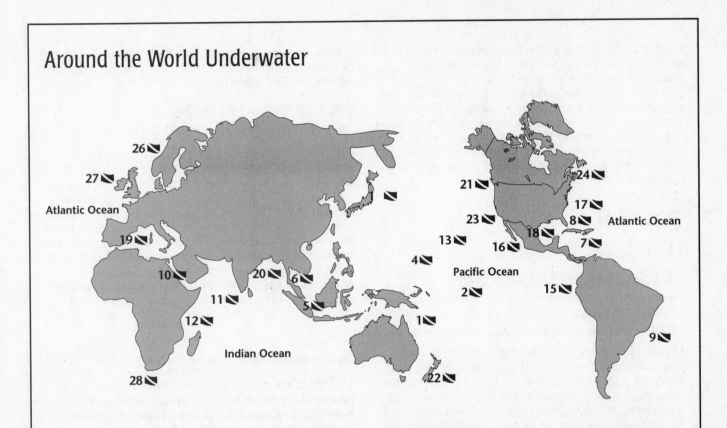

Fantastic underwater spectacles can be found in areas close to home or halfway around the world. Dive opportunities are frequently dramatic in freshwater quarries, lakes, rivers and springs. Jet travel and a proliferation of dive resorts and live-aboard dive boats now allow easy access to remote locations. Virtually all corners of the aquatic realm offer outstanding dive experiences. This section overviews some of the many dive sites around the world.

The World's Oceans

Most diving takes place in the ocean environment. The four major oceanic regions are, in order of decreasing size: the Pacific, the Atlantic, the Indian and the Arctic. The Pacific and the Atlantic are further subdivided into northern and southern regions. Projecting from, and occasionally cutoff from, these larger oceans are smaller bodies of water such as the Mediterranean, the Caribbean, the Coral and the Red seas.

On land, temperature is only one of the many factors that determines where plants and animals live; in the oceans it is the overriding one. Ocean temperatures range from -3°C/27°F at the poles to 30°C/86°F in the tropics. There are four main water temperature zones: polar, temperate, subtropical and tropical and between these zones are transition areas. Zone boundaries vary seasonally.

Polar seas have the coldest surface temperatures, ranging from -3 - 0°C/27 - 32°F. Polar regions have little temperature change and the clearest water of any ocean environment. Visibility is often measured in hundreds of metres/feet.

Temperate seas are cool or cold. Surface water temperature fluctuates more than any other zone. Temperature ranges from 0 - 21°C/32 - 70°F. These seas are often tinted green where up-welling of deeper nutrient rich water supports blooms of phytoplankton. These nutrients decrease water clarity. In temperate waters, the warmest temperatures are in the summer and fall, while the coldest temperatures are in the winter and spring. The best visibility may often be in winter, but calm periods can lead to excellent conditions at any time.

Rocky temperate shores are among the ocean's richest environments. The rocky shores provide a solid substrate for plants and animals to attach themselves against strong wave action. These rocky shores also play a part in the abundance of intertidal communities. The temperate zone's shore topography, strong tides, large tidal ranges and moderate climate lead to richer intertidal areas than in the other zones.

Subtropical seas are warm, but temperature fluctuates seasonally from 20 - 27°C/68 - 80°F.

Tropical seas have the warmest surface temperatures year-round: 24 - 30°C/75 - 86°F. Tropical water temperature and clarity change little annually.

Both subtropical and tropical seas are usually characterized by deep blue waters. This is due to a lack of nutrients to support phytoplankton.

Coral reefs, the largest structures made by living creatures on this planet, only occur in tropical and subtropical seas and oceans. Coral reefs are an interesting contrast between abundance and scarcity: they are the richest of marine ecosystems yet they are surrounded by warm surface waters that are among the most nutrient deficient on earth.

Three criteria categorize the world's dive sites: temperature zone as outlined above, closest major ocean and the location's significance as a recreational dive location. Random examples in each location illustrate the type of underwater environment and dive opportunities in each area. Seasons vary with location (with hemisphere in particular) and it is important to seek detailed information when planning a trip.

TROPICAL

PACIFIC

NE Australia (Barrier Reef, Coral Sea)

Water temperatures: Summer: 24-27°C/75-80°F Winter: 22-24°C/72-75°F

Visibility: 10-25 metres/30-80 feet, average 18 metres/60 feet

Features: Located off the northeast coast of Australia, the Great Barrier Reef is the largest structure on earth built by living things. As one of the most diverse coral reef ecosystems in the world, it is home to a wide variety of creatures, including giant clams, over 5000 species of fish and 500 species of coral. The dominant corals here are the branching corals, especially the delicate finger corals. The reef colors are due to the corals, not the sponge life, as is usual on Caribbean reefs. Many dive centers and resorts service the area and diving can be land-based from island resorts or from live-aboard dive boats.

The Coral Sea is located 240-320 kilometres/150-200 miles beyond the outer edge of the Great Barrier Reef where visibility may range from 15-60 metres/50-200 feet and averages 33 metres/100 feet. Rising from great depths to just brush the surface, these uninhabited atolls are oases in the clear blue ocean. Marine life from the surrounding waters congregates here. Divers may encounter diverse, prolific marine life, a variety of sharks and other large pelagic animals. Because of its distance from Australia, diving here requires the use of a live-aboard dive boat.

Melanesia (Fiji)

Water temperatures: Year round: 24-27°C/75-80°F

Visibility: 10-50 metres/30-150 feet

Features: Located just over 1600 kilometres/1000 miles north of New Zealand, Fiji consists of 300 islands, from big mountainous islands to small coral atolls. The three major diving areas are: the Western Region (Nadi, the Mamanucas, the Yasawa Islands and Vatuele), the Central Region (Yanuca, Beqa and Kadavu), and the Northern Region (Taveuni, Matagi, Laucala and Namena Islands and Savusavu). Visitors can explore shallow coral reefs, huge fish-filled caves and tunnels, and dramatic drop-offs studded with resplendent soft corals. An abundance of marine vertebrate life swarms in these waters from small tropical fishes to turtles, rays and sharks.

Notable dive sites include Astrolabe Reef, Bequ Lagoon, Rainbow Reef and the Somosomo Strait. Diving can be land-based or from live-aboard dive boats.

Polynesia (French Polynesia)

Water temperatures: Year round: 29°C/84°F

Visibility: 10-40 metres/30-120 feet

Features: Located just north of the equator, these islands lie half way between Australia and South America. There are three groups of islands: The Society Islands (which include Tahiti and Bora-Bora), Tuamotus, and Marquesas. The Society Islands are considered the most beautiful above water. Some of the most popular diving areas are in the Tuamotus group, especially Tikei and Rangiroa. Diving is best around the breaks in the fringing reefs that form tidal passes. Populations of large predators are attracted to the food-bearing currents in these passes. Diving can be land-based or from live-aboard dive boats.

Micronesia

Water temperatures: Year round: 29°C/84°F

Visibility: 10-60 metres/30-200 feet

Features: Located east of the Philippines and north of Melanesia these islands are arranged in groups: Carolines, Marianas, Marshalls, and Gilberts. Some of the best diving is in the Caroline group (Palau, Ponape and Truk).

Palau is best known for its hundreds of fascinating rock islands. Rock islands are mushroom shaped coral islets, topped with thick green foliage. Underwater, spectacular walls are covered with gorgonians and soft corals, from just below the surface to over 330 metres/1000 feet. Palau also has many fascinating marine lakes, renowned for enormous numbers of harmless jellyfish.

At the eastern end of the Caroline group, Ponape island is surrounded by a relatively untouched barrier reef with large fish populations. The reef passes are where divers find most of the exciting fish watching, where predatory fish converge on smaller schools of prey.

Truk Lagoon is the graveyard of Japan's World War II fleet. Over 100 sunken ships, planes and a submarine now dressed with colorful hard and soft corals, lie here. Truk is popular with wreck divers. Throughout the region, diving can be land-based or from live-aboard dive boats.

Indonesia & Malasyia

Water temperatures: Year-round: 24-27°C/75-80°F

Visibility: 10-45 metres/30-150 feet, average 18 metres/60 feet

Features: Indonesia comprises more than 13,600 islands and atolls. The smaller islands and remote reefs offer the best diving. The reefs here have an astonishing diversity of marine life matched by few other places in the world. It is hard to find greater numbers of coral and fish species anywhere else. Diving is land-based or live-aboard dive boat based.

Gulf of Thailand

Water temperatures: Year-round: 20-25 °C/70-78°F

Visibility: 10-45 metres/30-150 feet, average 18 metres/60 feet

Features: The Gulf of Thailand offers exciting diving. Resorts on the north, east and west coasts of the Gulf offer diving on spectacular coral reefs surrounding nearby islands. Shipwrecks from old junks to World War II and the present can be seen. Diving is mainly land-based, many live-aboard dive boats visit the Similan Islands.

ATLANTIC

Caribbean Sea

Water temperatures: Summer: 27-29°C/80-85°F Winter: 24-26°C/75-78°F

Visibility: 10-60 metres/30-200 feet, average 24 metres/80 feet

Features: The Caribbean Sea is bordered by Central and South America and a string of coral and volcanic islands. Each country has its own special history, cultural flavor and unique underwater attraction. The Caribbean offers a fascinating underwater variety of barrier reefs, fringing reefs, patch reefs, walls, canyons, caves, drop-offs, blue holes, pinnacles, and wrecks. Vibrant sponges color the coral reefs. Marine life abundance and diversity can change subtly from island to island. Caribbean reefs are geologically younger and less diverse in corals and fish life than their Pacific Ocean counterparts.

Diving is available through a wide variety of dive stores, resorts and live-aboard dive boats. Some islands offer excellent shore dive sites that are easily accessible by car, using well mapped and marked locations.

SE North America (Bahamas)

Water temperatures: Summer: 27-28°C/80-83°F Winter: 24-26°C/75-78°F

Visibility: 10-60 metres/30-200 feet, average 33 metres/100 feet.

Features: Located off the southeast coast of the Untied States, the Bahamas are comprised of 690 coral islands and cater to a wide range of diver preferences. Diving in the Bahamas can include shallow coral reefs, deep reefs, walls, caves, blue holes, abundant marine life, diving with wild dolphins, swimming with sharks, exploring shipwrecks and searching for sunken treasure. Diving is available through a wide variety of dive stores, resorts and live-aboard boats.

E South America (Brazil)

Water temperatures: Year-round: 24-28°C/75-82°F

Visibility: 9-45 metres/30-150 feet

Features: Most of the diving takes place along and off the coast north and south of Rio de Janeiro. Coral reefs and tropical marine life can be found off the thousands of miles of coastline. Away from the main coastal cities, many miles of coral reefs remain virtually unexplored.

INDIAN

Red Sea

Water temperatures: Summer: 24-27°C/75-80°F Winter: 20-23°C/68-73°F

Visibility: 15-60 metres/50-200 feet, average 23 metres/75 feet

Features: Bordered by Egypt to the west and Saudi Arabia to the east, the Red Sea is a rich and thriving coral reef environment. One of the most incredible things about the Red Sea is the striking contrasts of the land and sea. The lifeless desert moonscape of the Sinai Peninsula is a dramatic contrast to the prolific sea life lapping at its shores. Divers find delicate finger corals piled on top of each other, with colorful gorgonians and brilliant soft corals adding color to the reefs. Diving in the main body of the Red Sea is accessed through Egypt from live-aboard dive boats or from shore by car. The Gulf of Aquaba is accessible from Jordan, Israel or Egypt. In the Gulf of Aquaba many spectacular dive sites are also easily accessible by car, using detailed dive guide books.

Maldives

Water temperatures: Year-round: 27°C/80°F

Visibility: 10-40 metres/30-125 feet, average 24 metres/80 feet

Features: The Maldives are a long chain of atolls located off the southern tip of India. The outer walls of these atolls drop vertically into the depths. The best diving can be found in less than 15 metres/50 feet of water. Three types of diving are found here: diving in atoll reef passes where tides sweep in and out and pelagic fish gather, on outer drop-offs between major atolls, and in the shallow atoll lagoons. Many fish are endemic only to these islands and are incredibly tame. Diving can be land-based from small atoll resorts or from live-aboard dive boats.

Seychelles

Water temperatures: Summer: 27-28°C/80-82°F Winter: 25-27°C/77-80°F

Visibility: 10-30 metres/30-100 feet, average 24 metres/80 feet

Features: Located about 1600 kilometres/1000 miles off the east coast of Africa, the Seychelles are 115 mostly uninhabited islands at the top of a granite plateau rising out of the ocean depths. The reefs are spectacular formations made of granite boulders and monoliths that form arches, rock pinnacles and sheer walls, which are covered with sponges and corals. In addition to the tropical marine life found here, whale sharks are often seen.

SUBTROPICAL

PACIFIC

Hawaiian Islands

Water temperatures: Summer: 24-27°C/75-80°F Winter: 21-23 °C/70-74°F

Visibility: 10-45 metres/30-150 feet, average 33 metres/100 feet

Features: The Hawaiian Islands, located in the mid-Pacific, 20° north of the equator, are the most remote islands on earth, more than 3200 kilometres/2000 miles from the nearest major land mass. The lava from these volcanic islands has created underwater tubes, caves, arches and ridges. On and around these lava formations are stony corals. The water temperature here is too cool to support most reef building corals. The result is that these geologically young islands have a noticeable lack of corals compared to the Indo-Pacific and Caribbean regions. The vast stretches of deep ocean water surrounding these islands give divers a chance to see many deep water pelagic animals not commonly encountered elsewhere. Due to the island's isolated location, approximately 25 percent of the fish species are endemic.

Diving is available through a wide variety of dive centers, resorts and live-aboard dive boats. Most of the best dive sites are offshore or in remote areas and are accessible only by boat.

Japan

Water temperatures: Summer: 23-25°C/73-77°F Winter: 18-20°C/64-68°F

Visibility: 5-30 metres/10-100 feet

Features: Located on the west side of the Pacific Ocean, Japan consists of four large islands and many smaller ones. From north to south the archipelago stretches over 1,600 kilometres/ 1,000 miles. Japan has 160 national marine parks, more than any other country. The main island of Honshu offers some enticing diving in Sagami Bay, in the Izu Oceanic Park, 95 kilometres/60 miles southwest of Tokyo. A surprising richness and variety of marine life is found here. Rocks are covered with colorful invertebrate life, including soft corals and gorgonians. A variety of fish swim through forests of wire coral. About 120 species of octopus, squid, cuttlefish and other cephalopods live in these waters. Far to the south, the island of Okinawa has many worthwhile dives on the surrounding coral reefs. Diving is mainly land-based with some live-aboards available in Okinawa.

Galapagos Islands

Water temperatures: Summer: 18-29°C/65-85°F Winter: 13-24°C/55-75°F

Visibility: 10-45 metres/30-150 feet

Features: Straddling the equator off the coast of Equador, the Galapagos are largely uninhabited volcanic islands. Most underwater reefs are lava formations: caves, arches and ridges with a few scattered stony corals. Divers find a surprising range of underwater temperature and visibility as they move from island to island. Unique marine life is found here and tends to be incredibly tame. Of the animals that live here one third are endemic only to these islands, such as the Galapagos sea lions and marine iguanas. Deep water surrounding these islands brings in many pelagic animals. Diving is from live-aboard dive boats.

W. Mexico (Sea of Cortez)

Water temperatures: Summer: 21-27°C/70-80°F. Winter: 18-21°C/65-70°F

Visibility: 10-60 metres/30-200 feet, average 18 metres/60 feet

Features: The Sea of Cortez is located between the Baja Peninsula and the Sonoran coast of Mexico. Upwelling of deep cold nutrient-rich water is the foundation for the region's food chain. The Sea of Cortez is rich in sea life, with tropical, temperate and migratory species found here. The rocky reefs are home to large, colorful gorgonians, dozens of nudibranch species, anemones, sea stars, and more than 800 fish species. Popular dive sites include: Las Animas Island, Cabo Pulmo (the only living coral reef in the Sea of Cortez and the most northerly coral reef in this hemisphere), El Bajo Seamount (visited by mantas, whale sharks, hammerheads and sailfish), and Los Islotes (huge boulders that are home to a sea lion rookery).

Diving is from shore or boat with most dive stores, dive resorts, dive boats and live-aboards operating in the south from La Paz and Cabo San Lucas.

ATLANTIC

Bermuda

Water temperatures: Summer: 18-21°C/65-70°F Winter: 13-18°C/55-65°F

Visibility: 5-60 metres/20-200 feet

Features: Located in the mid-Atlantic, off the central coast of North America, Bermuda has marine life similar to that of the Caribbean Sea and the most northerly coral reefs in the world. There is not as much coral here as there is in the Caribbean, due to cooler temperatures. Over three hundred shipwrecks have been located here. Boat dives are required, since the dive sites range from several hundred metres/yards to over 16 kilometres/10 miles offshore.

Gulf of Mexico

Water temperatures: Summer: 27-29°C/80-85°F Winter: 21-27°C/70-80°F

Visibility: 10-60 metres/30-200 feet

Features: The Gulf of Mexico is bordered by the United States on the north, Mexico on the west and the Caribbean Sea to the south. Oil rigs in the Gulf provide many popular dive sites. The rig framework provides a vertical environment, offering a dramatic sense of scale, while providing a sanctuary for marine life. Under the rigs divers may find barracuda, grouper, huge jewfish, schools of spade fish, and smaller baitfish. Access to the rigs is from dive boats.

Mediterranean Sea

Water temperatures: Summer: 24-27°C/75-80°F Winter: 18-24°C/65-75°F

Visibility: 10-30 metres/30-100 feet, average 18 metres/60 feet

Features: To dive the Mediterranean is to dive not just the birthplace of scuba diving, but of civilization itself. Above and below water divers will probably see some evidence of an ancient civilization. Close to shore, craggy rocky reef formations are often home to some interesting invertebrate life. Diving is from shore or boat through local dive stores, dive clubs and a few dive resorts. Most diving here takes place from Spain, France, Italy, Greece, Cyprus and Turkey.

INDIAN

Andaman Sea

Water temperatures: Year-round: 20-25 °C/70-78°F

Visibility: 10-45 metres/30-150 feet, average 18 metres/60 feet

Andaman Sea diving is centered at Phuket Island. Liveaboards offer a chance to visit the Similan Islands, 80 kilometres/50 miles to the northwest. Gorgonians, corals and purple coraline algae camouflage the granite domes, boulders and monoliths that form alleys, archways, tunnels and caves. In addition to the tropical marine life found here, whale sharks are often seen. Colorful Indo-Pacific fish abound with pelagic species cruising through from the surrounding depths.

TEMPERATE

PACIFIC

NW North America (British Columbia)

Water temperatures: Summer: 10-12°C/50-54°F Winter: 5-10°C/41-50°F

Visibility: Visibility: 10-20 metres/25-70 feet, average 12 metres/40 feet

Features: The plankton-rich waters of Canada's western coast have diminished visibility, but support an abundance of marine life. The waters abound with invertebrates of extraordinary variety, size and color. Divers find giant Pacific octopuses 2.5 metres/8 feet long, sea whips 2 metres/7 feet long, nudibranchs 46 centimetres/18 inches long, and 30 species of seastars. British Columbia's 27,375 kilometre/17,000 mile coastline still has vast unexplored stretches. Diving is from shore or boat with many dive stores, resorts, dive boats and live aboards along the coast.

New Zealand

Water temperatures: Summer: 18-21°C/65-70°F Winter: 13-18°C/55-65°F

Visibility: Visibility: 10-45 metres/30-150 feet around offshore islands, average 18 metres/60 feet

Features: Under the cool, clean water you will find rich plant life, tremendously diverse fish populations, and a profusion of brightly colored invertebrates among the rocky reefs, underwater cliffs and caves. Three things stand out about New Zealand underwater: a great variety of kelps (red, green and brown) and coraline algae, the variety, profusion and color of the invertebrate life (sponges, anemones, bryozoans, sea fans, nudibranchs, crabs, soft corals, hydroids, etc.), and the fish life (96 species from 44 families found in the Mediterranean, Caribbean, Atlantic and Indo-Pacific).

One of the most popular dive areas is around Poor Knights Islands, about 24 kilometres/15 miles off the northeast coast of North Island. Diving is from shore or boat.

W North America (Channel Islands, California)

Water temperatures: Spring, Summer, Fall: 18-21°C/65-70°F Winter: 11-18°C/52-65°F

Visibility: Visibility: 10-30 metres/30-90 feet, average 18 metres/60 feet

Features: These eight mostly uninhabited islands of the coast off Southern California are surrounded by forests of golden brown giant kelp. Kelp forests host diverse and abundant marine life. Colorful invertebrates and a wide variety of fish life are found here. The kelp forest environment literally surrounds you. The marine life in the kelp forest is oriented horizontally along the rocky reefs and vertically on and around the kelp plants. Added attractions are the playful seals and sea lions found at many dive sites. Diving is boat based with many excellent single-day and multi-day dive boats available from ports along the mainland coast.

ATLANTIC

NE North America (Nova Scotia)

Water temperatures: Year-round: 10-13°C/50-55°F

Visibility: 3-15 metres/10-50 feet

Features: These waters of Canada's east coast are home to an abundance of kelp and colorful invertebrate marine life. The main attraction for divers, however, are the shipwrecks. The waters around Nova Scotia are littered with thousands of shipwrecks, most of which date to before the 20th century. The majority of these wrecks have yet to be found. Rough waters have taken their toll on the older wrecks with many of the old wooden sailing ships lost forever. Wreck divers properly equipped for this environment will be rewarded for their efforts. Diving is from shore or from local fishing boats that arrange dive charters.

Baltic Sea

Water temperatures: Summer: 13-18°C/55-65°F Winter: 4-10°C/40-50°F

Visibility: 10-25 metres/30-80 feet, average 18 metres/60 feet

Features: Shipwrecks and clear water are the attractions here. Ships from World War I and II can be explored. Well preserved wooden shipwrecks can be seen as well, some even dating to the 13th century. The slight tidal fluctuation, cold water and absence of wood boring mollusks account for the surprisingly good condition of these sunken ships.

Diving is available through dive stores, dive clubs and local boats.

W. Scandinavia (Norway, North Sea and Norwegian Sea)

Water temperatures: Summer: 13-18°C/55-65°F Winter: 4-10°C/40-50°F

Visibility: 10-25 metres/30-80 feet, average 15 metres/50 feet

Features: Divers can explore shipwrecks and encounter cold water marine life. Historical shipwrecks, many from World War II, can be found on Norway's North Sea coast. Norwegian fjords offer some incredible diving opportunities. In September, large gatherings of killer whales can be seen in the fjords near Lofoten, in the Norwegian Sea. Diving is available through dive stores, dive clubs and local boats.

INDIAN

South Africa

Water temperatures: Year-round by location 9-26°C/48-79°F

Visibility: 5-40 metres/16-130 feet, average 15 metres/50 feet

Features: Diving in South Africa occurs in the Indian Ocean along the east coast and in the South Atlantic along the southern Cape coast. To the north, waters are tropical, with corals, reef fish and ocean pelagics common to other parts of the Indian Ocean. Further south, temperatures drop, becoming temperate around the Cape.

The most popular Indian Ocean dive areas, such as those around the border of Mozambique and Protea Banks further south, are open ocean pinnacles. Large Potato cod, schools of jacks, and large gamefish such as tuna and billfish are common. Especially rich are shark populations, with many species, such as bullsharks, silvertips, hammerheads, tigers, and sand tigers seen on the same reefs.

In the area around the Cape, colder waters are home to Great Whites and other large sharks, in impressive numbers. A number of dive operators provide white shark dives. Diving in South Africa is shore-based, usually using rigid hull inflatables.

POLAR

Diving in polar regions is a highly specialized activity. Very little recreational diving takes place here, but some dive centers offer expeditions that provide divers with the opportunity to dive beneath polar ice. Visibility is frequently excellent and underwater ice formations can be dramatic.

FRESHWATER

Water temperatures: Vary with location and season, from 0-30°C/32-85°F

Visibility: Up to 60m/200 feet

Freshwater Springs

Features: Freshwater springs frequently offer excellent visibility. Aquatic life varies with location, but usually includes algae and bottom dwelling invertebrates. Fish species reflect geographical location and temperature. In North America, bluegill, crappie and largemouth bass are common to southern regions; salmonids, pike and smallmouth bass dominate in northern areas.

Throughout Europe, salmonids, cyprinids such as carp, roach and bream, and pike inhabit these waters. Many springs, particularly those in limestone substrates, have intricate cave systems which should be entered only by appropriately qualified divers. Many of the more popular springs are well served by dive centers.

Lakes, Reservoirs and Quarries

Features: Lakes vary in size from large ponds to inland seas. Dive opportunities depend greatly on the region: wreck diving, for example, is popular on the North American Great Lakes where many ships are preserved in excellent condition. Reservoirs are man made lakes. One of the most significant differences between the two is the presence of potentially hazardous outfalls and intakes in reservoirs. These are usually located adjacent to a dam at the deepest part of the reservoir. Maps published prior to the creation of a reservoir can be very informative regarding topographical features that are now underwater. Occasionally, buildings and even small towns, which were covered as the reservoir filled, may be encountered. The water levels in reservoirs fluctuates, often dramatically, consequently it is difficult for aquatic plants and invertebrates to establish themselves in the shallow margins. Thermoclines are more pronounced in freshwater lakes and reservoirs than in any other part of the aquatic realm. Bottom temperatures are frequently much lower than those on the surface and divers plan for the coldest expected temperature. Many flooded and disused quarries around the world have become popular sites with divers. Some of these have been specifically developed to attract divers.

Altitude Diving

Features: Many divers live in areas higher than 300 metres/1000 feet above sea level. These divers usually divide their interests between traveling to and diving popular dive destinations, and diving their local lake, quarry or reservoir. Altitude diving requires special procedures since dive tables become inaccurate above 300 metres/1000 feet. Divers learn these procedures by enrolling in specialty altitude diving courses or through local professional guidance.

Other than dealing with modified dive tables, high altitude divers may have to cope with special circumstances such as cold and hypoxia. Cold weather and water vary with seasons and geographic location, and hypoxia varies with altitude and personal adaptation. Hypoxia symptoms may occur after the end of a dive when the body returns to thin air after a dive. Divers should stop all activity and rest if they experience hypoxia symptoms. Divers can treat hypothermia by stopping all activity and warming up the body.

High altitude diving takes place at lakes and quarries from the European Alps to the North American Rockies and the South American Andes. Many local dive operators add small wrecks or other interesting structures to their local high altitude dive sites. They also offer dive table advice and rent altitude compensating dive computers.

River Diving

Features: Diving and snorkeling takes place in many rivers around the world. These don't have to be the aquatic-rich and exotic Amazon, but any river with a manageable current may offer an ideal body of water for a drift dive or snorkeling experience.

Divers report drifting down the Colorado river in the American Southwest, or coasting along a gentle stream in Italy. While the drift experience itself may entice these divers, marine life observation varies from one river to another. Some divers find pool areas within a river to conduct long dives with excellent freshwater visibility and marine life.

Recreational divers, photographers and researchers dive the world's large rivers regularly, including the Amazon, the Nile and the Mississippi. Divers, of course, evaluate river conditions and currents very closely before embarking on any activities there due to heavy current hazards and icing.

The Future of Diving

Five

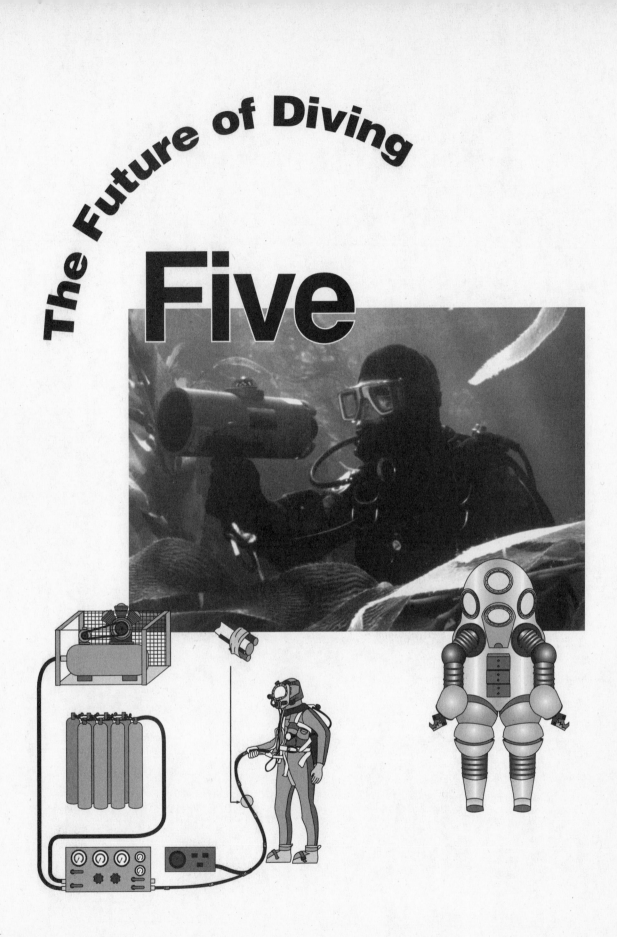

Emerging Technologies

Dive duration is independent of depth when using closed circuit rebreathers.

Introduction

In the early 1990s, *technical diving* emerged as a distinct diving niche that uses extensive equipment and rigorous protocols to go beyond the limits of recreational diving, but without the heavy gear, expense and massive demands of commercial diving. Technical diving sprang primarily from cave diving methods that were reapplied and broadened for open water applications. As technical diving has grown, it has tapped into other technologies from commercial, rescue, scientific, military and recreational diving, as well as computing, ultrasonics, hyperbaric/biomedical research and even space exploration technologies, to increase diver performance.

At this writing, technical diving still relies primarily on open circuit scuba (though more extensive than that used by recreational divers), however, the growing application of other technologies is spilling over into recreational diving. For its first five decades, recreational diving meant diving with compressed air — period. Yet now, recreational divers trained in its use can extend their no decompression time by breathing enriched air (nitrox). Although enriched air diving has been around longer than open circuit scuba, it wasn't until technical divers began using it that it passed into more mainstream use. Another example of technology moving from technical diving to recreational diving is the alternate second stage, which recreational diving picked up from cave diving in the early 1970s.

This process continues. Technologies that were once the exclusive domain of commercial, scientific and military diving have become common in technical diving, and some of these have started to edge their way toward recreational diving. Today, recreational divers face the promise of technologies that were once too complex for mainstream pleasure diving, too inaccessible due to cost, or out of reach simply because they had been dreamed of, but not created. The progression into recreational diving now marches so rapidly that by the time many people read these words, many of these "future" recreational diving technologies will be "present" recreational diving technologies.

Several technologies will change recreational diving, with four areas worth looking at in particular. Recreational divers use computing and electronics routinely now, though their potential has hardly been scratched. Closed circuit and semiclosed circuit scuba — both actually very old technologies — have some use in mainstream recreational diving, though for different reasons than in technical diving. Finally, one atmosphere hard suits may open the door to depths below 40 metres/130 feet to virtually anyone who wants to go, but without the rigors, risks, training or long decompressions associated with technical or commercial diving.

Dive Technology Milestones

1865 Benoit Rouquayrol and Auguste Denayrouze develop first open circuit demand scuba. It works, but doesn't benefit diving much because period compressed gas cylinders can't hold much pressure.

1876 Jules Verne publishes *20,000 Leagues Under the Sea* and "predicts" the development of scuba based on Rouquayrol's work.

1879 Henry A. Fleuss invents the first practical working scuba, an oxygen rebreather that conceptually differs little from modern oxygen rebreathers.

1892 Louis Boutan takes first underwater photographs by a diver.

1903 Sir Robert Davis invents submarine escape equipment based on Fleuss rebreather.

1908 John Scott Haldane publishes first dive tables.

1924 Joseph Peress builds early version of the hard suit with pressure compensating joints.

Louis de Corlieu invents first rubber fins for swimming.

U.S. Navy and Bureau of Mines begins testing helium as a deep diving gas.

1932 First snorkel for divers patented.

1935 Jim Jarrett uses Peress hard suit to explore the *Lusitania* wreck (100 metres/330 feet).

1936 First diver propulsion vehicle developed by Italian divers.

1937 Max Nohl dives to 128 metres/420 feet in Lake Michigan using heliox.

Wheland and Momsen of the U.S. Navy make chamber dive to 153 metres/500 feet using heliox.

1942- 1945 J.B.S. Haldane and Kenneth Donald of Royal Navy pioneer oxygen toxicity, semiclosed circuit scuba and enriched air diving. Combat divers use the first dry suits.

1943 Jacques Cousteau and Emile Gagnan invent the open circuit compressed air regulator.

1945 Arne Zetterström proves feasibility of hydrogen as a breathing gas by diving to 160 metres/525 feet, but dies during a decompression mishap.

1955 (approx.) Wet suit introduced.

1958 Submersible 35 mm Calypso camera introduced, which was the forerunner to the Nikonos.

1959 SOS Decompression meter, a mechanical forerunner of the dive computer, is introduced.

1963 In Cousteau's Conshelf II project, five divers live at 11 metres/36 feet for one month in the Red Sea.

1964 Sea Lab I puts four divers at 59 metres/193 feet for 11 days near Bermuda.

1968 Unisuit introduced in Sweden, ushering in the variable volume dry suit.

1969 Peress hard suit revived as JIM suit.

1970 Beckman introduces the Electrolung mixed gas closed circuit scuba. It is "ahead of its time," but provides a glimpse of what electronics can do to make closed circuit scuba widely practical.

1972 Commercial diving company Comex sends divers to 610 metres/2000 feet in chamber dive.

1976 JIM hard suit recovers television line at 440 metres/1450 feet.

1980 Duke University conducts simulated dive 650 metres/2132 feet using trimix.

1982 Phil Nuytten patents oil-filled rotary joint for hard suits, a major break through that becomes the basis of the Newt Suit. The second version of this joint is patented in 1985.

1983 Orca Edge and Decobrain I dive computers introduced — the first successful and widely accepted dive computers.

1987 Michael R. Powell Ph.D. completes first major series of hyperbaric test dives for recreational repetitive, multilevel diving to verify the Recreational Dive Planner developed by Dr. Raymond E. Rogers.

Wakulla Springs Project headed by William C. Stone, Ph.D., maps 5 kilometres/2.3 miles of an underwater cave system using heliox and trimix with open circuit scuba to depths of 98 metres/320 feet. The project sets the stage for the emergence of technical diving. The project also tests the CisLunar Mark I closed circuit scuba, setting the stage for wider interest in closed circuit applications.

1988 DSAT debuts the Recreational Dive Planner, Table and The Wheel, introduced and distributed by PADI. This is the first dive table exclusively for recreational no stop diving.

1992 Nikonos RS, first submersible single-lens reflex camera, introduced.

1996 Drager/UWATEC introduce semiclosed circuit scuba for applications in the 0 metres/feet to 30 metres/100 foot range. CisLunar unveils the Mark V electronic mixed gas closed circuit scuba, rated to 150 metres/500 feet.

Global positioning systems may be as small as a portable telephone.

Emerging Electronics

In the mid-1970s, prominent decompression experts held that it was "impossible" to make a practical dive computer. It could be done, but the result, they said, would be too big for the diver to carry and hideously expensive. The experts were right — at least at that time — but in less than a decade, that changed. By 1985, computers were commonplace, and by 1990, dive computers were small, relatively inexpensive and used by the majority of avid divers.

Some of the biggest immediate changes in dive technology will arise through or with dive computers. Computers with displays in the mask (heads up displays) have already debuted (thanks, in part, to transmitters that eliminate the SPG hose), with more on the way. Computers do more now than their counterparts of the late 1980s, and they will do yet more.

For one, electronic underwater *navigation* has barely been touched. Electronic transponder/finder systems have hit the recreational market, but these are crude compared to the potential. Leading edge developers for professional diving markets have developed systems that use two or three transponders so divers can always tell exactly where they are; the present barrier is cost.

Navigation based on transponders has the drawback that the diver or boat must deploy them. GPS (Global Positioning System) navigation permits accuracy to within a few metres/feet. This technology pinpoints location through a hand-held, inexpensive receiver that reads signals from satellite, and is commonly used by boaters, hikers and other recreationists. In diving, the limitation is that GPS signals don't penetrate water very well — but, researchers are trying to find a way to solve this. If (when) they're successful, the dive computer (or a separate GPS receiver) could easily become a sophisticated, highly precise

Hand held sonar helps divers locate under water features, such as wrecks or pipelines, even in limited visibility.

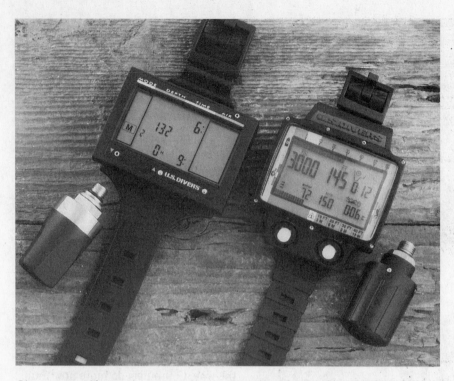

Dive computers with transmitters can monitor air consumption without a high pressure hose.

navigation tool that could be used anywhere on earth and requires no transponder or additional equipment.

Underwater electronics already in prototype and/or limited production suggest other possibilities: Divemasters (underwater or on the dive boat) can read data transmitted by each diver's computer: depth, no stop time remaining, air supply remaining, and location. Divers can type computer display messages on small keys pads and transmit them to other divers, or the boat.

Other electronics have potential benefits in the underwater environment. Through electronics, future cameras will require no film and have few or no moving parts. With no film to change, the camera body can be sealed in plastic, with contacts to download images from the camera's memory, and a water tight battery compartment that if flooded, won't flood the whole camera with it. The result could be an "unfloodable" camera.

Beyond these immediate promises, perhaps the most dramatic effects electronics will bring to diving will be those that no one has thought of yet.

Computing

It's not easy to say where dive computing on personal computers began — with technical divers who needed custom dive tables, or with recreational divers who wanted to keep their log books on their hard drives.

Either way, time has made both aspects of personal computing advance. As mentioned in the Equipment section, divers can choose from dozens of dive log softwares, including several that download data from the dive computer and permit the diver to adjust, within limits, dive computer variables.

Since technical divers use varying proportions of oxygen, nitrogen and/or helium to match a dive depth, duration and gas availability, not to mention varying blends during decompression,

Some dive computers interface with personal computers for information storage or dive planning.

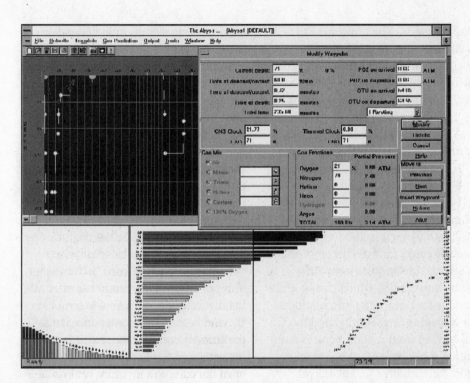

Abyss software allows divers to generate decompression profiles based on information they enter themselves.

they often find that suitable tables for a dive don't exist. To remedy this, they can generate custom tables using special software. Obviously at present this practice entails risks not associated with recreational diving, and requires extensive familiarity with decompression theory so as to use good judgment and assess the variables when generating tables. Nonetheless, this trend points to far-reaching potentials for diving: For example, it is possible to calculate a dive profile in a personal computer, then download the data into the dive computer for use underwater, with sufficient variables to handle contingency situations.

In the future, dive computers and software may have a common language, allowing divers to choose the dive computers and programs they prefer. Not only could it become common practice for divers to download their computers after each dive to assist divemasters in choosing the next dive site, but also the data collected could be

compiled into a central database, providing valuable information about typical dive profiles, DCI incidence and other relevant information.

Closed Circuit and Semiclosed Circuit Scuba

In a way, it's inaccurate to call closed circuit scuba an "emerging" technology because it was the first practical scuba (1879) and has been in use since that time. Until the invention of open circuit scuba in 1943, it was the *only* scuba; all other dives were made with helmet gear or hard suits. Although open circuit came to dominate scuba diving — virtually exclusively in recreational diving — closed circuit's stealth and efficiency characteristics made it useful in military and research diving. For those not familiar with the differences, it's worth reviewing the basic operation of open circuit, closed circuit and semiclosed circuit scuba.

Open circuit scuba is the equipment that all recreational divers are familiar with. The diver inhales a breath of compressed air or enriched air from the tank, then exhales the air into the water. The circuit is "open" in that it doesn't conserve exhaled air. Since the respiratory system only uses a fraction of the oxygen in each breath, the exhaled air still has most of the oxygen it had before the breath, but it is lost.

• *Advantages* — Open circuit scuba has several distinct advantages, which is why it has dominated recreational and technical diving. First it's mechanically simple, making it easy to learn to use, easy to maintain, and very reliable. Second, it only requires air, so it's possible to refill scuba cylinders anywhere with a compressor and at low cost. Third, assuming the cylinder is filled from an appropriate air or enriched air source, there's no concern during the dive that the unit will deliver a different gas blend.

Closed circuit scuba systems with heads up display in use during military training exercise.

• *Disadvantages* — The drawbacks to open circuit scuba are, first, that the diver has to carry a fairly large air supply, which is used faster as the diver goes deeper. This means a diver who needs to make a long dive, and/or a deep dive (as in exploratory technical diving) must carry an extraordinary number of cylinders. (For example, cave divers in the Wakulla Springs Project had to each carry 10 cylinders for 20-30 minutes bottom time at depths between 76 metres/ 250 feet and 91 metres/300 feet. This *did not* include tanks for their decompression gas.) Second, the bubbles sometimes scare shy aquatic life, which can be a disadvantage for naturalists and photographers/videographers. Finally, making multiple dives from a boat requires having either a compressor on board, or a cylinder for each dive for each diver.

Closed circuit scuba reuses exhaled gases. With closed circuit scuba, the diver inhales breathing gas (oxygen, enriched air or other blend) from a breathing bag, then exhales the gas, which flows through chemicals that remove carbon dioxide and returns to the breathing bag. The unit adds a small amount of oxygen to replace that which the diver consumed. The circuit is "closed" in that the exhaled breath is recycled, conserving the unused oxygen.

• *Advantages* — Closed circuit scuba uses comparatively small cylinders, and dive duration is independent of depth. With the most sophisticated types, the unit can change various gas proportions in the blend to minimize decompression, oxygen exposure and narcosis. The diver can get very long duration dives without carrying a lot of cylinders, especially when making deep dives. Since closed circuit has no bubbles, it's easier to approach shy aquatic life (this is also why combat divers on covert missions use closed circuit scuba). The gas supply and scrubber chemicals necessary for several dives can be carried in a small space.

• *Disadvantages* — Closed circuit scuba

has problems regarding inert gases in the breathing cycle. If the unit malfunctions and stops adding oxygen to the breathing gas, but the chemical scrubber still removes carbon dioxide, the diver can suddenly blackout without warning due to hypoxia. To avoid this, some closed circuit units use pure oxygen, but this restricts depths to 6 metres/ 20 feet or shallower. Alternatively, modern sophisticated closed circuit units use electronics to monitor oxygen and other gas content, and require special training and techniques more complex than open circuit scuba. Closed circuits gases may not be found as readily as air, and the diver must have access to scrubber chemicals as well. Maintenance isn't particularly complicated, but it is more involved and time consuming than open circuit scuba. Because of their design, number of components and (for some types) sophistication, they're more prone to malfunction than open circuit scuba.

Semiclosed circuit scuba combines some of the characteristics of open circuit with closed circuit scuba to give some of the advantages, and offset some of the disadvantages, of both. With semiclosed circuit scuba, the diver inhales from a breathing bag. The exhaled breath passes through chemical scrubber to remove carbon dioxide and returns to the breathing bag. The unit injects a small, constant flow of breathing gas (usually an enriched air blend) that periodically vents or streams fine bubbles. Semiclosed circuit reuses much, but not all, of the oxygen carried.

• *Advantages* — Semiclosed circuit scuba allows the diver to have a reasonably long dive with a small cylinder and scrubber material. Though the unit bubbles, it does so far less than open circuit, so it's still useful for approaching wildlife. Semiclosed circuit is much easier to learn to use than closed circuit, and its maintenance tends to be simpler than closed circuit. The use of a single gas blend simplifies dive planning, and greatly reduces the concern that the diver will unknowingly use all the oxygen in the circuit and suffer hypoxia. Semiclosed circuit is more prone to malfunction than open circuit scuba, but less so than closed circuit scuba (excepting pure oxygen closed circuit).

• *Disadvantages* — Semiclosed circuit scuba requires access to gas blends and chemicals. It has longer duration than open circuit, but shorter than closed circuit. Its maintenance is more extensive than open circuit. Because semiclosed circuit scuba uses a single gas blend that doesn't change during the dive, it has a depth limit of approximately 30 metres/100 feet (depending on the blend used) and it can't adjust for decompression, narcosis or oxygen exposure concerns.

As closed circuit and semiclosed circuit technologies evolve, doubtlessly they will have growing applications in recreational and technical diving. However, open circuit is far from gone. It's hard to predict precisely what their roles will be, but the best speculation for the immediate future seems to be:

• Thanks to its accessibility, simplicity, reliability, low cost and ease of maintenance, open circuit will remain the primary equipment used by recreational divers, and the main technology used when learning to scuba dive. It's reliability will also keep it the primary equipment used by technical divers, too.

• Semiclosed circuit's advantages over open circuit scuba are little bubble noise, and long duration dives for its size and weight. There are no reasons other than curiosity to use semiclosed circuit scuba. Given the added maintenance and setup (even though not complicated) and costs for gas blends and chemicals, in the immediate future semiclosed will be used primarily by serious underwater photographers and divers with special needs. A few people will enter diving using semiclosed circuit, but will probably find their diving opportunities relatively limited unless they also become qualified to use open circuit scuba.

• Closed circuit scuba will become frequently used in technical diving. Leading edge mixed gas units will open the largely unexplored 90 metres/300 foot to 150 metres/500 foot depth range to scientific and technical diving. It's unlikely that fully closed circuit will become simple enough and inexpensive enough to attract the mainstream leisure diver in the immediate future.

Hard Suits

Hard suits, also called "one atmosphere" suits represent a departure from mainstream diving. Many of diving's complexities — gas consumption, nar-

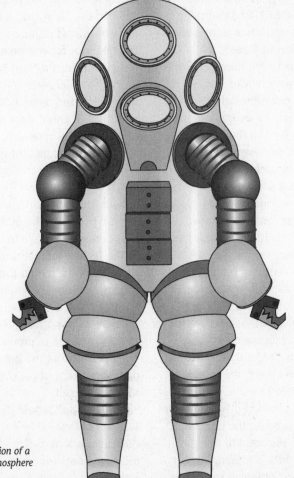

Graphic representation of a hard suit or one atmosphere diving system.

cosis, decompression — exist because pressure affects a diver's body. Hard suits, on the other hand, shield the diver from pressure; they are, in effect, very small human shaped submarines. A hard suit resembles armor more than a dive suit.

Although hard suits have only recently come to the forefront as an underwater technology with great promise and potential, like closed circuit they've been around for a long time. Dive historians generally cite the Lethbridge Diving Engine, designed and built by John Lethbridge in 1715, as the first example of the hard suit, as well as one of the earliest examples of successful underwater technology. Lethbridge's device was essentially a sealed wooden barrel with a glass viewport and openings that sealed with leather around the diver's arms. The diver lay face down in the "suit" suspended over the work area. According to records, in 1724 Lethbridge successfully recovered silver from a ship in 18 metres/60 feet of water.

Since the mid-1800s, dozens of inventors have drawn up hard suit designs; some were plausible, while others showed merely that the designer didn't understand pressure and diving. Beginning in the 1920s, however, hard suits that could perform useful work emerged. These were used for salvage, or attempted salvage on numerous wrecks.

One challenge that has plagued hard suits since their inception has been the effect of pressure on the suit joints. By the early 20th century, designers had mastered watertight ball joints and rotating joints that allowed a diver to move, but in all designs, as the diver descended increasing pressure put more and more force on the joint. Therefore, the deeper the diver went, the more strength was needed to move, until a depth was finally reached at which there was so much pressure on the joints that the diver couldn't move them.

The first suit with a pressure compensating joint was patented by Joseph Peress in 1922 and used by Jim Jarrett to dive the *Lusitania* wreck in 1935. In 1969, Underwater Marine Equipment Ltd. obtained the rights to the Peress suit and built the JIM suit, named after Jim Jarrett. The JIM suit, in its various designs, was the first widely used and commercially successful hard suit. Although the Peress/JIM joint design greatly reduced joint stress, it didn't eliminate it, so that although it went deeper than previous designs, eventually it reached a depth at which the joints were immobile.

In 1982 and 1985, Phil Nuytten of Hard Suits, Inc., patented a new hard suit joint that allows joints to move under far greater pressures than previous designs. Nuytten accomplished this, basically, by creating a depth-compensating joint that transfers the pressure off the joint to nonmoving parts of the suit. In the following two years, Nuytten developed the Newt Suit, which is the state-of-the-art in hard suit design. The implications for commercial diving are clear: a diver in a Newt Suit can dive to more than 300 metres/1000 feet, perform a job and ascend directly to the surface — without the expense and risks of a long decompression.

For all its capabilities, the Newt Suit remains too expensive and requires too much surface support for any widespread use in recreational or technical diving. However, the promise for pleasure divers doesn't lie in the Newt Suit, but in it's kid brother under development by Phil Nuytten (and possibly other inventors). Nuytten's patented joint combined with high-tech materials that are strong and lightweight may make it feasible to produce an affordable, practical to use hard suit for depths down to approximately 100 metres/330 feet.

Such a suit would make it possible to visit depths well below existing limits, and dives about as long as anyone reasonably wants (one atmosphere recirculating systems can support a diver for hours) without a need for decompression. A diver using a hard suit doesn't have flying after diving concerns, narcosis concerns or even squeeze concerns. A "sport diver" hard suit may well open diving to individuals who cannot dive due to physiological constraints (such as having a history of spontaneous pneumothorax). In fact, this technology would address many of the same needs addressed by mixed gas closed circuit scuba, but without the decompression concerns.

While hard suits will almost certainly have some application for recreation in the future, they're not going to replace scuba. For one, the costs and logistics will be considerably higher than for scuba, and second, a diver in a hard suit doesn't experience the environment as intimately as a scuba diver. Nonetheless, this technology may take divers places they might never have been able to visit without significantly greater expense, training, logistics and risk.

Aquatic World Awareness, Responsibility and Education

This photograph speaks for itself.

Introduction

Since people first began to explore our planet's waters using scuba, the richness of life they discover beneath the surface has fascinated them. The aquatic world provides the most densely productive environment on earth; every niche teems with diverse plants and animals.

In the early days of scuba, divers saw this realm as a source of seafood delicacies. Lobsters, scallops, crabs, fish and other highly prized food species were readily attainable by divers, and the sea's plenty seemed vast and limitless.

As time passed, attitudes about the environment and natural life shifted. Divers became leading proponents for the protection of aquatic ecosystems and their myriad creatures. With this shift in attitude, divers' activities have changed as well. Cameras have replaced spearguns as the accessory of choice; sight-seeing and aquatic life observation have replaced game-taking as the prominent activities. Divers now dive in a manner focused to minimize damage to the environment. Although there are still those divers who choose to seek out food species, even among these a responsible, respectful ethic prevails: that of take only what you'll eat, and eat whatever you take.

This growing sense of concern for the protection and nurturing of the aquatic environment among divers is no surprise. Divers, perhaps more than any other group of people, personally experience the underwater world — a world that is largely closed off and mysterious to virtually everyone else.

In reality, this aspect of diving is a part of what makes it so special for its enthusiasts. Divers also feel that this gives them a special responsibility. For they see, day after day as they dive, the changes and the damage occurring to oceans, lakes and rivers. To divers, something dumped or spilled into the waters isn't "out of sight, out of mind;" instead, it's there, it's visible, and its effects are clear.

Divers should not confuse recognizing the degradation of the underwater world with their having been the cause. There has been a great deal of confusion about the damage to coral reef systems from diver activity versus larger scale causes. In fact, a 1995 Coral Reef Alliance survey showed that a substantial number of divers mistook diver pressure as the major cause of coral reef damage.

In truth, divers do some incidental damage to coral reefs through touching or breaking corals. However, this type of problem is considered minor and recoverable (it happens in nature, too). The long-term damage to coral reefs — and other marine environments — is, in actuality, caused by the larger scale actions that typically affect overall water quality and the ability of marine species to reproduce and survive: pollution, dredging, oil spills, drift nets, and longline fishing. Noticing changes in marine life habitat and the numbers of animals living in a specific area; the destruction of coral reefs or kelp forests; or the loss of estuary areas through coastal overbuilding is unavoidable to someone who puts on a mask and ventures underwater.

Because of this, divers, as a community, are becoming true ambassadors for the underwater world, involving themselves in increasing numbers in underwater and beach cleanups; causes such as support for the U.S. National Marine Sanctuary and other marine park programs; and legislation actions such as those that have reduced the use of gill nets in Florida and California in the U.S. and provided protection to the endangered manatee.

Divers have also been among the chief proponents behind the efforts to protect and prevent the overfishing of the sea's top predator — sharks. Campaigns in Australia, the Bahamas and the U.S., with heavy involvement by the dive community, have been successful in reducing the threat to the ocean's most misunderstood — and, as an important keeper of a delicate ecological balance, one of its most necessary — creatures.

Project AWARE

Because of divers' special potential as advocates and protectors of the aquatic environment, in 1990 PADI introduced Project AWARE (Aquatic World Awareness, Responsibility and Education). The program, symbolic of PADI's commitment to protecting the underwater world, resulted in an increased emphasis on environmental education in

PADI's diver courses, PADI's production and business operations shifting to environmentally friendly practices, and the creation of the Project AWARE Foundation to fund aquatic environmental projects and research.

From the educational approach, nearly a million people each year are exposed to environmental awareness through interactions with PADI professionals. Project AWARE places new emphasis on environmentally sound approaches to dive practices, dive operations, and dive skills, especially buoyancy control. This emphasis led directly to new PADI specialty courses, such as Peak Performance Buoyancy, that showcase PADI's environmental and diver safety concern.

The Project AWARE concept continues to grow and is now a popular banner under which cleanups and educational projects are carried out. Such ef-forts, in conjunction with the U.S. Center for Marine Conservation, have resulted, for example, in the creation of the International Underwater Cleanup. Each year this event mobilizes thousands of divers around the world who participate in this effort to document damage to, and protect, the marine environment.

Project AWARE Foundation Small Grant

The Project AWARE Foundation is a non-profit, public benefit corporation designed to encourage and support aquatic ecology and education, to fund and assist worthwhile projects that will enrich humanity's awareness and understanding of the fragile nature of the aquatic world, and to support research and education in accordance with these

---

Project AWARE Mission Statement

The mission statement clearly identifies Project AWARE's goals:

- To provide PADI Members with information, including educational and support materials, to educate recreational divers on the aquatic realm and how to preserve it.

- To support the efforts of environmental organizations whose missions are aligned with Project AWARE.

- To support key environmental legislation.

- To incorporate environmentally sound practices throughout PADI's internal operations and to encourage the recreational scuba diving industry to do the same.

- To provide direct financial support (where possible) to environmental issues and organizations.

Project AWARE principles encourage responsible diver interaction with the environment. They are listed in "10 Ways a Diver Can Protect the Aquatic Realm:"

- Dive carefully in fragile aquatic ecosystems, such as coral reefs.

- Be aware of your body and equipment placement when diving.

- Keep your diving skills sharp with continuing education.

- Consider your interactions effect on aquatic life.

- Understand and respect underwater life.

- Resist the urge to collect souvenirs.

- If you hunt or gather game, obey all fish and game laws.

- Report environmental disturbances or destruction of your dive sites to the relevant authorities.

- Be a role model for other divers in diving and non-diving interactions with the environment.

- Get involved in local environmental activities and issues.

purposes. To fund all types of projects the Foundation has created the Small Grant Program.

The Small Grant Program funds projects of less than $500 (U.S.). Grant proposals are accepted on an ongoing basis and are reviewed each month by the Project AWARE Foundation Executive Committee.

Conclusion

Scuba diving has always been a source of pleasure, as the passport to the mysterious undersea world. Now, perhaps it is becoming more, for it can provide people everywhere a means to experience, firsthand, not only the beauty that exists beneath the surface, but also a very real and meaningful vision of just how much the world stands to lose if humanity doesn't succeed in the worldwide effort for preservation.

The aquatic environment *is* in peril, and divers have stepped to the forefront to strive for its protection.

CAREERS IN DIVING

Effective recreational instructors master the art of open water group control.

Underwater exploration has fascinated people for centuries. Many who experience the captivating subaquatic realm decide to make underwater adventure and discovery a regular part of their lives and one of the most effective ways to achieve this is to forge a career from their favored activity.

There are many ways to make a living while diving: recreational instruction, often considered a part-time hobby, has become one of the most effective; commercial diving, while perhaps not as viable as it once was, is still an obvious career in many people's minds; scientific and research diving provide opportunities for those with appropriate qualifications or ambitions; and military diving, which has given much in terms of equipment, techniques and procedures to other branches of diving, still provides many opportunities.

This section overviews the options available to divers interested in an underwater career.

PADI Continuing Education Course Flow

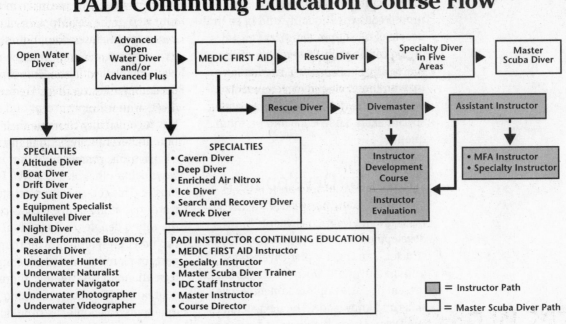

Open Water Diver → Advanced Open Water Diver and/or Advanced Plus → MEDIC FIRST AID → Rescue Diver → Specialty Diver in Five Areas → Master Scuba Diver

Rescue Diver → Divemaster → Assistant Instructor

Instructor Development Course / Instructor Evaluation

• MFA Instructor
• Specialty Instructor

SPECIALTIES
• Altitude Diver
• Boat Diver
• Drift Diver
• Dry Suit Diver
• Equipment Specialist
• Multilevel Diver
• Night Diver
• Peak Performance Buoyancy
• Research Diver
• Underwater Hunter
• Underwater Naturalist
• Underwater Navigator
• Underwater Photographer
• Underwater Videographer

SPECIALTIES
• Cavern Diver
• Deep Diver
• Enriched Air Nitrox
• Ice Diver
• Search and Recovery Diver
• Wreck Diver

PADI INSTRUCTOR CONTINUING EDUCATION
• MEDIC FIRST AID Instructor
• Specialty Instructor
• Master Scuba Diver Trainer
• IDC Staff Instructor
• Master Instructor
• Course Director

▨ = Instructor Path
☐ = Master Scuba Diver Path

Recreational Instruction

Introducing people to the aquatic realm is deeply rewarding.

Introduction

Recreational instruction is one of the most practical choices for individuals seeking a diving-related career. The potential to earn a living from an enjoyable pastime and access the exotic locations so often associated with the life of a scuba instructor attract many divers. Several factors have contributed to worldwide growth of recreational scuba and the subsequent career opportunity creation.

Humanity's interest in, and concern for, the global environment grows continually. People perceive diving as an environmentally friendly activity and it has therefore become more popular. The professionalism and effectiveness of dive retailers and instructors internationally have shown the nondiving public, through effective marketing and advertising strategies, that nearly everyone can enjoy scuba diving.

Technology advances and ongoing manufacturer development have improved equipment quality and fit so that people of all shapes and sizes can enjoy diving comfortably in a variety of climates. Dive professionals need to keep up with these ongoing developments to best serve today's divers. This requires specific skills, knowledge and personal qualities.

Instructor Development

Specific skills and knowledge are the most straight forward elements in the development of a recreational scuba instructor. The Open Water Diver course and the Advanced Open Water program present and develop fundamental dive skills and knowledge. The next step, Rescue Diver, directs the diver's attention towards others.

The Rescue Diver course, while rewarding, is demanding both physically and mentally. The course first develops and hones the self-rescue skills introduced in the Open Water Diver course and the Advanced Open Water program and then focuses on assisting other divers. Candidates develop accident prevention and management skills and

Complete academic instructional systems ensure effective classroom learning.

gain confidence by applying these skills in open water. This course is an important step in the development of a scuba instructor because accepting responsibility for others and knowing how to prevent and deal with accidents is part of becoming a Rescue Diver. Frequently, divers who willingly accept and enjoy this responsibility continue their education and eventually become instructors.

It is this responsibility that in many ways defines the role of a PADI Divemaster. This course is the next step towards becoming a dive professional and the rating denotes an individual who can accept responsibility for many aspects of planning and conducting safe recreational dives, whether shore or boat based. Divemaster training has four goals: to enable the candidate to organize and supervise dive activities; to develop the candidate's dive skills and knowledge to a level sufficient to become an instructor; to enable the candidate to function as an instructional assistant and, finally, to encourage and prepare the candidate for instructor training.

Divemasters may function as instructional assistants and qualify, provided they meet all other relevant prerequisites, to attend a PADI Instructor Development Course (IDC). The PADI Assistant Instructor rating, however, builds on a divemaster's skills and knowledge and, through independent study, classroom sessions and practical application, teaches candidates to construct and deliver teaching presentations and conduct PADI courses. This is an obvious and beneficial transition to the IDC. Additionally, PADI Assistant Instructors may, under qualified instructor guidance, deliver academic presentations on PADI courses and independently conduct certain PADI programs. These activities build confidence and increase familiarity with PADI systems, standards and procedures; qualities that enhance performance and increase the likelihood of success on the IDC.

Teaching takes place in confined water where students master skills in a controlled environment.

Prior to the IDC, candidates should have instructor-level dive theory knowledge and role-model watermanship, rescue skills and leadership ability. The IDC emphasizes development, not testing, and this creates a relatively stress free environment. Candidates learn how to teach the PADI System in the classroom and in the confined and open water environments. They also gain a complete understanding of PADI's educational goals, philosophies, standards and procedures.

The PADI Instructor Orientation Course (IOC), a shorter program, has the same goals as the IDC, but is only open to qualified scuba instructors from other certification organizations. Successful completion of an IDC or an IOC qualifies candidates to attend the PADI Instructor Examination.

The Instructor Examination (IE) evaluates a candidate's knowledge and skills to determine if they are sufficient to earn the PADI Open Water Scuba In-

structor qualification. Impartial PADI Worldwide examiners conduct IEs. The IE tests teaching ability, dive theory knowledge, skill level, understanding of the PADI System and attitude and professionalism. The goal is objective evaluation of the candidate's ability to meet specific certification criteria.

Good instructors never stop learning and a variety of instructor-level continuing education programs are available. PADI Specialty Instructor ratings qualify an instructor to teach divers the techniques involved in specialty areas of diving. PADI Night Diver, Ice Diver and Underwater Photographer Instructor ratings typify specialty qualifications. The PADI MEDIC FIRST AID (MFA) course qualifies instructors to teach an internationally recognized first aid program to divers. The IDC Staff Instructor qualification allows instructors to assist with IDCs. Master Instructor, a highly respected rating, denotes an instructor with significant experience, commitment and expertise. In an ever more competitive job market, advanced qualifications such as these can greatly enhance job prospects.

Where to Get Instructor Training

IDCs, IOCs and instructor-level continuing education courses are available from PADI 5 Star Instructor Development Centers, Career Development Centers and from PADI Colleges around the world. These facilities must meet rigorous training standards before running instructor courses. This process, and the fact that all candidates must pass an identical IE, assures that PADI Instructors receive quality and consistent training.

Dive Center Careers

PADI Dive Centers provide the majority of career opportunities for instructors. Most instructors realize that working

Divemasters help divers decide if the planned dive is within their capabilities.

knowledge, dive center owners look for employees with sales and communication skills and with training in scuba equipment repair and service. Basic knowledge of business procedures, such as how to complete sales receipts and rental documents, is essential. Computer skills, advertising knowhow and management experience also enhance employability. Professional attitudes and work ethic are important too. Many jobs need to be done to keep a dive center operating and instructors need to pitch in with the more mundane tasks. Teaching and diving comprise only part of working for a dive operation.

When discussing attitude, it is important to realize that many potential instructors have neither the financial need or the personal inclination to make scuba instruction a full-time career. Many choose to make scuba instruction a part-time endeavor. They enjoy scuba and scuba instruction and find that teaching part-time fulfills their need for prestige, recognition and, frequently, travel and/or equipment benefits. These individuals enjoy receiving pay for their avocation.

Dive Resorts

A high proportion of newly qualified instructors want to work at resorts because these locations allow instructors to work in highly desirable environments. Resorts place a premium on interpersonal skills. Generally, the instructor deals with large numbers of tourists and vacationing divers. Their skill levels differ greatly and the instructor needs to accommodate varying needs. The successful instructor helps divers enjoy themselves whether neophytes or experienced divers with hundreds of logged dives.

A large part of the business in most resort operations is the Discover Scuba Diving experience. This is a brief introduction to scuba diving including a closely supervised tour of a shallow

with an established center is usually more effective and rewarding than trying to operate independently. When shifting from diving recreationally to vocationally divers need to keep this in mind.

In addition to diving skills and

open water site. The emphasis is on fun and no qualification is issued. The instructor here is responsible for ensuring an enjoyable and positive experience. These experiences often motivate people to take up diving as a full-time recreation, but only if they enjoyed their dive in the first place. While one thinks of Discover Scuba Diving as a tropical activity, some resorts offer it in suitable locations in temperate climates. In some instances, potential divers get their first underwater experience in dry suits.

Other Opportunities for Divemasters and Instructors

When divers pay for dive services, particularly on larger vessels, the role of the divemaster is crucial. The captain has responsibility for matters concerning the vessel, but the divemaster has responsibility for most aspects of the dive operation. These duties may begin before departure with a roll call and include checking qualifications and log books, delivering a thorough briefing including logistical information and dive site details, checking divers in and out of the water and ensuring all divers are back on-board before departing the dive site. Divemasters frequently perform similar duties when organizing shore-based diving activities for dive centers or resorts.

Live-aboard dive boats, another potential source of employment, generally use fully qualified instructors to perform the duties mentioned above. On these vessels, when divers are typically on board for one or two weeks, the instructor's role may expand to include teaching continuing education courses. While the dive opportunities on these vessels are great, instructors will invari-

ably need to make sure that all aspects of the divers' trip are satisfactory. Here, more than anywhere else in the industry, employers place a premium on interpersonal skills and flexibility.

Cruise lines also hire divemasters and instructors. In most cases, the emphasis is on leading snorkeling tours and hosting other watersports. Except in special cases, opportunities to teach diving may be severely limited. Again, interpersonal skills are vitally important.

Many instructors find opportunities in schools and colleges. Physical education and science departments frequently encourage formation of a diving program or club and a professional presentation to the relevant faculty can be highly successful. The fact that many PADI programs qualify for college credit recommendations helps when approaching third level institutions.

No matter where the opportunities lie, instructors need to enjoy teaching and dealing with people. They need to have a sincere desire to help people of all ability levels learn to dive in a comfortable yet stimulating environment. They need to be at ease in front of groups of their peers and be able to communicate effectively and enthusiastically. While aspects of these qualities are learned or acquired, a large part depends simply on personal attitude.

Ultimately, with appropriate training and the right skills and attitude, there are many employment opportunities. Work is available all over the world. From ice diving in the polar regions, to freshwater locations in the midwestern United States, from Egyptian coral reefs to the pristine South Pacific, wherever there is water, it is likely there is an opportunity for a professional recreational dive instructor.

Commercial Diving

Surface supplied diving systems: "Standard" dress in the background was in widespread use up to 1980, eventually replaced by equipment similar to that in the foreground.

Commercial divers get paid for labor underwater, not for diving per se. Mainstream commercial diving specifically excludes scuba instruction, scientific diving, and police and military diving. In spite of overlap due to income (scuba instructors, technically, get paid for working underwater), the term *commercial diving* applies to the specific activities discussed in this section. When considering commercial diving as a career, it is important to recognize the type of labor and risks involved, to recognize the need for elaborate equipment and to look at the long-term income potential and job market.

Commercial diving is an arduous yet rewarding occupation. It demands quality training, self-confidence and significant fitness. It has associated risks, but these are often part of the attraction, an analogy might be drawn with becoming an astronaut. While there are obvious differences in the complexity of the training process and work undertaken, a diver leaving the safety of a bell to work on a well head and an astronaut leaving the safety of the shuttle to work on a satellite have much in common.

Commercial divers work on offshore installations such as oil rigs and barges, and on inshore civil engineering sites, hydroelectric plants and in harbors, lakes and rivers. Using band masks or helmets and umbilicals, quite different from recreational equipment, commercial divers maintain constant voice communication with the surface and their support personnel. Although they're diving, they focus on completing their tasks, not on enjoying aquatic life.

Underwater work varies and usually involves relatively simple jobs that may be difficult only due to their location. Poor visibility, cold water and strong currents often make a diver's job more difficult. Typical tasks include inspecting underwater plant, nondestructive testing of offshore and inshore installations, rudimentary cutting and tack welding (certifiable welding underwater requires setting up a pressurized dry environment at the work site and is a specialized and expensive undertaking), concreting, underwater pipeline "tie-ins" and a host of other, mainly manual, tasks specific to the location or operation. Many commercial diving instructors believe that it is easier, for example, to teach a plumber to dive than it is to teach a scuba diver to be a plumber.

There are two main branches of commercial diving: air diving and mixed-gas or "sat" (saturation) diving. Air divers typically work at depths as deep as 50 metres/165 feet and are usually tended directly from the surface. On offshore jobs, where depths approach the safe air diving limit, "surface

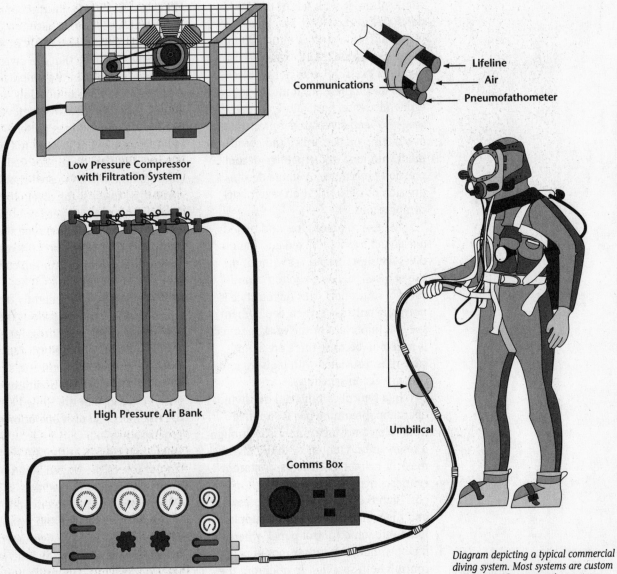

Low Pressure Compressor with Filtration System

High Pressure Air Bank

Communications

Lifeline

Air

Pneumofathometer

Comms Box

Control Panel

Umbilical

Diagram depicting a typical commercial diving system. Most systems are custom built to specific user requirements, so details vary considerably.

spreads" or wet bells are sometimes used. These are simply bells, open at the bottom, that provide safe transport to and from the dive site and a convenient stage for in-water decompression.

"Sat" divers may spend a month under pressure, living in a relatively spacious and well equipped chamber on the surface. They travel, under pressure, to the work site in a small "lockout" bell. Gas mixes used for "sat" diving vary with the working depth. Heliox (helium/oxygen) and trimix (helium/nitrogen/oxygen) are commonly used.

The idea behind "sat" diving is relatively simple: once a diver has become saturated with gas at the working depth (ref: section Two, The Physiology of Diving), required decompression time becomes constant. Any extended stay at depth (or pressure) does not require longer decompression. It makes sound economic sense, particularly in deeper water, to keep divers under pressure and avoid tying up personnel and equipment with long and repetitive decompression procedures. A single decompression has less risk than several decompressions.

Air diving procedures and mixed gas diving overlap. Mixed-gas "bounce" dives are short deep dives without the use of a bell, and with bottom times short of saturation. This diving style is normally only used when deployment speed is important or the work required is minimal, because there are significant risks associated with logistics and decompression schedules.

In a typical commercial air diving operation, breathing gas is supplied from a low pressure compressor through a reservoir and umbilical to the diver's mask or helmet. High pressure storage cylinders frequently provide backup gas. Both the low pressure compressor and the high pressure backup supply route through a control panel, where the operations supervisor monitors and controls both supplies. In addition, the diver usually wears a "bailout" cylinder

as a personal reserve, manifolded directly to the mask or helmet.

Diving procedures vary, but generally, commercial divers have a tender who assists with donning equipment and performing predive safety checks. A fully dressed standby diver, with another tender, must generally be on site and ready to enter the water on command. The standby should be equipped with adequate equipment to reach the working diver with minimal delay. An operations supervisor, with overall responsibility for diving activities, must generally be present and in control. The supervisor plans the dive operation, monitors dive depth and duration and ensures adequate communication and adherence to diving and safety procedures. The tender ensures that the diver has just enough slack in the umbilical to accomplish the task comfortably and constantly monitors the divers movement and breathing (bubble) pattern. The standby also needs to have full information on the dive site and procedures so that no time will be wasted should the need arise to assist the diver. Both the diver and the tender need to be fully conversant with manual rope signals to maintain communication (albeit limited) in the event of communication equipment failure.

Regulations are generally developed by government agencies that oversee worker safety standards. For example, in parts of the North Sea, an undeniably hostile environment, standards laid down by the HSE (Health and Safety Executive in the United Kingdom) are rigorous, and dive operation safety is generally good. OSHA (Occupational Safety and Health Authority) performs a similar role in the United States and again, the standards are high. In many warmer and less hostile environments, standards may be less stringent or nonexistent due to lack of government attention. In these cases, the individual dive contractor is responsible for diver safety.

Training is an important consideration for potential commercial divers. In an increasingly competitive occupation, the quantity and caliber of training have become crucial. In addition to basic air and mixed gas qualifications, potential divers will almost certainly need certification in diver first aid, plus qualifications in nondestructive testing and other specialty certificates to enhance job prospects. The nature of commercial diving also demands that divers are ready to work when there is work to be done. Many divers get their first break through polite persistence and being in the right place at the right time. When a big job comes up, companies hire. Reputation is also crucial in what is actually a relatively small industry. Those who perform calmly, quietly and efficiently get and keep the jobs.

Technological advances have had a major effect on the quantity of work undertaken by commercial divers. Efficient remote operated vehicles (ROVs) perform many tasks that used to be in the diver's realm. Design innovation in the offshore sector has reduced structure maintenance requirements and consequently the need for divers. The fact that the number of jobs has declined has made competition for commercial work intense. Divers seeking regular commercial work need quality training, determination and a little luck.

Scientific Diving

Careful notetaking and recording are fundamental tools for the scientific diver.

Divers go underwater every day somewhere in the world for research, scientific discovery and surveys. Scientific diving is a broad term that encompasses a variety of activities and people. One may consider archaeologists uncovering underwater artifacts in the Mediterranean scientific divers. The same is true of divers studying zebra mussel populations in the Great Lakes of North America, or coral formations in the South Pacific.

Underwater scientists for the most part use recreational scuba equipment and follow recreational scuba procedures. It is important to realize, however, that while these techniques and equipment are common in scientific diving, the dive activities are highly supervised and much of the diving is beyond the scope of recreational diving and a great deal more involved. Additionally, scientists use diving as a means to pursue their area of expertise; they are scientists first and divers second. Individu-

Water communication systems and navigation devices including relocation systems are regularly used by scientific divers.

ter scientists use extensive technology and submersibles to accomplish their goals. The Woods Hole Oceanographic Institution in the U.S., for example, uses large support vessels and submersibles to reach *Titanic* depths (3810 metres/ 12,500 feet).

The future has many new possibilities for scientific diving. As the human population expands, so will the demand for more food and mineral resources from the world's oceans and seas. Aquaculture, which has successfully flourished in Japan and other Asian countries requires some scientific diving to succeed (more on aquaculture in another section). As in any discipline, science, too, has its supply and demand, and as the demand for more oceanic research increases, so will scientific diving. The following activities describe some existing forms of scientific diving:

Geographic/geological. This also includes geological diving that attempts to understand our planet and how it works. Most of this diving took place by scientific and military teams that scoured the Earth's oceans and polar caps starting in the 1950s and continuing still. The data gathered by divers under the polar ice, the continental shelves, the Red Sea, the California submarine canyons and the world's coral reefs are still widely used and valid (since the Earth hasn't changed much geologically during the past few decades). These efforts yielded some outstanding discoveries. In 1977 the research submersible Alvin discovered, for the first time, life based on *chemosynthesis.* This is the synthesis of organic substances using the energy of chemical reactions and the process, unlike photosynthesis, can occur in a totally dark environment. Rapidly growing ecosystems of over 300 species based on bacteria are still being studied today.

This sort of diving is expensive and highly specialized, requiring government or large institute support. In addition to the world's governments, many institutions contribute to scientific div-

als interested in a scientific career need appropriate education in their chosen field.

In the United States, the American Academy of Underwater Sciences (AAUS) has set standards for scientific diving operations and certification courses. The Health and Safety Executive (H.S.E.) standards and procedures apply to scientific diving in the United Kingdom. There are, however, some instances where underwa-

ing worldwide. The Woods Hole Oceanographic Institution and the Scripps Institute of Oceanography in the U.S. are primary examples of these private institutions.

Biological. Marine biologists from around the world log thousands of dives each month to study various underwater life forms. These include hundreds of coral studies throughout the world's tropical and subtropical regions, and even more research on thousands of fish and invertebrate species worldwide.

Archaeological and historical. Mankind's fascination with maritime history hasn't waned through the ages. For this reason, hundreds of large and small expeditions to uncover buried sunken ships and early civilizations have taken place in the past 40 years or so. A great number of these expeditions have naturally taken place in the Mediterranean, which was a cradle of maritime civilizations for thousands of years. Other archaeological underwater digs have taken place in California's Channel Is-

lands, the Caribbean, the South Pacific and Europe.

Scientific, recreational and technical divers worldwide dive on a number of celebrated and lesser known wrecks in their quest for information and adventure. These include the Japanese fleet in Truk Lagoon, the Spanish Armada wrecks off Ireland's north and west coast and numerous other ships that went down dramatically with or without loss of life. While some divers go down on these ships with nothing more than a desire for adventure, others dive them looking for clues and scientific answers to satisfy historical or archaeological inquiry.

As long as scientific studies exist, so will scientific diving. The world's bodies of water constitute a rich and largely undiscovered realm that still requires a great deal of study and research. The major contributing factor to conducting these studies is funding, and as more money becomes available, so will scientific diving.

Military Diving

Introduction

Careers in military diving have a long and illustrious history. Since at least 332 B.C., when Alexander the Great used divers to clear the harbor at Tyre, military strategists have recognized the diver's important role. This recognition helped drive early dive equipment development as armed forces around the world used divers for various operations.

British Royal Engineers, in the mid-nineteenth century, tested early dive apparatus while clearing the remains of a sunken warship that was fouling a major fleet anchorage outside Portsmouth in England. Colonel William Pasley, in charge of the effort, formally recommended adoption of the Siebe standard diver's dress and helmet after this operation.

A similar surfaced supplied system based on the Mk V Diving Helmet, became standard U.S. Navy diving equipment. This system was employed for practically all salvage work throughout World War II and remained in use until 1980.

Military involvement with the development of scuba systems was and is still significant. Submarine escape equipment used by the British Royal Navy in World War I was based on an oxygen rebreather system, and by World War II, closed circuit equipment was in widespread military use.

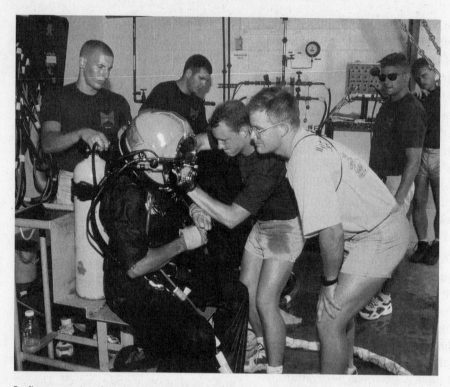

Predive preparations for a diver using Mk21 Mod 1 SSDS (Surface Supplied Diving System) while undergoing military training.

Warring navies of World War II developed several systems for military operations. The British and Italian navies in particular developed one and two-man submersible vehicles/submarines, which they used sometimes effectively on the enemy's anchored warships. The Italians in particular conducted several daring operations using divers and small submarines in the Mediterranean.

Another important military contribution to diving was made by a French naval officer and an engineer — Jaques Cousteau and Emile Gagnan. They created the first effective open circuit scuba, and after World War II, the aqua-lung became a commercial success. This equipment opened underwater exploration to anyone with reasonable physical fitness and appropriate training.

Military contribution to all aspects of diving, both commercial and recreational, cannot be overstated. Military diving careers have produced some of the most respected and productive people involved in diving today.

This section overviews some of the many military career opportunities. Specific information, except as otherwise noted, relates to the U.S. armed forces.

Training

Military training goals are to produce physically fit divers equipped for the rigors of diving in the armed forces. Candidates for diver training must be between 17 and 40 years of age and be enlisted in the armed forces. They must demonstrate appropriate academic aptitude, particularly in mechanics and mathematics, and they must pass a strict physical examination and test, including a pressure test, prior to enrollment in any diver training program.

Diver training in the military starts with the Second Class diver program. This includes theory and scuba and surface supplied training. A current trend in the armed forces is the formation of Consolidated Diving Units (CDUs). Second Class divers are assigned to a CDU and they build practical experience on various assignments before applying for First Class training. This program details compression chamber operations and dive operation supervision. Graduates of this course are adequately trained to organize and conduct military dive operations.

Saturation diving is a completely separate program. Divers may elect to undergo this training if they desire. Another option, for qualified corpsmen (emergency medical technicians), is to pursue the Diver Medical Technician (DMT) rating. This requires completing the Second Class curriculum and an advanced medicine program.

Experienced First Class divers may apply for the Master Diver qualification. This requires completing a rigorous written test on dive theory and medicine and two week practical examination on diving and dive management. A group of previously qualified

Master Divers evaluate the candidate's performance. This represents the top qualification for military divers.

As a final training option, Sea, Air and Land Special Warfare Teams (SEALS) undergo perhaps the most rigorous diver training program worldwide. The training qualifies the candidates as members of an elite, internationally renowned, offensive combat team that is capable of effective function in any environment.

Duties and Career Paths

The ongoing need for underwater reconnaissance, demolition, construction, ship maintenance, search, rescue, salvage and ordnance disposal worldwide has fueled demand for military divers. Units tend now to specialize, for example in the U.S. Navy three major units currently are Fleet Divers, Explosive Ordnance Disposal (EOD) and Sea, Air and Land special warfare (SEAL) teams.

Fleet diving involves inspection and repair of naval vessels, underwater construction and general search and recovery missions. All divers will, as a minimum, have completed Second Class Dive School.

These divers perform tasks such as hull cleaning, inspection and repair to a standard, in many cases, equal to that achieved in dry-dock. Construction, inspection, repair and removal of inwater facilities such as pipelines, cables and fixed structures is another major task for military divers. The divers regularly involved in these activities undergo additional training and are known as "Seabees," slang for Construction Battalion. Demolition jobs frequently involve the use of explosives, and here again, additional training is required.

Other duties include performing search and recovery missions and security swims to check for explosives or other devices that may be attached to ships or piers. In all cases where explosives are discovered, specially trained Explosive Ordnance Disposal (EOD) teams are called in to investigate, disarm and dispose of them.

Potential Future Developments

Current trends towards consolidation look set to continue. All branches of the U.S. Armed Forces, for example, will in future train divers at the one center in Panama City, Florida. Instructors from all branches of the military are stationed here. This center also houses the Navy Experimental Diving Unit, which has an enormous wet compression chamber capable of housing small submarines and has obvious value for specialized training or equipment testing.

As equipment becomes increasingly sophisticated, new military applications evolve. (The reverse is also true as military demand drives equipment development.) "Flyaway" saturation diving systems, that can be loaded on transport planes and flown to any location around the world are under development. Portable recompression chambers also allow teams deployed in remote areas to have appropriate facilities on-site to deal with almost any dive emergency.

Recreational, commercial, technical and scientific diving have all benefitted from military equipment and procedure development. From any perspective, divers with military backgrounds play an important role in shaping the future of diving.

Other Careers

Recreational, commercial, scientific and military diving provide many dive related career opportunities. Other options are available, and this section looks at some of these.

Search and Rescue

Police and fire departments around the world regularly face situations where dive capability can at best lead to successful rescue and at least facilitate effective underwater searches. In response to these situations, many departments set up specialized underwater units that are specifically trained to deal with the significant hazards that are often a factor in operations of this kind.

These units are usually formed by existing members of relevant departments who have an interest and perhaps some training in scuba diving. Many units get appropriate government funding and develop into truly professional operations, others frequently rely on volunteers from the local recreational scuba community.

The risk factor in dive operations of this nature can be high. Typical operations include: searching for and recovering submerged vehicles, responding to reports of drownings or missing boats on inland waterways and searching for weapons discarded after assaults or robberies. Often these dives take place in less than ideal conditions.

Aquaculture

With ever increasing demands on worldwide food resources and limited availability of arable and grazing land, aquaculture has become increasingly important in recent years.

In spite of a moderating influence due to environmental concerns, open sea net cages for rearing salmon and other important food species are an important economic part of many relatively remote maritime communities.

Fish farming using offshore net cages depends heavily on divers. Divers are responsible for regular stock inspections, mooring system and fish net maintenance and mortality removal.

Divers in this environment face particular challenges. Equipment is usually scuba, but many installations use lightweight surface demand systems with through wire communication systems. Currents make diving inside net cages hazardous because the net billows and changes shape creating possible entrapment risks. Open sea net cages can be up to 18 metres/60 feet deep or more, and in many cases, several cages are located next to each other so that divers perform multiple ascents and descents as they check each cage. This increases the risk of decompression illness.

In other forms of aquaculture, such as pearl farming, mussel or scallop rearing, divers simplify stock inspection and again perform useful work inspecting and maintaining mooring systems. As in scientific diving, divers working on aquaculture installations frequently have other useful skills or expertise. Individuals seeking careers in this field are more likely to succeed with additional relevant training and education.

Underwater photography is equipment intensive, competitive and highly rewarding.

Underwater Imaging: Stills, Video and Film

Successful underwater photographers, videographers and film makers forge careers that many divers envy. This is a highly competitive field that demands good training, experience and creativity. Many colleges and universities run photography programs that provide fundamental information, but there is no substitution for experience and determination.

As diving in general and recreational diving in particular become more popular, consumer magazines and other diving related periodicals demand more and more quality photographs. While many of the more dramatic cover photographs depict exotic and remote locations, quality photographs of interesting dive activity or aquatic life in a local river, quarry or lake may be equally marketable.

Additionally, many organizations produce promotional or educational videos. This medium is becoming more important because it integrates well with rapidly advancing computer technologies.

The film industry needs divers not only for the obvious role of underwater camera operator, but also for many related support functions: divers assist with elaborate and potentially hazardous underwater set construction; they are regularly required to support or perform stunts; they often double for actors and they are often needed for aquatic safety and rescue duties.

Journalism

Accurate writing and reporting are crucial to the success of the many specialist publications catering to recreational, commercial and other divers. For people interested in this career two elements are essential: writing skills and relevant experience.

Universities and colleges around the world offer writing courses. Many offer particularly beneficial programs geared specifically toward magazine article writing. It is also important to have something to write about. Many successful dive journalists started out with careers as instructors or commercial divers. Many combine the two roles as one career.

Send a query letter to determine a publication's specific requirements, editorial policies and pay rates. Many editors will accept and review unsolicited material, but others will simply return or ignore material sent on speculation. It is prudent to remember that most major magazines, for example, plan issues six to 12 months in advance. Be sure to time queries or submissions appropriately. It is also important to ensure that submissions match the editorial style of the publication by reading several issues before submitting anything. Providing relevant and quality photographs to support articles greatly increases the chances of publication.

Equipment Manufacturers

Equipment manufacturers are significant employers with extremely varied requirements. Engineers research and develop new products, skilled staff run and supervise the manufacturing processes, representatives sell the product to dive centers and other customers and efficient business managers control the entire process and ensure the company's success.

In most cases, a dive background is a useful, if not essential, qualification for many of these positions. This is particularly true for the manufacturer's representative. Comprehensive knowledge of dive equipment and the ability to discuss details with potential buyers are important.

As the dive industry grows, demand for equipment increases and equipment manufacturers increase production to keep pace. Opportunities in this area are set to increase.

There are many other diving related careers and opportunities. The salvage of an ancient shipwreck with a valuable cargo can make a fortune for a successful salvor. However, money lost through fruitless searchs more often than not outweighs the dramatic and occasional finds and archaeological concerns prohibit random excavations. Authors have written books on how to make money diving for golf balls, but this is not a career that most enthusiastic divers dream about.

Whatever the ambition, a determined approach and an appropriate education will ensure a rewarding and enjoyable career in diving.

Index

visibility 1-13, 1-14, 1-17
visible spectrum 1-14
visual reversal 1-15
vital capacity 2-7

W

warm-blooded 4-6
water 1-2, 1-9
water chemistry 4-7
wave height 4-10
waves 1-14, 4-10
Weddell seal 4-58
weight 1-7
weight, correct amount 3-45
weight system 3-42
wet suits 3-21
whales 4-54
whistles 3-90
wind 4-10

X

xenon 1-26

Y

Y valve 3-54

Z

zooxanthellae 4-27
Zostera 4-20